THE HAMPSHIRE TIGERS

Other books by Bryan Perrett

THE HAMPSHIRE TIGERS

The Story of
The Royal Hampshire Regiment
1945 - 1992

BRYAN PERRETT

Published by
The Royal Hampshire Regiment Museum Trustees
Serle's House Southgate Street Winchester SO23 9EG

in conjunction with
SYDNEY JARY LIMITED
9 Upper Belgrave Road Clifton Bristol BS8 2XH

First published September 1997

Publisher's editor: Lois Jary
© Text and maps The Royal Hampshire Regiment Museum Trustees
© Photographs as acknowledged

A catalogue record for this title is available from the British Library

ISBN 1 9011655 00 8

Designed, produced and typeset in ITT New Baskerville by
AVONWORLD LIMITED PO Box 568, BRISTOL BS99 1PZ

Colour and mono reprographics by BLACK CAT GRAPHICS,
Suite 36, 3rd Floor, Templar House, Temple Way, Bristol BS1 6HG

Printed and bound by The CROMWELL PRESS, Melksham, Wiltshire

Serle's House, Winchester, the home of the Regiment

There and back — the final parade at Winchester, 1992

Colours presented by the Colonel-in-Chief, Minden Day 1986

The Drums piled in Portsmouth Cathedral,
Minden Day 1991

It gave me enormous pleasure to be asked to write the Foreword to this history of the Royal Hampshire Regiment from the end of the Second World War until the end of its independent existence in 1992.

It was my singular honour to be Colonel-in-Chief of the Regiment from 1985 to 1992. I have affectionate memories of my visits to the Royal Hampshires during those years and vividly recall the pride which the servicemen and women I met had in their association with the Regiment, its past, its present and its traditions.

This history, with those covering earlier eras, is an invaluable record of the times and exploits of one of the truly great infantry regiments of the British Army.

Diana.

1997.

CONTENTS

LIST OF ILLUSTRATIONS

PREFACE

by

Brigadier R G Long CBE MC DL
Colonel of the Regiment 1987 - 1992

E very good regiment thinks it is special, and so it should. It is much more difficult to analyse the reasons, particularly for those who have not served in regiments other than their own. Defining a regimental characteristic is in any case better done by someone from outside, who can view it dispassionately.

However, this is not the place for impartial analysis; rather a subjective, though mature reflection of pride. There is no point in pretending that most members of The Royal Hampshire Regiment had their roots in the blissfully attractive countryside of Hampshire. The majority, both during and after national service, came from the urban areas of Portsmouth and Southampton. What was common to all was the strength of the county identity. There was pride in the fact that The Royal Hampshire Regiment was one of very few single county regiments alive up to the 1990s to bear the name of its county as its major title. Such a focus led to many advantages, not least in the pride of civic association. The Lord Mayor, Mayors and Chairmen of nine Freedom Cities, Boroughs and Districts in Hampshire, together with the Mayors of Bournemouth and Christchurch, former Hampshire Boroughs transferred to Dorset, all habitually visited the Regiment at home and abroad individually and collectively over much of the period covered by this history.   Indeed Christchurch granted the Regiment the Freedom of the Ancient Borough long after it was subsumed in Dorset; proof, if ever it were needed, of the strength of the Hampshire connection. And these visits by civic heads were no mere tokens. In nearly every case there were real rewards, particularly in Northern Ireland, when young soldiers drew strength from the fact that the mayor of their home town had taken the trouble to come to see them.

There is, however, more to it than civic connections, and this is the area harder to define. There was always a particularly warm relationship between officers, senior NCOs and soldiers. All regiments would claim this for themselves, but in the Royal Hampshires it genuinely was different. There was an abundance of wisdom among officers and warrant officers and particularly quartermasters, and an emphasis on teamwork, where every member of the Regiment was brought up, within its systems, to understand the part played by membership of the rank structure. A succession of commanding officers emphasized to new young officers that the worst crime of which they could be accused was the failure to care for the soldiers under their command. In the Royal Hampshires the teamwork seemed to take place instinctively and unselfconsciously, with a natural application of military principles. Two years compulsory military National Service was a test of the ability of the Regiment to assimilate a constant throughput and instill pride in belonging to Hampshire's County Regiment. This was successfully achieved because the Regiment took a pride in its National Servicemen. Though many National Servicemen were less than happy about military service, any discontent was focused upon the army and the government. Indeed, among the most fervent supporters of the contemporary Comrades' Association can be found former National Servicemen, proof not only that good times are easier to remember than bad, but that they were proud of the cap badge they wore.

For almost exactly half the period of this history, the two Territorial Battalions, and then the one, represented the Regiment in the county when the 1st Battalion was abroad. The TA was less structured and less formal than the regular army. There was nothing that the TA could not turn their hand to. Not many regulars have done beach landing exercises after a 24-hour sea crossing; not many regulars have taken part in a two-day exercise on entirely private land including formal and informal crossings of the River Thames. The Royal Hampshire TA did. And these men really were, by definition, from within the county, as the list of Drill Hall locations will testify.

It was typical of the Regiment that when orders came to amalgamate, after intense depression and sadness, the overwhelming majority decided that they would carry out their orders with dignity and, foremost, a consideration for those serving. The name of the Regiment lives on in the Princess of Wales's Royal Regiment (Queen's and Royal Hampshires). But only a fellowship giving rise to intense pride could engender such a widely-held feeling of bereavement at its passing.

This book tells the story of the Tigers' last 47 years. It is part of the history of the country, the army and the county. It was well worth writing.

AUTHOR'S INTRODUCTION

IT was while engaged in other aspects of my work, dealing mainly with the question of motivation, that I found myself coming into regular contact with The Royal Hampshire Regiment. After a while, it began to seem that if there was a point to be made the Hampshires had made it at one time or another in their long history. As one of the "Unsurpassable Six" British infantry regiments who fought at Minden they had turned the contemporary laws of warfare on their head by routing an overwhelming mass of French cavalry, then chased a large body of French and Saxon infantry off the field. At the Taku Forts in China, where the Royal Navy had already sustained a serious and humiliating reverse, the Regiment and the 44th (later the Essex) Regiment, carried the formidable defences at the first rush. In Tunisia during World War II the bitterly contested defensive battles fought by the 2nd Battalion at Tebourba, and by the Territorial 1st/4th, 2nd/4th and 5th Battalions, the last supported by 155 Battery RA, which, during the inter-connected battles of Sidi Nsir and Hunt's Gap, completely wrecked the Germans' strategic planning on two separate occasions. From such actions as these it was possible to draw the conclusion that once the Hampshires had been set a task nothing and nobody would be allowed to stop them performing it. They were, in fact, the most stubborn soldiers imaginable, but that should surprise no one with a sense of history, for they are descended from the same West Saxon stock that halted and ultimately turned back the Danish invasion of England. There were, too, men of Hampshire in the immovable Saxon shield-wall that brought William of Normandy so close to despair at Hastings.

It is, therefore, a great honour to have been asked to write the history of The Royal Hampshire Regiment during the forty-seven years between the ending of the Second World War and the implementation of an unfortunate government policy, euphemistically entitled *Options for Change*, in 1992. It is also a considerable responsibility and the task itself is a sad one, since this will be the final volume in the history of a great regiment.

It goes almost without saying that the world today is a very different place from that which existed in 1945. Change within the political, social, economic, technical and military spheres has been continuous and proceeded at a rate unparalled at any period in history. For these reasons the Regiment has been confronted with various situations which have differed considerably from its previous experience and which have demanded in turn the highest standards of professionalism and a remarkable degree of flexibility. The problems encountered in fighting an enemy in the jungles of Malaya or Borneo differ from those of a mechanised infantry battalion in Germany, which in turn differ from those experienced countering rural and urban terrorism in Ulster, yet the Regiment regularly made the necessary adjustments as a matter of course.

Nevertheless, for the story to be fully understood by succeeding generations it is necessary to point out that, although the background was one of constant change, there were strong continuous historical threads running through it and it was these that actually determined events.

The first was what has frequently been termed the "withdrawal from empire." Unrepresentative as it was of the British war effort, the fall of Singapore in 1942 can now be seen as a major turning point in world history. For millions of people in Asia it symbolised the decline of the colonial powers and their return was not universally welcomed even after Japan had been convincingly defeated. Neither the Dutch in the East Indies, nor the French in what became Vietnam, had been popular masters and when they attempted to re-assert their authority the result in both cases was a bloody and protracted war. The British managed their affairs rather better but the question of Indian independence within the Commonwealth had already been settled and during World War II some two million Indians had volunteered for service with the armed forces of the Crown on that understanding. When India and Pakistan achieved their independence in 1947 it was already apparent that every major British colony throughout the world would seek similar status, whatever the state of its political development. Recognising the reality of the situation the British government acceded to these requests, although sometimes the politicians with whom it had to deal were inclined to enhance their own local standing with claims that whatever disruption they managed to cause was part of some imaginary struggle for freedom; all too often, this meant the freedom for themselves and their cronies to impose tribal one-party government after independence and become very rich at everyone else's expense. Despite this, the British Army, with its wealth of experience, was, more often than not, able not only to break contact cleanly but also, in the majority of cases, preserve good relations between the former Imperial subjects and Great Britain. As HRH The Prince of Wales commented to the amusement of the Indian Parliament some years ago, there are now more people from India and Pakistan resident in the United Kingdom than there were ever British citizens living in the entire Indian sub-continent! The whole process of disengagement took approximately twenty-five years to complete, so that with the exception of the Hong Kong and sovereign base garrisons on Cyprus the Army had virtually withdrawn from east of Suez, from Africa and from the Mediterranean by 1970. On the way it had participated in a major conventional war in Korea, won a protracted struggle against communist guerrillas in Malaya, defended a difficult frontier in Borneo against incursions by neighbouring Indonesia, put down the Mau Mau uprising in Kenya, contained the Eoka terrorist movement in Cyprus and maintained law and order in the Caribbean. Yet hardly had this phase in its history been completed than it found itself called to the aid of the civil power in Ulster. Here, in 1969, the well-meaning but ill-considered activities of civil rights groups provided the detonator which caused the ancient hatreds and mutual distrust between the Protestant and Catholic communities to explode into violence. This proved to be the salvation of the various Irish republican terrorist gangs, who were then on the verge of virtual extinction. Although they spoke only for themselves, they wasted no time in declaring a war of national liberation, the Protestants' response being to set up terrorist gangs of their own. The task of the Army, therefore, was first to contain the terrorists, then erode their strength. There was no short-term solution and, inevitably, much of the burden devolved upon the infantry. By 1994 both communities had had enough of the cycle of murder and reprisal and the IRA, anxious to recover its strength, declared a ceasefire. In February 1996, however, it renewed its campaign of indiscriminate bombing and, at the time of writing, seems set to continue in its ways.

The second major historical thread running throughout the period was, of course, the so-called Cold War between the North Atlantic Treaty Organisation on the one hand and the former Soviet Union and its Warsaw Pact allies on the other. This began almost as soon as the defeat of Nazi Germany had been accomplished. While other nations disarmed and demobilised, the USSR continued to maintain huge armed forces and preach the Leninist doctrine of world revolution. For this reason a major part of the British Army has remained in Germany ever since as a safeguard against aggression. Nevertheless, when faced with the probable prospect of escalation beyond the nuclear threshold if it engaged in open conflict with the West, the Soviet leadership attempted to achieve its ends by surrogate means. Even before the defeat of the North Korean communist invasion of South Korea it had taken to providing active support for revolutionary guerrilla movements in colonial territories such as Malaya and Vietnam, usually through the agency of China. It failed in the former but in the latter it compelled the withdrawal first of the French and then of the Americans. The apparent success of this policy led to its being extended to Africa and other areas where communist sympathisers were supplied with all the arms and training they needed. Simultaneously, the Soviets quickly filled the power vacuum left by the British departure from the Middle East and equipped many of the Arab armies at a scale far beyond their wildest dreams. Superficially, the masters of the Kremlin were achieving their ends, for all of Eastern Europe, large areas of the Far and Middle East and many African countries were under communist influence or control. This apparent success, however, was illusory. In the Middle East the Arab-Israeli Wars revealed serious flaws in Soviet equipment and doctrine, while the West, having learned the lessons of Vietnam, stubbornly refused to be drawn by the bait of destabilisation in such countries as Angola and Ethiopia. By 1979, such was the Kremlin's mood of over-confidence that it decided to try an expansionist venture on its own account and invaded Afghanistan, the result being that it tumbled into its own bear pit. Historically, the Afghans have always reacted to any attempt at interference in their internal affairs with extreme violence and this occasion was no different. The Soviet Army found itself bogged down in an unwinnable ten-year guerrilla war among the mountains and in the end, having incurred tens of thousands of casualties and lost immense quantities of equipment, it pulled out, leaving the communist puppet government to its fate. The Soviet economy, already strained by world commitments and the cost of occupying Eastern Europe, had simply collapsed under the additional burden of Afghanistan. With almost unbelievable speed the Warsaw Pact disintegrated and the Soviet Union itself dissolved into its component units. The sinister forces that had threatened world peace for two generations had simply wrought their own destruction without the need for a latter-day Armageddon; and since they no longer existed, the need for the West to maintain large standing armed forces had also apparently disappeared.

The third strand which was to affect the Regiment's fortunes was socio-economic. The United Kingdom ended World War II with heavy debts to repay and, no longer being the "workshop of the world", its manufacturers were forced to compete fiercely in foreign markets that were once considered safe. Against this background the government introduced social welfare programmes that were costly but necessary. The problem was that every successive administration continued to broaden the scope of these programmes until they became all-embracing, regardless of expenditure, demographic trends and technical advances. To put the matter at its simplest, the burden of providing the welfare support for an ageing population, the unemployed and the unfortunate devolved upon fewer and fewer people of working age; and, because fewer people have been required in the workplace since the introduction of the microchip and the computer, the number of those who actually contribute is in fact a comparatively small percentage of the population.

In fairness to the Treasury, which has to raise the revenue needed by the government to implement its policies, these trends have long been apparent to its economists. The government, however, has to balance the Treasury's demands for economies against what is considered to be politically expedient, and in this scenario the armed services become the easiest and most obvious of targets. Thus, for the past forty and more years every diminution in overseas commitments and every slight lessening of tension has been used to reduce their size.

This, then, was the background to the final decades of The Royal Hampshire Regiment's independent existence. During this period the Regiment fought no major engagements but, as the following pages will show, it was regularly engaged on active service somewhere in the world against an armed and dangerous enemy, often producing spectacular results. In earlier wars the soldier had the reassurance of fighting with the support of the entire battalion structure around him, but in the sorts of conflict in which the Regiment became engaged after World War II the weight of responsibility at the point of contact tended to rest upon the junior officers and NCOs; more was asked of them than at any time before, and more was undoubtedly given. The Regiment has always contained officers like Cromwell's "plain russet-coated captain that knows what he fights for and loves what he knows," and soldiers who exemplify all the virtues of Kipling's universal Mr Thomas Atkins, caring not that their government's traditionally short memory does not prevent it from arranging a special train for them at the first sign of trouble. To them, with great respect, this book is dedicated, for they have formed the cutting edge of history and will continue to do so.

CHAPTER 1

THE FIRST BATTALION IN
BENGHAZI AND PALESTINE

1st return from Holland to train infantry replacements - warned for service in
Libya - Benghazi - expedition to Kufra Oasis - background to the Palestine
situation and Jewish terrorist groups - arrival of the 1st Battalion in Palestine
and nature of duties - the Hampshires become a Royal Regiment - the 1st Battalion
to be placed in suspended animation on completion of tour - Jerusalem - terrorist
ambushes - major terrorist attack on C Company foiled on Minden Day - return
to UK and suspended animation.

"IT is a truism that one can get used to anything," wrote the
compiler of the Battalion notes in the May 1946 issue of the
Regimental Journal. "It is being put to a hard test in Benghazi.
From this fringe of the world we can ponder the latest manifestations of peace - the strikes, riots and international arguments for
which we have all been fighting. When newspapers arrive, we
can see the headlines becoming larger and graver. When letters
arrive we have some idea of the alarms and excursions at home."

Peace, indeed, was not proving to be the unmixed blessing
that had been hoped for. At home rationing and austerity remained the order of the day with a rising tide of industrial unrest
thrown in for good measure. On the continent of Europe the
Stalinist administration of the USSR had already adopted its stance
of bullying intransigence; Italy and Yugoslavia were on the brink
of armed conflict over Trieste; there was a bitter civil war raging
in Greece; and millions of people, displaced by the Second World
War, either were still trying to make their way home or, if they

were frightened of what awaited them there, were being housed in camps until they could be absorbed by the Western nations. In the Middle East Jews and Arabs were preparing to kill each other in large numbers while in Egypt anti-British feeling was gaining ground steadily. In the Indian sub-continent the ancient hatreds of Hindu and Muslim resulted in mutual massacre as the grip of the Raj loosened in the run up to Indian and Pakistani independence; in the Far East the Chinese Civil War had still to run its course; the French in Indo-China were exchanging their first shots with the communist Viet Minh; and in the East Indies, now known as Indonesia, the returning Dutch, having assumed responsibility from Commonwealth, and on occasion Japanese, troops for internal security, were about to discover that their former subjects were beyond the control of the resources they could afford to deploy.

Infantry casualties in Normandy, and indeed throughout the campaign in North West Europe, had been so heavy that the loss had to be made good by breaking up some formations and transferring men from other arms of service to the infantry. Thus, in December 1944, the war-experienced 1st Battalion returned from the hard fighting in Normandy and Holland to Helmsley in Yorkshire to train gunners from the Royal Artillery and soldiers from other specialist arms in the skills of the professional infantryman. During this period it was commanded by Lieutenant Colonel J.M.Lee, DSO, who had commanded the 2nd Battalion during its epic stand at Tebourba, Tunisia, in 1942. In August 1945 Colonel Lee was succeeded by Lieutenant Colonel R.G.F.Frisby, DSO, MC (whose father, Colonel H.G.F.Frisby, had commanded the 1st Battalion in India 1928-1932) and the Battalion moved to Louth in Lincolnshire, where it was ordered to reorganise on an Indian Army establishment of "light scales" for service in the Far East as part of the 8th Indian Division. When the dropping of atomic bombs on Hiroshima and Nagasaki brought the war with Japan to a sudden and dramatic close it was then warned for service in Libya, where British troops were still occupying the former Italian colony pending its transition to what proved to be a short-lived constitutional monarchy. This involved a further reorganisation to conform with the standard British Infantry Battalion War Establishment, although the 8th Indian Division sign was retained on uniforms and vehicles throughout the ensuing tour of duty in North Africa.

BENGHAZI AND PALESTINE

The unsettled state of the world was mirrored within the Battalion itself, where the old sense of permanence was disturbed by constant comings and goings of officers and men. Those due for release under various schemes left by rota and were replaced by those who had been serving with other units, replacements drafts and repatriated prisoners of war. Familiar faces disappeared overnight, their places taken by others less familiar or only half remembered. Indeed, a more cosmopolitan "Hampshire" battalion it would have been difficult to find. Officers came from the Glosters, the Norfolks, the King's Royal Rifle Corps, the Royal West Kents, the Buffs, the Queen's, the Somerset Light Infantry and the Duke of Cornwall's Light Infantry. Many of the Hampshire officers had served with field service battalions during the war, including:

Lieutenant Colonel R.G.F.Frisby DSO,MC	N W Europe
Major A.H.T.Hogge	Italy
Major C.L.Thomas, DSO	Tunisia
Captain & Adjutant H.E.Wingfield, MC	Tunisia
Captain A.N.E.Waldron, MC	Tunisia
Major E.G.Wright, MC and Bar	Tunisia/NW Europe
Major A.R.Denne Bolton, MC	Tunisia
Captain (QM) F.Stone, MBE	Western Desert, Malta, Sicily, Italy, NW Europe, with prior service in Turkey (1921), Egypt, India and Palestine
Captain C.D.Darroch	Italy
Lieutenant C.A.Cuttress, MC	Italy
Lieutenant B.D.Fick, MC	Italy
Lieutenant W.R.B.May, MC	NW Europe

Pre-war Warrant Officers and senior NCOs serving with the Battalion on its departure from the United Kingdom included:

RSM R.Shave, CSM J.Sheridan, CSM G.Dodge, CSM H.Sharkey, CSM A.Bull, CQMS H.Plummer, CQMS J.Simpson, CQMS P.J.McAdam, CQMS B.Sargent, Colour Sergeant (ORS) D.Piggott and Sergeant S.Sutton.

The Battalion sailed from Liverpool aboard the former liner *Reina del Pacifico* on 21 November. Unpleasant rumours that the ship was "dry" proved to be based on fact but sufficient bottles had been smuggled aboard inside tunics and kit to mitigate the worst effects. During a stop at Algiers the officers enjoyed a brief run ashore, the consequence being a number of monumental hangovers next morning. Disembarking at Port Said on 1 December, the Battalion spent a fortnight in a tented camp at Qassassin in the Canal Zone drawing arms, support weapons and vehicles before moving by train to railhead at Tobruk and thence by road to Benghazi, which was reached on 19 December. With the exception of C Company, which was accommodated in billets near the town centre, it made its home in Berka Barracks. Neither time nor war had been kind to this structure, which had originally been built in the days when Libya was a province of the Ottoman Empire, but it was being rendered habitable by German and Italian prisoners awaiting repatriation who, one observer commented, could on occasion be galvanised "into laying as many as twenty bricks a day." By a remarkable coincidence one of the German prisoners was recognised by a Hampshire soldier as a man whom he had taken prisoner at Cassino.

Few would have wished to argue that Benghazi was one of the most exciting postings in the world. In addition to performing its share of garrison duties, each rifle company had to provide a twenty-four-hour on-call Desert/Air Rescue column of vehicles, medical support, personnel and rations for use in the event of a military or civil air crash in the desert. Ostensibly, boredom threatened to become the Battalion's real enemy, yet, as the Journal noted, "The Blue Lagoon is close by, its waters are warm and the bathing is good. An occasional ENSA party passes through; films, which have included recently *Henry V* and *Road to Utopia*, change every other night at the Garrison Cinema; the men have the Wavell Arms, the Sergeants and Officers their own clubs; there is a well-stocked library. The RAF are not always 'on strike,' and the mail call gives the bugler his moment of popularity, expressed in an ecstatic cheer. Additions to the comforts of the barracks and the welfare facilities in the town are continually being made. But one cannot go as far as one driver who remarked that he liked the place so much he was thinking of changing his religion."

There was also plenty of sport to be had including football, basketball, hockey, cross-country running, rifle shooting and a well-supported Battalion boxing tournament. Training was carried out in the Djebel Akhdar or the desert, where there were still plenty of traces to be found of the war which had raged across

North Africa. On 9 January 1946 a Guard of Honour was provided for General Sir Bernard Paget, the Commander-in-Chief Middle East, who unveiled two plaques in Benghazi commemorating the first and last Libyan campaigns of the Desert War. In June 1946 A Company began a two-month detachment in Tobruk. Despite heavy demands for guard duties, many people preferred Tobruk to Benghazi because of its better leisure facilities. On the other hand, "The harbour at Tobruk has not been touched since the end of the fighting and contains 174 wrecks above and below water which not only gives it a strange appearance but makes sailing a somewhat hazardous performance. Training was a problem owing to very extensive mining of the whole area; all movement except on roads and marked tracks was forbidden. 30,000 mines were lifted by German POWs under Royal Engineer supervision during our short stay."

For a fortunate few, the undoubted highlight of the Battalion's nine-month tour of duty in Benghazi was an operational trip to Kufra Oasis, approximately 700 miles to the south across the Great Libyan Sand Sea. Until 1941, when General Leclerc's Free French forces from Chad had captured it, this had been the Italians' most southerly outpost in Libya and it was about as far from civilisation as it was possible to get. Such a journey, like matrimony, was not to be entered into unadvisedly, lightly or wantonly, and the obvious precautions taken included fuel for 2000 miles, sand channels and the hiring of an Arab guide. The party, initially over forty strong and accompanied by Brigadier Acland of the British Military Administration in Cyrenaica, left Benghazi in a convoy of jeeps and three-ton trucks on 21 January.

To his surprise, Lieutenant Roger May had been handed a sun compass before departure and told he was the Navigation Officer. Despite never having handled such an instrument before he made few mistakes and quickly became proficient in its use. This was just as well since the guide, as the Journal relates, had his limitations: "The track became gradually more speculative as we progressed and our Arab guide was full of recondite and irrelevant conversation; he was an authority on camel locomotion, but could not conceive that these animals can cross places in which three-tonners would be irretrievably bogged. Soft sand was a perpetual difficulty and there were miles of rutted going like a switchback which did the wireless sets no good and jolted everyone considerably. Other hazards included badly-defined minefields like the one at El Haseiat in the centre of a wired 'box.'"

At times the sand channels were in permanent use and breakdowns became more frequent. It was decided to abandon some of these vehicles and pick them up on the way back. On occasion petrol consumption soared to one-and-a-half miles per gallon. By the time the party had reached Jalo Oasis, a former base of the Long Range Desert Group, resources had shrunk to the extent that two officers and eighteen men were sent back to Benghazi with all the non-essential stores, including the tents. After another sixty miles of soft going a calculation revealed that more fuel would be required to get the convoy to Kufra than the trucks could carry. Leaving Lieutenant May and five men to continue the journey with Brigadier Acland, the rest of the party also returned to Benghazi. Even so, by the time the remaining two jeeps and two three-tonners reached Kufra the spares situation had become critical.

Kufra supported a surprisingly large population. The former Italian fort now housed a French garrison consisting of one officer, one sergeant and six Senegalese privates armed with bolt-action single-shot rifles probably dating from the Franco-Prussian War; the legality of their continued presence was questionable but Acland was not inclined to make an issue of it. There was also a three-man RAF meteorological detachment which spent its days sending up weather balloons. On learning that this was to be relieved shortly Acland despatched a signal to Cairo requesting that the aircraft should also bring a list of necessary vehicle spares.

Altogether, twelve days were spent at Kufra. These were passed in what today would be called "hearts and minds" activity, arranging races for the children and other sporting events. The party attended several feasts given by Brigadier Acland, local sheikhs, merchants and the police. In due course the spares arrived and it became possible to return to Benghazi, the entire round trip having taken twenty-four days. Considering that the concept of adventure training was still in its infancy, it was a remarkable achievement. As intended, valuable lessons had been learned. The Brigadier's Arab cook, for example, could produce a meal on his primitive charcoal fire in a fraction of the time required by the Army's temperamental hydro-burners; but if one wanted a brew in a hurry, there was no substitute for a tin filled with petrol-doused sand, known as a "Benghazi cooker." To prevent indiscriminate fouling of the desert, latrines consisted of a hole, lined with a suitably cut hard-tack biscuit tin to prevent the sand flowing back. No matter how much sand was deposited on top of the spoil, these devices always became popular meeting places for hordes of hitherto-invisible flies. As for the ubiquitous "separately sited" urinals, their proliferation earned them the title of "desert roses."

In the autumn Colonel Frisby was informed that the Battalion would be moving shortly to Palestine, where he had already served with the 1st Battalion in 1939 and been awarded the Military Cross. By now, Palestine was not only in a state of growing unrest but had also become an area of considerable strategic importance, given the glowering attitude of the Soviet Union and the proximity of its troops to the oilfields of Iran, Iraq and the Gulf, the supplies from which, then as now, formed a vital component of the Western economic structure.

Palestine was a mandated territory and not a colony. The mandate to govern the country had been conferred on Great Britain by the League of Nations in 1919 following General Allenby's ejection of the Turks. Two years earlier the Balfour Declaration had favoured the establishment of a Jewish homeland in Palestine and this idea was also supported by the League, ignoring the fact that the 55,000 Jews actually living in the country were outnumbered twelve-fold by their Arab neighbours. Between the two World Wars Jewish immigration increased so dramatically that the Arabs, feeling they were being driven out, resorted to armed rebellion. By 1939 the revolt had, with some difficulty, been put down, although in a wish to avoid further trouble the British government agreed to limit Jewish immigration to 75,000 over the next five-year period then discuss the problem again. In the light of what was taking place within Nazi Germany this was bitterly resented by many Jews, although the majority, including Hagana, the disciplined self-defence force established with official approval to protect Jewish settlements during the early years of the mandate, co-operated willingly with the British war effort after the outbreak of the Second World War. A notable exception to this was the Stern Gang, also known as Lehi, a terrorist organisation which demanded immediate Jewish rule in Palestine. Its founder, Abraham Stern, was shot dead in a gun battle with police in 1942, but the organisation itself remained in being. A former follower of Stern's was Menachem Begin, a future prime minister of Israel and winner of the Nobel Peace Prize, who in 1943 became head of Irgun, another terrorist organisation with similar aims to Stern's. The following year Begin declared a formal revolt against the mandate with the reservation that as long as the British Army was engaged in hostilities against Nazi Germany its members would not become targets. That, however, did not stop regular bombing attacks on police posts.

With the ending of the European war in 1945 the situation began to deteriorate rapidly. Both Irgun and Lehi attracted large numbers of recruits, simultaneously reaching an accommodation with Hagana and the moderate Jewish Agency. When Ernest Bevin, the British Foreign Secretary, announced that immigration would be allowed to continue at the rate of 1500 a year, this figure fell so short of Jewish ambitions that the scale of unrest escalated at once. There was serious rioting and attacks on the police, the railway system and oil installations were intensified. By November the police were clearly unable to control the situation on their own and the Army was called on to assist the civil power. The troops were forced to open fire, killing several Jews, before order could be restored. After that the British armed services became the terrorists' major target. Ambushes and attacks on airfields and bases, usually carried out by groups equipped with stolen British weapons and uniforms, were followed by the murder or kidnapping of unarmed soldiers, the latter being held as hostages to the fate of convicted terrorists awaiting execution. In the summer of 1946 the Army responded with Operation Agatha, a major cordon-and-search operation that produced a haul of 600 weapons. Irgun's reply was to blow up the King David Hotel in Jerusalem with the loss of over ninety lives.

Concurrently, the Royal Navy was intercepting a series of coffin ships transporting thousands of Jewish refugees from Europe and escorting them to Cyprus where they were housed in temporary camps. This was a propaganda gift to the terrorists, who exploited it to the full among the influential Jewish-American community; Ben Hecht, the Hollywood producer, was particularly vocal on the subject, declaring that the angels sang every time he learned of the death of a British soldier. Under such pressures the American administration, well-intentioned but naive in the matter of Middle East politics, expressed its disapproval at the British handling of the situation.

By the autumn of 1946 there were no fewer than 27,000 British troops in Palestine, including the 1st and 3rd Divisions and the 6th Airborne Division. The average serviceman, knowing what the tragic passengers aboard the coffin ships had endured during the Holocaust, had every sympathy with their plight; what he found difficult to understand or forgive was the pleasure taken by the terrorists in killing British soldiers when his own country had offered sanctuary to tens of thousands of Jews and shed so much of its blood in overcoming the very evil that had created the Holocaust. Nevertheless, he maintained his disciplined calm even under extreme provocation; only on very rare occasions, such as the cold-blooded hanging of two British hostages, would individuals seek personal vengeance.

This, then, was the witches' cauldron that awaited the 1st Battalion when it sailed into Haifa aboard the *Winchester Victory* on 2 October 1946. It was first accommodated in a camp near the city and for the next two months was kept busy providing guards, manning roadblocks, and other internal security duties. At the end of November it moved to Transjordan (now Jordan) for brigade exercises lasting three weeks, it being difficult to hold conventional exercises in Palestine itself for obvious reasons. It then returned to a tented camp at Hadera, approximately half-way between Tel Aviv and Haifa, where it became part of the 1st Division's 2nd Brigade.

Here internal security duties were resumed with constant guards, checkpoint duties, roadblock manning, cordon-and-search operations, provision of escorts and railway patrols. There were times during the Battalion's tour of duty in Palestine, notably during its spell in Jerusalem, when 230 men were required for guard duty each night, with a further two companies on fifteen minutes' standby. On average, a full night's sleep in bed could be enjoyed once every four nights. There were periods, too, when in the interests of their own safety troops were confined to camp for weeks at a time unless they were on duty. Some men, to their own astonishment, found themselves thinking nostalgic thoughts about Benghazi.

There were, nevertheless, moments in which to take great pleasure. In December Colonel Frisby was able to inform the Battalion that HM King George VI had honoured the Hampshire Regiment as a whole by granting it the distinction "Royal" in recognition of its outstanding services during World War II. The King was known to have taken a personal interest in the Regiment and on one occasion had recommended a passing-out parade of officer cadets to study the 2nd Battalion's action at Tebourba, which he described as "a triumph of individual leadership and corporate discipline."

Naturally, opportunities for sport were severely restricted but the boxing team, led by Captain A.E.Amor, commander of Headquarters Company, did so well in the brigade and divisional events that one wag suggested substituting a pair of boxing gloves for the flag usually flown from the pole outside the Company HQ tent.

The Arabs caused few problems for the security forces but they could see where events were leading and as both they and the Jews began arming for the conflict between them, which had now become inevitable, large areas of Palestine passed from effective government control. In February 1947 Foreign Secretary Ernest Bevin, confronted with the impossibility of reconciling two implacably opposed factions and himself under pressure from the United States, handed the matter over to the United Nations and declared that Great Britain would relinquish her mandate the following year. The UN solution was to partition Palestine into equal halves, despite the fact that even at this stage the Jews amounted to only one-third of the total population. Nothing could have been more calculated to provoke the intervention of neighbouring Arab states after the British had left, inducing the first of a series of Middle East Wars, the consequences of which remain unresolved to this day. But that is another story.

In the meantime, Colonel Frisby had been posted to a staff appointment at GHQ Middle East Land Forces in January, having handed over command to Lieutenant Colonel Richard Chandler, DSO. Colonel Chandler had served with the all-Hampshire 128 Brigade in North Africa and Italy, first with 2/4th Battalion, then as Second-in-Command of the 5th Battalion during its stand against overwhelming odds at Sidi Nsir, and finally as a very distinguished commanding officer of the 1/4th Battalion in Italy. One of his first appointments was that of Captain Roger May, MC, to the post of Adjutant at the tender age of twenty-one.

In Palestine, as indeed elsewhere, information on terrorist activity was gathered through two channels, the military intelligence network and the civil police. Military intelligence relied largely on the interrogation of prisoners and covert surveillance; the Palestine Police, too, relied on interrogation and surveillance but also had its informers, including minor criminals promised immunity if they co-operated, those who sought the removal of personal enemies and, of course, those seeking financial reward. The Battalion's Intelligence Officer, Captain Sydney Jary, MC, received intelligence from Brigade on the need-to-know basis and this was applied operationally. It was difficult to gauge the accuracy of this by the results obtained since, by their very nature, the terrorists avoided any direct contact save of their own choosing; equally, many of their plans may have been foiled by the mere presence of troops.

On 20 March Colonel Chandler broke the news to the stunned Battalion that it was to be placed in a state of suspended animation, that is, disbanded save for a small cadre, thereby reducing the Regular element of the Regiment to a single active battalion. Ostensibly, there was no apparent logic to the decision, for the 1st Battalion was directly descended from the 37th Foot and had an unbroken record of distinguished service going back 245 years. The core of the problem was that the Army was stretched terribly thin by global commitments and this, coupled with the steady discharge of war-enlisted officers and men and the need to maintain new units such as The Parachute Regiment, meant that it lacked the manpower resources to maintain units at anything like their proper establishment. Therefore, since the Army was about to withdraw from Palestine within a year anyway, it seemed sensible that battalions due to return home shortly should consist of their suspended animation cadre and those due for release shortly thereafter, having posted the rest of their personnel to units remaining behind.

For the moment, however, the 1st Battalion The Royal Hampshire Regiment, now thoroughly accustomed to being cold-shouldered by the Jews, being pointedly ignored by the Arabs and the omnipresent graffiti inviting the British to go home in the rudest way possible, must soldier on. In mid-April it left Hadera for a dusty camp at Qastina, to the north of Gaza, coming temporarily under the command of the 3rd Division. During part of the first fortnight six of the nine rifle platoons were out on patrol for seven consecutive nights. There was one contact with a small terrorist group, one of whom at least was hit. The intensity of this operation curbed terrorist activity in the area to the extent that for the next fortnight the Battalion was simply required to provide guards for Divisional Headquarters.

At the end of this period it moved to the area of Jerusalem then designated Zone B, where some of its activities are described by the Journal: "Zone B contains the better class of residential area, some of which has been requisitioned from the Jewish population amidst profound protests, to house the deserving soldier; the whole zone is wired off like a perimeter camp, with three main gates which we guard zealously. Within the zone live many VIPs, including the GOC-in-C and various high government officials, which makes the task of security increasingly important. Through our gates travel all the important persons of the world, including the delegates of the United Nations Special Committee on Palestine. The task of inspecting vehicles and a host of different types of passes is extremely difficult, but it is with pride that we can honestly say that from every quarter, from the Press, from the Civil and from the Military, the men have earned an excellent name for efficiency and courtesy."

Shortly after arriving the Battalion carried out a major cordon-and-search operation in the Jewish quarter of the Old City. "Here we found a labyrinth of narrow streets and passages with houses, or more aptly dwelling places, built in a haphazard fashion for the last 2000 years. This old city has been destroyed several times and on each occasion the inhabitants either dug out their houses and continued to live in them, or built another house on top, so that in many cases people live four or five storeys down! The whole area is a warren of secluded dark passages and secret cellars; some of the underground tunnels are known to lead outside the city walls, and one even reaches Jericho nearly 15 miles away. In this area, which measures only about 500 yards by 500 yards, live three or four thousand Jews and within it would be possible to lose an entire brigade of troops. However, we did not lose a man, but found thirty-four suspected males and two malicious-looking female suspects."

During this period the Battalion's already declining strength was reinforced by a draft from the South Lancashire Regiment, the arrival of which reduced the frequency with which guard duties came round. Colonel Chandler departed for a staff appointment in Malta in July, his place being taken by his Second-in-Command, Major J.S.S.Gratton, who was granted the acting rank of lieutenant colonel.

There is every reason to believe that the Battalion was hurting the terrorists, for they now mounted several direct attacks upon it. First, a three-ton truck belonging to C Company was ambushed in Agrippa's Way. "Although the truck was riddled with 32 bullet holes, only two men, L/Cpl Heath and Pte Revill, were hit. The driver missed being hit by only an inch; two other men in the back of the truck both had their shorts 'holed' but escaped serious injury. Both L/Cpl Heath and Pte Revill were immediately sent to the British Military Hospital in Jerusalem, where fortunately they received excellent treatment. In the ensuing search of nearby houses for the thugs Pte Eades was very lucky when a further single shot grazed his chin. Several other incidents occurred around our infamous billet which we shared with D Company, and was bordered on one side by the Jewish Agency, the Municipal Gardens on another and Mamillah Cemetery on the other."

A further attack was mounted on a D Company patrol under Captain R.B.Waymouth which went to the assistance of a fire-bombed police car. As they scrambled out of their 15-cwt truck they were engaged with small-arms fire which was promptly returned, the result being the wounding and capture of a terrorist without loss.

August the First was, of course, Minden Day, the most important day in the Regimental calendar. Because of the Battalion's heavy operational commitments it was impossible to hold the usual celebrations, but Colonel Gratton was determined that the occasion should not pass unmarked. All ranks were provided with the traditional red rose to wear in their head-dress throughout the day and a souvenir leaflet describing the battle was distributed. Duties were reduced to a bare minimum, a special midday meal was produced and the officers were invited to enjoy a drink in the Sergeants' Mess. Uppermost in most people's mind was the opportunity to catch up on some lost sleep. The terrorists, however, had other ideas. The subsequent clash is described by Captain James Dunning, who was one of its participants:

"Just after mid-day, as Tiffin [lunch] was about to be served, a group of terrorists approached the perimeter wire and under cover of smoke and some covering fire threw a mattress onto the wire and attempted to get over it. Their intention was to catch the Battalion off its guard on this low-key Regimental holiday, force a breach in the wire, blow up a billet and escape into the surrounding residential area during the ensuing confusion.

"They did not count on the vigilance of the unlucky chaps detailed for the perimeter guard that day, who fired shots into the smoke. Hearing the firing, Second Lieutenant R.H.Arden, who as Orderly Officer was about to inspect the meal at C Company billet, told a handful of soldiers lining up for their grub to follow him. It must be borne in mind that all ranks carried their arms and ammunition with them at all times and were thus ready for action. Led by Arden they dashed from the billet to beyond the wire, that is, behind the terrorists, and opened fire at about 70 yards' range. With a couple of well-aimed rounds from his rifle Cpl Thurley killed one as he was running, whereupon the rest fled, leaving behind arms and explosives.

"Left by the wire were two brown paper parcels, which were assumed to be home-made bombs. They were. Each contained about 50 pounds of gun-cotton slabs. Captain Dunning, commanding C Company, then arrived on the scene and, fearing that the bombs might have time fuses, immediately set about disarming them. As it happened, they had been primed but not set and so were quickly rendered harmless.

"This was the first and only time during the whole period of the Palestine troubles that a major terrorist attack was completely thwarted without any casualties to our own forces and it could not have happened to any battalion on a more appropriate day."

The Journal takes up the story: "The official estimation was that 18 terrorists were taking part, of whom one was killed, five captured and three wounded but escaped. In addition a number of grenades and Sten guns were captured and the whole of the 250 pounds of explosives with which they intended to blow up the building. The same day the GOC, Lieutenant General G.H.A.Macmillan, wrote a congratulatory letter to the Battalion, and the action was highly praised by the Brigade Commander and the Chief of Police."

One of the escaping terrorists had the misfortune to cross the path of the Provost Sergeant, Sergeant Eager, who struck him so hard on the head with his revolver that the butt was damaged. The affair was to have an interesting sequel. Among those who interrogated the man was Captain May who, by 1979, had risen to the rank of Colonel and was serving in the Ministry of Defence, where he was visited by two Israeli officers. Through them he was put in touch with a Mr Arieh Eshel who had taken part in the attack. When questioned over lunch in a London club Eshel disclosed that nine members of Irgun had taken part in the raid with the aim of blowing up a building. He and his partner had provided covering fire and it was his partner who was killed. Two of their party had been wounded but got away and three including himself had been captured. They had not appreciated that it was Minden Day, nor the significance of the date; neither had they appreciated that the action took place within 100 yards of the Officers' Mess where the Battalion Colours were lodged. When Sergeant Eager's part in the action was described to him, Eshel said that he was the victim and displayed the resulting lump on his head. A friend of Mr Begin's, he had remained in custody until the end of the mandate in 1948 and had subsequently been rewarded with a senior post in the Israeli Diplomatic Service. A final postscript to the incident was provided by the Jabotinsky Institute in Tel Aviv which, in 1980, wrote to Colonel May via the Israeli Embassy in London, informing him that the attack had been mounted by Irgun as an intended reprisal for the execution of three terrorists on 29 July 1947.

By now the Battalion felt not only that it had the measure of its opponents, but also that its reactions were considerably faster than theirs. On occasion this could be taken to extremes, as in the case of the C Company subaltern who, observing a dressing gown behaving suspiciously in an outfitter's window, beat it to the draw and shot it full of holes.

The Battalion's tour in Palestine was now rapidly nearing its end. Having posted seventy men to the 2nd Middlesex and detached another eighty to extra-Regimental employment, it left Jerusalem in September and moved to Moascar in Egypt where it spent three weeks. On 22 October it embarked aboard the troopship *Otranto* for the uneventful voyage home.

This was to be the last homecoming of the old 37th, so the occasion was to be both nostalgic and memorable. As the *Otranto* moved to take up her berth at Southampton on 5 November she was played alongside by the Regimental Band. Waiting to welcome the Battalion on the quayside were the Colonel of the Regiment, General Sir George Jeffreys, the Mayors of Winchester, Southampton and Aldershot, and a large group of officers. Also present was Fritz, the Pyrenean Mountain Dog liberated from German ownership by the Battalion on D Day at Arromanches and now the Regimental mascot, of whom more anon.

After disembarkation leave the Battalion was posted to Purfleet in Essex, less two companies required for general duties at Woolwich. By January the departure of two further release groups had reduced its strength below viable levels. A Farewell Parade was held, during which the Colours were trooped for the last time, and on 17 February 1948 the suspended animation cadre, consisting of six officers and eighteen men, moved to the Regimental Depot at Winchester. Few entertained any real belief that suspended animation would be followed by resurrection. The supreme irony was that the Army was about to expand to manpower levels never previously attained in its peacetime history.

* * * * * * * * *

FRITZ - THE REGIMENTAL MASCOT 1944-1949

Magnificent was the only word one could use to describe Fritz, a fully-grown Pyrenean Mountain Dog weighing 122 pounds. Originally named Barri by his owner, a German officer, he and his master had been captured on D Day in Arromanches by Captain C.L.Thomas's platoon while the 1st Battalion was fighting its way inland from the beaches. Later, it became apparent that he had been trained to a very high standard indeed, combining obedience with a strong sense of guarding. Even-tempered and friendly, he was nevertheless a one-man dog who, on command, would pursue, bring down and pin anyone else; any would-be intruder who sought escape would have quickly discovered there was none, for Fritz could clear a six-foot barbed-wire fence without difficulty.

Shipped back to England with a batch of German prisoners, Fritz faced destruction or six months in quarantine kennels. A member of the WRNS, Leading Wren Elgar, decided that the former was unthinkable and undertook to pay the considerable quarantine fees herself. Deprived of his liberty, Fritz smashed up his first kennel but settled down in due course. In the meantime, Captain Thomas, now wounded and in hospital, contacted Major H.J.Jeffery at the Regimental Depot and asked him to find out what had become of the dog. Major Jeffery traced him and decided that he would make a fine Regimental mascot. Leading Wren Elgar was duly relieved of responsibility for the fees, which were raised by subscription within the Regiment, and, his period in quarantine over, Fritz duly reported to the Depot. There he became a member of the Regiment and, like any soldier, his kit was listed on his own Army Form H1157. It included two parade jackets, two brushes, one comb, one badge, one collar, two harnesses, two leads and one feeding bowl.

Fritz's appearances on formal parades, striding along beside his white-gauntletted Dog Major, were popular with members of the Regiment and civilians alike. During the visit of King George VI and Queen Elizabeth to Winchester on 17 May 1946 he was officially presented and was duly patted for the service he was rendering.

Fritz died in 1949. Anyone who has ever lost a dog knows only too well that there is no other in the world quite like it. It would have been a simple matter for the Regiment to have purchased another Pyrenean Mountain Dog, but he would not have been Fritz, with all his associations.

* * * * * * * * *

THE HAMPSHIRE TIGERS

CHAPTER 2

FROM WAR TO COLD WAR

The Regiment receives the Freedom of Aldershot, Bournemouth, Winchester and Southampton - 128 (Hampshire) Brigade in Austria - the 5th Battalion disbands - duties of 2nd and 1st/4th Battalions in Vienna - the 1st/4th Battalion disbands - the 2nd Battalion returns home - the 2nd/4th Battalion in Crete and Greece until disbandment - disbandment of 147 Regiment RAC - the 7th Battalion in NW Europe - move to Berlin and duties there - disbandment and laying up of Colours - introduction of conscription - the Cold War begins - changes in conditions of service and uniform - the 1st and 2nd Battalions merge to become 1st Battalion The Royal Hampshire Regiment (37th/67th) - the Regimental Book of Remembrance and Memorial Garden - the Freedom of Portsmouth - the 1st Battalion joins 31 Lorried Infantry Brigade in Minden - first post-war parade of Trooping the Regimental Colour on Minden Day - aspects of life in BAOR - Commemorative Memorial porch at Serle's House and presentation of a silver tiger to the City of Winchester - the 1st Battalion returns home - embarks for service in Malaya

Even before the last echoes of the Second World War had died away, and despite the fact that most of its battalions were still serving overseas, such was the pride of the people of Hampshire in their County Regiment that a number of local authorities decided to bestow upon it their respective Freedoms at the earliest opportunity.

A series of parades took place, beginning at Aldershot on 11 September 1945, then Bournemouth on the 13th, the City of Winchester on the 15th and finally the City of Southampton on 25 April 1946, during which these honours were conferred. On each occasion the Regiment was represented by detachments from all its battalions, the parade commander being Lieutenant Colonel James Lee, DSO. Scrubbed webbing, shining boots and well-creased uniforms produced an immaculate turnout, notwithstanding the difficulties presented by the contemporary battledress and the beret, khaki, general issue, which resembled an under-designed Tam o' Shanter and was probably the least attractive head-dress ever adopted by the Army. One unique feature of these parades was the presence together of the King's and Regimental Colours of no fewer than seven battalions. Another was that of Fritz, the Regimental mascot referred to in the previous chapter, groomed within an inch of his life and resplendent in his amber-fringed black velvet jacket embroidered with the Regimental badge, stepping out proudly with Dog Major W.Bradd behind the parade commander.

Each parade took the form of a march to the selected venue with Colours cased and the corps of drums silent. The Mayor or his Town Clerk then made a speech outlining the history and achievements of the Regiment before handing over a beautifully illuminated Freedom Scroll in its casket to the Colonel of the Regiment, General Sir George Jeffreys, who made an appropriate reply. The Regiment then exercised the rights conferred upon it by marching through the streets with Colours flying, drums beating and bayonets fixed. Solemn and moving as these occasions were, they were also intended as a demonstration of pride. There were many former members of the Regiment intermingled with the crowds lining the route, while among the civilians there were few whose families did not contain at least one member who had served with the Hampshires at one time or another. Thus, the Regiment was greeted with prolonged cheers and applause as it marched by, men raised their hats as a mark of respect, and the Branch Standards of the British Legion were lowered in salute as the Colours passed.

Meanwhile, the Regiment's battalions were continuing with their duties overseas. Immediately after VE Day the 128th (Hampshire) Brigade, consisting of the 2nd, 1st/4th and 5th Battalions, moved north from Italy to undertake occupation duties in Austria. They were initially nonplussed to be welcomed by their very recent enemies as heroes but soon discovered that the Austrians, living in mortal fear of Russian occupation as they were, viewed the British presence as a guarantee of their safety.

At first the Brigade was stationed along the Austro-Yugoslav frontier. Its duties involved implementing the directives of the military occupation authority, including the showing of horrific documentary films on German concentration and extermination camps for compulsory viewing by the entire adult population, the preservation of law and order, frontier patrols and the rounding up of the area's Nazi element. At this period the whole of Central Europe seemed to be on the move with columns of slave labourers and displaced persons trudging their way home, the Russians heading east towards the Red Army's zone and people from what had been the occupied nations of Western Europe walking in the opposite direction. There was, too, the distasteful task of repatriating Yugoslav prisoners of war who had fought for the Germans. These fell into two groups, the composition of which reflects many of the troubles afflicting the former republic today. First, there were the Croats who had formed the pro-monarchist Cetnik groups that had fought against Marshal Tito's mainly Serb communist partisans and ultimately co-operated with the Germans. Secondly, there were the Serb-hating Bosnian Muslims who had actually contributed an entire division to the Waffen SS. Naturally, the victorious communists were only too anxious to lay hands on these men, who harboured no illusions as to their probable fate. Nor did the Hampshires, but the decision had been taken at the highest political level and orders had to be obeyed, however much they went against the grain. The hand-overs were made to grimly jubilant partisans, bristling with weapons, at frontier posts, and the captives would be marched out of sight. All too often, a burst of firing would follow within minutes. Fifty years later, yet more chapters have been written in the bloody history of ancestral hatreds between Serb, Croat and Bosnian Muslim.

In other respects, life in Austria was very pleasant. The picturesque countryside had not been fought over, there was fishing for those who could find the time and tackle, the beer was excellent, and, the demands of the war having removed all the males of military age, the new arrivals found themselves surrounded by interested maidens of bashful fifteen, matrons of fifty, and all ages between. The official *diktat* was one of no fraternisation with the former enemy, but neither this, nor the Cook Sergeant's legendary infusions of bromide into the cookhouse tea buckets, nor vigorous exercise, made much impact on the situation.

The 1st/4th Battalion, commanded by Lieutenant Colonel A.G. Ryshworth-Hill, MC, settled into its quarters in the quaint old town of Bleiburg, establishing its headquarters in a nearby schloss. The owner, a grumpy nobleman, took strong exception but was ignored. In an ill-considered attempt to re-establish his standing and prestige locally the man approached Regimental Sergeant Major G.I.Bugden with a demand that the Quarter Guard should turn out whenever he appeared. Once his blood pressure had subsided sufficiently to permit speech, the RSM responded to the effect, more or less, that the Hampshires were not the chorus from some Franz Lehar operetta; that the Quarter Guard was fussy about whom it turned out for; and that the nobleman was not on the list; or words with a similar meaning.

In August 1945, following inter-zonal boundary changes, the Brigade moved one hundred miles eastwards to the Austro-Hungarian frontier, the 2nd Battalion being initially based at Freidberg then Bad Gleichenberg, the 1st/4th at Furstenfeldt and the 5th at Hartberg. The Brigade's duties involved frontier patrols and manning checkpoints, bringing it into direct contact with the Red Army for the first time. Cordialities were somewhat restricted by the language barrier, and on the Russian side soon disappeared altogether, undoubtedly on the orders of higher authority. Further contacts were restricted strictly to business. Sometimes the Russians would be co-operative, but at others they would be surly and obstructive in identical circumstances; most people found their psyche quite impenetrable.

The effects of the release programme now began to make themselves felt. The 5th Battalion, commanded by Lieutenant Colonel P.R.Sawyer, MC, since the departure of Lieutenant Colonel A.Boyce, DSO, in September 1945, received the order to disband the following January. Of the original thousand officers and men who had left England with the Battalion in 1942 only six officers and 174 men remained. On disbandment some 250 men were posted to the 1st/4th Battalion, the strength of which had also begun to decline.

At the end of November the 2nd Battalion, commanded by Lieutenant Colonel J.P.Fowler-Esson,DSO, MC, moved to Vienna, which, like Berlin, had been divided into Allied occupation sectors. Here, its function was to perform guard duties, including the ceremonial guard at Schonbrunn Palace, the former summer residence of the Hapsburg emperors, through the portals of which passed innumerable senior officers and important political figures. In view of the presence of American, French and Russian troops in the city an extremely high standard of turnout was demanded and given on these occasions. During the Christmas festivities the Battalion played host at a party for 2000 children who otherwise had little or nothing to celebrate in the cold, grey world of 1945.

At the end of January 1946 the 1st/4th Battalion replaced the 2nd in Vienna, performing the same functions. The daily requirements for guard duty amounted to 110 all ranks, but despite this the Battalion was brought to the highest standards of drill and turnout. One of the high points of the period was a Guard of Honour mounted at Schonbrunn Palace, with the Regimental Colour on parade, to welcome a visit by the Chief of Imperial General Staff, Field Marshal Lord Alanbrooke. As luck would have it, it was snowing lightly on the day and until the last possible moment a small squad was kept busy flicking flakes from the guard's berets, shoulders and boots. The Field Marshal, having inspected the guard and expressed himself well pleased, then entered the Palace, doubtless wondering why the Hampshires were apparently immune to the snow which now covered his own uniform.

With one short break the 1st/4th remained in Vienna until July. One of the various ceremonial duties carried out was the changing of the guard at the Headquarters of the Allied Control Commission, located at the Palace of Justice. The Battalion provided a guard of 100 men who marched behind the Regimental Colour with bayonets fixed to the magnificent square fronting the building where, amid much ceremony, responsibility was formally handed over to the French 6th Chasseurs Alpins. So high was the 1st/4th's reputation for precise drill and overall smartness that it was asked to participate in the Vienna Military Tattoo, during which 150 warrant officers, NCOs and men gave a drill demonstration without any word of command being given, any necessary signals being communicated by flashlight from a control tower.

In July the 1st/4th Battalion, commanded since 15 May by Lieutenant Colonel James Lee, DSO, returned to Furstenfeldt and there made preparations for its dispersion and disbandment, which took place on 1 September.

The old 128 (Hampshire) Brigade had now ceased to exist. The 2nd Battalion remained in Austria for a further eighteen months, sometimes dispersed to carry out border patrols along the Yugoslav and Hungarian frontiers, and sometimes undertaking further periods of guard duty in Vienna. At the British Troops Austria Small Arms Meeting in October the Battalion team won the prestigious Steele Cup Championship. In November Lieutenant Colonel J.H.H.Robinson, DSO, OBE, took over command on the departure of Lieutenant Colonel Fowler-Esson.

On the rare occasions that the Battalion was concentrated at Tessendorf Barracks, Klagenfurt, it became possible to do a modest amount of training and a very popular ski school was organised during the winter months. At the beginning of 1948 the Battalion again moved to Vienna for the now familiar round of guard duties and on 1 March it took part in the ceremony of changing the guard at the Headquarters of the Inter-Allied Control Commision. The Battalion had already received a warning order that it would be returning to England and within a fortnight of this parade postings to other units reduced its strength to 175 all ranks. On 15 March a special train conveyed the depleted 2nd across Europe to the Hook of Holland, whence it sailed to Harwich. Posted to Bulford, it assumed the duties of Training Battalion for the Wessex Brigade (The Devonshire, Gloucestershire, Royal Hampshire, Dorsetshire, Royal Berkshire and Wiltshire Regiments).

Elsewhere, VE Day had found the 2nd/4th Battalion supervising the removal of German prisoners from Crete. This task lasted until August, when the Battalion moved to Yannina for two months and then to Patras in the Morea where it occupied very pleasant quarters within a hundred yards of the sea. In March 1946 it moved into billets just outside Athens. Here its function was to restore order in the event of trouble during the Greek elections, but these passed off quietly enough. This uneventful if enjoyable year in the Battalion's life, during which it suffered from the usual constant drain on its manpower, was punctuated by the need to provide a Guard of Honour for Field Marshal Viscount Montgomery's arrival at Hassani airfield on 1 December. On 3 January 1947 the Battalion held its last ceremonial parade and was then dispersed. Its Commanding Officers during this period were Lieutenant Colonel F.Mitchell, DSO, MC, until 16 September 1945; Lieutenant Colonel J.L.Spencer, DSO, OBE, MC, until 3 January 1946; Lieutenant Colonel P.H.Man, OBE, MC, until 29 October; and Lieutenant Colonel H.T.Roberts until disbandment.

In North West Europe the first Hampshire unit to disappear was 147 Regiment RAC, commanded by Lieutenant Colonel W.B.Blain, DSO. 147 had been formed from the Regiment's

10th Battalion in November 1941 and, equipped with Churchill tanks, had fought in the infantry support role from Normandy onwards, being disbanded in October 1945.

The 7th Battalion, commanded by Lieutenant Colonel D.E.B.Talbot, DSO, MC, was leading the advance of the 43rd (Wessex) Division on Bremerhaven when Germany surrendered. Some measure of the ferocity of the battles which the Battalion had fought since it landed in Normandy eleven months earlier can be gauged by the fact that over one thousand men had passed through its ranks, the majority of whom had been killed or wounded.

After contributing a contingent to the XXX Corps Victory Parade in Bremerhaven itself, the Battalion moved to the small town of Winsen, halfway between Hamburg and Luneburg, where it performed occupation duties. The Germans, having accepted their defeat philosophically, gave no trouble; rather, it was the groups of displaced persons, and the Poles in particular, who were inclined towards acts of revenge and had to be kept in order.

Colonel Talbot left in June, handing over to his Second-in-Command, Major D.B.Rooke, MC and Bar, who was promoted lieutenant colonel. In October the Battalion moved to Soltau, where it took possession of a former cavalry barracks that had recently been used to house displaced persons. Suitably cleaned up, this was named Bournemouth Barracks.

The 7th continued with occupation duties in Soltau until March 1946, when it moved to Berlin, being housed in comfortable barracks in the suburb of Spandau. It was given particular responsibility for preserving order in the Tiergarten area, in which the four Allied sectors met. This area was the haunt of deserters from all four armies, black marketeers, thugs, pimps and the rest of the Berlin underworld. The Battalion maintained a company group permanently stationed there, its patrols reacting so swiftly to the first signs of trouble that the activities of the criminal element were always kept under tight control.

Notwithstanding the fact that Berlin still presented a scene of almost total devastation, it offered numerous compensations, including excellent sporting facilities. The great Olympic Sports Stadium was at the Battalion's disposal; there was rugby football, soccer and hockey, indoor swimming, badminton and tennis. In the evening and at weekends there were plenty of clubs, cinemas and theatres to be found among the ruins.

On the first anniversary of VE Day, Colonel Rooke commanded the British contingent, consisting of the 7th's Colours and Escort, Royal Marines and an RAF detachment, during an Inter-Allied parade down the famous Charlottenburg Chaussee. Predictably, the Russians again trotted out their new Josef Stalin III heavy tank, which had caused such alarm among the Western Allies when it was first unveiled at the Berlin Victory Parade the previous September. The tank was armed with a 122mm gun which, when fitted to earlier models, was known to have cracked open the armour of the formidable Tiger at impressive ranges, and this meant that every Western tank in contemporary service was outgunned. Furthermore, the JS III, with its low, domed turret and sharply angled hull armour, apparently presented the optimum possible ballistic defence against kinetic energy attack. Yet, if the impassive Slavonic faces of Russian senior officers watching both parades betrayed the merest hint of gloat, this was not justified by subsequent experience on the battlefield. Nevertheless, the appearance of the vehicle at the Berlin parades of 1945/46 provided a very sharp spur indeed for Western weapons designers. For the infantry, it was apparent that the conventional anti-tank gun had a very limited future and that henceforth successful anti-tank defence would depend increasingly on chemical energy (i.e. shaped charge) weapons and the development of delivery systems to make them effective at longer and longer ranges.

The Battalion's last major parade took place on 24 May 1946 at Gatow airfield where it provided a Guard of Honour, complete with the Regimental Colour, to welcome the South African Field Marshal Jan Smuts who, though he had fought against the British during the Second Boer War, had remained a firm friend of the United Kingdom ever since. The following month it moved to Luneburg, where it disbanded.

On 20 July the 7th's Colours were laid up in St Peter's Church, Bournemouth, the Battalion's home town, following a very moving parade which was cheered by a crowd several thousand strong as it marched from Central Station. First, the Regimental Band being overseas, came a band provided by the Regiment's own Army Cadet Force units; then Dog Fritz, by now well used to great occasions; then the Colour Party, with Colours flying and bayonets fixed in accordance with the Freedom granted the previous year; then a forty-strong detachment from the Battalion itself, consisting of men on leave; and, finally, 300 members of the Comrades' Association, representing two generations of soldiers with an honourable record of service in three wars.

A most important factor which was to affect both the Regular and Territorial Armies during this period of change was the introduction of National Service. True, the need to provide an Imperial garrison for India had gone, but in other respects the Army retained its worldwide commitments and there was the additional need to maintain substantial armed forces in West Germany to counter the Soviet Union's barely-veiled expansionist threats. With a foresight notably absent in considerations of national defence during recent years, Prime Minister Clement Attlee's government authorised the expansion of the Regular Army to a strength of 305,000 men, with teeth arms consisting of 77 infantry battalions (excluding Gurkhas), the Royal Armoured Corps with 30 regiments, the Royal Artillery with 69 regiments, and the Royal Engineers with 23 regiments, plus supporting services. The very idea of peacetime conscription was politically dangerous, but it was the only way in which the required manpower targets could be achieved. Attlee, moreover, was inclined to trust to the basic common sense of the electorate and experienced no difficulty in guiding the 1947 National Service Act through Parliament. The Act originally provided that with effect from 1 January 1949 young men aged eighteen were liable to serve one year with the Colours and six years on the reserve. The full time commitment was subsequently increased to eighteen months and then, following the Defence White Paper of 31 August 1950, to two years followed by three-and-a-half years in the Territorial Army. In the event, most men entering the Territorial phase of their service availed themselves of a £50 Bounty payable if they volunteered to serve for four years; many of them chose to enlist for further terms. The result was that, during the 1950s and early 1960s, Regular battalions were able to operate at full strength and Territorial battalions, while losing something of their all-volunteer character, consisted almost entirely of fully-trained, experienced personnel.

The timeliness of the government's measures became apparent in March 1948, when the Soviets began a sustained campaign of harassment against the British, French and American garrisons of Berlin. On 22 June they severed all land communications between Berlin and the Western Allies' respective zones of occupation in West Germany, clearly anticipating that the garrisons would be withdrawn. The West, however, was not inclined to submit to such bare-faced bullying and Berlin was supplied by air until the following year when the Russians, accepting defeat, lifted their blockade. Nevertheless, Soviet aggression continued, using surrogate means. When, in June 1950, communist North Korea invaded its southern neighbour, the United Nations despatched troops, including a British contingent, to the latter's defence. Faced with this additional commitment the Army had to resort to recalling some of its Regular reservists, of whom a large proportion were former prisoners of war, so that by the end of 1951 it had approximately 400,000 men under arms plus an expanding Territorial Army in reserve.

Changes were also taking place in the daily life of the Army. Save for the Brigade of Guards, which had a heavy programme of ceremonial duties to perform, suggestions that the infantry should revert to its 1914 Full Dress scarlet for parades and walking out were never seriously considered. Officers were required to purchase No 1 Dress (Blues) which were worn when dining in the Mess on weekdays. Blues were also worn by the Orderly Officer for Guard Mounting and evening duties. For specific ceremonial parades on which it was desirable that the Escort to the Colours and the parade orderlies should also wear Blues, the Quartermaster, having obtained the necessary authority, would indent for the temporary loan of dress items and accoutrements from the theatre pool. During this period the official dress for Bands became No 1 Dress, which was provided at public expense; subsequently, over a period of years, regiments, keen to emphasise their esprit de corps, provided Full Dress for their Bands. In the late 1940s the hideous khaki beret - "that abomination" as Montgomery called it - was replaced by the smarter dark blue beret that has remained part of working dress ever since. At the same time other ranks were permitted to open the neck of their battledress blouses, which were now worn with a collar and tie; shortly after, a much improved version of the blouse, with tailored lapels, became general issue. The new shirts were made from a hard-wearing material known as "angola drab." When new, their coarse fabric was calculated to drive the most dedicated hermit into a frenzy, but after being laundered a few times they became wearable. Curiously, despite the trend towards smarter uniforms, they continued to be issued for over thirty years. Under Montgomery's influence, the War Office also accepted the point that discipline would not collapse instantly if soldiers in barracks slept between sheets like other citizens; less enthusiastic about the idea were the Company Quartermaster Sergeants, who had to account for these items during their weekly journeys between their stores and the local laundry. Curiously, the boxing of blankets after Reveille, once necessary as a hygienic precaution, continued for many years. Simultaneously, the War Office also accepted that the provision of reading lights above a soldier's bed space was not necessarily the first step on the slippery slope to decadence.

Under Colonel Chandler, the 2nd Battalion had continued in its role as Training Battalion to the Wessex Brigade at Bulford. During 1949 it began accepting fortnightly intakes of National Servicemen, putting them through their basic training and then posting them on to the regiments in the Wessex Brigade to whom they had been badged.

By now it was apparent that the War Office had no intention of re-instating the two-battalion Regular establishment of the Regiment. On 11 August 1949, therefore, the cadre of the old 1st Battalion merged with the 2nd Battalion to bring into being the 1st Battalion The Royal Hampshire Regiment (37th/67th), which retained both Stands of Colours.

At Bulford, the new 1st Battalion's shooting and boxing teams continued to do well. At one time the shooting team had the unique distinction of holding both Queen Victoria trophies, that for units abroad having been won by the old 2nd Battalion in Austria. In the ring, the boxing team won the Salisbury Plain District Championships.

Colonel Chandler left the Battalion on 31 October 1949, command being assumed by Major C.A.T.Halliday until the arrival of Lieutenant Colonel R.H.Batten, DSO, OBE, on 3 January 1950. On 6 May Colour Parties from the 1st and 4th Battalions and the 14th Parachute Battalion, together with a Guard of Honour provided by the 1st, were present at two commemorative ceremonies held in Winchester, both of which were attended by the Mayor and Corporation of the City and the Lord Lieutenant of Hampshire, the Duke of Wellington, KG. The first took place at the Cathedral where, after the re-dedication of the city's War Memorial 1914-18 / 1939-45, the Regiment's *Book of Remembrance*, containing the names of 2094 of its members who had made the ultimate sacrifice for their country and county during the Second World War, was emplaced in its bronze-framed case and plinth designed by Major P.R.Sawyer, MC,TD, and entrusted to the care of the Dean and Chapter. The second took place in front of Serle's House, the Regiment's Headquarters, where the Lord Bishop dedicated a Memorial Garden containing a central flagstaff, rose bushes from Minden and a tree from Ploegsteert Wood. After this, the Regimental Flag was broken and wreaths were laid at the foot of the staff by one of the Regiment's Royal Hospital, Chelsea, Pensioners, seventy-seven-year-old Colour Sergeant D.Prior, and Captain F.H.Waldren, the latter on behalf of the Comrades' Association, twelve of whose Branch Standards were on parade. Even today, despite its proximity to the bustling city centre and the passage of heavy traffic nearby, the Garden, with its Regimental flag floating quietly above, retains a great sense of peace and tranquillity. Together, the Garden, the *Book of Remembrance* and the publication of David Scott Daniell's third volume of the Regimental History, covering the years 1918-1954, constituted the Regimental War Memorial. All came into being as a result of private subscriptions contributed by members of the Regiment, past and present, families, friends and organisations of every kind throughout the County and beyond.

On 20 May 1950 the Regiment was honoured with the Freedom of Portsmouth. The parade included detachments from the 1st and 4th Battalions, the 14th Parachute Battalion and 524 Light Anti-Aircraft/Searchlight Regiment RA (the old 7th Battalion) and members of the Old Comrades' Association; sadly, Dog Fritz was not there to lead it, having died the previous year.

The training role could be repetitious to the point of boredom and it was, therefore, with something of a sense of relief that the 1st Battalion received orders to join the British Army of the Rhine as part the 7th Armoured Division's 31st Lorried Infantry Brigade, in which, for the first time, it would perform the role of a lorried infantry battalion. It left Bulford on 21 February 1951 bound, by a happy coincidence, for Clifton Barracks, Minden, which had been built on the site of the French camp prior to the battle almost two centuries earlier. Many members were thus able to walk across the battlefield, covering the same ground on which the old 37th's disciplined volleys had blasted the French Household Cavalry into ruin and broken the nerve of Contades' white-coated infantry.

FROM WAR TO COLD WAR

On 17 April the Battalion provided a Guard of Honour and band for the visit of Field Marshal Viscount Montgomery, now Deputy Supreme Commander Allied Forces Europe, to Rhine Army's Headquarters. Having subjected the guard to so thorough an inspection that its members felt every detail of their turnout was being evaluated by his sharp eyes, the Field Marshal expressed himself well pleased.

Minden Day was celebrated by the first post World War II parade of Trooping the Regimental Colour. Distinguished guests included the corps, divisional and brigade commanders, the salute being taken by the Colonel of the Regiment. The parade lived up to the highest traditions of the Regiment, high praise on the bearing and steadiness of the Battalion being received from many visitors. This reflected the greatest credit on everyone who took part and, in particular, RSM W.R.Watton, for the excellence of the drill for which he was mainly responsible. During the evening a dinner and an all-ranks dance were held.

By now the Battalion had settled into the BAOR routine which it was to follow for the rest of its tour in Germany. Individual and specialist training was carried out during the worst of the winter months, followed by sub-unit, battalion and brigade exercises as spring turned to summer, culminating in a major exercise in the Soltau area in the autumn. German barracks were considered to be infinitely superior to their counterparts in the United Kingdom, such items as cigarettes could be obtained at a fraction of their usual price at home, and with the German cost of living still low and a contemporary exchange rate of DM12 to £1, it was possible to avail oneself of the undoubted bargains that were to be had in the local shops. The most common purchases were suitcases with which to go on leave, radios and sports equipment, all of superior quality. To restrict the drain on sterling the troops were paid in paper scrip, issued in various denominations from 3d upwards. Known as Baffs (British Armed Forces Special Vouchers), they were of use only in barracks and such establishments as the NAAFI and Salvation Army Clubs and the AKC's cinemas, although they could also be used to purchase a reasonable quantity of Deutsch Marks from the Regimental Paymaster for outside activities. There were sports facilities of every kind, including skiing in the Harz Mountains and sailing on the Baltic. The general opinion was that Germany had become an excellent posting.

On his promotion to Brigadier, Colonel Batten handed over temporary command to Major T.G.Tucker and in October 1951 the Battalion moved to Luneburg. On 23 November Lieutenant Colonel R.G.F.Frisby, DSO, MC, who had last commanded the 1st Battalion in Libya and Palestine 1945-46, assumed command for a second tour.

The year 1952 marked the 250th anniversary of the founding of the Regiment. This was celebrated throughout the Regiment, and in Winchester by two special events which took place on 16 August. Detachments of the 1st and 4th Battalions and the 14th Parachute Battalion paraded with the 4th's Colours and ten branches of the Comrades' Association to watch General Lord Jeffreys unveil an elegant Commemorative Memorial porch and door to Serle's House. This not only complemented the architecture of the house perfectly, but also provided a visually satisfying link between it and the Memorial Garden. The Regiment's principal architect, who conceived the plans of both the Memorial Garden and the Commemorative porch and door, was Major P.R.Sawyer,MC,TD. Later in the day the parade marched to the Guildhall, where the Colonel of the Regiment was able to repay some of the kindness shown by the city over so many years by presenting the Mayor, Councillor Miss Doris Edmeades, with a suitably inscribed silver tiger. The tiger was the distinction conferred on the 67th by King George IV in 1826 when the Regiment returned home after twenty-one years continuous service in India and, naturally enough, its members were referred to thereafter as "The Tigers." When the 67th became The Hampshire Regiment's Second Battalion, the tiger was retained in the combined insignia and, by association, the nickname was accorded to the Regiment as a whole.

During the autumn of 1953 the Battalion received its first Pay Team, under Paymaster Major C.G.F. (Chalky) White, MC, Royal Army Pay Corps. This considerably eased the burden of some Regimental officers, notably that of the Company Seconds-in-Command, who were no longer required to hold Imprest Accounts or become involved in the detailed work of Pay Parades.

In the meantime, Colonel Frisby had received orders to the effect that the 1st Battalion was to perform an operational tour of duty in Malaya, where a State of Emergency had been declared in June 1948 following a dramatic increase in the number of terrorist attacks carried out by communist guerrillas.

For the last few months of its time in Germany, therefore, the Battalion set about learning as much as possible about Malaya, its people and terrain, the nature of its enemy, and the weapons and techniques of jungle warfare, including survival. On 29 October it left Luneburg for Fowler Barracks, Perham Down, where it remained for the next six weeks, during which tropical clothing was issued. Colonel Frisby left the Battalion on promotion and was replaced by Lieutenant Colonel P.H.Man,OBE,MC.

On 18 December the Battalion embarked aboard the troopship *Dunera* at Southampton, the scene being no different from countless other departures for active service in the Regiment's long history. Among those who came aboard to wish its members good luck and a safe return were the Colonel of the Regiment, Brigadier Cadoux-Hudson,MC, accompanied by the Lord Lieutenant of Hampshire, the Duke of Wellington, KG, the GOC Aldershot Command and the Mayor of Southampton. On this occasion, the Band was sailing with the Battalion and from an open deck it played the ship away. The quayside was crowded with waving families and friends, struggling bravely to seem cheerful, with mixed success. The tugs fussed and hooted to pull the *Dunera* clear, cast off, and the gap between the ship and the quay began to widen slowly. Then the screws began to bite, churning up foam at the stern as the vessel moved out into Southampton water. For those aboard, ahead lay the open water of the Channel and a new and vigorous chapter in the Regiment's annals.

* * * * * * * * *

THE HAMPSHIRE TIGERS

THE NATIONAL SERVICE SOLDIER

The National Serviceman holds a unique place in the history of the British Army, and therefore in that of all its component regiments and corps. His attitude to the Army itself was ambivalent. Most joined shortly after their eighteenth birthday unless they had obtained deferment to complete their education. To some extent it helped that the commitment was universal and part of life's cycle at the time, but they resented being dragged away from the comforts of home, their jobs and their girlfriends. On the other hand, they were secretly glad of the chance to prove that they were the same men as their elder brothers, fathers and uncles who had fought in World War II, and their grandfathers who were veterans of the Great War, with whom they would now have something in common.

If a National Serviceman asked to serve in The Royal Hampshire Regiment because of family associations his request would probably be granted. On arrival at the Depot his first impression was that the Army was a great leveller. He was handed brown paper and string and told to send his civilian clothes home. Then, the incorruptible military barber, usually a silent man deaf to discreet suggestions and imprecations alike, would remove 80 per cent of his hair. Now looking distinctly odd, he would be herded to the Medical Inspection Room where, on a production line basis, he and his fellows were injected time and again by the Medical Officer's equally taciturn staff. Worse was to follow as, day by day and week by week, he was chased by sergeants and corporals through an apparently endless routine of drill, weapon training, drill, physical training, drill, lectures about the Army and current affairs, drill, assault courses, drill, map reading, drill, fatigues and more drill. In the evening there was the equally endless round of bulling boots, shining brasses and blancoing of webbing, followed next morning by billet cleaning and kit inspection. He was, in fact, being put through exactly the same training syllabus as the young Regular recruit and it was a shock to the system, even for those with previous experience in cadet forces. Suddenly, the National Serviceman found himself catapulted into the company of others from every conceivable walk and condition of life and, with the realisation that he needed their help to get by, and vice versa, a sense of comradeship began to grow. The constant exercise gave him such a voracious appetite that he supplemented his regular meals with large quantities of food in the NAAFI canteen. There, a cup of tea could be purchased for 2d, a sausage roll for 4d, a meat pie for 7d, a big fry-up for 1/3d and a pint of beer for 9d. If these prices seem impossibly low even by the values of the time, it must be remembered that the National Serviceman's basic pay was just £1.8.0d per week, of which he received only £1, the rest being retained in "credits" as a contingency against "barrack room damages" until he left the Depot. In these circumstances, his spending in the NAAFI had to be carefully controlled since he also had to purchase boot polish, Brasso, Blanco and dusters from his own funds. Even so, he began to increase in weight, putting on muscle rather than flab. The end of his period of basic training was marked by a passing-out parade attended by his parents. During this, his turnout now immaculate, he would swing proudly past the saluting base, knowing that he had successfully passed through one of the most testing times of his life. For their part, his parents were suddenly confronted with a young man who was somehow bigger, and certainly fitter, tougher and more self-confident, than the nervous youth who had left home some weeks earlier.

Shortly after arriving at the Depot the National Serviceman would have an interview with the Personnel Selection Officer, who would assess his aptitudes and abilities for further training. In addition to riflemen, there were requirements for mortar, machine gun and anti-tank gun specialists, drivers, signallers, clerks, armourers, storemen, equipment repairers and all the other trades that ensured the smooth running of an infantry battalion. Thus, on completion of his basic training, he would be posted to the 1st Battalion, which would hold Special-to-Arm training cadres on the 3-inch mortar, medium machine gun and anti-tank weapons. Non-infantry specialist training courses for clerks, equipment repairers and so on were held at external Schools of Instruction and the Battalion would put in bids for vacancies on these.

The Personnel Selection Officer would also assess the suitability of men for Potential NCO and Potential Officer training. The Potential NCO would complete his specialist training before going on an NCO cadre course, after which he would be posted to the 1st Battalion, which would naturally want to assess him itself before awarding promotion. For the Potential Officer, the road was much harder. First, he would have to pass through the

Depot's own Unit Selection Board, which would weed out the least likely candidates. Then, he would attend a rigorous three-day examination by the War Office Selection Board at Barton Stacey. At least half the candidates would fall at this fence or be told to return in three months. If the Potential Officer passed, he would be sent to Eaton Hall for a sixteen-week course before he was commissioned. The course was never less than gruelling and Officer Cadets lived in daily fear of being returned to their units as being in some way unsuitable. Those who failed the selection process were usually granted three choices: they could transfer to the Royal Army Education Corps, in which they would, in due course, achieve the rank of sergeant; they could elect to study Russian at the Army's language school and transfer to the Intelligence Corps; or they could soldier on in the regiment of their choice. Most opted for the last, usually earning one or two stripes before their two years with the Colours ended, and many were subsequently commissioned during the Territorial phase of their service.

The newly commissioned National Service officer might believe that he had left Eaton Hall trailing clouds of glory, but on arrival at his regiment he discovered that once again he was at the bottom of a ladder. In the messes of the most august regiments National Service subalterns were required to keep to their own kind, speak when spoken to, not get under the feet of the senior subaltern or the captains, give the majors a wide berth and never, on any account, approach the Commanding Officer directly. The National Service subaltern posted to the Royal Hampshire Regiment found himself in an altogether friendlier and more constructive environment. It was a shock for him to suddenly find himself subjected to the hard, speculative stare of the entire platoon of trained soldiers for whose training and well-being he had become responsible, especially as many of them were older and more worldly-wise, but this was tempered by the support and advice of his platoon sergeant and section leaders. Provided he listened to them, gave of his best, admitted his mistakes honestly, dealt fairly with his men, shared their hardships and played sport with them, he would have few serious problems. Again, provided he displayed a commonsense attitude to rank and mess etiquette, he would enjoy his off-duty hours.

Indeed, on reaching the 1st Battalion, the majority of National Servicemen would discover a more relaxed and friendly regime than that of the Depot. To their surprise, they discovered that Warrant Officers and NCOs were inclined to steer them away from trouble rather than into it. During a 1st Battalion Commanding Officer's Parade an NS soldier made a mistake, thereby incurring the wrath of the RSM.

"What were you before you joined the Army, lad?" bellowed the latter.

Puzzled, the soldier considered the matter carefully before replying:

"A civilian, sir!"

In many regiments there would have been a universal intake of breath in anticipation of the heavens opening to deliver the expected thunderbolt. In the " 'Appy 'Amps," however, things were done differently. The RSM spread his arms in despair and the parade dissolved in involuntary laughter.

The National Service soldier retained his ambivalent attitude throughout his period with the Colours. The Army was taking two years of his life and since there was nothing to be done about it he was usually determined to enjoy them. He was irreverent, inclined to see the funny side of everything and took delight in puncturing pomposity. He could irritate his Regular counterpart beyond measure by repeatedly telling him how many days he had left to do or pointing at the crosses on his demob wall chart. Perversely, he was outstandingly good at whatever task he was given to do. On parade, on exercises or on active service, he was indistinguishable from his Regular colleagues of the same age. In particular, on active service in Korea, Malaya or any other of the world's troubled areas, he would, for all his youth, display soldierly qualities that would earn him the sincere admiration of senior officers.

As time passed his pay improved marginally and by degrees. Passing a trade test would give him another 6d per day, as would completion of one year's service, and for the last six months he would be paid at Regular rates; in 1954 this meant that a Private with one trade was rewarded with the princely sum of £3.6.6d per week.

On 5 April 1957 the Minister of Defence, Duncan Sandys, announced that conscription would be progressively reduced until 1960, after which there would be no further call-up. The 1st Battalion held a Farewell Parade for its National Servicemen on 30 October 1962, following its return from the West Indies. "It was indeed a moving sight," recalled the next issue of the Journal, "to see the last 50 of many thousands of National Servicemen march off the square to the strains of *Auld Lang Syne*, with the Battalion conveying a symbolic message of thanks by presenting arms." Before they left, the Commanding Officer presented each of the men with a Regimental tie to remind him of the occasion and of his service with the Regiment. When they had gone, there was a sense of loss on both sides.

* * * * * * * * *

CHAPTER 3

MALAYA 1954 — 1956

Origins and course of the Malayan Emergency - training at Kota Tinggi - the first terrorist kills - Bentong - operations in Pahang State - further kills - move to Wardieburn Camp, Kuala Lumpur - location of Companies within Selangor State - Operation Nassau begins - selection for trials with FN-FAL rifle - messages of congratulation regarding Operation Nassau - terrorist counter-attack - distinguished visitors - re-training - operations in Johore State and return to Selangor - the action at Ulu Langat - record number of kills by a British battalion in a single engagement during the Emergency - "Typical Hampshire effort!" - reinstatement of Y and Z Companies - further operations and kills - revenge of a scorned female terrorist - reflections on leaving Malaya and return home - reception at Southampton

The situation which found the 1st Battalion on the high seas bound for Malaya had its roots in the catastrophe which had overtaken the British and Imperial forces during the Malayan Campaign of 1941/42. Following the Japanese victory a clandestine British unit known as Force 136 had organised the delivery of arms and equipment to the Malayan People's Anti-Japanese Army, a guerrilla force which had been raised by members of the largely-Chinese Malayan Communist Party. By 1945 the MPAJA was 7000 strong and the intention was that it should be used in support of the projected British invasion. When Japan surrendered before that invasion could take place the MPAJA was stood down in December 1945, although some 4000 of its members illegally retained their weapons. For a period the communists attempted to gain power by political means but failed to make any headway and by the end of 1947 had decided to employ force.

Their plan was based on the successful guerrilla campaigns

waged by Mao Tse-tung in China. During the first phase, armed groups would establish themselves in secure bases in inaccessible areas, namely the jungle which covered three-quarters of the Malayan Peninsula. The second phase would involve raids of increasing intensity against targets such as plantations, road and rail communications and police posts, gradually establishing a domination over the villages. Once the countryside was in their hands, the guerrillas would initiate the third and final phase, which would consist of conventional operations against the British security forces. According to Mao's gospel, the guerrilla should swim among the population like a fish in the sea, drawing his food, supplies and recruits from friendly villages; if there were villagers who disliked the idea, they could be murdered or terrorised into providing active assistance. This philosophy was mirrored in the organisation of the communist forces which, despite the fact that they called themselves the Malayan Races Liberation Army, drew their support almost exclusively from the Chinese community. In overall command was the Politburo, which formulated policy and co-ordinated operations, its leading military figure being Chin Peng, who had served with the MPAJA and been decorated by the British for his trouble. Below this, the most important element was the District Committee, which was responsible for supplying rations and recruits for the regular terrorist groups in its area, and for re-constituting them if they sustained serious casualties. Responsible to the District Committee were the Min Yuen, who lived in the villages and helped to provide food, and the Li Ton Ten, who enforced discipline within their community by means of execution and torture as well as carrying out minor acts of sabotage and subversion. Yet, despite the essentially sound structure of its organisation, the MRLA suffered from a number of serious handicaps which were ultimately to prove fatal. First, it would have to function in virtual isolation, since the Royal Navy vigorously patrolled the Malayan coastline and the border with Thailand was closely watched. Secondly, outside the Chinese community it enjoyed very little support, the slightly larger Malay population being at best indifferent to its aims. Thirdly, apart from a few local vegetable gardens, the armed groups in the jungle depended entirely on the villages for their support, and if this link were to be cut they ceased to exist. Fourthly, the British had no intention of making a present of Malaya, with its rich resources of rubber and tin, to the communist bloc. Finally, while it was appreciated that British prestige in the Far East could not be restored to the levels it had enjoyed prior to the fall of Singapore, a great deal of lost ground could be recovered by demonstrating the determination and ability necessary to overcome the terrorists.

Following several attacks on planters, a State of Emergency was declared on 18 June 1948. The Emergency Regulations conferred the right to detain without trial, an essential provision in view of the communist intimidation of witnesses, the right to search property without a warrant, which produced useful intelligence and inhibited the accumulation of food stocks, and the imposition of curfews on villages known to be supporting the insurgents, the last involving the inhabitants in some degree of hardship. Most important of all was the introduction of identity cards for everyone over twelve years of age. These had to be produced to obtain food and their issue not only curtailed the terrorists' freedom of movement outside the jungle but also made it extremely difficult for them to live in the villages. Together, these measures forced Chin Peng to withdraw into the jungle by the spring of 1949.

Nevertheless, the overall security situation was far from satisfactory. Guerrilla raids were regular and frequent, resulting in 649 civilian deaths by the end of that year, plus 250 people reported missing without trace. The insurgents began mounting attacks on village police posts, but these were countered by rapid reaction forces from nearby army bases. By now there were seventeen British, Gurkha and Malay battalions operating in Malaya and, although these killed over 1000 insurgents, captured 600 and received the surrender of 300 more during the same period, Chin Peng's District Committees were able to sustain a flow of recruits that made good the loss. At this period the security forces tended to react to a contact with large-scale cordon-and-search operations and the terrorists, warned by their supporters, often managed to evade the net. Clearly a more subtle approach was needed.

On 5 April 1950 Lieutenant General Sir Harold Briggs arrived to take up the newly-created post of Director of Operations. As well as greatly improving liaison and co-operation between the armed services, the police and the civil authorities, he introduced what became one of the decisive measures of the anti-terrorist campaign, namely the New Village scheme. Chin Peng's

41

principal support lay among the 500,000 Chinese squatters who had been living in camps on the edge of the jungle since the world recession of the 1930s. Over a two-year period the squatters were moved into some 400 New Villages, where they were given construction materials, the title to their property and the cash sum of $100. The New Villages also contained schools, clinics and shops and were protected by a perimeter fence and a police post. Food was escorted into the villages but none was allowed out. At a stroke, the measure dealt with many Chinese grievances and support for the MRLA dwindled to the extent that its larger gangs had to be dispersed into smaller sub-units in order to feed themselves. In addition there were now twenty-six infantry battalions deployed against them, plus supporting arms.

Chin Peng, appreciating that he was faced with a major crisis, escalated his campaign of violence. In 1951 the security forces sustained their highest casualties to date and 668 civilians were either murdered or vanished without trace. During the same period 1078 terrorists were killed, 121 were captured and 201 surrendered, but MRLA morale was given a tremendous boost when, on 6 October, Sir Henry Gurney, the High Commissioner, was ambushed and killed in his car.

Shortly after this, on Briggs's return home, General Sir Gerald Templer took up the combined appointment of High Commissioner and Director of Operations on 2 February 1952. The keynote of his policy was winning the hearts and minds of the whole population, and particularly the Chinese element, by convincing them that the government not only had the will and the means to defeat the terrorists but also that it was, in fact, the communists themselves who were hindering economic development, the latter point being emphasised by increased demand for Malayan rubber and tin caused by the Korean War.

Templer's troops went over to the offensive during the spring of 1952. For obvious reasons, the terrorists sited their bases no more than a few hours' march from the villages upon which they relied for food, the two being connected by comparatively few trails. By now, intelligence sources knew which villages were still supplying the communists and ambushes were laid on the trails, steadily eroding the enemy's strength in a series of small engagements. By these means, 1155 terrorists were killed in 1952, 123 were captured and 257 gave themselves up. The weapons most commonly used in these encounters were the No 5 (shortened) version of the Lee Enfield rifle, the Bren light machine gun, the Australian Owen gun, the American M2 carbine, the silenced Lanchester carbine, the 9mm Browning pistol, shotguns and the No 36 grenade. The British Sten sub-machine gun was intensely disliked because of its tendency to jam or discharge itself without the slightest provocation, and because it was wildly inaccurate beyond a few yards' range.

The MRLA was now under intense pressure. Its recruits began to hate the system which kept them deep in the jungle for no apparent purpose. Half-starved, their resolve weakened by airdropped leaflets and broadcasts from low-flying aircraft that promised amnesty and reward, they began to desert in growing numbers. Many were only too glad to talk, with the result that communist supporters in the offending villages suddenly found themselves being rounded up. Some were sent back into the jungle to talk their erstwhile comrades round, while others, known as SEPs (Surrendered Enemy Personnel), guided security force patrols to their former bases.

The effect was to force the MRLA even deeper into the jungle and further reduce the size of its gangs. To counter this the security forces recruited expert Dyak and Iban trackers from Sarawak. In matters of jungle lore and survival, no Chinese terrorist could hope to compete with these men, who were extremely good at their job and very dangerous opponents. From March 1953 onwards the helicopter was used to insert troops deep into the jungle. This further demonstration that the security forces' reach extended everywhere was a further blow to the terrorists' morale. Nevertheles, the MRLA, while under unremitting pressure, was still far from being beaten and would certainly resume its campaign of destabilisation given the slightest chance.

Christmas Day 1953 had proved to be something of a mixed blessing for the 1st Battalion The Royal Hampshire Regiment. The Mediterranean might project a gentle image to the holidaymaker, but it also has a vicious temper when roused. For two days the *Dunera* pitched and rolled wildly, so that the ample Christmas dinner provided by the vessel's owners was enjoyed by some but eaten with dogged determination by most. At Port Said, the first port of call, no shore leave was permitted as relations between the United Kingdom and Egypt were deteriorating rapidly and British troops were largely confined to the Canal Zone. Once within the Suez Canal the traditional barrage of inter-unit insults took place between those on board and those ashore. "Get your knees brown!" bawled the Grenadier Guardsmen lining the banks. "What's it like to have a home posting?" yelled the Hampshires, feeling that they had had the better of the exchange.

Much of the ship-board time was consumed with physical training to maintain the Battalion's level of fitness, lectures and familiarisation with the No 5 Rifle, which was fired from the ship's rail at floating balloons thrown over the stern. Some time ashore was permitted at Aden, where the sun-scorched, barren red rocks of the extinct volcano Shamsan towered over a warren of shops selling luxury goods at duty-free prices, and again at Colombo, where the tattooists were kept busy inserting subcutaneous, and subsequently painful, tributes to mothers and girl-friends; sometimes, alas, the affections of the latter did not out-last the tour of duty, leaving the chagrined wearer with a perma-nent reminder of his misplaced devotion, plus the need to supply a convincing explanation for the benefit of future conquests.

The *Dunera* docked at Singapore on 15 January 1954, be-ing met by Lieutenant Colonel P.H.Man, OBE, MC, who had flown out some days earlier. On disembarkation the Battalion moved to Nee Soon Camp, where it spent the next six days drawing stores, zeroing weapons and sewing insignia onto tropical uniforms. On 21 January it left Singapore Island for the Far East Land Forces Jungle Warfare Training Centre at Kota Tinggi in Johore State, where companies settled down to an intensive four-week training period culminating in a four-day exercise. Here they were intro-duced to the jungle, taught how to live and move in it, and how to cope with the sense of disorientation it induced; how to establish platoon bases, patrol and select ambush sites; how to interpret animal and bird behaviour that betrayed the near presence of other humans; and how to rely upon the senses of sight, hearing and smell for survival. They learned how to employ the same stratagem as bird watchers entering a hide, noisily inserting an entire company or platoon into a suspect area and then ostenta-tiously withdrawing from it a day or so later, leaving behind an ambush section that would lie beside a trail until its prey came into view, then kill in a rapid burst of fire. They learned that if ambushed themselves they must immediately respond with every weapon at their disposal and win back the initiative. They learned, too, the cruel fact of jungle warfare that wounding often pro-duced better results than killing since a wounded man sometimes required the support of two or possibly four of his comrades to carry him to safety, and that the trail of blood slicks he left could well point the way to a terrorist base camp. In sharp contrast, they learned that their own wounded would be picked up by ambulance on the nearest road or lifted out by helicopter from a suitable clearing.

It might be thought that the FARELF Training Centre was located in an area relatively free from terrorist activity, but this was far from being the case. It was during A Company's four-day exercise that Lieutenant J.L.Freeman-Cowan, commanding No 2 Platoon, A Company, was alerted by the characteristic chatter of disturbed monkeys some distance ahead on the track along which his patrol was moving. Weapons cocked and ready, the patrol advanced cautiously until three terrorists suddenly broke cover. Firing a warning shot, Freeman-Cowan shouted "Bandits!" and, dropping to one knee, opened aimed fire with his carbine. Beside him, Corporal Powell also engaged the fleeing targets. Two of the terrorists vanished amid the trees but the third was killed by a shot through the head. He was subsequently identified as Lee Sin, an area secretary of the communist party and therefore a very important person indeed. This was only the second time since the Emergency began that a battalion in training had scored a kill. "Mr Lee had been underground in the jungle since 1949 and, unfortunately for him, he is now 'underground' somewhere else," commented the compiler of A Company Notes in the next issue of the Regimental Journal. Within the company itself Freeman-Cowan and Powell became known by the respective nicknames of "Killer" and "Deadeye."

During the latter half of February the Battalion left Kota Tinggi and moved 300 miles up-country to its operational area, Bentong in Pahang state, where it came under the command of 18 Independent Infantry Brigade (Kuala Lipis), commanded by Brigadier D.E.B.Talbot, DSO, MC (late, the Queen's Own Royal West Kent Regiment), who had commanded with great distinction the 7th Battalion in Normandy, Holland and Germany 1944/45. The Battalion relieved the 1st Battalion The Queen's Own Royal West Kent Regiment. Initial deployment was: Bentong - Battalion Headquarters, Headquarter Company and C Company (Major C.G.T.Mumford, MC; Sungei Penjuring - Support Company (less the Mortar Platoon) and D Company (Major P.A.T.Halliday); Sungei Pertang - A Company (Major G.J.A.Dewar, MBE);

Sabai - B Company (Major F.M.Shaw); Genting Sempah - Mortar Platoon (Captain C.D.Darroch).

Companies immediately found themselves committed to the unremitting process of constant patrolling and ambushes. By now, everyone had slipped into the jargon in which the jungle became the "Ulu" and the enemy were known as CTs (communist terrorists). Patrols varied in length from between two and three days, in which those involved would be self-sufficient, to two or three weeks, during which supplies would be replenished by air drop. Sometimes, when the jungle offered no identifiable features to the pilots, a small clearing had to be cut at an agreed map reference. Such a task required the felling of tall, mature timber using axes, chain saws and explosives. Ambushes could last for days and involve the participants lying silent in their fire positions for hours on end until relieved. More often than not they produced no results at all, but sometimes they produced excellent results and therefore had to be maintained. The jungle compatibility of the attached Iban trackers was a constant source of wonder. They pulled fish from streams by hand and were adept at turning apparently tasty snakes into snacks which no one wanted to share. They had a strong sense of humour that reached hysterical levels whenever a fully-equipped soldier came close to drowning in a river or swamp. Their interpretation of tracks was uncanny. From a few marks on the ground they could tell how many people had passed by, how long since, their sex, whether they were laden and much else besides; they were seldom, if ever, wrong.

Naturally, the lion's share of this work was undertaken by the rifle companies, but the personnel of HQ and Support Companies also did their share of jungle bashing. At Genting Sempah (3940 feet above sea level) was the Bentong Pass at the State Boundaries of Selangor and Pahang, on the Kuala Lumpur - Bentong main road. Here the forty-four strong Mortar Platoon, the senior NCOs of which were Sergeants Haines, Taylor and Morton, was given a number of operational tasks. These included taking over the security escort of food convoys at the State boundary, and providing two road patrols daily between first and last light along the route Genting Sempah - Bentong and return, each consisting of two armoured cars and two open Escort Dodge 15-cwt trucks; one of these daily patrols would be given the additional task of searching the road verges, culverts and embankments on foot to a depth of one hundred yards for likely terrorist road ambush positions. The Mortar Platoon remained at Genting Sempah until 3 May 1954 when it rejoined Support Company at Sungei Penjuring. The Platoon's log recorded a total of 7050 miles on road patrols and escort duties and 66 miles on foot. No CTs were encountered by the patrols but those on foot took a certain amount of "positive hate" from the numerous baboon colonies, each of which apparently possessed an unlimited supply of missiles!

One of the major problems encountered when firing 3-inch mortars in the jungle was the close proximity of the water table. The firing of the "bedding in" rounds to secure a firm and stabilised base plate for the mortar could be a protracted and frustrating affair. This was particularly true of the 4.2-inch mortars which supplemented the Platoon's standard 3-inch mortars later in the tour. Whatever the calibre, it was sometimes necessary to construct log platforms, reinforced with metal ammunition containers, before the base plate held firm.

In Pahang State a typical deployment and employment drill of the Platoon when firing mortars in the jungle was:

(a) The Platoon Commander and part of the Platoon would "march in" some five to ten miles, the first two or three of which would probably be through a rubber plantation before the jungle proper was entered.

(b) Having reached and secured the base plate position for the mortars, possibly chosen from an air photograph or a patrol report, the Platoon Commander would radio for a section of mortars plus crew to be brought in by helicopter (usually a Royal Navy S55) to an LZ secured and possibly cleared by the Platoon. Dependent on the nature of the shoot, the helicopter would probably make two or three ferrying flights with ammunition and stores. On one shoot, which started on the night of 21 May 1954, the task given was to carry out intermittent and harassing fire over a designated number of map squares, by night, for three consecutive nights, from last light to first light.

Perhaps, for the terrorists, the mortar bomb, out of all the types of shells and bombs directed at them, was the most terrifying. Its approach was relatively silent and, in the jungle, it would detonate in the trees, scattering a large amount of lethal shrapnel. On occasion, the Battalion's operations would also be supported by the 25-pdr guns and 5.5-inch howitzers of the Royal Artillery, by air strikes and, during a major operation the course of which will be described later, by naval gunfire.

If there was one group of people within the Battalion who were more affected than the rest by the demands of jungle warfare it was the smokers. Smoking was usually permitted at the patrol commander's discretion and, on the march, ten-minute smoke breaks were a great morale booster. Nevertheless, tactical situations existed in which it was absolutely forbidden. An example illustrating the necessity of this was provided by one patrol which was alerted by the smell of tobacco smoke which could only come from a CT source. Stealthily, the patrol was closing in for the kill when, by the worst possible luck, a radio check alerted the enemy; by the time the assault was launched the CTs had gone. When smoking was allowed, pipes were considered best for dispersing flying insects, but there was no substitute for a cigarette end when it came to detaching the ever-intrusive leeches.

There were few days when everyone was not doing something, and those were devoted to sport of one kind or another. Within and around company bases administrative personnel and those "resting" between long patrols carried out gate and perimeter checks at the New Villages, enforced curfews and undertook daily food denial patrols, usually at the point where the rubber plantations met the jungle. In these respects the British soldier abroad has always been a fine ambassador, especially where children are concerned. He is generally genial and likes to address those to whom he is talking by name; if the subject's name is unknown it matters little, as the soldier will give him one. Thus, Ludwig or Otto will serve very nicely in BAOR and in the Middle East Abdul and Mustafa are firm favourites. In Malaya, however, the complexities of Chinese, Malay and Tamil nomenclature inhibited their use so, in the friendliest possible spirit, the Hampshires bestowed an honorific John upon every male whose pass or baggage required examination.

There were several identifiable strands which ran throughout the Battalion's entire tour of duty in Malaya in 1954 and which are evident in both the company and platoon notes submitted to the Journal, and in the memories of the participants themselves. First, Colonel Pat Man is always remembered by those who served under him as a vigorous and inspiring leader. Accompanied by WOI W.R.Watton, formerly of the Irish Guards and the Royal Military Academy, Sandhurst, he regularly visited the company bases, listening to the stories of the patrols that had just returned, providing motivation for those about to go out and convincing everyone of the value of the contribution each of them was making to the overall success of the anti-terrorist campaign. The second was the intense rivalry which existed between companies and indeed between individual platoons to have eliminated the greatest number of CTs. The third was that everyone preferred to be out and "ulu-bashing" rather than in the company base camps, regardless of the discomforts of the jungle, wading chest-deep through swamps and rivers, or being soaked for hours on end by rain so heavy as to be beyond the range of the average British imagination. The fourth was the part played by the young National Service officers and soldiers who made up over half the Battalion's strength. Most of the latter arrived in Malaya with between a year and eighteen months of their service to complete, and it was by no means uncommon for a National Service corporal to serve as acting platoon sergeant or for a National Service private to command a section during operations. They proved to be every inch their fathers' sons, displaying remarkable qualities of courage, stamina and leadership. As group release dates approached and they began departing for the UK, their Regular comrades were not only saddened by their leaving but also worried by what Fate might have in store for these twenty-year-old veterans. Often, the parting handshake would be accompanied by a gruff "You'll be back!" from the Regular; the "I hope" was never said but it was meant and understood. Colonel Pat Man put it another way. Anxious to retain their services, he spoke to each departing draft in the hope of encouraging them to enlist for an additional three-year engagement. "Out here you are in the jungle but you are among friends," he said. "Where you are going is another jungle in which you will find that you have no friends."

To describe in detail the circumstances of every kill and capture made by the Battalion would require a book in itself. Within the space of a single chapter it is only possible to record the major events of what was a most active tour of duty, reflecting the highest credit upon the Regiment itself.

At one time the Bentong district had been a hotbed of MRLA activity, but over the previous three years the security forces had obtained the upper hand and the remaining CTs did their best to avoid contact. In April 1954 Nos 10 and 11 Platoons of D Company, under the Company Commander, Major P.A.T.Halliday, subsequently Mentioned in Despatches, surrounded and destroyed an enemy camp, killing all five occupants. As three of the dead were later identified as a District Committee member, a Branch Committee secretary and a Branch Committee member, the camp was probably used as an intermediate level headquarters. Messages of congratulation were received from the High Commissioner, General Sir Gerald Templer, the GOC Malaya, Lieutenant General G.K.Bourne, and the Commander 18 Infantry Brigade, Brigadier D.E.B.Talbot. In May and June the Battalion's operational responsibilities were extended to include those of the neighbouring 6th Battalion The Malay Regiment, which had been withdrawn for routine re-training. This meant establishing a small tactical headquarters under Major J.S.S.Gratton, the Battalion Second-in-Command, in the absent unit's area and meant that the Hampshires were now dispersed across an acreage equivalent in extent to three-quarters of their home county.

On 6 May 1954 members of a draft in training with Support Company, which also carried out the role of Training Company, surprised and killed two terrorists. A Company, commanded by Major G.J.A.Dewar, MBE, added to their own score by killing another CT on 23 May. Three days later B Company opened their batting when Corporal Palmer, Privates Byrne and Hallett of No 4 Platoon, together with a Chinese liaison officer named Tony, wounded and captured a District Committee member. On 1 June a patrol, consisting of Sergeant Kisby and Privates Lamb, Peckham and Higgins, also struck, killing a CT in the same area.

July, August and September were less productive. A Company killed two terrorists in August and a Support Company training draft a further one in September. "Bandits are becoming harder than ever to find," mused the compiler of the Battalion Notes. "There are two main reasons for this. Firstly, in Bentong District the communist organisation is now very thin on the ground. The two bandits killed by A Company were the last members of a gang which once consisted of at least twelve terrorists. The second reason is that the communists are very much on the defensive and are more concerned with keeping body and soul together than on making life unpleasant for the Security Forces. It is an excellent thing therefore that we have troops constantly in the jungle because sooner or later they get to know this. It keeps them moving and in a jittery frame of mind. From all reports the bandits are becoming short of food. A large number of their jungle cultivations have been found and destroyed: six by B Company during a 26-day operation in August. The Battalion will not be satisfied, however, until all the Bentong District CTs have been eliminated."

In July 1954 C and D Companies were temporarily detached to the Kuala Lipis area to operate firstly under the 2/7th Gurkha Rifles and then the 2nd Battalion The King's African Rifles. Minden Day was celebrated with Beating of Retreat, parties and football matches. Most of the wives made the journey from Kuala Lumpur to Bentong under an escort provided by the Mortar Platoon at Genting Sempah and were accommodated by local civilians and planters, with whom the Battalion was on the best possible terms. Elaborate arrangements to fly in roses from Sumatra were thwarted by bad flying weather, so inferior local roses had to be obtained at the last minute.

In November another terrorist was killed by B Company, bringing the total number of CT eliminations to twenty-five. At the beginning of December the Battalion moved to Wardieburn Camp, Kuala Lumpur, changing places with the 1st Battalion The Somerset Light Infantry. During the period 23 March to 1 December 1954 all the rifle companies had been out in the jungle for a minimum period of 130 days out of 277. Sixty-eight air drops were received in the jungle in addition to the four days' rations carried in by every man and the numerous food-carrying parties organised for silent re-supply. Forty-five men were evacuated by helicopter from the jungle direct to the British Military Hospital, Kinrara, owing to sickness or injury, and six complete company operational insertions were mounted by helicopter. What pleased the Battalion most was the fact not one single terrorist incident took place in the Bentong District while it was present. Neither it, nor the civil population, sustained any casualties as a result of enemy action. In appreciation of the fact the local police, planters and civilians presented the Battalion with a magnificent traditional Malay sword and two kris (daggers), all in antique silver-worked scabbards.

For the forthcoming operations in Selangor State, the Battalion came under the command of 26th Gurkha Infantry Brigade, 17th Gurkha Infantry Division. With the exception of A Company, which was located at Kuala Kubu Bahru, 40 miles to the north, and C Company, some 60 miles to the south at Sepang, the entire Battalion was concentrated at Kuala Lumpur. The bright lights of Batu Road, the amenities, social life, opportunities for sport and the chance for the married men to spend more time with their families were all obvious advantages after having served for so long in a remote area and enabled everyone to spend an enjoyable Christmas. Less welcome was the fact that, with the exception of 22nd Special Air Service Regiment, who were constantly busy about their own business, the Hampshires were the only battalion in the Federal capital, since this meant providing the High Commissioner's and GOC Malaya's ceremonial guard and other duties.

The first kills of 1955 were made by A Company. The Company had been operating in the Selangor jungle since December, mounting ambushes and patrols intended to eliminate the local gang leader, Heap Thong, and his followers. On 18 January five terrorists attempted to ambush a No 1 Platoon patrol commanded by Second Lieutenant J.D.Walne. "The leading scouts, Private Hamilton and Lance Corporal Elverson, heard a CT weapon misfire and, together with Brasap of the Sarawak Rangers and Kim, our interpreter, opened fire at the hidden bandits. The Bren-gunner, Private Barton, joined in with Second Lieutenant Walne, Lance Corporals O'Gorman and Sweet (Medical Orderly) and circled the CTs and killed two of them at 15 yards range. The other three escaped. No one of the patrol was hurt, but a bullet struck the patrol commander's compass which was on his belt."

A week or two later another of No 1 Platoon's patrols had a further contact. "Corporal New thought it was his last day in the jungle before demob. He was returning to base camp when he came across four CTs resting. Private Brochet, the signaller, saw them first and was pointing them out to Corporal New when Lance Corporal Sweet saw them begin to move and opened fire. Unfortunately his weapon jammed after one round. The others in the patrol - Privates Biggs, Rowland and Hurst - followed up but the CTs escaped. Much to Corporal New's annoyance, we spent three days searching for the bandits!"

January found the rest of the Battalion deployed for a major terrorist drive, codenamed Operation Nassau, which lasted from December 1954 until September 1955. The course of this and its very satisfactory results are described by Colonel Man.

"Kuala Langat is the most southerly district of Selangor. It is about 35 miles from east to west and 25 miles from north to south. Its population of rather over 60,000 is predominantly Malay but includes important Chinese and Indian minorities. It is famous for two swamps, North and South, of which the South Swamp was the focus of the operation. The South Swamp covers an area of over 100 square miles and is virtually trackless except for the western end where logging is carried on. The swamp, except after heavy rain, for the most part appears dry until you go inside. When you do, you sink up to your ankles, knees, waist and sometimes deeper into mud and water. It is entirely jungle with trees going up to 150 feet and thick undergrowth giving a visibility of seldom more than 30 yards and often less. Silent movement is almost impossible and biting insects of every sort thrive in profusion. Other things, including soldiers, exist; they do not thrive.

"All round the swamp is a belt of cultivated land consisting for the main part of rubber, oil palm or coconut estates and smallholdings. In addition there are considerable areas under cultivation, in particular, tapioca. The swamp has from the beginning of time been a sanctuary for the hunted and was again so used by the communist terrorists from the start of the emergency. The terrorists built themselves camps on log platforms inside the swamps and terrorised the civilian population outside into supplying them with food and even luxuries. Several attempts were made to deal with them but with no conclusive result.

"On 29 September 1954 a Chinese boy aged 15 was murdered outside the swamp by a terrorist gang who gave as their reason that they wished to strike at his father. Having beheaded the boy with nine blows of a parang in front of his 11-year-old brother, they kicked the body and returned to the swamp. On the same day two tappers were murdered equally brutally in the same area. Fear, which hitherto had the district in its grip, mounted and the feeling of helplessness increased.

"The first phase of Operation Nassau began on 21 December 1954 and lasted only until 9 January 1955, but in it was sown one of the most important seeds of victory for it initiated the strict food control which was to last throughout the operation. This control was achieved by a system of rationing, convoys, gate checks and searches. At the same time C Company under Major I.F.R.Ramsey (The Dorset Regiment), who were already based at Sepang, began operations in the swamp.

"The second phase began at 06:00 hours on 9 January 1955 with the noise of gun and mortar fire, the drone of aircraft and the crash of exploding bombs. Battalion Tactical HQ was established at Telok Datoh alongside the District Officer and Police Commander and B and D Companies, under Major V.T.G.Liles and Major J.E.Little-Jones respectively, together with the Mortar and Machine Gun Platoons, were committed to the battle.

"The plan for this phase was simple. We should shell and bomb the swamp day and night and make the lives of the 37 terrorists inside such hell that they would either surrender or leave the swamp and be killed by ambushes outside laid by us and the Police. This did not work. In the first place the swamp was some 60 miles round and so we were very thin on the ground, and secondly the terrorists were quite prepared to stay put and take what was coming. This they did. Food collecting parties did come out from time to time, but the local inhabitants were too afraid to report their movements and such information as was received arrived too late.

"The plan, therefore, was modified. The bombardment was restricted to night harassing only. Ambushes continued to be laid outside the swamp and patrolling there was stepped up in an attempt to raise civilian morale. In addition, patrols began to penetrate more and more deeply into the swamp and were arranged so that there were always soldiers inside day and night looking and listening for signs of terrorists.

"January came to an end, then February and March arrived without a contact and with little information of CT movement. It was a trying period involving intense effort, much discomfort and no concrete results whatever. Then, on 17 March, a piece of attractive information was received. Another ambush was laid for 48 hours; nothing happened; the ambush party was relieved; another 45 hours elapsed and then three terrorists appeared. As is almost always the case the terrorist party did not behave as expected and was actually walking back towards the swamp when Sergeant Morris of No 8 Platoon, C Company, and his merry men came out of their position and opened fire standing - thick undergrowth made any other firing position impossible - at a range of 80 yards. They killed two of them and wounded the third; he was killed later in the operation. The two dead terrorists had taken part in the boy's murder. The first two pins appeared on the map and local morale rose a little."

This, in fact, was the first occasion on which CTs were killed using the new Belgian-designed FN-FAL semi-automatic rifle, which replaced the No 5 (Short) Lee-Enfield in the rifle companies, the Battalion having been selected as the only unit in the Far East to carry out operational trials. Half of those issued possessed a normal sight and the rest an optical sight; the latter tended to fog over in the humid jungle environment and the recommendation was that it was best dispensed with. When taken into British manufacture the weapon became universally known as the SLR (Self-Loading Rifle); ceremonially it had not a lot to offer in that its configuration meant arms had to be shouldered rather than sloped, but on balance the opinion of its users was that it was an excellent tool of the trade which gave the rifle section a greatly increased punch.

Colonel Man's narrative continues: "Another month crawled by and then, in the late evening of 22 April, information was received that terrorists were to contact loggers inside the swamp soon after dawn next day. No 4 Platoon, B Company, under Second Lieutenant J.E.Horton, took on the job and moved some 8000 yards in pitch darkness along the narrow gauge logging railway, stepping from sleeper to sleeper well knowing that a false step could well mean a broken leg. They got there, however, and at first light two ambushes were laid. The loggers arrived but did not spot either ambush party despite the fact that they were working virtually on top of them. A terrorist was seen and was immediately shot and killed by Private Collins. So, after three and a half months of intense activity by three companies the total bag had reached three.

"May was comfortably blank despite determined and sustained effort and then in June the tide began to turn. D Company's No 11 Platoon, commanded by Second Lieutenant Jim Kellie, had a chance contact in the swamp - in fact, they hit an occupied camp without knowing it, killing one terrorist and capturing another. A few days later one of C Company's ambush parties, consisting of Corporal Thorne and three men from No 8 Platoon, having been on the job for four fruitless nights, were told on the fifth morning, just as they were going back to camp, that two terrorists had been seen within the last half-hour. They gave chase, killed one and wounded and captured the other. In the same month No 3 terrorist in order of importance, together with his girl friend, surrendered. They told us that one terrorist had died of fever aggravated by starvation, that another had been murdered in a quarrel over food, that the murderer had been tried, condemned and beaten to death by his comrades, and that our food control measures were proving most effective. They gave, in fact, two reasons for surrender, the first being Security Force pressure and the second lack of food. The score, therefore, was now 12 and only 25 remained.

"Towards the end of the month the Commanding Officer told the GOC 17th Gurkha Division, our operational master, that, granted two extra companies, there was a sporting chance that the operation would be finished off by 15 August, the day on which the Battalion was to withdraw from Operation Nassau and start re-training. Two companies of the 1st Fijian Infantry Regiment arrived on 7 July and started operating next day. A major effort employing every available man, together with air bombing, began on the 14th and ended on the 21st. Results: nil. Another major effort began on 24 July and on this day three terrorists surrendered giving the same reasons as the first two. One of these was the No 2 terrorist and he knew the No 1's camp. At first light, therefore, on 25 July No 4 Platoon, B Company, under Second Lieutenant J.E.Horton, with the surrendered terrorist, entered the swamp and marched until late afternoon. They found the camp with four terrorists inside, attacked it and killed three, including the No 1; the one survivor surrendered two days later. In the meantime the 1st Fijians killed two out of two in another camp and then two singletons and by Minden Day the score had reached 23. By 15 August a further three had surrendered, leaving eleven survivors split up into twos and threes with no communication, no food, no contact with the outside world and virtually no hope.

"The 7th Battalion The Malay Regiment then relieved the Battalion which withdrew to Kuala Lumpur for re-training. During the next three weeks the 7th Malay captured two of the eleven and seven surrendered and at midnight on 20 September the operation came to an end. Two days later H.H.The Sultan of Selangor declared the whole area of the operation White, meaning that all restrictions were lifted and that the inhabitants could live their lives as normal human beings without curfews, without rationing, without the sound of gun and mortar fire, without the crash of bombs and without fear. Operation Nassau had paid off."

Among the many messages of congratulation received by the Battalion was one from the High Commissioner, Sir Donald

MacGillivray, KCMG, MBE: "Hearty congratulations to all of you on your recent success in Operation Nassau. Conditions in the Kuala Langat Swamp must be as bad as any in Malaya and the dogged way in which your men have kept up the pressure over many long months deserves the highest praise." The Director of Operations, General Bourne, also sent a message: "Eight eliminations in two days in Operation Nassau is your reward for months of hard and extremely arduous patrolling in one of Malaya's worst swamps. In the past year the successful operations carried out by the Battalion have done much to improve the emergency situation, firstly in West Pahang and recently in the swamps of Kuala Langat. Well done, and good luck to you in your future operations."

It would have been very surprising indeed if the terrorists, who were losing face steadily throughout Operation Nassau, had not made at least some attempt to hit back, but even their best effort came to nothing. This took place some four days after D Company's No 12 Platoon, under Lieutenant B.R.C.Street, had taken over an ambush site. Most of the platoon was resting in its base camp when, at about 01:45, four terrorists managed to penetrate it, the sound of their movements drowned by falling rain. Private Paddy O'Callaghan, a very young Regular soldier, was slashed about the head and feet but managed to shout a warning. Rolling from his hammock, he grappled with a CT and succeeded in wresting his carbine from him, after which the attackers, suddenly finding themselves in a disturbed hornets' nest, faded away. Captain Ian Palmer, RAMC, the Battalion's most excellent doctor, made an extremely gallant night march in the swamp to attend O'Callaghan and spend the night with the Platoon, the patient being evacuated by helicopter after first light. O'Callaghan required a short spell in hospital but emerged to learn that he had been awarded the Military Medal for his courageous and prompt action.

In the meantime, 100 miles to the north, A Company had been slowly but steadily adding to its total of kills. Its final contact with the enemy in this area took place during the early hours of 9 August when four CTs walked into a multiple ambush site manned by No 2 Platoon under Sergeant Pike. Corporal Turkington's section opened fire, dropping three of the enemy, but the fourth escaped. However, only one of the terrorists had been killed and another, though wounded, managed to throw a grenade which killed Private John Ainsley and slightly wounded Corporal Turkington and Privates Bartlett and Dykes. Sergeant Pike was quickly on the scene with two more of the platoon's ambush parties and put an end to the matter. Shortly after, the Company joined the rest of the Battalion at Wardieburn Camp for re-training. Pike and Turkington were both Mentioned in Despatches and later the former was awarded the Military Medal.

With the passage of time the Battalion's personnel had been turning over steadily as National Servicemen and time-expired Regulars left and were replaced by fresh drafts, so that by now comparatively few remained of those who had arrived in Singapore aboard the *Dunera*. The process, however, was slow and enabled continuity to be preserved. Even before Operation Nassau had got fully into its stride the 1st Battalion The Royal Hampshire Regiment had earned itself a reputation in Malaya as being second to none. This meant that it received a stream of distinguished visitors including, on 28 February 1955, Sir Anthony Eden, the Foreign Secretary and Deputy Prime Minister, accompanied by the Chief of Imperial General Staff, Field Marshal Sir John Harding, GCB, CBE, DSO, MC, and the GOC Malaya Command, Lieutenant General Sir Geoffrey Bourne, KBE, CB, CMG. The party arrived by helicopter, met all the available officers and warrant officers and inspected a B Company patrol under Lieutenant D.A.Protheroe, about to go out. During March the Battalion received two visits from the Director of Infantry, Major General C.L.Firbank, CB, CBE, DSO, who expressed himself well pleased with what he saw.

Such popularity was very welcome, but it also had its price, which in this case was the curtailment by ten days of the re-training period granted the Battalion after Operation Nassau. Re-training actually meant some weeks out of the line when no operations were undertaken, these being used to rest, repair and make good weapons and equipment, re-classify on the range, catch up on administration and remind everyone of such neglected arts as drill and turnout. Unfortunately, the re-training period also included the Brigade Commander's Annual Administrative Inspection, the preparations for which involved large quantities of paint, whitewash, boot polish and Brasso. Hard on the heels of this was the GOC's Parade, during which Colour Sergeant W.Butt, MM and Sergeant R.Tombleson received the Long Service and Good Conduct Medal from Major General J.R.C.Hamilton, CBE, DSO,

Chief of Staff HQ Malaya Command, who also took the Salute. Few people enjoyed the re-training period and it was with some relief that orders were received for the four rifle companies and a tactical headquarters to fly south to Kluang for operations in Johore State on 5 October 1955.

Johore was the favourite stamping ground of the terrorists and General Bourne had personally selected the Hampshires with a view to bringing the situation under control. Unfortunately, although three rifle companies were always active in the jungle at any one time, this proved to be the least productive period of the Battalion's entire tour in Malaya. There were two reasons for this. First, at the higher command levels there were frequent changes of mind and plan which resulted in those on the ground being repeatedly mucked about. Secondly, there was no contact whatever with the enemy, and it is tempting to speculate whether the local CTs, having been warned of the Battalion's by-now fearsome reputation, simply decided to stay even further out of harm's way.

At the end of November the Battalion moved back to Kuala Lumpur, with HQ, C and Support Companies at Wardieburn Camp, A Company and the Draft Training Wing at Kuala Kubu Baru, and B and D Companies at Kajang, about 15 miles south of the capital. Together, the re-training period and the Johore experience had induced a feeling of frustration. That, however, was to change radically when a composite company under Major J.M.Symes, MC, achieved one of the most spectacular coups of the entire Malayan Emergency. Major Symes describes the course of action in his memoirs, a copy of which is held in the Regimental archives at Serle's House.

"At 17:00 hours on Saturday 10 December 1955, Derek Sowerby, the District Special Branch officer in Kajang, arrived at our camp in his grey car. He asked for troops to be made available to attack a group of high-ranking terrorists believed to be attending a course of political instruction in a jungle camp near the village of Ulu Langat. There were possibly seventeen CTs in the camp, including Chan Lo, the Selangor State Committee Secretary, Wahab, a District Committee member, and Sarlip, a Branch Committee secretary. Derek thought that some of the terrorists might be out of camp between 08:30 and 16:30 hours collecting supplies from supporters in the rubber, while the rest were in camp attending the course. He could give us only an approximate location of the camp. He was prepared to let us have as a guide an ex-CT, whom we named George, who had actually been to this camp. George knew that the camp was to the south-east of Ulu Langat in very hilly country and that it was about 600 yards from the rubber/jungle edge. It was small and very well concealed and was on a steep spur running south to north. The spur was flanked by two streams which joined up to the north of the camp. About 150 yards beyond the streams to the west and east were two parallel ridges running north and south. The camp was protected by a large log at the north end. There were possibly three sentry posts: one a hundred yards to the north; one a hundred yards to the south; and one by the waterpoint on the stream west of the camp. There were two main escape routes, one to the east and one to the south. George did not think the CTs would go north since they would soon be in cultivated rubber. He considered that the only possible approach was from the north-west between the log and the waterpoint.

"George knew of a route to the camp from the village of Sungei Long and wanted to approach by this route, but the Police were ambushing in that area and could not be warned or withdrawn in time; so we needed to find a route which would bring us as quickly as possible onto George's route north-east of the ambush area. This meant approaching from the west, i.e. over the River Langat which at that time of year was in spate. We therefore needed a bridge and there were two possibilities. Either we went to the village of Ulu Langat and crossed the river there, or we crossed by the bridge near the village of Bukit Raya. We discarded the Ulu Langat option since the villagers were known to be CT sympathisers, so we were left with the bridge at Bukit Raya. One of Derek's police officers, Inspector Alias, knew the route from the bridge to the River Sub, and from there through the jungle to George's track, when we would be about 2000 yards south of the camp area. It seemed as if our approach to the camp would be painless. Another Special Branch officer, Inspector Shahir, would accompany us and act as interpreter between us and George. Dick Sowerby offered another ex-CT to act as George's escort and we accepted this offer.

"I calculated the distance from the debussing point to the suspected camp area to be about 5000 yards as the crow flies. As I aimed to keep to the jungle tracks as far as possible, I estimated the total distance to be covered to be about 6000-7000 yards. From the debussing point we had first of all to cross about 1000 yards of rubber, and the bridge. The rubber plantation was Chinese-run, which meant that there would be considerable undergrowth to slow us up, since the Chinese did not worry very much about husbandry as British planters did. We would also be slowed up by the bridge, which was reported to be not very strong, and for safety's sake we would have to cross in single file. Marching in pitch darkness in dirty rubber is not fun, nor is crossing a wonky bridge. I decided to base-up for the night after we had crossed the bridge and reached the rubber/jungle edge. The jungle in this area was a mixture of primary and secondary.

"It is difficult to be dogmatic about marching speed in these types of country. Some say that in neglected rubber an average is about 1700 yards per hour, and in primary and secondary jungle it is seldom possible to move at more than that speed, but it is more likely to be about 1000 yards per hour. But to allow for the extreme hilliness of the country I considered 500 yards per hour to be a good average. Even at that speed, as it turned out, the signallers with their man-pack sets had difficulty keeping up and to help them their colleagues carried their personal equipment. There was also a constant need to check progress by counting paces, and by compass bearings, which further reduced our speed.

"I had optimistically hoped to be able to cordon and attack the camp on the evening of 11 December, but the more I thought about it the more I realised it would require a great stroke of luck to be able to do so. Though George said he knew where the camp was, we had to get to his track first, then carefully approach the camp area, cordon it, which we anticipated would take two-and-a-half hours, move the assault force into position, then attack.

"I felt I would need at least three platoons to be able to cordon and attack a camp with up to seventeen CTs in it. On standby in Kajang were No 6 Platoon of B Company (Lieutenant J.B.Bretherton) and No 10 Platoon of D Company (Sergeant G.R.Hogan). The nearest platoon was No 4 Platoon (Second Lieutenant D.L.Stephens) at Cheras, nicely situated on the route to the bridge. There was a curfew daily from 23:00 hours on the road Cheras - Ulu Langat, so there was no point in moving before that time. I decided to embus at Kajang at 23:30 hours, pick up No 4 Platoon and then debus on the road near the track leading to the bridge over the River Langat. I asked Derek if he could provide four Police four-ton vehicles, since military lorries had a particularly distinctive whine which was well known to everyone including the CTs, and which would carry some distance in the still of the night. He agreed to do this.

"We would travel light. We would take rations for 24 hours only, but no cooking stoves. We would not take washing kits, as soap suds floated about 400 yards before dispersing. Nor would we take matchetes or similar cutting implements, because the sound of chopping carried a considerable distance in the jungle. There would be no smoking and there would be radio silence. To get things moving I gave out orders to the platoon and section commanders of Nos 6 and 10 Platoons, and to the platoon commander of No 4 Platoon, who had arrived from Cheras.

"It was now about 20:15 hours. Activity in the camp was kept to a minimum so that suspicions that something was afoot would not be aroused. At 23:30 we set off. All went well until we started to cross the bridge. It started to sway alarmingly after the first two or three men had stepped onto it and I had to order that there would only be one body on the bridge at a time. It therefore took twenty minutes for the company of 120 men and two dogs to cross. We then formed up and marched through the rubber, and at 02:40 I ordered a halt. We lay down just inside the jungle edge, where we rested until 05:45 hours. We took bearings from scrubland on the jungle edge and found that we were further east than we had meant to be. We turned more to the north, came out in the rubber, and headed for the River Sub. Inspector Alias thought that a track which he found was the one he was looking for but, when we took bearings from a hill, we estimated that we were still some distance from the river so we stopped for a cold breakfast. During this halt Captain Len Chandler, D Company's Second-in-Command, and Inspector Alias went out to ascertain where we were and returned to say that we were not all that far from the Sub. At 10:30 we continued our advance. We reached and crossed the Sub, where we replenished our water bottles, the metal caps of which had been exchanged for rubber ones to eliminate any noise.

"Our next halt was made about 500 yards further on, just before we reached the jungle edge, where the track suddenly became very steep and rough. Inspector Alias, aged 43, found the going very tough. We plodded on for the next three hours. The only incident of note was when the leading scouts had a nasty brush with hornets. Luckily no one was stung but it was interesting to see how quickly one could move in the jungle if one had to! At about 15:30 George announced that we were near his track from Sungei Long. We halted, and I sent George with two soldiers as escort to make sure it was the right track. I gave the order for everyone to have a cold meal while we were waiting and used the time to go over the details of the move into the cordon etc with the officers and NCOs. Twenty minutes later George returned with the good news that we were on the right track. It was about 15:30 hours and I knew that there would not be sufficient time to find the camp and position the cordon and attacking force before dusk, let alone attack it. The company packed up and moved about two or three hundred yards along the track. I sent Second Lieutenant David Stephens with George to find the camp. When they returned at last light they said they had heard voices, and so we knew where the camp was.

"According to the information I had received in Kajang, the camp should have been four to five hundred yards from where it actually was. I decided to stay where we were for the night and to move about four hundred yards further north early next morning, and to carry out a further recce from there.

"On arrival at the new base area next morning, I went out with George, Shahir, Len Chandler and Private Jones, my wireless operator, to confirm George's news and settle the final details. Sure enough, we heard the sound of chopping and voices. We were on the ridge to the west of the camp and could see the log. It was now about 09:00 hours. I sent George and Len back to the base to start the moves into the cordon positions and to bring up the assault parties. It took George about three hours to put Nos 4 and 6 Platoons into position. They were not allowed to move forward of a line which George pointed out to them. He then brought Len Chandler and No 10 Platoon up to about seventy yards from the CT camp. While Inspector Shahir, Private Jones and I were watching the camp we saw three CTs including one woman but we could not tell how many there might be altogether. My wireless operator, the three platoon operators, the dog handlers and dogs, under the command of Colour Sergeant Taylor, were left in the base area.

"We had one particular piece of good luck. It started to rain at about 09:00 and it stopped at 12:00 hours. This covered any noise made by the main cordon party. It stopped at the wrong time as the most difficult part of the cordon operation - the move of half of No 10 Platoon - had still to take place. George, however, put them in position without any alarms and rejoined me. The final operation was the move forward to the start line of the assault force. A short distance below us was a track running parallel to the camp and I felt this would make a good start line. We started to get into position at 12:30 and were ready to go at 13:10. When we reached the track we were pleased to note that our movements had been covered by the noise of the stream.

"The going between the track and camp was very rough. There was first of all a very steep slope down to the stream, and then a very steep slope up into the camp. My main worry now was making up my mind about the right time to launch the attack. I knew there were at least three CTs in the camp - I had heard voices but did not know whether they belonged to others or not. I did not know whether the food parties had gone out. I did not know whether the exclusion order on the tappers had been extended, though Inspector Shahir thought it would have been since nobody had heard from us. I felt on balance I should attack at once.

"The assault party consisted of four groups of four or five. The northern group, under Len Chandler, was to go straight down the hill to the stream to cut off any sentry who might run that way. After the attack they were to move into the camp and cover the northern edge by the log. My group, consisting of myself and the Police, Sergeant Hogan's group (he was No 10 Platoon Commander), and Corporal Smith's group from No 10 Platoon, were to advance in line on the camp. The move forward was to be as quiet as possible. My group was to deal with equipment and documents, Hogan's group would go through the camp to the eastern side, and Smith's group to the southern side. When the camp was cleared the rest of No 10 Platoon, which was in the cordon, would be called forward to fill the gap on the western side of the camp.

"At 13:20 hours I gave a hand signal to advance. There was a very loud noise of snapping twigs, but no reaction came from the camp. When we had made about ten yards down the slope and were about twenty yards from the camp I yelled 'Charge!' and fired at the cookhouse basha. There was a few seconds' delay while the whole assault party fired towards the camp and then we all slithered down the slope, crossed the stream and started to climb the steep slope into the camp. Some were lucky to find the steps leading from the water-point. The rest of us were soon in the camp and Len's group joined us shortly afterwards. A shotgun was fired at us.

"The camp was a mess. There were documents galore, abandoned clothing, but no packs or weapons. The CTs had tried to get out of the trap. The cordon had started firing by the time we got into the camp and, from the sound of it, the CTs were moving east and south. A party of eight which headed south was greeted by a burst of fire from No 6 Platoon and at least three were killed. The five survivors turned east and tried to break through No 4 Platoon. All died. The firing died down and I ordered the cordon parties to close in on the camp. There were six bodies in front of No 4 Platoon and five in front of No 6 Platoon. I ordered the platoons to search for any more in their respective areas. A female, one of two in camp, was found lying wounded in a thicket. When John Bretherton, commander of No 6 Platoon, tried to bandage her leg, she just spat at him and would not be bandaged. The other female had been killed.

"I sent a message to Colour Sergeant Taylor to bring his group from the base to the camp. I then reported the success to Battalion Headquarters in Kuala Lumpur. I just said 'I have figures One Two.' It was thought I said 'One or two,' but we soon got that right. I asked for a carrying party to bring out the bodies and the booty. I was given 70 local Home Guards. The captured female had to walk. Our sole casualty was Corporal Smith, who was slightly wounded under the arm by splinters from a tree which was believed to have been hit by Bren gun fire.

"On 22 December a combined patrol of Nos 5 and 11 Platoons visited the camp area to search for any items we might have missed. They captured Sarlip, the Chinese Muslim Branch Secretary of the Ulu Langat area. He had been wounded in the action and gone to ground in thick cover. He stated that there were no other CTs in the camp."

Altogether, eleven terrorists had been killed, including Chan Lo, and two had been captured, together with a large haul of intelligence material, three rifles, two shotguns, one carbine, one Sten, two pistols, four grenades, 478 rounds of ammunition and ten packs. The action was the most successful security operation mounted since 1951 and also resulted in the greatest number of terrorists eliminated by a British battalion in a single engagement throughout the Emergency. Over fifty messages of congratulation were received, the sources of which are recorded elsewhere. Perhaps the most gratifying was from the Battalion's former Commander, 26 Gurkha Infantry Brigade, Brigadier C.S.Howard, DSO, OBE, now Deputy Director of Military Training at the War Office. It read: "Terrific - well done - typical Hampshire effort!" In other words, a thorough appreciation of the situation had been made, based upon all the available information; a viable plan had been put together, discarding the least suitable alternatives yet allowing for every contingency; and, above all, maintenance of the objective had been the hallmark of every phase of the plan's execution. Major Symes, a Guernseyman who had already been awarded the Military Cross for a clandestine mission to the Channel Islands during World War II, received a Bar to the award; the Military Medal was awarded to Corporal H.T.Smith and Corporal J.H.Wheeler.

For those not engaged in operations, Christmas was observed in the traditional manner with the officers waiting upon the men and football matches. Colonel Man, feeling that the Battalion should equally reflect the traditions of the old 1st and 2nd Battalions, perpetuated those of the latter by re-designating C and D Companies as Y and Z Companies in the New Year, a step which was welcomed throughout the Regiment as a whole, although it caused some temporary confusion in higher headquarters.

Meanwhile, having returned from Johore to Kuala Kubu Bahru in December 1955, A Company's No 2 Platoon brought in the bodies of their arch-enemy Heap Thong and his girl friend Ng Soo Lin, who had been killed in a police ambush. The company opened its own account for 1956 on 2 January when No 1 Platoon killed two CTs in Templer Park. On 17 January the platoon added two more kills to its score. With the assistance of a tracker dog this latter success was pursued to a house in Rasa where a quantity of food intended for the terrorists was discovered; the two female occupants were subsequently awarded lengthy prison sentences. By now there were clear signs that the communists were beginning to crack. On 27 February an entire CT unit, the Kerling Armed Work Force, consisting of six men and five women under the command of one Chee Sang, surrendered to the police. As a result of this enormous quantities of food were recovered from terrorist dumps throughout the area. One survivor of Heap Thong's gang came in to surrender on 2 March and twelve days later two more were killed by a small patrol under the command of Corporal J.Clark, who was awarded the Military Medal.

For the next few months most of A Company's operations were directed against Teck Koo's South Perak gang of CTs to the north of Kalumpang. On 16 May No 3 Platoon came upon Teck Koo's camp, believed to contain eight or ten terrorists, and was emplacing its cordon prior to attacking when Lance Corporal Brian Swain was shot dead by an enemy sentry. Thus alarmed, the rest of the terrorists fled, but not before one of them had been killed. This was to be the Company's last contact before it was finally relieved at the beginning of August. Fortunately, there exists an interesting analysis of its achievements throughout the tour:

"More than 50 camps and 75 cultivations were found, largely as a result of Auster (light aircraft) reports, and all of them with CT traces less than a week old. For two-and-a-half years the platoons averaged 18-19 days in the jungle each month. No 3 Platoon were in the jungle at one stage for 25 days out of 29 - and they were on one occasion in the jungle for 21 days on end. On average, it took 50 days' patrolling to achieve one kill. During the Company's stay in Ulu Selangor, the CT organisation was reduced by 31 and very much disrupted, and the local population showed their appreciation by the presentation of a Kelantan silver bowl and salver, and a silver rose bowl, to all ranks of the Company. The Company were top scorers in the Battalion with 18 kills - 31 per cent of the Battalion total."

Meanwhile, B, Y and Z Companies had been equally busy. On 12 January B Company's No 5 Platoon, commanded by Second Lieutenant David Bolam, was moving toward a rendezvous with the Assault Pioneer Platoon, with whom they were to set up an ambush on the edge of the rubber; a small party of men were briefly glimpsed moving among the trees some 200 yards distant. Bolam, a popular National Service officer noted for his dash and aggression both on operations and the rugby football field, moved forward with Sergeant Albert Westall and three others to investigate. Coming upon fresh tracks, he spotted three terrorists and charged forward to close with them only to be shot and killed by a fourth CT whose presence had not been detected. Sergeant Westall at once assumed command and decided to press home the attack, deploying his men under a heavy fire from the enemy which slightly wounded Private Rawles. Westall hit two terrorists in succession, then closed with and killed the man who had wounded Rawles. Of the two remaining CTs, one crawled away to die of the wounds he had received and the other made good his escape. One of the dead was found to be the local CT leader, Liew ah Kang, a noted murderer and the self-styled "Terror of Kajang," who had been on the Wanted List for many years. For his leadership, quick thinking, determination and marksmanship, Sergeant Westall was awarded the Military Medal.

In February Y Company's No 7 Platoon, who had somehow acquired an ancient piece of Japanese ordnance with which to dignify their basha, were responsible for another successful coup. On 20 February a middle-aged CT female named Ah Tan gave herself up at the Ampang Road Police Station in Kuala Lumpur. During her interrogation she talked willingly, revealing that her group, consisting of eleven men and herself, had been in the jungle for five years. She had been the mistress of the group leader, Ah Foot, who was expected to inherit the State Secretary's mantle of the late Mr Chan Lo, and was a very nasty piece of work in his own right. Unwisely, Ah Foot had made it perfectly clear that her personal attentions were no longer welcome and suddenly the combined teachings of Marx, Lenin and Mao were swept aside by a burning desire for revenge. Ah Foot, said the lady, had recently left their camp with seven of the men and she would gladly lead the security forces to it.

In the circumstances, speed was of the essence. At Wardieburn Camp, Second Lieutenant E.W.Hoare's No 7 Platoon, C Company, had just returned from a ten-day food control operation at Cheras and were starting to enjoy their rest when, at 10:00, they were alerted for the operation. By noon they were leaving the camp, fully armed and briefed, and forty-five minutes later they met a police inspector, Ah Tan and a Chinese interpreter at a water conduit. Ah Tan directed them to march up the conduit. After an hour's steady progress it began to occur to Hoare and others that the conduit, flanked as it was by thick secondary jungle, was an ideal site for an ambush. The CTs still possessed the ability to mount such ambushes and in fact had done so twice only recently, inflicting heavy loss on other units. Were they being led into a trap? At 14:00, however, Ah Tan stopped beside a stream that passed under the conduit from a steep re-entrant on the left. She said that the camp was near the head of the re-entrant on the left of the stream and described the position of the sentry post. In the circumstances, Hoare could only plan on the basis that she was telling the truth.

"A quick calculation showed that there were sufficient troops to cordon the whole valley with gaps of not more than 20 yards between men. Sergeant Baines, with No 1 Section, would take the mouth of the valley, No 2 Section the high ground on the east bank of the stream, and No 3 Section would take the west bank. The assault party, which was made up of Second Lieutenant Hoare, Corporal Foster, Privates Holloway, Ellison, Scobell, Stoneham and the police inspector, would assault from the far end of the valley towards the water conduit. Privates Alner and Burton were briefed to take over guard of Ah Tan from the moment the assault began.

"No 2 Section was the first to move out, followed by the assault party and No 3 Section. Doubly cautious now, the men moved with practised ease into the less dense primary jungle covering the eastern ridge. This was the vital part of the whole operation. In places, the going became steep and slippery and even the specially designed jungle boots began to slide. Each man knew that to catch hold of even a sapling for support would cause a disturbance amongst the treetops likely to be seen by the ever-watchful bandits; it was better to measure one's length on the solid earth. Fortunately, it began to rain. The men smiled at each other. 'This must be our lucky day,' they thought as the noise of the rain spread across the jungle.

"Slowly, almost stealthily, the cordon began to take shape. Gradually, one by one, No 2 Section were dropped off and then, at an indication from Ah Tan, the assault party formed up. Once they were in position, No 3 Section came past and the remainder of the cordon was completed. The rats were in the trap. There only remained for the assault party to flush them out - or to kill them. At a gentle hand signal, they moved off....

"There were seven men in the assault party, advancing through the jungle towards an unknown enemy. Somewhere in their path was an enemy camp. In the camp there were any number, from three to eleven, of armed and desperate terrorists. Perhaps there were more. Perhaps there were none at all.

"They advanced, steadily and in line. Occasionally a man was held up by a vine or a creeper, but freed himself and caught up with the others. The silence taughtened the nerves. Seven stomachs began to flutter with suspense and men looked at their neighbours, each admiring the other's apparent lack of fear. Suddenly, quite unexpectedly, they saw a basha. A shot rang out as Private Scobell shot the first bandit he had ever seen.

"Two bandits had been sitting, Chinese fashion, cooking a meal of rice. Scobell's first shot took one of them in the back of the skull. The other, groping helplessly for his weapon, received a volley from the assault group. When they picked him up there were seventeen bullet holes in his body. He was very dead.

"For seconds there was silence, only to be disturbed by yet another volley of FN fire from the right of the line. This time it was the sentry who died. Some strange instinct had prompted him to run back towards the camp instead of attempting to make good his escape by running in the opposite direction. Once again the FN had saved the hangman a job.

"The assault party pressed on into the jungle for a short distance. Having determined that there were no further bandits and not wanting to walk into the cordon, they returned to the bandits' camp. A runner was despatched to the cordon and the battle was over . . . .

"The march out took about two hours. The platoon was met by its transport just as the light was fading. At the Ampang Road Police Station the bodies were left in a grotesque pile on the well-lit lawn in front of the building. They were left there all night in full view of the public - a warning to other would-be communists."

The surviving terrorists in Selangor became even more wary after this episode. As contacts, and consequently kills, became rarer, the major part of the companies' efforts was directed into the food denial role. It became possible to send small parties on local leave to Port Dickson or enjoy the Royal Navy's hospitality aboard warships off the coast for short spells. In the spring it was learned that the Battalion's tour of duty in the Far East was to end in August, and that following leave in the UK its next destination would be Germany, where it would become the mechanised infantry battalion of an armoured brigade.

Sadly, Colonel Man, who was awarded the Distinguished Service Order, plus the Selangor Meritorious Service Medal by the Sultan of Selangor, would not be bringing the Battalion home. Instead, he was to take up an appointment in the War Office with the rank of Brigadier, his place as Commanding Officer being taken by Lieutenant Colonel A.H.T.Hogge, who had just returned from a period in temporary command of the 2nd Battalion The Royal Welch Fusiliers. Colonel Man had made many friends for the Hampshires among colleagues from all three services, the civil administration, the police and the civilian community. On the day of his departure Kuala Lumpur station was packed to capacity with those wishing to make their farewells; so much so that he came close to missing the train altogether and, after a spirited sprint along the platform, managed the scramble aboard the last carriage, much to the relief of Mrs Man. By a happy coincidence the next stop down the line was Kajang, where B and Z Companies had turned out in force.

It remained for Colonel Tony Hogge to complete the process of disengagement and handover to the 1st Battalion The Rifle Brigade. In August the Battalion was given a wonderful send-off from Kuala Lumpur, being played away by the band of The Royal Lincolnshire Regiment. After staging at Nee Soon transit camp, it moved by companies to Singapore docks, where it embarked on three troopships for the voyage home: Battalion Headquarters, HQ Company and B Company aboard the *Empire Orwell*, Y and Z Companies aboard the *Captain Cook*, and A Company and Support Company (less the Mortar Platoon, which flew home) aboard the *Empire Clyde*.

After spending so long in Malaya, it was not surprising that many felt a twinge of loss as the ships cleared Singapore harbour. An unknown member of Y Company put it best: "The veteran of Malaya is a soldier. Proud of a superb physical fitness, conscious of a real sense of adventure, he has not allowed hardships or discomfort to blunt his alertnes. He has dealt with repulsive leeches, myriads of insects, snakes, rain and short rations all in his stride. He has lived and slept under the tall canopy of the jungle for long unbroken periods. He has learnt the sounds and the feel of the jungle, so that the brightly-coloured birds, the monkeys and even the insects have a message for him as he tracked his enemy. He has carried and cooked his own food, rinsed his clothes in the clear jungle streams. When the test came and he contacted the enemy he emerged triumphant. Looking back on it, it was a man's life and it appealed to men." Typical, perhaps, of that feeling was young Private Paddy O'Callaghan, MM, who had come out a boy and earned the sincere respect of his older peers. He never forgot the comradeship he had enjoyed and subsequently presented his old company with three silver cups for inter-platoon football, hockey and athletics competitions.

There was, too, a sense of a job well done, for the Emergency was now well under control. In fact, the previous December Chin Peng had held a secret meeting with Tunku Abdul Rahman, the Chief Minister of the Malayan Federation, and offered to end his campaign of terror in return for recognition of the Communist Party. The Tunku declined and shortly after the British government cut the ground from beneath the terrorists' feet by announcing that Malaya would be granted its independence in 1957. Thereafter, in response to the Tunku's offer of a general amnesty, the remnant of the MRLA drifted in to surrender and in 1960 the State of Emergency was officially ended.

Because of the probability of active hostilities in the Suez Canal Zone, of which more anon, the enjoyable voyage home was made around the Cape with ports of call at Aden, Mombasa, Cape Town and Dakar, taking six weeks. The *Captain Cook* and the *Empire Clyde* docked in Liverpool a week before the *Empire Orwell* reached Southampton and those aboard therefore missed the tremendous welcome accorded to the rest of the Battalion in its home port. The combined bands of the 4th and 5th Battalions (TA) played the ship alongside, where a crowd of families and friends, several hundred strong, was waiting. As soon as the gangway was in place a large number of distinguished officers and civic dignitaries went aboard, including the Colonel of the Regiment, Brigadier G.D.Browne, OBE; the Deputy Colonel of the Regiment, Colonel R.Chandler, DSO; Lieutenant General Sir Geoffrey Bourne, the former General Officer Commanding Malaya Command; Lord Ashburton, Vice Lieutenant of Hampshire; the Commanding Officer, Lieutenant Colonel A.H.T.Hogge, who had flown home; Brigadier P.H.Man, DSO, OBE, MC, Brigadier R.G.F.Frisby, DSO, MC, Brigadier R.H.Batten, CBE, DSO, Colonel C.A.T.Halliday, OBE, Lieutenant Colonel P.R.Sawyer, MC,TD, commanding the 4th Battalion, Lieutenant Colonel B.B.von B.im Thurn, DSO, MC, Lieutenant Colonel C.C.Smythe, OBE, MC, Major H.J.Jeffery, the Regimental Secretary, the Mayor of Southampton, Alderman Mrs K.E.Cawte, and the Mayor of Winchester, Councillor Paul Woodhouse.

In July Brigadier Browne had received a personal letter from Lieutenant General R.H.Bower, CB, CBE, Director of Operations in Malaya, and he relayed the contents of this over the ship's public address system:

"Last night we said good-bye to the 1st Battalion of your Regiment on Kuala Lumpur station and we were all very sorry to see them go. I thought you would like to know how very well they have done during their two and a half years in Malaya, and how much I shall miss them. They displayed tremendous drive and energy in their jungle operations and right up to the last moment Colonel Hogge had every available soldier that he could lay his hands on actually out on the job. He has displayed tremendous personal energy and drive in spite of the recent lull in contact with the CTs. However, they have a total of 65 CTs to their credit and are really responsible for the 'liberation' of Selangor State - a task which we hope finally to complete by the end of the year."

Traditionally, the Officers of HM Customs stand aloof and unsmiling on such occasions. Major Symes and his family, for example, had all their crates opened and rummaged through, and were released only when the search failed to reveal clandestinely imported supplies of tin or rubber or dutiable items among them. Such needless episodes apart, the warmth of the welcome home provided a fine note upon which to end a memorable tour. Shortly after, the Battalion dispersed on leave. It would have no formal presence in the United Kingdom, but would re-assemble as individuals in Münster, Westphalia, whence its Advance Party had already gone some weeks earlier.

* * * * * * * * *

ROLL OF HONOUR — MALAYA 1954 - 1956

Major A.E.Amor	B Company
Major C.J.G.Mumford, MC	Attached, HQ Malaya Command
2nd Lieutenant D.W.Bolam	B Company
Lance Corporal B.D.Swain	A
Lance Corporal R.C.Watton	A
Private J.R.Ainsley	A
Private P.J.Archer	B
Private W.Hill	C
Private P.W.Masterman	Z
Private B.D.Smith	A

The names on the Roll of Honour are recorded in the Regiment's Third Book of Remembrance "1946 Onwards" in Winchester Cathedral

* * * * * * * * *

HONOURS AND AWARDS — MALAYA 1954 - 1956

Distinguished Service Order
Lieutenant Colonel P.H.Man, OBE, MC
Bar to Military Cross
Major J.M.Symes, MC
Military Medal
CQMS M.Pike
Sgt   G.Westall
Cpl   H.T.Smith
Cpl   J.H.Wheeler
Cpl   J.J.Clark
Pte   P.P.O'Callaghan
British Empire Medal
Cpl   L.C.Bentley
Mentioned in Despatches
Lieutenant Colonel P.H.Man, OBE,MC
Lieutenant Colonel A.H.T.Hogge
Major P.A.T.Halliday
Major V.T.G.Liles
Major G.J.A.Dewar, MBE
Captain A.H.T.Smith
Captain J.E.Tull
Captain C.D.Darroch
Captain J.Berry, RA Ch D

Lieutenant J.E.Horton
RQMS L.B.Edmonds
Sgt M.Pike
Sgt K.Wood
Sgt D.Henderson
Sgt J.G.Morris
Sgt J.A.Wiles
Sgt R.W.Remsberry
Sgt G.F.Townsend
Sgt G.A.R.Westall
Cpl R.D.Turkington
Cpl G.F.Savage
Cpl K.P.Faithful
Commander-in-Chief's Far East Land Forces Certificate of Merit
Sgt J.A.Wiles
The Sultan of Selangor's Meritorious Service Medal
Lieutenant Colonel P.H.Man, DSO, OBE, MC

* * * * * * * * *

SOURCES OF CONGRATULATORY MESSAGES
RECEIVED BY 1st BATTALION
THE ROYAL HAMPSHIRE REGIMENT
FOLLOWING THE ACTION AT ULU LANGAT

His Excellency the High Commissioner for the Federation of Malaya; Tunku Abdul Rahman, the Chief Minister for the Federation of Malaya; the Mayor of Winchester; General Sir Charles F.Loewen, KCB, KBE, DSO, Commander-in-Chief Far East Land Forces; Lieutenant General Sir Geoffrey K.Bourne, KBE, CB, CMG, General Officer Commanding Malaya Command; Major General R.N.Anderson, CBE, DSO, General Officer Commanding 17th Gurkha Division; Major General J.R.C.Hamilton, CBE, DSO, Chief of Staff, Malaya Command; Major General E.S.Lindsay, CBE, DSO, Principal Staff Officer to the Director of Operations; Major General C.L.Firbank, CB, CBE, DSO, Director of Infantry, the War Office; Brigadier C.S.Howard, DSO, OBE, Deputy Director of Military Training, the War Office; Brigadier H.T.Alexander, OBE, Commander 26th Gurkha Infantry Brigade; Brigadier J.S.Vickers, DSO, Commander 63rd Gurkha

Infantry Brigade; Brigadier J.L.Brind, DSO, Commander 159th Infantry Brigade; the Commissioner of Police, Federation of Malaya; Pahang State War Executive Committee; Kuala Lumpur District War Executive Committee; Kuala Langat District War Executive Committee; Bentong District War Executive Committee; Kluang District War Executive Committee; HQ Squadron 11th Hussars (Prince Albert's Own); 1st Battalion The Queen's Royal Regiment (West Surrey); 1st Battalion The Royal Lincolnshire Regiment; 2nd Battalion The Royal Welch Fusiliers; 1st Battalion The South Wales Borderers; 1st Battalion The Queen's Own Royal West Kent Regiment; 1st/6th Gurkha Rifles; 1st/7th Gurkha Rifles; 2nd/7th Gurkha Rifles; 1st Battalion The Northern Rhodesia Regiment; 3rd Battalion The Malay Regiment; 7th Battalion The Malay Regiment; Depot The Malay Regiment; 1st Battalion The Fiji Infantry Regiment; 93rd Squadron RAF Regiment (Malaya); Depot The Royal Hampshire Regiment; Lieutenant Colonel F.F.Laugher, OBE, MC, The Dorset Regiment; Lieutenant Colonel J.H.Penrose, MC, GSO1 HQ Malaya Command; Wing Commander P. de L. le Cheminant, DFC, Wing Commander (Flying) Kuala Lumpur; President, Comrades' Association, Bournemouth; Mr J.Theophilus, Bhutan Estate; the Rev T.J.C.Roberts, OBE, ACG, FARELF; Mr J.Voin, Rinchang Estate; Mr J.C.Mathison, Kajang Estate; Mr J.Mills, Karak Estate; Mr J.Hunter, Bukit Cheraka Estate; and Mr J.Paton, Permatang Estate.

* * * * * * * * *

LIFE IN THE JUNGLE

A soldier's life in the jungle was never easy. It could be the harshest of environments. It was squalid, claustrophobic, unfriendly and was always physically demanding. However, survival was always possible as water was readily available. Soldiers under training on entering the jungle for the first time were full of imagined fears, but they adjusted remarkably well to the unfamiliar and sometimes dangerous life.

To assist quick identification all soldiers wore either red or yellow hatbands with the company shape on the front of the jungle hat - a triangle (A), a rectangle (B), a circle (C) or a square (D).

Hats were turned inside out before leaving barracks and reversed on entering the jungle. The two colour bands were alternated from time to time.

Other dress, equipment and food was left to personal choice. Efficiency, comfort and weight were the criteria for choice. A heavily laden soldier with four days' rations could be carrying 60lbs. For a signaller or Bren gunner the weight was even more. Soldiers shaped their jungle hats with parachute cord for individuality and also retention when hooked by "wait-a-whiles."

While some soldiers slept on the ground, not always easy in the Kuala Langat South Swamp, many slept in canvas hammocks produced by the unit contractor Mohammed Ibrahim. Parachute cord was used to give the hammocks the necessary tension, to keep up the basha roof which was an issue poncho or a piece of plastic cloth and to mark the camp perimeter in lieu of vines.

The Army machete was too large and unwieldy. It was quickly discarded by most. In its place were locally manufactured parangs. The Iban trackers were very good at producing ornamental handles and cases. Clearing a DZ was very hard work. Large trees could be felled with parangs but accidents happened when they glanced off iron-hard wood. Chain saws would speed up the process but a large DZ would need Homelite saws and even explosives. Few parachutes were carried out of the jungle. Most had been damaged by the drop or were far too cumbersome to be carried far. Usually the colourful parachutes were ripped up and soldiers would retain one or two segments as jungle bedding.

Whilst British, Gurkha and Malay rations were available in a variety of packs, most soldiers discarded in barracks those items they did not need or personally like. Soldiers would bash up in pairs and put their combined mess tins to good use. A jungle all-in stew or curry was usually produced to accompany the evening brew of tea. There was not much time to cook as it would be dark early. At Stand To all cooking had to cease, all lights were put out and there was no smoking.

Whilst in the jungle, a small party would remain in base camp whilst the rest were patrolling or ambushing. When not on sentry duty the long humid daylight hours would be spent either in sleeping or reading some dog-eared, lurid novel with those by Hank Jansen being the favourite. Such novels were passed from hand to hand.

Insect life was very varied. Mosquitos and leeches were the

ever-present irritant. Hornets, when disturbed, would cause a patrol to scatter rapidly, many soldiers receiving unpleasant stings.

In the dense secondary jungle with ferns up to ten feet high red ants reigned everywhere and were studiously avoided where possible. Sometimes, in the early hours of the night, delightful fireflies would be seen. During the day an incredible variety of other insects of all shapes and colours were visible. The best was the long stick insect which, like many other insects, were nicknamed weirdies by the soldiers. As darkness descended, the insects would set up a cacophony of sounds, the most piercing being the one which sounded like a sawmill in operation.

Animal life was usually nothing more than sounds such as the Wha! Wha! gibbons in the tree tops. In Pahang traces of elephant spoor were seen, sometimes quite close to camp. Most frequently encountered were the wallows of jungle pigs. Snakes were rarely seen and no soldiers were ever bitten. One hamadryad (King Cobra) caused consternation in a base camp as it emerged from a basha.

Fitness was all-important. Cuts and grazes went septic very easily. Those who had impetigo were daubed with gentian violet. Efficient evacuation of casualties was essential for reasons of morale and confidence, but whether an LZ had to be constructed, or the injured man had to be carried out, it sometimes took a long time to get him to hospital. One shaved before marching out, but not in the jungle, although everyone did their best to keep reasonably clean.

Major J.D.K.Kellie

* * * * * * * * *

THE MYSTERIOUS EAST

"Animal life in the camp includes an occasional cobra, and thereby hangs a tale of the Mysterious East. We have a Tamil kitchen boy, a small dark-skinned chap who claims that a small amulet, permanently attached to his left upper arm, gives him immunity from snake bite and all other jungle dangers. Being level-headed Britishers, we are normally sceptical about such things, but after seeing him allow a real live cobra with hood upraised to bite him several times on the hand, with no apparent effect, we are not so sure. Colour Sergeant Harry Barnard was eager to try it himself, but we persuaded him that we lose most of our CQMSs that way and he reluctantly declined the experiment."

Extracted from Support Company Notes, November 1954

* * * * * * * * *

A TALE OF TWO TIGERS

In November 1955 Second Lieutenant J.L.Fellows was leading a twenty-strong patrol in close, mountainous jungle when the leading scout, Private Gillespie, was suddenly confronted by a large and extremely angry tiger which sprang out at the patrol from behind a fallen tree trunk. It continued to roar, snarl and spit at the men as it circled through the undergrowth and showed clear signs that it was on the point of springing. Recognising that such an attack could well result in death before the animal could be dealt with, Fellows reluctantly authorised the firing of a single round. This struck the tiger behind the foreleg and it sheared off into the jungle. Although the blood trails were subsequently followed no further trace of the animal was found.

Some 30 yards from the scene of the encounter the patrol discovered the cause of the tiger's fury between the roots of an enormous tree - two cubs, about ten days old, less than a foot in length and still with their eyes closed. They were carried back to the company base, where Colour Sergeant Harry Barnard tried unsuccessfully to feed them on condensed milk, and thence taken to Kluang, where the British Military Hospital provided baby food and feeding teats which were fitted to lemonade bottles. This arrangement was not at first to the cubs' liking. The problem was solved by the Medical Officer with a length of feeding tube through which a mixture of milk and codliver oil was fed by means of a syringe for the first few days.

In course the cubs were transferred to a room in the officers' mess at Wardieburn Camp, Kuala Lumpur. They travelled by train from Kluang in a crate marked Mess Silver. When this suddenly became internally active the escorting officer, Captain W.G.Alderman, was forced to describe its real contents to an understandably curious fellow passenger; whether his story was believed is not recorded. At Wardieburn the cubs took to the bottle in a big way and began to grow so rapidly that professional help became a necessity. The Army is a wonderful institution in that within any one unit it is almost always possible to find just the right man for a particular job, and the 1st Battalion The Royal Hampshire Regiment was no exception. Serving in the War Dog Section was Private Brick, who had grown up in a circus and whose father was a lion and tiger tamer. Handing over his dog, he assumed responsibility for the cubs and raised them as fine healthy animals consuming five pounds of meat per day each, that is, five times the soldier's standard ration. Despite this, they developed a slight tendency to draw their hindquarters. Advice was sought from a Game Warden from Pahang State, known to keep a tigress of his own in his spare bathroom. Almost the first question he asked on arrival was, "Where do they swim?" At first light the next day the Assault Pioneer Platoon started constructing and had by last light completed a cement-lined swimming pool. By day, the cubs were seldom out of it, and their hindquarters problem disappeared.

Some undoubtedly saw the cubs as magnificent and entirely appropriate successors to Dog Fritz, leading the Regiment's formal parades through Winchester and elsewhere beside suitably uniformed Tiger Majors. The less romantic foresaw strenuous objections from the police and the civic authorities. Furthermore, the Officer Commanding the Depot had got wind of the idea and he did not want them padding about the place; it would, he thought, unsettle the townspeople. Nevertheless, the enthusiasts persisted and War Office permission was sought to pursue the matter, with one cub only. Being somewhat unorthodox, the request took considerable time making its way through the official channels, so that it was only within a few weeks of the Battalion's tour ending that the following signal was received: "For 1st Royal Hampshires. Regarding your request to bring back home one tiger cub as Regimental Mascot at public expense. Much regret cannot approve. We are advised that tigers are seldom if ever steady on ceremonial parades!!!"

Colonel and Mrs Man had named the male cub Nassau and the female Rose. Photographers and children came to see them regularly, but as they continued to grow they were moved into a pen into which few save Private Brick were inclined to venture.

Although they showed no signs of becoming vicious they remained feral animals and had to be respected as such. Their games became rougher until a playful swipe with a paw could result in torn clothing. Clearly, the moment had come to say goodbye to the orphans and, as a result of contingency plans made while the War Office's response was awaited, the Regent's Park Zoo paid for them to be air-transported to London. Rose was predeceased by Nassau and when she herself died in the mid-1970s she was the oldest tigress in captivity in North West Europe.

* * * * * * * * *

THE PADRE AND THE REGIMENTAL CHAPEL

On arrival in Pehang State we met for the first time our Padre who would remain with us for the whole of our Malayan Emergency tour. Those who have "followed the drum" in war or combat situations will know what an inestimable service a "field" Padre can give to the morale of a battalion. We were so fortunate in securing the services of John Berry, RA, Ch D, a man of unlimited courage and devotion to duty to all ranks in the Battalion. His Land Rover, in which he travelled without escort whenever he could, was painted white with a large Royal Army Chaplains' Department badge and the motto "In This Sign Conquer" . In the opinion of anyone serving in the 1st Battalion, he did just that. In Wardieburn Camp he arranged the refurbishment of the Regimental Chapel necessitated by the departure of The Somerset Light Infantry on handover. In Malaya one "inherited" much from regiments who had "gone before". The altar installed, which was used in Bentong, came to us from The Green Howards; the lectern came by courtesy of The Royal West Kents, adorned with a banner to match the new altar cloth presented by Major and Mrs C.G.T.Mumford; a prayer desk, together with altar rails, came from the Suffolk Regiment. To give the Chapel a sense of our own identity, a National Serviceman who modestly wishes to remain anonymous, carved a Regimental crest which hung above the chancel, thereby putting the seal to the Church of the 1st Battalion The Royal Hampshire Regiment. Each Sunday morning the week began in the Regimental Chapel, and then the indefatigable Padre set forth with his inseparable driver, Corporal (later Sergeant) F.P.Zakary, to administer Holy Communion to all "outstation" platoon and company operational bases in the Battalion's area — very much a dawn-to-dusk labour of love.

* * * * * * * * *

THE BAND AND CORPS OF DRUMS

The Band, under the Directorship of Bandmaster Fidoe and Band NCOs Colour Sergeant Ernie Butt, MM, Sergeant Bailey and Sergeant Roberts, and the Corps of Drums under Drum-Major Gray and, later, Drum-Major Bryant, carried out many exemplary performances of the Ceremony of Beating Retreat. With a joint strength of over fifty musicians, they really were an imprsssive display which captivated large audiences on all major and minor padangs (public squares of grass or hard ground in villages, towns and cities) in the States of Pahang and Selangor. In addition to their musical role, both the Band and the Corps of Drums had combat training: for the Band, armed road escort duties, and for the Corps of Drums, operational patrolling in the jungle.

Around the periphery of Kuala Lumpur there was quite a large French community engaged in rubber production, tin mining, and so on. They were particularly appreciative of the Band and Corps of Drums' ability to play, in French quick-time, that stirring bugle march *Sambre et Meuse*. Entering the apparently indolent port of Dakar, French West Africa, at 9am on a Sunday morning en route home to England at the end of our Mayalan tour, the Band and Drums, which had been marshalled forward in the ship's bows, suddenly struck up with *Sambre et Meuse* — within the space of a few minutes, the quayside was a mass of applauding spectators.

CHAPTER 4

THE TERRITORIAL BATTALIONS
1947 — 1967

Reactivation of the Territorial Army - the 4th Battalion reactivated - winning the China Cup - the 5th Battalion reactivated as 14th Battalion The Parachute Regiment - training drops - reverts in title and role to 5th Battalion - other Territorial units with Regimental lineage - ceremonial duties - the 4th and 5th Battalions amalgamate to become the 4th/5th (TA) Battalion - training commitments - support from the civil community - the 4th Battalion at Camp 1954 - increased co-operation with the Regular Army - government policy regarding the Territorial Army's teeth arms - Farewell Parade and disbandment

As we have seen, the process of demobilisation after World War II seriously affected even the strength of Regular units, and, concurrently, for a brief period, no Reserve Army existed that could be called upon in an emergency. In 1946, therefore, the government decided that the Territorial Army should be re-activated. There were at that period thousands of recently demobilised men who, while only too thankful to have survived the war, sorely missed the close companionship of the service. As individuals and in small groups they converged on drill halls to enjoy this anew on drill nights, training weekends and at the fourteen-day annual camp. In some areas officers hoping to join had to take their place on a waiting list. There were, too, interested volunteers, attracted by the combination of military training and a good social life. The purely voluntary aspect of the Territorial Army was maintained until the Defence White

Paper of 31 August 1950, which defined the National Service-man's commitment as being two years with the Colours followed by three-and-a-half years in the Territorial Army. In the event, most men entering the Territorial phase of their service availed themselves of the £50 Bounty payable if they volunteered to serve for four years. Many of them also chose to enlist for further terms, the result being that until well into the 1960s Territorial units were able to operate at full strength.

Thus, while it was inevitable that the Territorial Army should complain at having to wait for modern equipment until the Regular Army's requirements had been met, at battalion and brigade level it was much the more experienced of the two and, had it ever been mobilised during this period, it would have become a formidable force very quickly. In 1950 its ranks were filled with men whose tunics bore the medal ribbons of World War II, including the Africa, Italy, Burma and France and Germany Stars, the Territorial Decoration or the Territorial Efficiency Medal, plus a few men with the General Service Medal with Palestine clasp and, in some cases, gallantry awards. After that date further ribbons appeared on the tunics of National Service volunteers, including those issued for the Korean War, the General Service Medal with clasps for Palestine 1945-48, Malaya, Cyprus and the Suez operation, and the Africa General Service Medal for service against the Mau Mau terrorists in Kenya. Even those National Service volunteers who had not been posted to an active theatre had usually served in an infantry battalion and acquired at least one skill. By the late 1950s, therefore, although the number of World War II veterans had begun to tail off, most units could boast that at least 90 per cent of their members had served at least two years with the Regular Army.

In January 1947 The Royal Hampshire Regiment was authorised to re-activate its 4th Battalion, and as the old 2nd/4th had still to disband this ensured a certain degree of continuity. On 20 June the Battalion Colours were marched from Serle's House to the Battalion Headquarters at Newburgh House, Winchester, and handed over to the Commanding Officer, Lieutenant Colonel F.Mitchell, DSO, MC, a former 4th (TA) Battalion officer who had commanded the 2nd/4th Battalion in Italy and Greece 1944/45, at a ceremony attended by the Colonel of the Regiment, General Sir George Jeffreys, and the Mayor of Winchester. On 27 November Colonel Mitchell held his first

Commanding Officer's parade, at which nine officers and forty-three other ranks were present. From this point onwards the strength of the 4th increased steadily until it was able to send detachments to Regimental parades and on 31 October 1948 four officers and twenty-one other ranks represented the Battalion at the King's Review of the Territorial Army in Hyde Park.

Colonel Mitchell handed over command of the 4th to Lieutenant Colonel C.A.T.Halliday, OBE, on 1 April 1950. At Bisley later that year the Battalion team won the prize most coveted by every Territorial unit in the country, the China Challenge Cup, awarded for the best results in the Inter-Divisional rifle and light machine gun match. As every winner before and since has discovered, winning the trophy was one thing, taking it home quite another. Standing four feet high and proportionally broad, the China Cup was an astonishing example of the silversmith's craft that required four men to carry it while a fifth carried the lid. The 1952 Annual Camp was remarkable in that it was joined by the Regiment's Z Reservists, giving a total strength of some 1200 officers and soldiers. During 1955 the entire 43rd (Wessex) Division went to camp together and took part in Exercise Effen Down. This had a nuclear warfare scenario and was held on Salisbury Plain, lasting four or five days. Those adjudged to be casualties were evacuated through the usual medical channels to hospital (or the notional cemetery) and then returned to their units as reinforcements.

The 5th Battalion was re-activated as the 14th Battalion The Parachute Regiment (5th Battalion The Royal Hampshire Regiment (TA)) on 17 October 1948 during a ceremony held in the forecourt of the Civic Centre, Southampton, with which city the Battalion had deep-rooted historical links. Two Guards of Honour and Colour Parties were on parade, one from the Regiment's 1st Battalion with the old 5th Battalion's Colours, which were then entrusted to the 14th Battalion The Parachute Regiment by the Colonel of the Regiment, Brigadier P.H.Cadoux-Hudson, MC, who had succeeded General Sir George Jeffreys that January.

The new unit recruited so quickly that within months it became the strongest Territorial battalion in Southern Command. The undoubted glamour of the Red Beret certainly helped, but in the final analysis the paratrooper was simply an infantryman who arrived in battle by a different means. Thus, once they had acquired the necessary standard of fitness and parachuting skills the old hands experienced no difficulty in settling into their new role. The Battalion was initially commanded by Lieutenant Colonel A.G.F.Monro, TD, The Parachute Regiment, until October 1949, then Lieutenant Colonel R.G.F.Frisby, DSO, MC, until October 1951, then Lieutenant Colonel H.D.Nelson-Smith, MC, and, finally, Lieutenant Colonel H.W.Le Patourel, VC.

During the 1949 Annual Camp, held at Windmill Hill, parachute training was carried out from Halifax aircraft, the exit from which was through a hole in the floor. Following the parachute drop, the Battalion marched past and was addressed by the Minister of State for War, The Rt Hon Mr Emanuel Shinwell. On 29 July 1950 it made a training drop at St Aubin's Bay, Jersey, after which it was inspected by the Lieutenant Governor of the island, Lieutenant General Sir Arthur Grasett. The following year it repeated the 4th Battalion's achievement by winning the China Cup at Bisley. The 1952 Camp was held in Germany, where the Battalion was dropped from USAF C82s and C119s onto a dropping zone close to the River Weser. During The Queen's Coronation in 1953 the Battalion covered a section of the East Carriage Road in Hyde Park, The Queen's Colour being carried by Lieutenant R.Hoare, escorted by CSM Riddler, Sergeant Poulton, Lance Corporals Marsh and Kearley and Private Cronen. Later in the year it took part in the largest airborne operation to be held in the United Kingdom since the end of World War II.

By 1956 sufficient imperial and global commitments had been shed for the government to reduce its expenditure on both the Regular and Territorial Armies. The Regiment was not seriously affected by this, the first of many cuts, the main effect of which was that, parachute training being extremely expensive, the 14th Battalion The Parachute Regiment was converted back in title and role to the 5th Battalion The Royal Hampshire Regiment (TA) with a territorial area including Southampton, Bournemouth, Eastleigh and the Isle of Wight. The actual ceremony took place at Chickerell Camp near Weymouth on 15 July 1956, when the Colours of the old 5th which, it will be recalled, had been entrusted to the 14th Battalion on its formation, were handed over to a Colour Party from the new 5th.

Three more of the Regiment's former Territorial battalions were re-activated during this period, although they all remained within or passed into the orbit of the Royal Regiment of Artillery. Their lineage forms a most complex subject since they were involved in many changes of title and role in the period between their re-activation in 1947-49 and disbandment in 1968, as indicated in the following table:

1947

59th Anti-Tank Regiment RA (TA) Portsmouth
Princess Beatrice's (Isle of Wight Rifles)
Heavy Regiment RA (TA) Newport, IoW

joined in 1948 by

642 LAA/SL Regiment RA (7th Bn The Royal Hampshire Regiment) (TA) Bournemouth

1949

383 Duke of Connaught's Own Hampshire (DCRH) AT Regiment RA (TA) Portsmouth
423 (M) HAA Regiment RA (Princess Beatrice's Isle of Wight Rifles) (TA) Newport, IoW
642 LAA/SL Regiment RA (7th Bn The Royal Hampshire Regiment) (TA) Bournemouth

1967

383 (Duke of Connaught's Own Hampshire) Regiment RA (TA) Portsmouth
HQ (Princess Beatrice's IoW Rifles) Battery
457 (Wessex) Heavy Air Defence Regiment RA (TA) (Hampshire Carabiniers Yeomanry) Newport, IoW
"P" (Royal Hampshire) Battery, 383 (Duke of Connaught's Own Hampshire) Regiment RA, (TA) Bournemouth

If, perhaps, some of the latter-day unit titles seem unwieldy and confusing, it should be remembered that they represented an attempt by units, at a time when cut-backs and amalgamations had become commonplace, to preserve their identities and with them their links with the past.

On 6 April 1957 the Regimental Depot and the 4th and 5th Battalions provided a Guard of Honour for the visit of The Queen and the Duke of Edinburgh to Romsey, which was celebrating the 350th anniversary of the borough being granted its first charter. The future, however, was by no means secure. In 1961 further economies were imposed on the Territorial Army, involving the amalgamation of the 4th and 5th Battalions to create the 4th/5th (TA) Battalion. The effect of this was to deprive the equivalent of a full battalion, officers and men alike, of the opportunity to continue their service. On 29 June 1963 the 4th/5th Battalion was honoured with the presentation of new Colours by Admiral of the Fleet Earl Mountbatten of Burma at Broadlands, his home at Romsey. The following year Lord Mountbatten further honoured the Battalion by agreeing to become its Honorary Colonel. On 26 July 1965 the Battalion provided a Guard of Honour at Newport for the visit of The Queen to the Isle of Wight.

The Territorial soldier's commitment was to attend a minimum number of drill (i.e. training) periods during the year, plus his unit's fourteen-day annual camp. Drill periods took place on one or two nights per week and weekend training also counted towards fulfilling the commitment. From the early 1950s each year's training followed a fairly predictable pattern. There were regular weekends during which range days were held or field firing practised; other weekends might be devoted to attacks on Royal Naval, Army or RAF establishments, probing their security. Most men contributed far more time than was required, partly because they enjoyed the comradeship, and partly because the pay provided a welcome and sometimes vital supplement to their civilian income. A fixed rate was paid for drill nights, but at weekends and at camp the Territorial was paid at Regular daily rates, which had now begun to rise slowly but steadily.

The standing of the Territorial within his community was high. He brought a breath of Army life into his civilian workplace and was described, justly, as being "twice a citizen." The best employers, fully approving of what he was doing, paid his wages in full while he was at camp; others made up his Army pay to the level of his civilian wages; others paid his wages but deducted the period of camp from his holidays; the meaner-spirited paid him nothing at all. Securing the continued support of employers therefore became a most important aspect of every Territorial Commanding Officer's job. Equally important was maintaining the support of the soldiers' wives and families. They were invited to range days and, with the assistance of the Band, these always developed into pleasant social events despite the fierce rivalry between companies and individuals for trophies and challenge shields. Likewise, at Christmas, each company held two parties, one for the wives and the other for the children, the climax of the latter being the arrival of Father Christmas by Land Rover or motor cycle. The relationship between local councils and Territorial units within their area was always excellent. For example, at a formal parade on 15 March 1952 the Borough of Basingstoke adopted B (Basingstoke) Company of the 4th Battalion, and on 11 November 1957 the Borough of Andover did likewise for the Battalion's D (Andover) Company, an adoption being a lesser civic honour than a Freedom but the highest that could be conferred on a sub-unit of the County's Regiment.

From time to time the routine of the Regiment's Territorial battalions was punctuated by the need to provide contingents for Regimental occasions, some of which have already been described, plus the Sovereign's Birthday Parade in Winchester and the Territorial Jubilee Parades of 1958. Companies usually paraded locally on Armistice Sunday and after the parade the Mayor would pay a visit to the messes and the canteen.

For the greater part of their post-World War II existence the Regiment's Territorial battalions produced their own Commanding Officers, who were supported by the Regular element of the Regiment with a Permanent Staff consisting of a training major, adjutant, quartermaster, RSM and a Permanent Staff Instructor (Warrant Officer, Colour Sergeant or Sergeant) to each company. It was the Permanent Staff who set up the camps so that the Territorials could arrive and start training immediately. As time passed and the number of Territorial officers with active service experience began to decline, it became the custom in some regiments to appoint a Regular Commanding Officer and dispense with the training major. The Hampshires, however, were fortunate in possessing sufficient officers with the appropriate qualities so that during the twenty-one years which elapsed between Colonel Mitchell's appointment in 1947 and disbandment in 1967 the 4th Battalion was commanded only twice by a

Regular officer, and the 4th/5th Battalion was always commanded by Territorial Army officers.

The high point of every Territorial battalion's year was its annual camp. Here, considerations of space inhibit mention of every camp that took place, but that of the 4th Battalion at Penhale Camp, near Newquay, Cornwall, in May 1954 will serve as a good representative example, especially as it took place in what hindsight enables us to see as the Territorial Army's Golden Era, when its strength and levels of experience were at their peak.

Penhale Camp was perched on top of a high cliff across which a rain-laden Force 9 Atlantic gale howled for the first three days, sending spume from the bursting spray below over 200 yards into the lines. The general opinion was that "Whoever built this camp was a master craftsman, and whoever sold it to the government was a genius!" Training, however, was not interrupted and with the arrival of better conditions actually became enjoyable.

For the rifle companies the training programme during the first week included individual training and classification on the open range, followed by section and platoon training. The weekend was given over to a cross-country run, social events including a Guest Night, and a Church Parade. Training during the second week was at company level and culminated in a battalion exercise. The training was strenuous but left sufficient time and energy for other activities, including an All Ranks Dance and the Battalion Football Competition. Distinguished visitors included the Army Commander, Lieutenant General Sir Ernest Down, KBE, CB, the GOC 43rd (Wessex) Division, the brigade commander and, of course, the Colonel of the Regiment.

The training requirements of Support Company were somewhat different but its members clearly enjoyed themselves as much as the riflemen and the various platoon reports in the Journal reveal the pleasure taken in exercising their respective skills.

For the Assault Pioneer Platoon, "The first part of camp was devoted to mine training, and the latter half of the week was spent at Wyke Regis Bridging Camp, Weymouth, on watermanship. Apart from the more serious side of training, fine weather and outboard motors lent a seaside holiday atmosphere to work with assault boats. Booby-trap training during the second week of camp was enjoyed, but enthusiasm was dampened somewhat when one section was intercepted with 24lbs of guncotton for a section exercise in the barrack room. What Assault

Pioneers will do for a bang!"

The Medium Machine Gun and 3-inch Mortar Platoons moved to Okehampton, Devon, for field firing on 11 May. "Here," wrote the machine gunners, "we successfully completed some field firing and gave the 'Drainpipers' [their deadly rivals, the mortar crews] a demonstration of our skill which we hope they appreciated. Finally, we rounded off a successful fortnight by winning the Inter-Platoon Cup and celebrating in the British Legion Club, with Sgt Chillery as MC and Sgt Pendrill at the piano."

Not to be outdone, the Mortar Platoon went into action on the morning of the 12th. "First we did Individual Mortar Shooting, HE and Smoke. During the afternoon we gave a demonstration of battery fire to the MMG Platoon with wireless control, which went off very well; in all, we fired 264 bombs and had no mis-fires and only a few blinds. The blinds were dealt with by two members of the Assault Pioneer Platoon and the CSM. The climax was the blowing up of the remainder of the gun-cotton, which resulted in a terrific bang; it was only after we arrived back at Penhale Camp that we found we had exploded the CO's Atom Bomb for the Battalion exercise by mistake. Our apologies for this error."

This being the first camp of the year, the Anti-Tank Platoon was confronted with several 17-pdr anti-tank guns from which the thickly-applied preservative grease had to be cleaned. Simultaneously, the platoon's Oxford carriers (turretless Stuart light tanks that served as towing vehicles for the guns) had to be brought up to operational standard. Once these chores had been completed serious training began for field firing at the Royal Armoured Corps' Gunnery Ranges at Lulworth, to which the platoon moved on 12 May. "On arrival," recalled one of its members, "we were in danger of disorganising a big demonstration, and to avoid this we were allowed to enter the camp by way of the main gate, where the road had only just been re-laid with new tarmac. The inevitable happened, and a Stuart was forced to do a slight turn on it whereupon the guard commander nearly executed a war dance." A few conciliatory words from the platoon commander were not considered acceptable, but an evening's conciliatory work with a heavy roller seemed to leave honour satisfied. Next morning the platoon began a very full programme of field firing, engaging tank hulks at various ranges. Of necessity, two days' firing had to be concentrated into one because The

Queen was expected off the Dorset coast the following day and, since ricochets from hard targets often flew out to sea, the Ranges were to be temporarily closed. The Anti-Tank Platoon therefore finished what had been an enjoyable and successful camp a day early.

During the early 1960s aid to the civil power in the event of nuclear war was added to the training syllabus, involving courses at Millom, Cumbria, where civil defence and radioactive fallout monitoring techniques were learned. During this period, too, the 4th/5th Battalion regularly sent a detachment to take part in the Nijmegen Marches. Co-operation between the Regular and Territorial Armies had also reached new levels. For example, in 1966 the Battalion was joined at camp by members of the 1st Battalion, with which some of its members carried out their own camp commitment. Also present at this camp were a party from the destroyer HMS *Hampshire*, emphasising the good relationship which always existed between the Royal Navy and the Regiment. It was, in fact, due to the courtesy of the Royal Navy that the 4th/5th Battalion was able to end each year with a training weekend on Jersey, Guernsey or Alderney, where the residents, aware of their strong links with the Regiment, were always most kind and welcoming.

The end of the old Territorial Army, as known and loved by its members, came very suddenly in 1967. Harold Wilson's administration, plagued by poor economic housekeeping and desperately short of the funds necessary to fulfil its programme, sought even deeper cuts in the armed services. The Army's Chief of Staff was ordered to save £20 million from his annual budget or lose four major Regular units, and since his responsibility was to preserve the first line of national defence he naturally turned to the Territorial Army. By coincidence, the annual cost of this also amounted to £20 million, and it therefore offered superb value for money. Despite this, the Ministry proposed not merely the further reduction of the Territorial Army's teeth arms, but their complete elimination, leaving only elements of the service arms, most of which were already tasked with the rapid reinforcement of Rhine Army. Naturally, the idea was difficult to sell. Local brigade commanders were told to hold weekend seminars for their Territorial officers, these usually being addressed by a travelling circus of senior officers and civilian lecturers. Two arguments were put forward. The first was that few World War II veterans now remained and that the numbers of National Service volunteers had also begun to dwindle; true, plenty of keen young volunteers were still coming forward, but they needed training and the cost of bringing them up the required standard was prohibitive. Few Territorial officers were willing to accept this, the general feeling being that the problem could be solved quickly and easily by even closer co-operation with the Regular Army and an enlarged Regular Permanent Staff. The second argument, namely that world tension had decreased to the point that a Reserve Army was no longer necessary, was so patently flawed as to be received with laughter, since at the time a major part of the United States' strength had already been absorbed into the bloody conflict in South Vietnam and therefore could not be deployed in Europe, should the need arise. Furthermore, within a year the Warsaw Pact was to demonstrate the true nature of the new, relaxed world order by forcibly stamping out the first glimmers of freedom in Czechoslovakia with a full-scale invasion. Most officers were well aware that the Ministry was simply carrying out the instructions of its political masters; what they resented was being patronised with blatant clap-trap. Curiously, neither the Ministry nor the politicians learned anything whatever from the experience, and a quarter of a century later they would repeat their mistakes on a truly heroic scale.

The government, in fact, had already made up its mind on the fate of the Territorial Army. When the necessary measure passed through Parliament by the slimmest possible majority it was already apparent that political expediency had become a more valuable coinage than in Attlee's day, and was set fair to become common currency. Colonels-in-Chief were discreetly requested to use their influence and Colonels of Regiments lobbied hard, but Wilson had expected this and was suitably prepared. What took him completely by surprise was the vehement anger with which the electorate reacted to the proposal, not least among members of his own constituency party. The government was forced to think twice, although its response could hardly be described as generous. Where once there had been a battalion, there would now be a company, dedicated to the immediate reinforcement role. In a lower category of reserve it became possible to preserve some sub-units with very limited facilities, the vindictive philosophy of the thwarted Whitehall mandarins being that if men wished to serve let them prove it by doing so without pay;

many did. Not a great deal had been salvaged from the wreckage, but it provided a foundation upon which to build for better times.

All over the country parades took place as the Territorial battalions of county regiments laid up their Colours, having received the formal thanks of the civil authorities for the services they had rendered. They were deeply sad occasions, for although the crowds clapped and cheered as they always did, everyone understood their significance and there were some tears to be wiped away as well, usually from the eyes of middle-aged men who had spent some of the most significant years of their lives in those same battalions. The Farewell Parade of the 4th/5th (TA) Battalion The Royal Hampshire Regiment took place on 19 March 1967 in Winchester under the command of its Commanding Officer, Lieutenant Colonel P.D.T.Powell, OBE, TD. In addition to the Mayor of Winchester, the Lord Mayor of Portsmouth and the Mayors of Southampton, Bournemouth, Aldershot, Andover, Basingstoke and Romsey were present. The ceremony started with a Service of Dedication at St Thomas's Church, which was conducted by the Battalion's Chaplain, the Rev J.H.N.Llewelyn. After this the Battalion, led by the Band, marched via High Street to the Guildhall for the official Farewell Ceremony with 140 officers and soldiers on parade. The parade then moved to the Regimental Memorial Garden at Serle's House and in the presence of official guests and a large number of friends the Colours were handed to the Colonel of the Regiment, Major General R.H.Batten, CB, CBE, DSO, DL, for safe keeping at Regimental Headquarters.

After the disbandment of the 4th/5th Battalion a number of officers and men joined the newly created B (Hampshire) Company 1st Battalion The Wessex Volunteers or The Hampshire and Isle of Wight Territorials; the latter unit, in fact, had a very short life and was disbanded in 1968. Others found their way into Territorial units of service arms. Others, again, not wishing to change their allegiance, simply left the Territorial Army, wondering whether the wholesale destruction that had been wrought would indeed safeguard the future of four major Regular units; and, if so, for how long.

* * * * * * * * *

TERRITORIAL BATTALIONS
OF THE ROYAL HAMPSHIRE REGIMENT 1947-1967

4th (TA) BATTALION THE ROYAL HAMPSHIRE REGIMENT

May 1947	Lieutenant Colonel F.Mitchell, DSO,MC
April 1950	Lieutenant Colonel C.A.T.Halliday, OBE
April 1953	Lieutenant Colonel T.G.Tucker, MC
April 1955	Lieutenant Colonel P.R.Sawyer, OBE,MC,TD,JP
April 1959	Lieutenant Colonel B.Gater, TD

April 1961   Amalgamation with the 5th Battalion (TA)

14th BATTALION THE PARACHUTE REGIMENT (TA)
(5th BATTALION THE ROYAL HAMPSHIRE REGIMENT)

Oct 1948	Lieutenant Colonel A.G.F.Monro, TD, The Parachute Regiment
Aug 1949	Lieutenant Colonel R.G.F.Frisby, DSO, MC
Oct 1951	Lieutenant Colonel H.D.Nelson Smith, MC
Oct 1954	Lieutenant Colonel H.W.Le Patourel, VC

15 July 1956 Reverts in title and role to
5TH BATTALION THE ROYAL HAMPSHIRE REGIMENT (TA)

	Lieutenant Colonel H.W.Le Patourel, VC
Nov 1957	Lieutenant Colonel G.J.A.Dewar, MBE

April 1961   Amalgamation with the 4th (TA) Battalion

4th/5th (TA) BATTALION THE ROYAL HAMPSHIRE REGIMENT

April 1961	Lieutenant Colonel B.Gater, TD
April 1962	Lieutenant Colonel J.B.Young, OBE,TD
April 1965	Lieutenant Colonel P.D.T.Powell, OBE,TD

April 1967   Disbanded on the reorganisation of the Reserve Army

* * * * * * * * *

CHAPTER 5

MÜNSTER AND LEMGO
1956 — 1959

Origins, course and consequences of the Suez Crisis - the Sandys Defence White
Paper and its effects on the Army - the 1st Battalion arrives in Münster - M3
halftracks manned by 105 Squadron RASC - aspects of contemporary theory
and tactical practice relating to mechanised infantry - visit of Generalleutnant
Dr H.Speidel - Münster Horse Show Week - the Battalion moves to Lemgo -
relations with civil population and ceremonial occasions - autumn manoeuvres
1957 - compliments from the Netherlands 4th Division and commander of 1
BR Corps - 105 Squadron replaced by A Squadron 14th/20th King's Hussars -
the Saracen APC - personalities and sporting achievements - uneasiness regarding
redundancy - the Depot to close and new badge imposed - autumn manoeuvres
1958 - Lieutenant Colonel Hogge succeeded by Lieutenant Colonel Hastings -
convoy shot up by farmer - "dismounted" anti-terrorist training in the Harz
Mountains and march back to Lemgo - bicentenary commemorations of the
Battle of Minden - the Battalion returns to the UK November 1959 - marches
through Winchester January 1960 - embarks for the West Indies.We left the 1st
Battalion about to go on leave following its return from Malaya, after which it
was to re-assemble at its BAOR station of Münster, Westphalia. Before proceeding
further, however, it is necessary to examine a series of events which were to have
a profound effect upon its history, and indeed upon that of the Army as a whole,
during the succeeding years

As luck would have it, the Anglo-Egyptian Treaty of 1936,
under the terms of which British troops were stationed
in the Canal Zone, expired in 1956. In October 1954 agreement was reached that they would be withdrawn and that their

bases in the Zone would be preserved and maintained as British property. By June 1956 the last soldier had gone and HQ Middle East Command had been transferred to the troubled island of Cyprus.

Concurrently, Colonel Gamal Abdel Nasser, who had become virtual dictator of Egypt following the revolution of 1952, needed funds with which to finance his Aswan High Dam project. He shamelessly played off the Free World against the Soviet bloc, but in July 1956, after he had begun re-equipping his army with Russian weapons, the British and Americans withdrew their support. His immediate response was to nationalise the Suez Canal with a view to appropriating its dues. Diplomatic pressure having failed to change his mind on the subject, the government of Sir Anthony Eden, who was now Prime Minister, took the view that he would have to be taught a sharp lesson, by force of arms. At a secret meeting it was decided that the United Kingdom, France and Israel would co-operate and a plan was drawn up. This would involve the Israelis attacking the Egyptian army in Sinai, following which the British and French would effect landings at Port Said with the apparent motive of separating the combatants and ensuring the security of the Canal along its length.

It was 31 October before preparations were complete and the plan was implemented, despite strenuous American urgings against direct action. In the event, the Israelis disposed of the much stronger Egyptian forces in Sinai in a matter of hours and, as agreed, halted their advance ten miles short of the Canal. The British and French airborne and amphibious landings, codenamed Operation Musketeer, took place on 6 November. During the subsequent breakout the troops had advanced almost halfway along the Canal, latterly without meeting the slightest opposition, when they were instructed to halt in compliance with the terms of an apparently inexplicable ceasefire. The United States had threatened to bankrupt the British economy unless hostilities ceased, and Eden had bowed to the threat.

At a stroke, the fiasco destroyed the Great Power status of the United Kingdom and France, both of whom had been publicly humiliated. It was said that after the Battle of the Somme in 1916 the British never quite trusted their national leaders again, and the Suez debacle tended to reinforce this view. Likewise, the consequences of Suez throughout the Middle East can be compared to those of the fall of Singapore during World War II in that British influence was so damaged that it could never be fully regained. Nasser, able to claim that he had withstood the combined might of the United Kingdom, France and Israel, became the hero of the Arab world. Others followed his lead until, to the chagrin of the US State Department, the majority of Arab nations, their armies re-equipped with Soviet weapons and trained by Soviet advisers, slid effortlessly into the communist sphere of influence.

Eden, broken by the disaster, resigned the Premiership in January 1957 and was succeeded by Harold Macmillan, who, as Minister for Defence and then as Chancellor of the Exchequer, had long been keen to reduce the size of the armed services and end conscription. His own Defence Minister, Duncan Sandys, quickly gave substance to these proposals in his Defence White Paper of 1957, the effects of which were to shake the Army from top to bottom. The main provisions of his policy can be summarised as follows:

1. There was to be greater reliance on nuclear deterrence.

2. The last National Serviceman would be called up in 1960.

3. The Army was to be smaller. The infantry, having already been reduced from the 1951 level of 85 battalions to 77 battalions, mainly by the disbandment of regiments' junior battalions, was to be reduced further to 60 battalions. The Royal Armoured Corps was to lose 7 of its 30 regiments and the Royal Artillery, having already lost 14 regiments on the disbandment of Anti-Aircraft Command, was to lose another 20. As far as the infantry was concerned, these reductions would be effected by amalgamation between neighbouring regiments or between regiments with similar historical backgrounds, for example the Light Infantry, to create "large" regiments with several battalions. As already described, similar reductions would take place within the Territorial Army.

4. Though smaller, the Army would be more flexible, a phrase which would become commonplace in the years to come whenever further reductions in its strength were

contemplated. In this context it required the creation of a central strategic reserve which the RAF would fly to wherever it was needed. Unfortunately, the RAF was also being severely cut back and it lacked the aircraft to perform the role. Thus, though official policy was to dispense with as many overseas bases as possible, it became necessary to create new bases in Kenya, Aden, the Persian Gulf and Malaya to house the troops that would be needed. Government explanations as to why the central strategic reserve should begin its life dispersed around the globe lacked something in their conviction.

5. As the re-armament of West Germany had begun in 1956, it was proposed that Rhine Army should be reduced to 45,000 by 1959, by which time it was anticipated that the Germans would be able to make a substantial contribution towards their own defence. This attracted strenuous protests from the the Germans themselves, since the infant Bundesheer had yet to find its feet — it had, for example, plenty of experienced senior officers and newly-commissioned subalterns, but very few officers of middle rank. Further protests came from other NATO allies, including Belgium, Holland and Denmark, where memories of German occupation were still painfully fresh, and who saw continued stability in a strong British presence on the Continent. In the end, a compromise figure of 55,000 was reached.

This, then, was the prevailing situation when the 1st Battalion The Royal Hampshire Regiment, having travelled as individuals to BAOR in accordance with recently introduced movement procedures, reached Münster in December 1956, where it relieved the 2nd Battalion The King's Royal Rifle Corps as the mechanised infantry battalion of 20th Armoured Brigade, 6th Armoured Division. It was quartered in Oxford Barracks which, though of sombre Wilhelmine construction, possessed central heating, tiled bathrooms and parquet flooring and were very comfortable.

Münster was an old Catholic cathedral city in Westphalia onto which industry and a major railway junction had been grafted and because of this there were still traces of war damage, although these were fast disappearing as the "German economic miracle" began to unfold. It possessed a fine medieval market place with excellent shops, pleasant tree-lined walks where the old Vauban-style fortification had been levelled, and a lake, the Aa See. There was an AKC cinema, a good NAAFI Club and a Salvation Army bookshop, plenty of pubs, cafes and restaurants but very few places of evening entertainment. This mirrored the personality of the average Münsterlander, a rather self-contained, dour character who spoke in Platt Deutsch dialect. His city had been a military district headquarters even in the Kaiser's day and, having long since become used to the presence of troops on his streets, his attitude to them was one of cool indifference.

Operationally, the role of the Battalion, in common with that of BAOR as a whole, was the defence of Western Europe against a Warsaw Pact offensive westwards towards the Rhine. The scenario was a nuclear, biological and chemical threat. The threat of nuclear weapons taught the troops the need for comprehensive concealment in woods and farms, the need to dig in with overhead cover and the use of armoured vehicles for protection against flash. The Battalion learned to keep vehicles and weapons operational in sub-zero temperatures, and respirators were worn each week. The role was a challenge, albeit an interesting one. As one member of B Company put it, "An infantry company just can't be taken out of a Malayan jungle and made into an armoured infantry company ready to fight a war in Europe by the alteration of its name. It has to be re-moulded and shaped, forgotten techniques have to be re-mastered and entirely new ones first of all learned and then perfected. It all takes time and demands a great deal of practice, hard work and concentrated training."

Equally, those responsible for formulating the Army's doctrine on the employment of mechanised infantry had still to reach the firm conclusions that only experience would bring. They had accepted that operations would be conducted at a much faster pace than in the old days of lorried infantry, and they were prepared to listen to those who had already made extensive use of mechanised infantry during World War II, hence the use of the American term armoured infantry. Yet innate conservatism still reigned when it came to the question of armoured personnel carriers. Logic suggested that APCs, drivers and maintenance facilities should all be organic elements within the establishment of a mechanised infantry battalion. The War Office, however, regarded the standard infantry battalion establishment as being graven in stone and preferred to attach other units to perform these tasks. Thus, the tactical movement of the Battalion was to be carried out in M3 half-tracks manned by 105 Squadron Royal Army Service Corps, commanded by Major F.Workman, RASC, who was inevitably nicknamed Ticket. This consisted of four troops, one of which was attached to each rifle company, adopting its letter, and a REME Light Aid Detachment. Likewise, because of the need for improved communications, V Troop 6th Armoured Division Signals Regiment, under Sergeant F.Kemp, Royal Corps of Signals, was also attached to the Battalion. These sub-units became fully integrated into the Battalion and identified themselves with it in every way.

Each of the Battalion's rifle companies wore the 6th Armoured Division's mailed fist flash and was affiliated to one of 20th Armoured Brigade Group's armoured regiments, of which there were initially four - the 3rd Carabiniers (A Company) at Osnabruck, and the 14th/20th King's Hussars (B Company), 17th/21st Lancers (Y Company) and 2nd Royal Tank Regiment (Z Company) at Münster. When, in the summer of 1957, the 14th/20th King's Hussars left to become the armoured regiment of 11th Infantry Brigade Group at Hohne, B Company, now lacking an affiliation, took over the role of Training Company from Support Company, with much reduced strength. The Mortar Platoon attached one of its sections to each of the three remaining rifle companies, but the Anti-Tank Platoon existed only on paper, it being deemed pointless to issue the Battalion with anti-tank guns in the presence of so much friendly armour. The same considerations applied to the Medium Machine Gun Platoon, although it retained its weapons until the autumn of 1957, simultaneously carrying out Battalion reconnaissance and traffic control duties.

Having settled in during the last weeks of the old year, the Battalion began 1957 with the rifle companies visiting their affiliated armoured regiments, where they were introduced to the Centurion tank and quickly learned by hard experience that, even in peacetime, tanks were dirty and very dangerous. This was particularly so when tired troops were riding on the engine decks at night, since the heat rising from the engine could make them so drowsy that they were in real danger of falling off into the path of the tank behind. Perversely, those sitting in the centre of the engine decks, while safer, received the suspension's full response whenever the tank crossed a hummock and could be flung into the air. Likewise, those who chose to sit on the turret risked being swept off by branches, and anyone who touched the main armament after live firing would sustain severe burns.

For their part, the rifle companies were told what was expected of them. In open country, the tanks would normally lead. However, where the axis of advance passed through close country or villages these would have to be cleared first by the infantry because in such circumstances the tanks were clearly vulnerable to the enemy's concealed bazooka anti-tank teams. At night, too, it would be the infantry who provided security for the tank harbours while the tank crews got on with their replenishment and maintenance tasks. There were at the time two aspects of mechanised infantry tactics which were provoking debate in the international professional press. The first posed the question as to whether the best results could be obtained by mechanised infantry fighting mounted or dismounted. Collective experience suggested that mounted action only produced good results against a beaten, disorganised enemy who was already in flight, and the obvious conclusion was that most actions would be fought dismounted after debussing from APCs in the proximity of tactical startlines. On the other hand, *if* the ground permitted, movement in APCs onto the objective under close supporting fire had obvious advantages, since the infantry could then dismount before the enemy surfaced. Views tended to be coloured by the type and numbers of APCs in use. Clearly, a vehicle which could keep up with tanks across country, and with its own firepower, enhanced the tactical use of the infantry in it. The second was who, tanks or infantry, commanded during which phase of any operation. Colonel Hogge had already emphasised to his companies that in the field they would become tactical sub-units of the armoured regiments to which they were attached and therefore subordinate to them. For their part, regimental and squadron commanders fully appreciated that in certain situations the decisions were best left to professional infantrymen. For example, if a wood on the flank of an advance had to be cleared, one or more tank troops might be placed at the company commander's disposal to provide fire support and he would be left to carry out the task in his own way. In other words, the rules of common sense would apply. From these initial meetings at all levels there stemmed an excellent and extremely friendly working relationship between the rifle companies and their armoured regiments that was to last throughout the tour, despite changes in affiliation - A Company to 5th Royal Inniskilling Dragoon Guards; Y Company to the 9th Queen's Royal Lancers; and Z Company to the 3rd Royal Tank Regiment and, almost at the end of the tour, to The Royal Scots Greys in which the Duke of Kent was serving as a troop leader.

Meanwhile, the Battalion had entered the BAOR training cycle. Many of the old Malaya hands who had not been looking forward to a German winter found it to be something of an anticlimax. In February 1957, however, a three-day survival exercise was held in unexpectedly arctic conditions which Colonel Hogge claimed he had booked well in advance. The following month the companies carried out section and platoon training at Sennelager. In April preliminary infantry/tank training took place at Soltau. Gallipoli Day, 25 April, was marked by a Commemorative Service, followed on 27 April by the Ceremony of Beating Retreat by the Band and Drums, which proved to be a very popular event as the Battalion possessed the only Corps of Drums in the Division.

Annual classification courses were fired at the huge Putlos Ranges in Schleswig Holstein on the Baltic coast, where troops from many NATO armies were also present, including some of the Bundesheer's first intakes. June found Y and Z Companies training with their affiliated armoured regiments at Sennelager, where they were visited by Generalleutnant Dr H.Speidel, Commander Allied Land Forces Central Europe, accompanied by the commander of I BR Corps, Lieutenant General H.E.Pyman, CB, CBE, DSO, the commander of the 6th Armoured Division, Major General D.S.S.O'Connor, CBE, and the commander of 20th Armoured Brigade Group, Brigadier A.W.A. Llewellen Palmer, DSO, MC, ADC. Having watched the training with considerable interest, General Speidel, himself a former Panzergrenadier, made a number of complimentary comments to Colonel Hogge before leaving.

Those remaining in Münster took part in an excellent Queen's Birthday Parade in which the Corps of Drums provided a frontage of eight side-drummers for the massed bands of the brigade. Containing as it did such a high proportion of cavalry, augmented by the 1st Regiment Royal Horse Artillery, it was understandable that equitation events should form an important part of the garrison's social life, culminating in the Münster Horse Show Week at the end of June. This was held at Dorbaum, a training area on the edge of Münster, and attracted entries from all over northern Germany, Holland and Denmark. Daily, each regiment took it in turn to establish a tent on the show ground, and at night there were cocktail parties and dances in the various messes. The Battalion was charged with running the Ball, which took place in a transformed Officers' Mess and was attended by some four hundred guests, including the divisional and brigade group commanders, the last of whom emerged blinking into the sunlight at 07:00 the next morning, expressing opinions that it had been the "Ball of the Year."

On 20 August 1957 the Battalion moved to Lemgo, a small town in the hills to the west of Hamelin and the Weser, in accordance with a revised NATO policy known as the "New Posture," under which units were stationed as close as possible to their designated mobilisation area. Here the Hampshires quickly made themselves at home in a way that would not have been possible in Münster. They were the only unit present and not only policed themselves efficiently but also took an active interest in the town's affairs, joining its various sports teams and rifle club. Numerous friendships were formed and in due course there were a number of marriages to Lemgo girls. The Burgermeister and prominent citizens were invited to the Mess as a matter of course and were greatly impressed by the officers' scarlet mess dress which, on the Battalion's return from Malaya, the Colonel of the Regiment had indicated should be reintroduced, thereby giving the Regimental tailors a great deal of pleasure but rather less to those who had to adjust their monthly "standing order tailor's bill"! So impressed was the Burgermeister on his first visit that, when proposing that the hospitality should be returned in the Ratskeller, he enquired hopefully, "You will wear the red coats, ja?" Granting him his wish might have contravened regulations, but it conferred much prestige on the Rat as a whole and was therefore wonderful public relations.

Notwithstanding heavy rain, the Battalion's first formal parade in Lemgo, too, was an occasion that warmed the German heart. The Battalion still held both the 1st and 2nd Battalions' Colours and on 5 September the Regimental Colour of the 2nd Battalion was Trooped in the presence of General Sir Dudley Ward, KCB, KBE, DSO, Commander-in-Chief British Army of the Rhine, the commanders of 1 BR Corps, 6th Armoured Division and 20th Armoured Brigade Group, and Colonel Richard Chandler, DSO, Deputy Colonel of the Regiment, watched by over three hundred German civilians. Photographic evidence confirms that even though the Regiment as a whole had always taken great pride in its ceremonial, this parade, commanded by Colonel Hogge, achieved an exceptionally high standard, thanks to the painstaking rehearsals carried out under the direction of RSM W.R.Watton. The Regimental Colour was carried by Second Lieutenant R.N.Tillard, with Sergeant W.Hanna and Sergeant R.Page as Escort, and Guards Nos 1 to 5 were commanded respectively by Major C.L.Thomas, DSO, Major P.Branwell, Major J.H.Fitzsimon, Captain W.R.Dugmore and Major E.G.Wright, MC. The occasion was also notable for the fact that, quite unofficially and for the first time for very many years, the Corps of Drums wore their pre-war Full Dress scarlet jackets, albeit with No 1 Dress hats; this unauthorised initiative earned the Battalion a rocket from on high, though hardly one to grieve over. In passing, it is worth recording that the Band and Corps of Drums became firm favourites with the people of Lemgo, who always applauded them strenuously whether they were giving an official public performance or simply marching through the streets.

The major manoeuvres of the year, designed to exercise the 20th Armoured Brigade Group under notional nuclear conditions, began on 10 September. It rained continuously and without mercy.

"Work, both by day and night, started off at a high tempo," noted the Journal, "but it soon became evident that with the country in such a water-logged state, the damage being done by the tanks was more than could be tolerated in peacetime even by a manoeuvre-hardened German population. Main roads became quagmires impassable to civilian traffic through mud left by tanks; verges and tracks disintegrated and tanks were sinking so deep in agricultural land that even field drains were being broken. To anyone viewing with the eyes of a countryman the aftermath of an armoured regiment's passage, the results in places were almost sickening. As a result, the Corps Commander called a halt to the manoeuvres before the entire area took on in fact the appearance of nuclear devastation which in theory it had acquired already in the imagination of the umpires."

It was an apparently disappointing end to the training year, compensated to some extent by the Battalion being required as mechanised infantry in support of a Dutch armoured unit, the Prins Alexander Regiment, in place of a Dutch infantry battalion stricken by Asian flu. Initial difficulties with language had been overcome by the third day, during which the final attack was put in with such dash and crisp co-operation that Major General P.Gips, commanding the 4th Netherlands Division, was delighted, presenting Colonel Hogge with a ceremonial cane and describing the Hampshires as "The best British battalion in the Dutch Army!" Some days later Colonel Hogge received a copy of a letter written by Lieutenant General Pyman to Major General O'Connor.

"Major General Gips called on me this morning. He came to express his great gratitude to, and admiration of, the 1st Battalion The Royal Hampshire Regiment which co-operated with an armoured regiment and other elements of his division last week at Sennelager.

"Will you please pass this information to the Royal Hampshires and tell them that I am very pleased with their excellent performance, which I know had to be undertaken at very short notice and not without sacrifice.

"I feel certain, too, that The Royal Hampshire Regiment will have benefited from this novel experience. It affords another example of the splendid spirit of this Battalion and it sets a standard of comradeship between allies which I know 4th Netherlands Division will long remember."

This exercise ended the training year, although firing the next year's rifle and light machine gun classification took place during the early winter months. The major operational change at this time was the withdrawal of the by-now elderly half-tracks and the return of 105 Squadron to more traditional RASC duties. Their place was taken early in 1958 by A Squadron 14th/20th King's Hussars, two of whose sabre squadrons had converted to the APC role while the third provided the armoured element of the British brigade in Berlin. Sad though the Hampshires were to see 105 Squadron go, they had already worked with the Hussars when the latter were stationed in Münster and the renewed association was to prove a happy one. A Squadron was equipped with the Saracen APC, based on an Alvis six-wheeled chassis that could withstand the loss of two wheels to mine damage, provided that they were not on the same side. It had a small turret housing a .30-inch Browning machine gun and an enclosed body of armour plate that was not only proof against non-armour-piercing small-arms fire and shell splinters but would also provide a degree of protection against flash, burns and fallout on a nuclear battle-field. The problem was that the Saracen, like the Austin Champ, was rather more camel than horse, having been designed by a committee to fulfil the Army's universal requirements for an APC. It performed well enough in an urban environment, in the Middle East and on the roads of Malaya, but it could not cope easily with the mud of the North German Plain, the result being that it was not always able to keep pace with the tanks across country.

This tour of duty is always remembered by those present as being one of the most satisfactory and rewarding of their entire service, and for this reason mention should be made of the Battalion's most prominent personalities. Many of the Company Commanders had seen distinguished war service. In A Company Major D.J.Warren, DSO, MC, commanded during the greater part of the tour. Major H.E.Wingfield, MC, Major C.L.Thomas, DSO and Major J.E.B.Conder, MC, all commanded B Company at some stage, while Major W.B.Thomas, DSO, MC, the Regiment's last Brevet Lieutenant Colonel, commanded Y Company during the later stages of his tour. For a while Major E.G.Wright, the holder of two MCs, commanded Headquarters Company.

After holding the post of Adjutant for three years, Captain John Darroch's departure on handing over in Münster was marked by a comment in the Journal that "His immaculate presence will be sorely missed." His successor was Major J.E.Tull, succeeded by Major S.G.B.Matthews, who in turn handed over to Captain J.D.Wellings on 1 October 1958. At the end of 1957 Major F.R.A.Read, the Quartermaster, handed over to Captain H.A.J.Plummer on posting to the Depot. Captain Plummer remained as Quartermaster throughout the Lemgo and Caribbean tours with conspicuous success. The Battalion never lacked for anything and nothing ever seemed to ruffle him. The Rev R.C.Desch, MBE, joined the Battalion in the summer of 1957. He had been the Padre of the 5th Battalion during the closing stages of the war and was universally welcomed.

It was unique for a Regimental Sergeant Major to return for a second tour, but WOI W.R.Watton did so, from June until November 1957. On his return he was greeted by all ranks with genuine pleasure, an outstanding tribute to an outstanding soldier and leader. He was succeeded by WOI H.L.Barnard, known as Harry to all and sundry unless he was within earshot, a man of vigorously robust personality which he impressed forcefully on the Battalion. As a hockey goalkeeper he was triumphant, terrifying opposing forwards and his own defenders equally. He was presented with his sword by the officers and this, subsequently known as the Barnard Sword, was carried by the RSM until 1992 and is now in the Regimental Museum. The Orderly Room was run by Sergeant (later WOII) Waterman from 1957 to the end of the BAOR tour and included, as well as numerous National Servicemen, three members who later made their mark - Lance Corporals West and Mordaunt, both fine rugby players like the Chief Clerk, became lieutenant colonels in due course and Orderly Room Corporal Kirby became Chief Clerk himself later on. The Bandmasters during this period were WOI G.Fidoe followed in April 1958 by WOI J.Plant. The Band Colour Sergeant was Colour Sergeant W.Butt, MM, and the Drum Major was Colour Sergeant R.E.Bryant, a magnificent figure on parade. Among other stalwarts were Sergeant Bill Bailey, Sergeant Rube Roberts and Corporal "Lofty" Ferris, who was to become Drum Major in years to come. Between July and September 1958 the Band appeared in public on no fewer than seventy occasions.

The Service Support was notable and those attached from the various Corps were, as always, welcomed and fully integrated into Battalion life. WOII Apperley, ACC, Staff Sergeant Deacon, REME, and the inimitable CSMI "Dinger" Bell, APTC, all made their mark, as did the Pay Team.

Among the best remembered people from the Lemgo tour was Mrs Kate Lean Varcoe, a widow. As the WVS representative in the Battalion, she ran a quiet room with tea and coffee, being much loved and respected.

One of great benefits of serving in BAOR was the excellent sporting facilities. During this period the Battalion contained many outstanding sportsmen, although the problem as always was getting the best team together for any particular game. Rugby football was enthusiastically embraced, the team being led by Lieutenant John Morrish at first and then, during 1958 and 1959, by Captain Tim Wellings with RSM Harry Barnard as trainer. Sergeant Andrews, later President of Leicester Rugby Football Club, Sergeant Baines, ORQMS Waterman and Private Ponsford were the other organisers. The highlight of the 1958/59 season was a four-day tour to Berlin, where the team defeated that of the 1st

Battalion The Royal Scots, the subsequent winners of the Rhine Army Cup. In total, the rugby team played twenty-four games during this season, and the fact that it lost only four speaks for itself.

In 1959 the hockey team under Captain J.R.E.Laird did well to reach the BAOR final, where they lost to 35 Corps Engineer Regiment. The team for the final was WOI Barnard, Corporal Hine, Corporal Breton, Corporal Arnold, Captain Laird, Lieutenant Palmer, Lieutenant Stevens, Bandsman Begum, Sergeant Roberts, Private Teasdale and Corporal Chester-Walsh.

The Association Football team had its successes and it was a mark of the time that the players included Private Fisher (Millwall and Portsmouth), Private Somers (Chelsea) and Private Taylor (Portsmouth). During the 1958/59 season Lance Corporal Sevier, the team captain, Lance Corporal Lightly and Lance Corporal Fisher all played for BAOR.

Much other sport was played and Lieutenant M.G.P.Chignell had great success on the squash court and on the cricket field, where Drum Major Bryant and Corporal Kirby also performed to good effect; and among many others, mention must be made of Second Lieutenant Oldaker, a National Service officer, who was still playing for the Regiment in 1992. In the field of athletics Private Pullinger produced spectacularly successful results with the shot, discus and hammer, becoming Army Hammer Champion in 1958 and 1959 as well as holding the Army and Divisional Hammer Records. Lance Corporal Tiltman held the Divisional Long Jump Record and also qualified for the BAOR Championships each year. Sergeant Cripps and Corporal Withers were conspicuous with some courageous middle distance running. The cross-country team did particularly well, winning all its matches and the 20th Armoured Brigade Group and 6th Armoured Division Championships.

The shooting record during the years 1957-59 was most satisfactory. In 1957, the first year back from Malaya, the team only finished tenth overall in the Rhine Army Meeting, although Colour Sergeant Pike, Sergeant Turner, Sergeant Fazackerly and Sergeant Beveridge won the Sten Match, Colour Sergeant Pike being the individual runner-up. There were also successes on the range in 1958 when WOII Pike and Colour Sergeant Hyatt won the Rhine Army Bren Gun Pairs; Sergeants Beveridge (20th), Henderson and Private Veck were in the Rhine Army Hundred while Staff Sergeant Deacon REME (14th) and WOII Hanna (20th) were in the Rhine Army Pistol Twenty. In 1959, the Battalion beat every other unit in BAOR except the Rifle Brigade. The Young Soldiers Team event was won easily by Lance Corporal Coyne, Privates Dyer, West, Veck, Holdway and Robbins. The Corporals and Privates team was second and the Warrant Officers and Sergeants team third in their respective events. The SMG team were third in their event. Eight firers were in the Rhine Army Hundred — Major Nicholson, Captain Bretherton, Staff Sergeant Deacon REME, Sergeant Wheeler, Sergeant Blake, Corporal Robinson, Lance Corporal Coyne and Private Veck, the last two being second and third respectively in the Young Soldiers class. At Bisley in 1959 Lance Corporal Godfrey and Private Driscoll won their class in the LMG Pairs; Captain Bretherton, Sergeant Blake, Sergeant Turner and Sergeant Wheeler were runners-up from 121 entries in the Falling Plate competition. Perhaps the greatest enthusiast and best all-round shot was WOII Paddy Hanna, who was still shooting for Great Britain many years later, and whose Company team was always the one to beat in the Battalion Skill-at-Arms Meeting.

Superficially, therefore, the Sandys Axe had left the 1st Battalion untouched, although by the beginning of 1958 some worrying trends had already become apparent. Within the infantry as a whole there had always existed a need for more trained junior officers, NCOs and soldiers than were available, so at this level the amalgamation of two battalions presented few problems to their successor. On the other hand, such an amalgamation left a surfeit of those holding Field or Warrant rank and, for the first time, the new word "redundancy" began to cast its chill shadow. These uneasy feelings were reinforced by the news that, as part of the economy drive, the Depot was to close in September, its place being taken by the establishment of a small Regimental Headquarters in Serle's House, and that thereafter its functions would be performed by a newly-formed Wessex Brigade Depot at Exeter. Although as positive an outlook as possible was preserved, there were those who began to suspect a move towards one of the new "large" regiments, the battalions of which could, in future, be axed with far less public protest than those of county regiments with over two centuries of service to their credit. If anything, the imposition of a Wessex Brigade cap badge on 17 May 1958 tended to reinforce such suspicions. The new badge, a

Wyvern surmounting the word Wessex, was promptly named "The Pregnant Prawn." Some of its wearers quickly discovered that the beast's right foreclaw could be bent upwards to meet its nose, thereby cocking a snook at authority; amusing as such attempts at animation were, they did not survive the notice of Warrant Officers and Sergeants. Some of the Wyverns worn by the officers were made from melted down Mess silver and suitably hallmarked. Buttons and all other badges remained Regimental.

During 1958 a Battalion Patrol Competition was instituted and teams were sent to participate in the Nijmegen Marches. In other respects, the training cycle followed the usual routine, save for changes of affiliation as armoured regiments left or joined the brigade group. By now the Battalion had acquired a reputation of being second to none at its job, as is demonstrated by a letter Colonel Hogge received from Lieutenant Colonel Gill, commanding the 4th/7th Royal Dragoon Guards, 7th Armoured Brigade, to whom A Company, commanded by Major David Warren, was temporarily attached during August.

"Whoever conceived the idea of sending your A Company to join my Regiment on the training area recently deserves a pat on the back. It was a brilliant piece of good fortune for us, for indeed it is many years since we had the good privilege to work at tank/infantry co-operation with a company of that calibre. They were fun to work with, and even nicer it was to work with someone who knows what he is doing."

The final exercise of the training year took place in the area of Brilon, south of Paderborn, shortly after. "We went off with our affiliated armoured regiment, 5th Royal Inniskilling Dragoon Guards," recorded A Company, "with whom we had some preliminary canters before starting on Exercise Velvet Glove II. This exercise was a battle between 20th Armoured Brigade and 4th Guards Brigade. Despite the fact that we were cast in the role of Fantasians, we set out to smarten up our Guardsmen friends. At first light at the start of the exercise, the Company moved out with C Squadron of the 'Skins' to a hide near a river, and prepared to cross it. Before long, Major Warren, commanding the Squadron/Company Group, gave the order to move forward to the river with a view to crossing it. Soon we were moving forward in Saracens behind tanks and, despite hostility by certain German farmers, successfully crossed the river with no sign of any enemy.

"However, exercises being what they are, we were told that we must go back to the other side and wait for some Guardsmen to arrive. Two and a half hours later they did arrive, and once more we set off in our 'amphibious' APCs across the river and, after a sharp encounter with the Coldstream Guards, secured a bridgehead and quite a lot of kit belonging to the Guardsmen."

On 31 October the Regiment's oldest member, former Private Alf Hawker, celebrated his 100th birthday, as described elsewhere.

Such events provide a reminder that a Regiment is a living institution that evolves continuously through the generations yet, though faces may change, retains its identity and sense of family. On 3 January 1959 the 1st Battalion said goodbye to Colonel Tony Hogge on his promotion and departure for a Staff appointment in the Ministry of Defence. When the 1st Battalion left Malaya it had the reputation of being among the best jungle warfare units to have served there during the Emergency; now, still under his command and in a comparatively short space of time, the Battalion had earned a similar reputation as being a hard-driving, efficient mechanised infantry unit.

Simultaneously, Colonel Hogge had also been responsible for a number of developments which would be of benefit to the Battalion. For example, much of the silver, having made the journey to Malaya and back and then to Münster and Lemgo, was damaged and in need of very expensive repair. An unofficial pig farm was therefore set up, the animals being fed with the cookhouse swill, and the profits were paid into the Commanding Officer's Fund. In due course sufficient had been amassed to crate up the silver and deliver it to Garrards of Regent Street, who also trained the Officers' Mess silverman in how to maintain it. Likewise, as a result of the enthusiastic urgings of Major J.E.Little-Jones, who also took a party of skiers to train with the Norwegian Army, the Battalion acquired a ski lodge at Gurkhausen in the Harz Mountains. This induced considerable enthusiasm for the sport among regular skiers and beginners alike, so much so that it became possible to form a Battalion Cross-Country Relay team, prominent members of which were Second Lieutenant Withers, a National Service Officer who also fenced for Great Britain with the foil and épée, Sergeant Withers, and Privates Booth and Oliver. By no means least was an affiliation established in 1957 between the Battalion and a mechanised infantry unit of the Belgian Army, the 1er Bataillon de Carabiniers Cyclistes, resulting in regular exchange visits between the various messes.

Colonel Tony Hogge understood and embraced the ethos of an armoured formation. He had a great sense of fun and was a far-sighted officer who visualised the new Regular Army and the sort of men who would join it, and gradually up-dated old views and methods. He was much missed and was given a noisy send-off during which, having escaped through the barrack gates, he found his route through Lemgo lined by the Saracens of A Squadron 14th/20th King's Hussars, each of which marked the progress of his car with a thunderflash.

His successor was Lieutenant Colonel M.C.Hastings, DSO, who had been commissioned into the Devonshire Regiment in 1936. During World War II he had served with his Regiment's 2nd Battalion in Malta, Egypt and Sicily in 231 Malta Brigade alongside the 1st Hampshires, where he was wounded, then re-joined for the campaign in North West Europe. Subsequently he had served as Brigade Major to 3 Commando Brigade Royal Marines at Ipoh, Malaya, and as a company commander with 1st Devons against the Mau Mau terrorists in Kenya. He was then posted to the Tactical Wing of the School of Infantry at Warminster, the commandant of which at the time was Colonel R.G.F.Frisby. In 1957 he had returned to 1st Devons, now a mecha-nised infantry battalion based at Celle, as Second in Command, and remained with the 1st Battalion Devonshire and Dorset Regi-ment after amalgamation until it left for Cyprus in October 1958.

Hardly had the 1959 annual training cycle begun when the Hampshires came under fire for the first time since they left Malaya. During a night march on 9 April a twenty-strong packet of vehicles, using only convoy lights, took a wrong turning on the Sennelager training area and arrived in the farmyard of one Gerhard Welschon, where it began to turn itself round. The re-sponse of Herr Welschon was to fling open a window and blaze away with a Walther 6mm automatic pistol, puncturing a water trailer. When Colonel Hastings ordered his jeep's lights to be switched on to identify the source of the shots, this attracted fur-ther firing, as a result of which a driver, Private David, was slightly wounded in the arm. The German civil police seemed to regard the incident as being unremarkable and only took action when Colonel Hastings threatened to have the farm surrounded. The man Welschon was then taken to Paderborn in a police car, where he was charged with negligent wounding; his excuse was that he had mistaken the convoy for a motorised gang of poultry thieves reputed to be active in the area.

During the greater part of June the Battalion held a series of "dismounted" anti-terrorist exercises in the Harz Mountains in preparation for its next posting, which was then believed to be Cyprus. This was a terrific release after being cooped in APCs for so long. At the end of this unusual period of training, the Battalion marched back to Lemgo in temperatures exceeding 90°F, covering 84 miles in four days, played through the various towns along the way and back into barracks by the Corps of Drums in the absence of the Band, which was performing at the Royal Tournament.

On 2 July A and Y Companies gave a demonstration of mechanised infantry tactics on the Soltau training area for a group of distinguished visitors including the Chief of Imperial General Staff, General Sir Francis Festing, GCB, KCB, DSO, the commander of I BR Corps, Lieutenant General Sir Michael West, KCB, DSO, and the commander of 20th Armoured Brigade Group, Brigadier d'Avigdor-Goldsmid, OBE, MC.

Uppermost in the majority of minds throughout the Regiment were preparations for the celebration of the Bicentenary of the Battle of Minden. These began on 27 July with a magnificent banquet held at the Guildhall, London, in the presence of the Queen Mother, Princess Margaret, the Duchess of Gloucester and the Lord Mayor of London. Also present were the Colonels of all the Minden Regiments and the Master Gunner, St James's Park. Of the 640 officers and guests who attended the dinner, about one hundred belonged to the Royal Hampshire Regiment, including:

> Lieutenant Colonel Martin Hastings and his Second-in-Command, Major I.Methven, MBE, Major General R.H.Batten, CBE, DSO, Brigadier Cadoux-Hudson, MC, Brigadier R.Chandler, DSO, Brigadier R.G.F.Frisby, CBE, DSO, MC, Colonel A.H.T.Hogge, Major H.J.Jeffery, Lieutenant Colonel J.M.Lee, DSO, Brigadier P.H.Man, DSO, OBE, MC, Major General W.H.C.Ramsden, CB, CBE, DSO, MC and Lieutenant Colonel P.R.Sawyer, OBE, MC, TD, JP.

On 31 July the 1st Battalion held a ceremonial parade at Lemgo in honour of the Colonel of the Regiment, followed by a drum-head service. An excellent Minden Day Lunch, including beer for everyone, was served after the parade and during the evening the Sergeants' Mess held their Minden Ball, at which Brigadier Browne and Brigadier Man were guests.

On 1 August, the actual anniversary of the battle, the focus of events moved to Minden itself where, at 09:30, an exhibition dedicated to the battle was opened in the town's museum. At that moment, two hundred years earlier, the routed French army was streaming through the streets. On the battlefield the six British infantry regiments most responsible for their defeat had finally halted. The sky was beginning to clear but a high wind persisted, making it difficult for the Ensigns to control their bullet-riddled, unwieldy six-foot-square Colours. Of the 37th Regiment, which had gone into action 506 strong, only 208 officers and men remained on their feet, their hands and faces blackened by burned powder, suddenly weary from loss of sleep and reaction, uncaring for the moment that they were responsible for one of the British Army's greatest feats of arms. Their reward was to fire a *feu de joie* and, for the few that lived on into old age, a medal from the Regiment.

For such reasons, therefore, the emphasis on 1 August 1959 was on commemoration rather than celebration. At 11:00 the principal ceremony of the day took place at the battlefield memorial. A Guard of Honour, commanded by Lieutenant R.N.C.Pannell, was provided by all the Minden Regiments, the 1st Battalion's contingent consisting of a corporal and six privates. Since Minden was also a German victory, the Bundesheer also provided a Guard of Honour. It would have been appropriate if the latter had included the direct successors of the Hanoverian Royal Guard and Hardenberg's Regiment, which had shared the fortunes of the day with the six British regiments, but they had ceased to exist when Hanover, having joined the losing side during the Austro-Prussian War, was stripped of its Army in 1866. During the ceremony music was provided by the Royal Hampshires' Band and Drums, together with a German Army band. Brigadier Browne, representing the Colonels of all the Minden Regiments, laid a wreath, and Colonel Hastings did likewise on behalf of the Regiment. Afterwards the parade marched through the town and was entertained to lunch by the civic authorities. During the evening both bands gave a concert at the Domhof.

Next day, Sunday, the Band and Drums marched through Lemgo and beat Retreat at the Sportplatz before a large and appreciative crowd. The Bicentenary celebrations were concluded on the evening of 3 August with the Officers' Minden Ball, among the guests at which were Major General G.C.Hopkinson, DSO, OBE, MC, commanding 6th Armoured Division, and Brigadier d'Avigdor-Goldsmid, OBE, MC.

For some months there had been rumours that the 1st Battalion's next tour of duty would, in fact, be in the West Indies, and now these were confirmed. For some the prospect conjured visions of blue seas, palm trees and rich American ladies searching for Hampshire husbands; others, better informed, were aware that some serious soldiering lay ahead. The period following the Minden celebrations was, therefore, devoted to ensuring a smooth handover to the 1st Battalion The Argyll and Sutherland Highlanders, this being completed during the first week of November. The Battalion's departure from Lemgo for the Hook was clearly regarded as a major event. Major Peter Waterman (then WOII ORQMS) remembers marching the cased Colours to the station as senior member of the Escort. On the way he was very moved to notice two elderly Germans stand to attention and remove their hats as the Colours passed by. Each of the Brigade's armoured regiments had provided a Sergeants' Mess bar at the station and 3 RTR's Corps of Drums played the train away. On arrival in the UK the Battalion took up temporary accommodation in Bhurtpore Barracks, Tidworth. Here, khaki drill uniforms were issued and tailored, inoculations given and the Battalion brought up to a strength of nearly one thousand men. Most people caught up with their leave and were able to spend Christmas at home. On 21 January 1960, a typical wet, grey, mid-winter day, the 1st Battalion exercised its Freedom rights by marching through Winchester with bayonets fixed, Colours flying and drums beating. Six abreast, it swung down the High Street from the Upper Barracks to the familiar strains of *The Farmer's Boy* and the Regimental March of the old 37th, then to the bugle march *Mechanised Infantry* as it returned by way of Southgate Street to the Lower Barracks Square. Despite the miserable weather the crowds were there as usual, shops and businesses turned out and even the Assize Court at the Castle was adjourned for the occasion. At the

Guildhall, the Salute was taken by the Mayor of Winchester, Councillor Mrs P.A.T.Lowden, the Lord Lieutenant of Hampshire, the Duke of Wellington, KG, the Colonel of the Regiment and the High Sheriff of Hampshire, Sir Hugh Smiley, Bart. Before embarking on the *Dunera* at Southampton on 3 February, the Battalion was addressed by the Colonel of the Regiment and the Mayor of Southampton, who wished them bon voyage, a successful tour and a safe return. Once again, in the words of the old recruiting song that had led so many men into the ranks of the 37th Regiment in Marlborough's day, the Hampshires were bound "o'er the hills and far away."

* * * * * * * * *

THE REGIMENT'S OLDEST SOLDIER

Former Private Alf Hawker had, with the connivance of the recruiting sergeant, added a year to his age in order to join the 67th Regiment. In December 1879 he had taken part in the epic defence of the Sherpur Cantonment, outside Kabul, against an Afghan force outnumbering the garrison by at least ten to one. He was probably the last survivor of the Second Afghan War, but for all that he became a centenarian his mind remained clear and his recollection sharp. He remembered the intense cold and short rations endured at Sherpur; the light shed by the new star shells illuminating the howling ranks of the enemy; his best friend, Private Lever, being hit beside him; and that, because of his apparent invulnerability, the troops had nicknamed their commander, the future Field Marshal Lord Roberts, The Iron Man on the Wooden Horse. After twelve years' service, too few to qualify for a gratuity or pension, he had left the Army with £12 in his pocket, the accumulated savings of a shilling-a-day soldier at 6d a week. When he chose to retire at the age of eighty-three he was working as a stoker. On the day of his centenary he received congratulatory messages from The Queen and from the Colonel of the Regiment. The Secretary of the Comrades' Association, Major H.J.Jeffery, also called on him at his home in Stratford in the East End of London, to present him with a cheque for £5, which he promised not to waste on beer, and a painted wall plaque of the Regimental Crest, which he hung on his bedroom wall. At the request of the Regiment, the local officers of the British Legion continued to keep an eye on his welfare. Alf Hawker died on 5 December 1962 aged 104 years.

* * * * * * * * *

THE HAMPSHIRE TIGERS

CHAPTER 6

THE DEPOT 1945 — 1948

Layout of the Depot - return of the Depot Party - Major H.J.Jeffery and succeeding Commanding Officers - functions of the Depot - Colours of the Royal Militia Island of Jersey - Dog Fritz - the winter of 1946/47 - HMS *Pandora* - visit of General de Lattre de Tassigny to Winchester College - the *River Clyde*'s nameplate - aspects of recruit training 1951-58 - Coronation duties and Royal visit to Winchester - last ceremonial parade and closure - new Regimental Headquarters

The Depot of The Royal Hampshire Regiment occupied the Lower Barracks, Winchester. It incorporated Serle's House, a barrack block, a chapel and several smaller buildings including a Guard Room at the entrance from Southgate Street, an indoor miniature range and a gymnasium, and the Lower Square. The Officers' Mess was located next to the Green Jackets' Officers' Mess at the southern end of the Upper Barracks Square. The Sergeants' Mess occupied the ground floor of Serle's House, beneath the Depot Commander's office and the Orderly Room, and the top floor of the building housed the Regimental Museum. This accommodation scale, however, was only intended to cope with peacetime recruitment and training for the two Regular battalions, and training assistance for the Militia and Territorials. It lacked the space and training facilities required for the General Mobilisations of 1914 and 1939, so, on both occasions, it vacated the Lower Barracks, Winchester, for Albany Barracks, Parkhurst, Isle of Wight.

THE HAMPSHIRE TIGERS

The Depot Party, commanded by Major H.J.Jeffery, returned to Winchester in November 1945. Major Jeffery had enlisted in the Regiment's 3rd (Militia) Battalion in June 1905 and three months later became a Regular soldier. Prior to World War I, he served with the 2nd Battalion in Bermuda, with the 2nd Battalion Mounted Infantry in South Africa, and in Mauritius. After joining the 1st Battalion in February 1914 he accompanied it to France with the BEF and was taken prisoner during the Battle of Le Cateau. His services while a prisoner of war earned him the Meritorious Service Medal. After repatriation in 1919 he joined the 3rd Battalion at Catterick and was selected as Regimental Sergeant Major direct from Sergeant, an astonishing achievement. He served as RSM with the 1st Battalion in Turkey and Egypt, and then with the 2nd Battalion until he was promoted Lieutenant (QM) in August 1926. Three months later he rejoined the 1st Battaliion in India, taking part in the North West Frontier campaign of 1930. Following promotion to Captain (QM) in 1934 he was posted to the 2nd Battalion, with which he served in Palestine during the troubles of 1936-37. Appointed Quartermaster of the Depot in March 1937, he remained at Winchester until the outbreak of World War II, when he joined the Isle of Wight Infantry Training Centre at Albany Barracks, Parkhurst. In October 1941 he returned to the Depot Party, being appointed its commander and remaining so until his retirement in 1947. During World War II he also played the major role in organising the Regiment's Prisoner of War Fund, the residue of which was passed to the Comrades' Association for benevolent purposes after the war. A man of great energy and determination, his life was dedicated to the Regiment and even after his formal retirement he continued to serve it in a number of important capacities, including Regimental Secretary, Secretary of the Comrades' Association, Editor of the Journal, and Committee Member of the Hampshire and Isle of Wight Military Aid Fund. Major Jeffery died on 31 March 1980 in his ninety-third year.

Succeeding Commanding Officers of the Depot were:

Major E.R.S.Westropp	August 1947
Major C.A.T.Halliday	November 1948
Major H.D.Nelson-Smith, MC	January 1950
Major D.J.Warren, DSO, MC	Autumn 1951

THE DEPOT 1945 — 1958

Major F.M.Shaw	Autumn 1954
Major T.H.N.Keene	August 1956
Major H.E.Wingfield, MC	November 1957 until closure 1958

The Depot's functions were legion, the most obvious being the training of recruits for the Regiment's Regular battalions. In the immediate post-war years, however, War Office policy was that recruits should receive their initial training at Primary Training Centres before going on to Infantry Training Centres. The Regiment's recruits therefore reported to No 37 PTC, commanded initially by Lieutenant Colonel J.M.Lee, DSO, which was at first based in the Upper Barracks. This system had never been intended to cope with the increased numbers generated by National Service and within the infantry a reversion was made to training recruits at regimental depots. On 6 December 1951 the first recruit intake since the war, consisting of forty-three National Servicemen and potential Regulars, were personally greeted by the Commanding Officer when they reported to the Depot. From this time on, in addition to the Commanding Officer, the Depot Staff included an Adjutant, a Quartermaster, a major in charge of recruit training and two training subalterns with NCO instructors, an Orderly Room, cooks, drivers and Officers' Mess staff. As the ultimate beneficiary, the 1st Battalion always posted its best instructors to the Depot. The vital and main function was to convert civilians, be they Regulars or National Servicemen, into trained soldiers able to take their place in a rifle section in the Regular battalion.

It was quite usual throughout the Army for the advantages of Regular enlistment to be pointed out to National Service recruits. Their reaction, as described elsewhere, tended to be ambivalent, but on one occasion during Major David Warren's period as Commanding Officer of the Depot no fewer than twenty-three National Servicemen from a single intake transferred to Regular engagements. Not surprisingly, Major Warren received not a few interested telephone calls from offices in Whitehall, demanding to know what The Royal Hampshire Regiment was doing right that other people apparently weren't!

Although its strength never numbered much more than two hundred officers and men, the Depot was the hub of the Regiment's collective life and therefore its home. In addition to this primary role of training recruits, the Depot was responsible for a number of other functions. It provided accommodation if required for any officer or soldier between courses in the UK and the 1st Battalion overseas; it was the home of the Regimental Band when it was away from the Battalion on UK duties, and it was of course the repository for a great deal of Regimental property not needed by the Battalion in its overseas role. It provided permanent accommodation for bachelor members of the Regular permanent staff in the two Territorial Battalions at Southampton and Winchester, and it was the occasional week-end training rendezvous for members of the Territorial Battalions.

All time-expired Regulars and National Servicemen ending their two years' service spent their last few days at the Depot, handing in their kit and completing their documentation. Not infrequently the Depot staff also found themselves acting as mediator over some welfare problems between soldiers serving abroad and their home-based families. So diverse were the Depot's roles that at one time a sailing cruiser and an officer's hunter were housed within the barrack walls!

The Regimental Depot always cherished its very special relationship with the Regimental Comrades' Association. The Commanding Officer was automatically the Association's Chairman and on the occasion of the Annual Reunion it was the Depot that provided the venue for the Standard Bearers' Competition and the Memorial Garden service, and from whence the Comrades marched through Winchester to their dinner at the Guildhall. The Depot was always held in high regard by the Comrades, for whom it was, of course, their Alma Mater.

Externally, the Depot provided the link between the War Office and the Regiment on non-operational matters. It was closely involved with the County's civic and religious authorities regarding such matters as Freedoms, Royal visits, Armistice Day parades and other occasions requiring a Regimental presence, and it entertained local dignitaries at cocktail parties and guest nights in the Officers' Mess, at which the Band of the 4th (TA) Battalion usually performed.

Something of interest was generally taking place at the Depot. In April 1946, just prior to the disbandment of the 11th (Royal Militia Island of Jersey) Battalion The Hampshire Regiment, a Colour Party and Escort under Major C.A.B.Rule were accommodated at the Depot. They had come to take back to

Jersey the Colours of The Royal Militia Island of Jersey which, since November 1941, had been placed in the safe custody of the Bishop's Chapel, Wolvesey Castle, Winchester. After a short service that preceded the ceremony, the Lord Bishop of Winchester handed back the King's Colour to Captain R.L.Reed and the Militia Colour to Captain F.S.Prince.

The Depot was also home to Dog Fritz who, when he was not leading parades, sometimes undertook charitable work. In November 1946 he attended a People's Dispensary for Sick Animals show in the grounds of the Royal Hospital, Chelsea, held on behalf of the Allied Forces Animal Welfare Memorial Fund, winning second prize in the "Dog You Would Like Most To Take Home With You" class. He also made some excellent collections during Winchester's Commando Week, and in July the following year returned from the War Dog Show at Wembley with a full collecting box and several rosettes. In the meantime, like everyone else, he had somehow managed to get through the memorable winter of 1946/47, during which a chronic fuel shortage coincided with endless weeks of arctic weather. With tacit official approval, almost every wooden fence in the Depot was fed into fires and stoves in an attempt to keep warm.

By the summer of 1948 the Depot had been firmly re-established with its own and Regimental flags flying from twin poles near the Guard Room. On the Guard Room verandah hung the highly polished ship's bell of HMS *Pandora*, discovered on a camp at Sutton Veny, Wiltshire, by the 12th Battalion in 1915. How it came to be there remains a mystery, for *Pandora*, a 2250-ton cruiser of the Pelorus Class, completed in 1900, had been sold for scrap a year earlier.

On 22 June 1949 General Jean de Lattre de Tassigny, commander of the then Western Union Land Forces and a future Commander-in-Chief of the French forces in Indochina, visited Winchester College, the Cadet Corps of which provided a Guard of Honour. This had been prepared by RSM J.Baxter of the Depot, who shared in the General's congratulations on its steadiness and drill.

In 1950 the Regimental Museum received one of its most prized exhibits from the family of the late Captain E.Unwin, VC, CB, CMG, Captain of the *River Clyde*, who presented the ship's name-plate to the Regiment. This remains prominently displayed, together with the ship's chronometer, port light (the starboard light is at the RMA Sandhurst) and other Gallipoli trophies.

Some aspects of recruit training during the late 1950s are recalled by Major Jim Kellie, one of the training subalterns at that time:

"At any one time there were four platoons training in pairs - Minden and Tebourba, Gallipoli and Salerno. The four platoons overlappped for four weeks of their training cycle. Competition was intense within a pair and the platoon sergeants strove to make their platoon the best of the intake. RSM W.R.Watton's influence on the standards at the Depot was immense. The standard of discipline was very high. Few recruits were discharged on medical grounds and none of them was ever in really bad trouble. Courts martial were unknown. At the very worst the Depot Commander might have to award seven days' detention in the Guardroom. The quality of recruit produced at the end of the ten weeks' training was very high indeed. Turnout was first class, as was both foot and arms drill, these results being a credit to their instructors and the Regiment - so much so that recruits took part in the Queen's Birthday Parade outside the Guildhall in Winchester. Each intake passed out ceremonially in the presence of their families with a band on parade, then attended a short service of dedication in the Chapel. During these passing out parades awards were made by the distinguished senior officer taking the Salute. These included a Certificate of Merit for the best all-round recruit, awards for the best rifle and LMG shots and, later, a physical training medal and an inter-platoon cup. On one occasion, the judges sitting at the Castle, faced with an intricate legal problem and knowing that a passing out parade was about to take place, requested that the Band should remain silent, fearing that the delicate balance of their deliberations would be disturbed by martial music; being a good neighbour, the Depot agreed.

"Most of the shooting was done at Chilcomb Range, three miles away. Many of the recruits reached Marksman standard on the rifle and the LMG. Some were Marksmen on both weapons. Their instructors, one or two of whom were National Servicemen themselves, were dedicated and highly motivated. In 1958 the Depot won the Recruit Match at the Aldershot District Small Arms Meeting beating, among others, the Depot's barrack neighbours, The Green Jackets. One of the team's best shots was Private Norman West, a very young regular who, many years later, reached the rank of lieutenant colonel in The Duke of Edinburgh's

Royal Regiment."

Understandably, the Depot was extremely busy during 1953, the year of The Queen's Coronation. "On Coronation Day," recalled the author of the Depot Notes for the Journal, "there was a parade to the Cathedral in the morning and in the evening we 'held the Ground' in the Broadway for the Carnival Procession, whilst several harassed men under the RSM helped to marshal the fantastic army of floats on the Upper Square. The Band and Drums had a busy day, being on both parades. In addition, the Drums escorted the ox to its roasting site. On the day following the Coronation, the Band and Drums played The Queen's and Regimental Colours of the 1st Battalion, The Queen's Colour of the 4th Battalion, and the Depot and 4th Battalion Coronation Street-lining Detachments, through Winchester back to the Depot on their return from duty in London. During that afternoon the Sergeants' Mess gave a very successful party to the children of the Depot which they all seemed to enjoy. In the evening the Band gave a concert in the Memorial Garden.

"As a climax to the civic celebrations in Winchester the Mayor arrived in procession to watch the Band and Drums beat Retreat. The weather for once was excellent and a very large crowd, estimated at about 2500, lined the square and sat on the bank to see what was undoubtedly a very impressive spectacle. The Band and Drums beat Retreat on the square once again on 18 June and a large crowd came again to see an excellent performance."

On 25 July 1955 The Queen and the Duke of Edinburgh paid a formal visit to Winchester. "The Depot was given the honour of providing a street-lining party of one officer (Lieutenant J.R.E.Laird) and 64 ORs. This party, which had to be found from the NCOs and recruits of Minden Company, whose recruits had only 17 days' service, put up a very good performance. The Depot throughout Her Majesty's visit acted as the base for Service street-lining parties and bands, and also for the extremely smart Guard of Honour found by the 4th Battalion. At one stage the Adjutant, who was acting as marshal of the various comings and goings, was somewhat shaken to find the Band of HMS *Ariel*, which was expected, being followed into barracks by a seemingly endless procession of pre-Service and nursing cadet contingents who were definitely not expected!"

The Depot also provided a contingent for the Guard of Honour, commanded by the Adjutant, Captain P.B.Chambers,

MC, required for The Queen's visit to Romsey on 6 April 1957, the details of which have been recorded elsewhere. On 7 July that year it organised a shoot for the Home Guard, which was on the point of being stood down for the last time.

By the spring of 1958 it was known that the Depot would be closing later that year and the Commanding Officer, Major H.E.Wingfield, MC, decided to make its its final months as memorable as possible. At the passing out parade on 18 April, therefore, there was a slight departure from recent tradition in that the Salute was taken by the Mayor of Winchester, Councillor Miss E.M.Barnes, who then spoke of the Regiment's links with Winchester and the high esteem in which it was held by the townspeople.

Simultaneously, with the ending of National Service already scheduled, it had become of paramount importance to secure a flow of Regular recruits for the Regiment, and for this the Depot laid the groundwork. Both the *Southern Daily Echo* and the *Hampshire Chronicle* published lengthy articles on the subject. A shop window display was arranged in Newport, Isle of Wight, and displays, complete with weapons and soldiers, were staged in the foyers of the Forum Cinema, Southampton, and the Odeon Cinema, Winchester. Portsmouth and Bournemouth were also targeted and the Recruiting Officer paid visits to the Isle of Wight, Jersey and Guernsey. This was the start of the operation known as KAPE, or Keeping the Army in the Public Eye.

The last ceremonial parade at the Depot took place on 3 September. It was a combined passing out parade for the last two recruit platoons and a formal leave-taking of the Depot Party from Winchester, with the recruit platoons wearing battledress and the Depot Staff No 1 Dress. The Colours on parade were those of the 3rd Battalion, carried by Lieutenant M.G.P.Chignell and Second Lieutenant A.G.K.Esdaile. The Salute was taken by the Colonel of the Regiment, Brigadier G.D.Browne, CBE, accompanied by the Mayor of Winchester, Major General Councillor F.W.H.Pratt, CB, CBE, DSO, MC. Also present were Major General Branwell-Davis, CB, DSO, GOC Aldershot District, the Officer Commanding Solent Garrison, the Brigade Colonels of the Wessex and Green Jackets' Brigades, and the Mayors or Council Chairmen of every local authority throughout the County.

The parade took the customary form of inspection, march past in line, and advance in review order, followed by an address from the Colonel of the Regiment and the presentation of awards. After this there was a march past in column of route, followed by a march off in slow time to the tune of *Auld Lang Syne*. The buglers of the 1st Battalion's Corps of Drums then sounded the Last Post while the Depot Flag was lowered, leaving the flags of the 1st, 4th and 5th Battalions still flying to symbolise that while the Depot had left the County, the Regiment had not.

There remained a little tidying up to do. The Regiment became a corporate member of the Hampshire Club, across the road from Serle's House, so that officers visiting the new Regimental Headquarters would have facilities for meals and a bedroom. The surplus silver in store at the Depot was sorted through, some pieces being retained, others auctioned at a Regimental Dinner in October, about 200oz being put aside for making a statuette and other purposes, and those items which were broken, badly damaged or unsaleable being sent to a silver contractor.

On 31 December 1958 the Depot closed. Its training functions were taken over by the newly-created Depot, The Wessex Brigade, at Topsham (later, after refurbishment, redesignated Wyvern) Barracks, Exeter. The Regiments of the Wessex Brigade were: The Devonshire and Dorset Regiment; The Gloucestershire Regiment; The Royal Hampshire Regiment; and The Duke of Edinburgh's Royal Regiment - Berkshire and Wiltshire. The "Brigade" system of recruit training lasted until the autumn of 1974 when it was changed to a "Divisional" system and the Wessex Brigade regiments became part of The Prince of Wales's Division. Thereafter, all Royal Hampshire Regiment recruits reported on joining to the latter's depot, located at Whittington Barracks, Lichfield, Staffordshire.

On 1 January 1959 a newly designated Regimental Headquarters was established in Serle's House. There were two official retired officer appointments: Brigadier R.Chandler, DSO, as Regimental Secretary (RO2); and Major G.A.Greenway, MBE, as Assistant Regimental Secretary (RO3). Two clerical staff and a caretaker completed the total staff of the Headquarters, which was still required to perform the same administrative and liaison functions as the old Depot. The Regimental Museum was moved from the top floor of Serle's House to the ground floor, where it remains. What had been the Depot's accommodation in the Lower Barracks was converted to house the Record Offices of the RAMC, RADC, QARANC and WRAC.

Serle's House is now all that remains of the Depot. The former Officers' Mess was already starting to slide down the hill when the Depot closed and was demolished in 1960. Its successor, which served as the Green Jackets' Sergeants' Mess, was itself knocked down in 1995 during the civilian development of the Upper Barracks. At the time of writing, much of the former Depot remains visible, although Nature has begun to encroach. The Lower Square, from which the sounds of the Regiment's marches and the shouted commands of many RSMs penetrated the Castle's courtroom, can still be traced. The old barrack block, though largely intact, is empty and in a state of disrepair. It is, perhaps, a sign of the times that the Guard Room, once avoided like the plague by soldiers with minor sins to hide, has been rescued from ruin by a private purchaser who is converting it into a desirable residence!

* * * * * * * * *

CHAPTER 7

THE CARIBBEAN AREA
1960 — 1962

Voyage to the Caribbean - prevailing situations in British Guiana, Jamaica, the Bahamas and British Honduras - A Company in British Guiana - adventure training to Kaiteur Falls - the Jamaica companies - the Henry Gang affair - casualties and Area Commander's Commendation to Pte Barnes - Y Company at Nassau - Cuban landing on Cay Sal - C Company temporarily reactivated when Y Company withdrawn to Jamaica - Z Company in British Honduras - donation of launch *Lord Nuffield* - the Band performs in Caracas at the celebrations commemorating 150 years of Venezuelan Independence - Lieutenant Colonel D.J.Warren, DSO, MC, assumes command of the 1st Battalion - Belize devastated by Hurricane Hattie - relief operations - Bn Tac HQ, B and Y Companies arrive - Y Company remains in British Honduras as garrison - operations against the invading "Belize Liberation Army" - riots in Georgetown, British Guiana - A Company restores order - arrival of Bn Tac HQ and B Company - visit of Lord Mountbatten and letter of appreciation - Birthday Honours awards to Major Matthews and Captain Tillard - the 1st Battalion performs the British Army's last ceremonial parades in Jamaica - returns to the United Kingdom by air

The 1st Battalion's voyage to the West Indies was a pleasant one during which the emphasis was on placed on maintaining physical fitness and weapon training, including live firing. After calling briefly at Las Palmas in the Canary Islands, HMT *Dunera* disembarked the Battalion at its various destinations around the Caribbean: A Company at Port of Spain, Trinidad, from whence it was flown onwards to British Guiana;

Battalion Headquarters, HQ and B Companies at Kingston, Jamaica; Y Company at Nassau in the Bahamas; and Z Company at Belize City, British Honduras, now itself known as Belize.

At each of these locations there existed either the possibility of civil unrest or an external threat, or both, and in the northern part of the area seasonal hurricanes could cause immense damage and loss of life, usually accompanied by widespread looting. Training for internal security duties was therefore high on the agenda.

British Guiana was a sparsely inhabited colony in which most of the population lived close to the coast, the mainstays of the economy being logging, sugar and bauxite. Much of the interior consisted of savannah, swamp or high mountain ranges with jungle covering the lower slopes. There being very few roads, the best means of transport was by the numerous rivers. Comparatively few Europeans lived in the colony, the greater part of the population consisting of the African and East Indian communities, between whom there existed feelings of enmity. The East Indians were the more politically aware of the two and in 1953 Dr Cheddi Jagan's People's Progressive Party won a general election. However, because of Dr Jagan's communist sympathies, the British Government decided to suspend the constitution. When unrest broke out among the East Indians in Georgetown, the capital, the Colonial Office despatched troops and warships. The situation quietened down to the extent that it became possible to hold another general election in 1957. This was again won by Dr Jagan, who was, for the moment, pursuing a less controversial policy, and a third election was due to be held in 1961.

Jamaica was on the eve of achieving her Independence in 1962 and presented an apparently stable regime to the world. Internal security, however, was menaced by militant Rastafarians, a religious group which believed that Emperor Haile Selassie of Ethiopia represented a divine presence on Earth. They wanted to establish a homeland for themselves in Ethiopia but received little sympathy from the Emperor's government. Next, they sought to establish themselves in Liberia which, it will be recalled, had been founded by liberated slaves in the nineteenth century, only to receive a similar response. Now, with Independence in the offing, their ambition was to make Jamaica a Rastafarian island, a number of them being prepared to impose their views by force if necessary. It was, in fact, believed that sympathisers in the United

States were smuggling arms to them; trouble was considered to be a strong probability

As a millionaires' playground, the Bahamas were stable and prosperous, although some of the heavily outnumbered white population were nervous about the possible course events might take following Independence. A more tangible threat was posed by neighbouring Cuba, where Fidel Castro's Marxist guerrillas had ousted the corrupt Batista regime in 1959 and, to the fury of the Washington State Department, established a strident communist presence on the very doorstep of the United States. With the support of the Soviet Union, the Cubans, cocky and belligerent, had become such a potential source of instability throughout the region that the Bahamian government willingly paid the expense of maintaining a British military presence in its islands.

British Honduras, lying between Mexico to the north, Guatemala to the west and Honduras to the south, supported a mixed population of 140,000, of whom about one-third lived in the capital, Belize City. With a coastline consisting of mangrove swamps and much of the interior still dense forest, the colony offered few attractions other than its strategic location. Nevertheless, the government of Guatemala, anxious to create a diversion from its constant internal problems, periodically laid claim to the territory, and even marked British Honduras on their maps as "the lost province of Belize," although the line of the border had been formally agreed the previous century. In 1948 the Guatemalans made such threatening noises that the Colonial Office rushed troops and a cruiser to Belize City. Although no invasion took place, the decision was taken to station a small garrison there as a deterrent. In 1957 a similar situation arose but when the garrison was reinforced the Guatemalans once again spread their hands in injured innocence. Despite this, they had certainly not lost interest and would undoubtedly take advantage of any weakness.

So widely was the Battalion dispersed across the entire Caribbean Area, and so difficult were communications, that Colonel Martin Hastings took to referring to his more distant Company Commanders as "The Independent War Lords." Telephone and radio communication being virtually impossible, routine business between Battalion HQ and outstations was by means of what became known as the twice-weekly Safe Hand Mail, more urgent matters being processed by the civilian Cable and Wireless Company at the cost of ninepence a word, a figure so appalling that outstations' expenditure on signals was restricted to £40 per month. Even with the assistance of Cable and Wireless, the fact that most transport was by sea within the area meant that requests for stores could take up to six weeks to fulfil.

A Company had flown in from Trinidad to British Guiana in a two-day airlift on 18 and 19 February 1960, relieving a company of The Worcestershire Regiment at Atkinson Air Base, 28 miles upstream from Georgetown on the east bank of the Demerara River. Here the Company Commander, Major W.R.Dugmore, simultaneously assumed the role of Officer Commanding Troops British Guiana, and occasionally received gratifying letters from the War Office which addressed him as "OC British Forces South America."

The intense heat and high humidity required a period of acclimatisation, after which individual and section training commenced, together with show-the-flag patrols to the remoter inhabited areas, often made through the bush. The Company shared the base with the US Air Force's Aerial Survey Team No 5, with whom it got on so well that the latter flew individuals on local leave to the United States, free of charge. One of the Company's major assets in an environment where entertainment was in short supply was undoubtedly the Wives' Club, which provided regular Bingo sessions and plenty of good home cooking for voracious consumption during the interval.

"It always rains in June so we have the Queen's Birthday Parade in April instead," ran a local shibboleth. "We certainly had the parade," recalled the compiler of the Company Notes, "a big affair with our soldiers, the Police and the British Guiana Volunteer Force involved. As soon as 'Fall in the Officers!' was given, the heavens really opened in true British Guiana fashion and no one present is likely to forget the prolonged soaking. Needless to say, it was perfectly fine on The Queen's official birthday in June!"

Halfway through the year the Commander Caribbean Area, Brigadier D.W. Lister, CBE, DSO, MC, issued orders to the effect that the Army was to take over Public Duties in Georgetown from the police and that a major parade was to be held. "A Guard Changing Ceremony followed by Beating Retreat was decided upon, the former along the lines of the daily ceremony at Buckingham Palace. The first thing was to try and get the Band over. Of course, it had to be on a 'no cost basis' and their flight was eventually arranged by the US Air Force who flew a special mission from their base in Georgia to Atkinson via Jamaica. Then there was the white No 3 Dress. A blithe signal from Caribbean Area announced its despatch via Miami on 3 August. On 17 August - the parade being two days later - it still had not arrived and frantic signals were flashing all round the Caribbean. Hope had been abandoned when it suddenly arrived by Pan American at 1 am on the day before the parade, having apparently been lost in Panama, of all places. To say that Colour Sergeant Robinson nearly went round the bend over the last minute dhobi (laundry) and tailoring problems would be an understatement and an hour before the march-on the participants were still sitting in their underpants waiting for the freshly laundered white uniforms! But all went off in splendid style and no less than 7000 people turned up. The Guianese are a simple people who love a show and their enthusiasm for the Changing the Guard Ceremony and the subsequent Retreat was heart-warming and made all the trouble worthwhile." Much of the credit for this parade must go the CSM, WOII R.Sargent.

British Guiana also offered plenty of scope for adventure training. The Company's first exercises in this field took place in May and June when the rifle platoons made an eighteen-hour steamer trip up the Berbice River and marched across the Berbice Savannahs to the bauxite town of Mackenzie on the Demerara for the 60-mile boat journey back to Atkinson. The actual distance covered on foot was 40 miles in two days over an area resembling Salisbury Plain save for the myriad flies and heat so intense that No 1 Platoon consumed 1200 cans of beer.

Later in the year the Company paid the first of several visits to the remote and spectacular Kaiteur Falls which, with a single drop of 741 feet, are among the highest in the world. Normally they are only seen by those who can afford the cost of a seaplane excursion from Georgetown, but the A Company parties decided to make the journey across country.

"The fact that vehicles can only get to a point 26 miles away means that the Falls are only approachable by a combination of foot-slogging and movement by frail-looking flat-bottomed boats known locally as 'ballahoos.' There are two intermediate Falls before the base-camp one-and-a-half hours' climb from Kaiteur is reached and at these points portages are necessary.

"The first party went at the wettest time and got plenty of

practice crossing innumerable creeks and rivers. The second party was more fortunate although seven of them, including the Company Commander, were nearly ship-wrecked when their boat struck a submerged rock at night in the middle of a river. They had to 'get out and push' when the boat stuck fast and then had to be left for over an hour as the boat was taking in water at an alarming rate. Various eyes glinting in the moonlight may or may not have been alligators and anacondas, but no one was very sorry when they were eventually rescued. The Kaiteur Falls, when eventually reached, were certainly an unforgettable sight."

This routine, involving training, show-the-flag patrols, ceremonial duties and adventure training, was to continue throughout 1960 and 1961 with A Company making itself sufficiently at home for several of its members to marry local girls.

Meanwhile, Battalion HQ, Headquarters Company and B Company had relieved the 1st Worcesters at Up Park Camp, near Kingston, Jamaica, on 29 February 1960. After the inevitable fatigues which accompanied settling in and familiarisation with the local terrain and situation, internal security training began. Guards and duties were a constant problem and at one stage WOII Goldsmith, CSM B Company, was finding eighty-five men daily for them. Guards were provided for King's House, the Governor's Residence, Trafalgar House, the residence of the Commander Caribbean Area, and the Ordnance Depot, as well as Guards of Honour for visiting VIPs, including the Rt Hon Ian McLeod, the Secretary of State for the Colonies.

Colonel Hastings made a point of visiting his out-stations regularly and had flown some 44,000 miles when he handed over in July 1961. On 20 June 1960, while he was in British Guiana, Major J.M.Symes, MC, the Battalion's Second-in-Command, was summoned to Area Headquarters. There he was informed that the threat of Rastafarian violence had increased and was being taken very seriously. The threat was centred on a group known as the Henry Gang who had established a training camp in one of three possible sites in the Red Hills, close to Kingston. The intention was to eliminate the gang before it could do any damage. The operation would be under police control and the Hampshires were required to cordon and search the most likely site the following morning. At Major Symes' disposal were Headquarters Company, Major J.E.B.Conder, MC, including elements of Support Company, and B Company, Major W.R.B.May, MC. The

Company Commanders, some of the senior NCOs and a few Regulars among the lower ranks were Malayan veterans, but the experience of the rest was limited either to BAOR or initial training. Each man was armed with an SLR and three twenty-round magazines, but because of the nature of the operation weapons would not be loaded and magazines would remain in pouches. B Company was to form the cordon and the camp site would be searched by Headquarters Company. During the afternoon Colonel Hastings returned from Georgetown and approved the plan.

In the event, forming the cordon, with the men in pairs, one looking inwards towards the camp and one outwards, proved to be difficult because the whole area was covered with dense scrub that seriously restricted vision and movement. Unfortunately, while the cordon had been emplaced in accordance with instructions, the camp, in fact, lay outside it. The situation may well have been further confused by the presence of several Special Branch police officers in civilian clothes. The gang, flushed out either by the police or the West India Regiment, ran uphill into the cordon, firing as they came. Privates Brian Metherell and David Philpott were killed and Privates Barnes and Satterley were wounded. Both wounded men recovered and Private Barnes received the following Area Commander's Commendation for his presence of mind:

"On 21 June 1960 Private Barnes was acting as runner at B Company HQ during an operation to cordon a Rastafarian camp in the Red Hills. About 11:15 hours he was given a written message by the Company Commander to deliver to 2nd Lt Jacks, commanding No 5 Platoon. While taking this message, Barnes was shot at close range in the chest by a gunman and severely wounded.

"On being shot, he fell to the ground and feigned death, at the same time concealing a full magazine which he had been removing from his pouch. While lying on the ground, Barnes had his rifle taken and his bayonet removed from his scabbard. Private Barnes was then left lying wounded. He continued with his message, reporting to Sergeant Townsend, the Platoon Sergeant of No 5 Platoon, stating that he had a message from the Company Commander for the Platoon Commander. Only when he had passed over the message did Barnes state that he had been wounded.

"Private Barnes' conduct, both at the time of the incident

and immediately afterwards, has been an inspiration to the re-mainder of the Company. His devotion to duty was of the highest order."

The funeral of Privates Philpott and Metherell was attended by a representative of the Governor, who was away, Mr Manley, the Prime Minister, and the Commander Caribbean Area.

Three bodies were discovered in the camp, buried on top of each other in a common grave. It was thought that these deaths had resulted from a disagreement between Jamaican and imported American terrorists. A full-scale search for the gang commenced at once, involving HQ and B Companies and the Jamaica Police Force, reinforced by Y Company at the end of June, plus the West India Regiment, for which the Hampshires had a high regard. This operation lasted about three weeks, involving extensive searches inland and coastal patrols in RASC launches. The local population was helpful and supportive at every level, to the ex-tent that it seemed as though all of Jamaica's resources had been mobilised against the criminals. For example, at one stage B Com-pany Commander was travelling in a West Indies Sugar Com-pany (WISCO) vehicle talking on a WISCO radio to Captain J.L.Freeman-Cowan, piloting a private aircraft, as well as one of his patrols searching the coast in a WISCO launch. On another, a Hampshire patrol, believing that it had part of the gang penned in a cave and receiving no answer to a surrender call, had no hesitation in blasting the interior with an anti-tank round from a 3.2-inch rocket launcher; unfortunately, when the smoke cleared the cave was found to be empty. In due course the Henry Gang was captured by the West India Regiment, brought to trial and executed. In overall terms, the affair seems to have exercised a calming effect among the wilder Rastafarian elements.

Thereafter, life on Jamaica returned to a more normal pat-tern. At times during their training cycle the rifle companies used a tented camp on Lord Brownlow's estate at Moneague, ten miles from the resort of Ocho Rios on the north coast of the island. While they were there, they were generously permitted by the owner, a Mrs Simpson, to use her beautiful private beach, "Laughing Water." Further training was also carried out on the estate of the actor Errol Flynn near Port Antonio. Both compa-nies also carried out adventure training exercises in which they climbed to the peak of the 7504-feet Blue Mountain. In Jamaica, and indeed throughout the Caribbean Area, swimming, all forms of water sport and cricket, the last played with gusto and noisy support, were universally popular. Hampshire being a maritime county, many men were able to meet relatives and friends serving in the Merchant Navy aboard the British cruise liners calling at Kingston, notably the SS *Mauretania.*

During the first half of 1961 the Jamaica companies and the Band were kept busy with a variety of duties, including the provision of a Guard of Honour for the visit of Prime Minister Harold Macmillan on 30 March, and another for Princess Alice, who enjoyed an annual holiday in Jamaica and honoured the Regiment by taking tea in the Officers' Mess. Next came a Battalion Tattoo, run by Major W.R.B.May, MC, attended by the Governor and most of Kingston, during which Y Company provided the highlight with a reconstruction of the Gallipoli landing from the *River Clyde,* the "ship" having been reconstructed around the body of a three-ton truck. The Annual Administrative Inspection followed, then the Queen's Birthday Parade and a Battalion exercise.

Y Company (Major M.F.A.Wilson), it will be remembered, had originally been based in Nassau, where it had arrived during the early days of March 1960. It was popular alike with the resident population and the American tourists, so that when its members were not training hard they were being royally entertained in places normally frequented by the seriously rich. Night exercises in the Blue Hills, intended to sharpen up movement and evasion, lost much of their point when numerous girl friends arrived on the training area in their cars. In addition, Bahamas Airways allowed a 90 per cent discount, which meant that a return ticket to Miami cost just 34 shillings (£1.70p).

In April, however, the Cubans seemed inclined to provoke an incident when they landed a party on a tiny desert island named Cay Sal, situated 200 miles from Nassau but only 35 from Cuba, and left after planting their flag. The island was only notable in that the eccentric millionaire Howard Hughes owned a fishing lodge there, and its population consisted of three fishermen. The Cuban incursion was a typical communist ploy designed to assess a potential enemy's resolve by provoking a reaction.

The reaction consisted of the prompt despatch of Lieutenant M.J.Martin's 7 Platoon from Nassau to Cay Sal by seaplane, together with 700 rounds of ammunition. Having thus learned where everyone stood, Havana's bearded, cigar-smoking revolutionaries suddenly lost interest in Cay Sal. The platoon therefore spent an enjoyable week training, fishing and swimming, after which they were withdrawn. In the process they learned from a seaplane pilot that they had become the toast of Miami, where the violently anti-Castro press reported the incident as "an angry twitch of the lion's tail."

Together, the Henry Gang incident and the Cuban incursion had convinced the War Office that the Caribbean Area should be reinforced and in June 1960 B Company 1st Battalion The Duke of Edinburgh's Royal Regiment arrived in Nassau to relieve Y Company, which returned to Jamaica. By December 1960, however, the situation was considered stable enough for the DERR company to be withdrawn and the Hampshires were again ordered to assume responsibility for the Bahamas. Because of other commitments, this was more easily said than done, but a solution was found by posting a reactivated C Company, under Major J.D.Wellings, to Nassau. The company establishment, including WOII H.Robinson as CSM and Colour Sergeant J.Cheeseley as CQMS, consisted of a headquarters and a single platoon from Kingston who rotated on a three-monthly basis. On 12 January 1961 a Guard of Honour under Second Lieutenant H.D.H.Keatinge was provided for the opening of the Bahamas Legislature by HE The Governor and Commander-in-Chief, Sir Robert Stapledon, KCMG, CBE, who complimented it on its turnout, drill and steadiness.

Z Company, commanded by Major H.W.Parry, had arrived in British Honduras on 26 February 1960 and settled in at Airport Camp, some nine miles from Belize City. As well being at full strength itself, attachments included a section each of 3-inch mortars and Vickers medium machine guns (supplemented later by a section of Mobat anti-tank guns and 0.5-inch Browning machine guns for airport defence) because of the potential threat posed by Guatemala, plus an MT detachment and personnel from the Royal Engineers, RASC, REME, RAMC, RAPC and ACC. The camp included a 25-yard range, and a 600-yard classification range was situated four miles away. Training was carried out in an area called the Mountain Pine Ridge, the lower slopes of which were covered with jungle and the upper slopes with pine forest. Sports facilities included soccer, cricket, riding, basketball, and golf; occasionally, too, a launch would be hired for a swimming trip to the offshore Cays, swimming from the coast itself being impossible because of the mangrove swamps. Recreational facilities in Belize included three cinemas, clubs, restaurants and cafes.

Three weeks after arriving Z Company was required to provide a Guard of Honour for the arrival of The Princess Royal in the colony and a guard for Government House during her stay. Major Parry had emphasised to everyone that the Company's presence in British Honduras was, whenever necessary, to provide help for the people of the country, so that when serious training commenced in April one of the most important tasks was to prepare a hurricane contingency plan in conjunction with the civil authorities and the emergency services. Hurricanes Abbe and Donna led to this being activated twice during 1960 but on both occasions they passed by at a safe distance.

In December Major S.G.B.Matthews took over Z Company when Major Parry retired to civilian life. During the Malayan Emergency Harry Parry had been employed on intelligence duties. He played a fine game of hockey, and cricket to a very high standard. He left behind two legacies in British Honduras. The first was to bequeath his name to a 700-foot waterfall he came across on Mountain Pine Ridge and which, being subsequently visited by most of the rifle platoons, became known as the Parry Falls. The second came about as a direct result of a discussion with Lord Nuffield, who had most generously asked what he could contribute to the company's welfare. It was decided to have a thirty-foot diesel launch built, as this would make trips to the Cays possible without the need to hire civilian craft. The vessel, capable of carrying thirty men and their stores for a week, was launched the following year by Miss Marjorie Thornley, the Governor's daughter, and appropriately named *Lord Nuffield*. As we shall see, the launch was to perform operational as well recreational roles.

Throughout 1961, in addition to its training commitments, Z Company made numerous show-the-flag patrols through the jungle to Mayan villages, where many of the inhabitants existed in a state of drunken euphoria induced by locally distilled rum costing 4/6d (22p) a pint! Hammocks were taken back into use and, inevitably, comparisons with Malaya were made; on balance, it was considered that Latin American insects were uglier and more vindictive than their Malayan counterparts. Ceremonial duties included the provision of a Guard of Honour for the

Governor and Commander-in-Chief, Sir Colin H.Thornley, KCMG, CVO, at the opening of the first British Honduran Parliament on 23 March 1961. In July the hurricane contingency plan was again activated when Hurricane Anna swept across the coast 60 miles south of Belize, causing some flooding but little serious damage.

Meanwhile, the Band, under WOI J.Plant, had become the most travelled members of the Battalion, regularly visiting the outstations, often by warship, and performing a full range of ceremonial duties. On 3 July 1961 it was flown in three RAF Shackletons to Caracas, where it was accommodated in the Presidential Guard Barracks (with free use of the Canteen!), in order to participate, together with a naval detachment from HMS *Lynx*, in a major international parade commemorating Venezuela's 150 years of independence from Spain. The parade was witnessed by no fewer than 230,000 spectators and included colourful contingents from many Latin American nations. "The British contingent," commented the Military Attaché in Caracas, "really were superb and received tremendous praise both from the Venezuelans and the British community. All of the latter were deeply moved by the sight of the Band and the Armed Guard of the Royal Navy marching down that enormous parade ground. Although only a comparatively small contingent, their effect on everybody was the reverse."

While in Caracas the Band also beat Retreat in the Olympic Stadium and later at the Caracas Sports Club, then played at the Tomb of the Liberator, Simon Bolivar, in the Pantheon, where a wreath was laid by Field Marshal Earl Alexander, KG. It was rewarded not only with ample hospitality bestowed by Venezualans and British alike, but also with a remarkable and rather interesting letter of appreciation, recorded elsewhere, which was forwarded by the Military Attaché to Brigadier Lister, Commander Caribbean Area, and thence to Colonel Warren.

During July 1961 Colonel Martin Hastings, having been appointed AA and QMG Headquarters Amphibious Warfare in the United Kingdom, handed over command of the 1st Battalion to Lieutenant Colonel D.J.Warren, DSO, MC. For a little while longer, life in the Caribbean Area continued much as before. No one could possibly have imagined what lay in store during the next few months.

On the morning of 30 October the Miami weather bureau

Sticks of gelignite and gun cotton intended for use in the repulsed attack on the 1st Battalion on Minden Day, 1947 at Rehavia, Jerusalem.

C and D Company billets in Jerusalem, 1947. The front of the building has been destroyed by terrorists just before the arrival of the Regiment. It was from here that troops of C Coy rushed out to repel the terrorists on Minden Day, 1947.

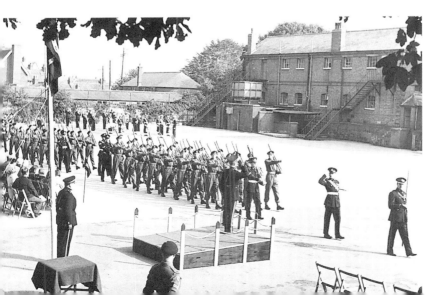

A Passing-Out Parade of National Servicemen at the Regimental Depot, Winchester, 1950.

Above: Rose and Nassau, tiger cubs in the care of the 1st Battalion, Malaya

Left: Major Jim Symes, MC and bar.

Below: A parade to mark the 200th anniversary of the Battle of Minden, Lemgo, 1959

1962: Looters are arrested in Georgetown, British Guiana

Lord Mountbatten,
Chief of Defence Staff,

Lt Col David Warren,
CO 1st Battalion

Maj Sandy Wilson,
OC A Coy

British Guiana,
February 1962

Lord Mountbatten receives the salute at the Presentation of Colours, 1 August 1963. He wore a Minden rose with his naval uniform.

Mud — a characteristic of mechanised exercises in BAOR. A 1-ton armoured 'PIG', Soltau 1964.

The Inner German Border. A Border Patrol with a British Frontier Service Officer

The Torrey Canyon disaster.
Pte Waxman dispersing oil
at a Cornish beach.

Band Sergeant Major Bill Bailey.
UN Tour, Cyprus, 1968-9

Sergeant John Wheeler, MM
Queen's Medallist, 1965

The Thetcher Memorial

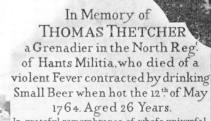

In Memory of
THOMAS THETCHER
a Grenadier in the North Reg.t
of Hants Militia, who died of a
violent Fever contracted by drinking
Small Beer when hot the 12th of May
1764. Aged 26 Years.

In grateful remembrance of whofe univerfal
good will towards his Comrades, this Stone
is placed here at their expence, as a fmall
teftimony of their regard and concern.
Here fleeps in peace a Hampfhire Grenadier,
Who caught his death by drinking cold fmall Beer,
Soldiers be wife from his untimely fall
And when ye're hot drink Strong or none at all.

This memorial being decay'd was reftor'd
by the Officers of the Garrifon A.D. 1781.
An honeft Soldier never is forgot
Whether he die by Mufket or by Pot.

The Stone was replaced by the North Hants
Militia when difembodied at Winchefter,
on 26th April 1802. in confequence of
the original Stone being deftroyed.

And again replaced by
The Royal Hampshire Regiment 1966.

The final parade which wasn't. This was expected to be the last occasion on which the Colours were paraded before amalgamation with the Gloucestershire Regiment. Uniquely, Capt Harry Barnard, Quartermaster, was entrusted with the Queen's Colour, (Lt Peter Hughes carrying the Regimental Colour).

Public duties at Buckingham Palace

The final royal occasion for the 4th/5th Battalion: Guard of Honour for HM The Queen, Cowes, with Maj George Fulford, 1965.

The end of the 4th/5th Battalion, 19th March, 1967. The Colours are marched into Serle's House.

One of the last troopships, EMPIRE KITTIWAKE, prepares to sail for Singapore from Hongkong with the Advance Party of the 1st Battalion.

The aftermath of riots. Members of the 1st Battalion search a car at a road check in the Falls, Belfast   Note the paving stones torn away to form barricades.

NORTHERN IRELAND, August 1969

Lt Col Roger May briefs Denis Healey, Secretary of State for Defence

reported that a major hurricane, codenamed Hattie, had shifted from its north-westerly course and was now heading west, straight for Belize City, leaving just six hours to prepare for its arrival. The Central Disaster Committee met immediately, issued the appropriate warnings and activated its contingency plans. Whatever might happen when Hattie struck, it was clear that, initially at least, an enormous burden would fall on the shoulders of Z Company. Including attachments, the Company numbered 113 all ranks, of whom 60 were normally in Company HQ or administrative staff and only 53 in platoons, these assets being quickly reorganised into a Support/Reconnaissance Platoon, 10 Platoon and an ad hoc 11 Platoon formed from men usually employed on administrative duties. In addition, there were 23 wives and 23 children. The first task, therefore, was to round up the families from their quarters in Belize and transport them to the camp where, with the troops, they took cover in the only hurricane-proof buildings — the combined cookhouse/dining hall and store, and the tiny brick-built radio hut, which could just about accommodate six people. The families were brought in under a prepared evacuation plan, less Vicky Edbrooke, wife of Captain Don Edbrooke, RAMC, who had to be left in Belize hospital to produce a baby. Captain Edbrooke was on duty at the camp and she and the baby, both fit and well, were rescued by Lieutenant R.D.Hanscomb and his men after the hurricane. Mrs Friedel Hanna, the wife of the CSM, was in charge of the families and performed nobly, eventually taking them all back to Jamaica after the hurricane. Like the rest of the Company, they lost virtually everything they owned.

By the time Major Matthews and CSM Hanna left Police Headquarters in Belize at 21:00 hours that night, Hattie had already begun to make her presence felt. Through deserted streets in which the wind ripped with ever-increasing fury, they made their way back to camp. As Paddy Hanna relates, few of those present were likely to forget the hours which followed:

"Winds in excess of 180 mph struck the colony and there was nothing one could do about it. This high wind was accompanied by heavy rain which was moving horizontally - a very odd experience indeed. After some hours of high winds and heavy rain, there came an eerie lull. Heavy dark clouds encompassed the whole area giving a feeling of claustrophobia. The lull lasted for around two hours. It was tempting to assume that the storm was over and that it would be safe to break cover. Suddenly, the wind got up and the rain came down once more with the same ferocity as before - only this time, there was an added dimension. There were ten-foot tidal waves coming in off the sea. Within a couple of hours the entire town of Belize and the adjoining countryside was flooded to the extent that it was difficult to distinguish between land and sea."

The worst period of the hurricane was between 03:00 and 08:00 on Tuesday 31 October. By 10:00 it had become possible for a man to stand upright without clutching a companion and the shelters were unbattened. Vanished radio aerials were quickly replaced and for the next thirty-six hours Lance Corporal Clayforth, Royal Signals, who was subsequently awarded the BEM, remained at his set continuously, providing the colony's only reliable link with the outside world, which learned that British Honduras had sustained a major disaster and would require international assistance if wholesale tragedy was to be averted. This link was by means of morse transmissions British Honduras - Bermuda (RN ship) - Portishead, Somerset - HQ Jamaica, and it was by these means that The Queen's message of sympathy for the people of British Honduras was received.

The contingency plan required Z Company to perform four tasks, viz:

1. To establish communications with the outside world.
2. To clear and report on the serviceability of the airfield.
3. To open the road between the airfield and Belize.
4. To prepare to send columns up-country to assist stricken areas.

It was soon established that the airfield could receive aircraft, although it now lacked a radio and control tower. This information was re-broadcast internationally by HQ Caribbean Area for the benefit of those despatching relief flights.

Re-establishing communications between the airfield and Belize proved to be much more difficult, as the road was under five feet of water and blocked by fallen trees. The Support/Reconnaissance Platoon under Lieutenant Robin Tillard, with WOII Head, REME, as boat engineer, set off in the *Lord Nuffield*. Lieutenant Bobby Hanscomb and 10 Platoon, ably supported by Second Lieutenant Colin Coates, RAEC, who was only in British

Honduras to carry out ACE examinations, were to open the road to Belize. An earlier reconnaissance of the road under Sergeant Grace suggested this would be impossible, so high had the water risen. After incredible adventures both parties reached Belize late at night, Lieutenant Robin Tillard and Corporal Rumbold nearly coming to a sticky end when the *Lord Nuffield* smashed into the damaged town bridge.

Major Matthews met the Governor, Sir Colin Thornley, who had taken command and declared a state of emergency, at Police Headquarters. Belize was a scene of utter devastation. Because of the high water table, many houses were built on stilts and these had simply been washed and blown away. Others stood with roofs wholly or partially blown off and gaping windows. In the garden of CSM Hanna's quarter, located some 200 yards from the sea, lay a large sailing boat. Telegraph poles and lamp posts leaned at drunken angles. All the public utilities, including the water sup-ply and telephone systems, had been wrecked. Amid streets cov-ered with a layer of thick black mud between ten and fifteen thousand homeless people wandered in stunned bewilderment. Bodies were being discovered regularly and the criminal element had already started to loot. The police and civil service were doing what they could and the Boy Scouts were running an effi-cient official messenger service. As the hurricane had passed to the south of Belize the Governor believed that two smaller towns, Stann Creek and El Cayo, would have suffered severely and di-rected that columns should be sent there at first light. The Hampshires therefore returned to camp, the falling water level rendering the journey marginally less difficult, and, satisfied that the route between the airfield and Belize would remain open, Major Matthews was able to plan the following day's operations.

At first light on Wednesday 1 November he left camp with Lieutenant Tillard's platoon, heading for Stann Creek. By 11:30 they had reached the Sibun river only to find that a forty-foot span of the bridge had been washed away. Having ordered Tillard to get to Stann Creek by any means possible, Major Matthews returned to Belize.

Tillard divided his platoon into three groups. One, under Sergeant Page, was ordered to swim the river and, if necessary, march the 37 miles to Stann Creek; the second was also ordered to cross the river and continue clearing obstacles on the road; and the third, under Corporal Clarke, Royal Engineers, who was to be awarded the BEM for his part in the operation, was to re-pair the bridge. By 04:30 next morning all the platoon had reached Stann Creek and established a base in the police station.

The town had indeed been extensively damaged but was in a better state than Belize. Tillard took an immediate grip on the situation, requisitioning all food supplies which were then placed in a central store to prevent further looting. He then made it clear that, with the exception of the old and sick, those who wanted to eat would work, and organised a strict rationing system. Work was organised on a task system under local foremen who were issued with the appropriate ration coupons for their gangs. In this way much of the town, including the damaged jetty, was put back into working order while the platoon cooked, supervised food queues and oversaw the landing of relief supplies from two American warships, the USS *Antietam,* a helicopter carrier, and the USS *Bristol,* a destroyer, which were lying off-shore.

Simultaneously, 10 Platoon under Lieutenant R.D.Hanscomb had been ordered to El Cayo but suddenly found itself temporar-ily isolated by flash floods between Teakettle Bridge and Roar-ing Creek. For the moment it could only give what help it could locally. Private Ray, despatched back to Belize with a situation report, demonstrated a remarkable degree of initiative by cover-ing the 35 miles on foot, swimming, paddling a dugout canoe and finally hitching a lift.

It was now known that aid from all over the area was being flown to Belize. Some of the problems encountered in handling the greatly increased volume of traffic are recounted by Paddy Hanna:

"At the airport, commanded by Lieutenant M.J.Martin and Second Lieutenant Coates, RAEC, all forms of lighting and com-munications had been knocked out of action, which made life very difficult when receiving aircraft at night. These were mainly transport planes carrying supplies, tentage, etc, all in answer to our SOS via ships at sea. Aircraft suddenly appeared from all parts - the USA, Mexico, Guatemala, El Salvador and Jamaica. The problem facing us at night was that we had neither runway lights nor any form of radio communication with the aircraft and it was necessary to get these planes down safely. It was solved by placing army and civilian vehicles, with headlights on, along either side of the runway, thus creating a flarepath."

Meanwhile, in Jamaica, the frigate HMS *Troubridge* had been hurriedly loaded with relief supplies on Tuesday 31 October and, having embarked Captain Kellie and thirty-six Hampshires, plus a number of staff and technical personnel, set sail for Belize that night.

Brigadier Lister and Colonel Warren had boarded the only available aircraft, a Bahamian Airways DC3 piloted by Captain Easy, whose performance was well beyond the call of duty, and flown into Belize on 1 November. By now looting in the town had reached ungovernable levels and since everyone in Z Company was working round the clock only Second Lieutenant B.T.Wigmore and a single section could be spared to discourage the criminal element. The task was tackled with great courage but it was an impossible one. The following morning, therefore, the Governor handed over responsibility for restoration of law and order to Colonel Warren, who set up his headquarters in the police station. As those of their quarters which had not been wrecked had been thoroughly looted it was also decided that Z Company's families should be flown out to Jamaica. Most arrived possessing nothing but the clothes they travelled in.

At 04:15 on Thursday 2 November the first elements of Major Roger May's B Company began arriving by air, followed later by the rest of the Company and Major D.M.Russell with Y Company. This took the strain off the exhausted Z Company and enabled the rule of law to be re-established fairly quickly. A curfew was imposed and one or two looters had to be shot but, as CSM Paddy Hanna relates, the exercise of sheer moral authority often won the day.

"I remember being called to an oil supply depot where looting had been reported. I set off hot-foot with a few soldiers. On the way we met a crowd of people who had obviously just come out of the depot and were carrying drums of fuel. On seeing us they tried to scatter but we rounded them up and marched them, and the drums, back to the depot. I made them put the drums down and told them all to sit on the tops. This they all did except for one evil-looking individual who challenged my instruction and took issue with me. However, with a little Irish Persuasion and the Sergeant-Major look, he thought better of it and then joined the others. I then made them all look up to Heaven and ask the Lord for His forgiveness for looting!"

HMS *Troubridge* also reached Belize at first light on 2 November. While Captain Kellie's detachment immediately set off to assist in restoring order, the ship's engineering staff buckled to, starting generators, repairing ovens for baking bread and restoring the radio station to working order.

At Airport Camp, only the few hurricane-proof buildings remained habitable and it was necessary to establish a tented transit camp very quickly. The magnitude of the devastation to British Honduras was clearly beyond the resuscitation capacities of the over-stretched 1st Battalion HQ and three rifle companies, supported by the mobilised British Honduras Volunteer Guard under its Commandant, Lieutenant Colonel D.N.A.Fairweather, all now fully deployed on a multitude of post-hurricane relief tasks. From the UK Strategic Reserve came the 1st Battalion The Worcestershire Regiment, commanded by Lieutenant Colonel P. Hall, DSO, the leading elements of which arrived in Belize on 6 November, having flown the Atlantic in RAF Transport Command Britannias to Kingston, Jamaica, and on from there in an assortment of aircraft including British West Indian Airways Viscounts and RAF Shackletons. Also from England, to give technical support to the British Honduras Public Works Department, came 12 Field Squadron, Royal Engineers under Major A.J.Notely, MBE, who arrived in Belize in a DC7 freight aircraft on the evening of 5 November. In addition, Washington placed the USS *Antietam* at the Governor's disposal. The Americans' good humour, generosity and efficiency made a lasting impression on the hard-pressed Hampshires. In particular, the carrier's forty-eight helicopters must have saved innumerable lives by lifting casualties from inaccessible areas and carrying food and stores to isolated communities, and her medical teams assisted in a mass inoculation programme which undoubtedly averted a major epidemic.

Everyone turned his hand to everything, so that few could say what they would be doing in a few hours' time, let alone next day. The dead were buried and refugees cared for, roads were cleared by supervised gangs, guards were mounted on the prison, the bonded warehouse and supply depots, transport was requisitioned and put back into working order, and the public utilities restored. By degrees, some semblance of normality began to reappear after four weeks' gruelling work. Here are just some of the tasks undertaken by the Battalion during the emergency:

Major T.S.W.Reeve-Tucker, the Second-in-Command, assisted by Miss Joan Whittington, MBE, of the British Red Cross, organised the relief supplies which came pouring in, and Lieutenant Hugh Keatinge was appointed the colony's Deputy Minister of Food, controlling the distribution of food purchased by the government.

Captain Kernohan, RAMC, and the Battalion medical orderlies dealt with a constant stream of casualties, including 600 in one day alone, and administered 4500 inoculations. At one stage the Battalion was running five feeding centres, feeding 12,000 people with three meals a day. Over a four-week period a total of 180,000 meals were served. At the St Ignatius Refugee Centre Sergeant Smith, Corporal Kelly and their section administered, organised and guarded up to 3500 refugees, while two battalion cooks with an American field cooker fed them all. Corporal Allen and his section, Privates Crouch, Griffin and Cabell, cremated 94 bodies discovered in the Belize area, including one found in a tree. In Jamaica, under Major P.Branwell the Band ran an extremely efficient Air Movements Centre while Colour Sergeant Joe Turner and the rear party not only supported the Battalion from afar and carried out all the necessary duties, but also manned a transit camp for up to 1000 men, including the 1st Battalion The Worcestershire Regiment on their way to British Honduras.

There were many more examples, of which considerations of space alone prevent inclusion. Recorded elsewhere is a typical agenda for the daily conferences held by Colonel Warren for the heads of government departments and services, and this will give the reader some idea of the universal scope of the operation.

Hurricane Hattie had claimed the lives of 262 people yet, when the colony had been similarly devastated some thirty years previously, the death toll had been ten times that figure. Thousands owed their lives to the thoroughness of the contingency planning, and to the quick reactions of the Hampshires. Some weeks after the event, Colonel Warren received the following letter from the new Governor, Sir Peter H.G.Stallard, KCMG, CVO, MBE:

"Dear Colonel Warren,
"I am writing on behalf of the Government and people of British Honduras to thank you officially for the splendid services of the 1st Battalion The Royal Hampshire Regiment during the emergency following Hurricane Hattie.

"I have seen for myself since December the contribution made in maintaining law and order and I have heard about the notable exploits at the height of the emergency, such as Major Matthews's dash into Belize City and Lieutenant Tillard's dash to relieve Stann Creek. You must be very proud of the Battalion's achievements which, if I may say so, were in the best traditions of the British Army."

By the time the Battalion had returned to the United Kingdom everyone thought they had heard the last of Hattie. Major Matthews, however, had not. He was hauled before a Board of Enquiry and invited to account for the losses at Airport Camp, totalling some £4.5 million. He could not, but regretted them just the same. Facing professional ruin, he took up serious smoking for several days until a benevolent Quartermaster General announced that he had decided to write off the losses. A general comment was that if Matthews couldn't take a joke he shouldn't have joined! Later, he was posted to Central Africa, where, as in Hampshire, hurricanes hardly ever happen — instead, he experienced an earthquake!

The Command and Control organisation in British Honduras after the "Captains and the Kings" had departed was the establishment of a small Garrison Headquarters and Staff commanded by Colonel K.H.Stevens, MBE, late Royal Engineers. Y Company, commanded by Major C.D.Darroch, had been reinforced when B and Z Companies departed for Jamaica. In addition, it had a full strength Support Platoon with 3-inch mortars (Corporal R.Feeney), medium machine guns (Sergeant J.Loader) and Mobats (Corporal J.Rumbold).

Major Darroch records: "I counted myself incredibly lucky to have taken over the new Y Company. At least two-thirds of the men were of the last National Service intake - many had had their 'call-up' deferred on grounds of apprenticeship, etc. There was so much talent in the way of carpenters, joiners, pipe fitters and so on. We had inherited a virtually devastated Airport Camp with hutted sleeping accommodation virtually nil and tents being used in lieu until eventually new prefabricated wooden huts were shipped into Belize from Jamaica. Whenever their operational or training deployment permitted, the 'artisans' of Y Company built themselves their new camp. Initially, sandfly insects were a major problem, despite sandfly/mosquito nets, necessitating, in order to get a reasonable night's sleep, wearing one's trousers and shirt. With the arrival of Hattie, the Colony's bird population had left. The birds took their time to return, and consequently the insects took over. It was not until a considerable time after the return of the birds that Nature's balance was restored and the scratching stopped. Overhead fans and air conditioning had yet to be installed. Despite such adversities, morale throughout the tour remained incredibly high."

At 19:10 on the evening of Sunday 21 January 1962 Major Darroch received a radio message from the Garrison Commander in Belize, ordering him to despatch the Stand-by Platoon to Punta Gorda as quickly as possible. Information had been received that twenty Guatemalan soldiers had crossed the border and had hauled down and burned the Union Flag which was flying at Pueblo Viejo. The Guatemalan soldiers were reported to be moving in the direction of San Antonio and Punta Gorda. The scene of this activity was in Toledo province in the south of the colony. This area was one of the most isolated in British Honduras and was accessible only by sea and light aircraft. The provincial capital, Punta Gorda, was connected to two other small towns, San Pedro Columbia and San Antonio, by the only road. In other respects the terrain was similar to the secondary jungle of Malaya, with mangrove swamps and steep-sided hills and some cultivation beside the road.

Support Platoon, commanded by Second Lieutenant B.T.Wigmore, was promptly despatched aboard the government vessels *Patricia* and *Colette,* casting off at 22:00. At first light on 22 January the remainder of Y Company was deployed as follows: 7 Platoon (Second Lieutenant R. Ashenden) at Airport Camp as a guard against any attempted *coup de main* by Guatamalan paratroops; 8 Platoon (Second Lieutenant J.K.West) on stand-by to move to El Cayo; 9 Platoon (Second Lieutenant J.M.Perret) on internal security duties in Belize City. During the morning Captain F.D.J. Dickenson, Y Company's Second-in Command, and Major Guy Lewis, the Military Intelligence Officer (Belize), flew to Punta Gorda in a light aircraft. Captain Dickenson set up his operational headquarters in the police station. The intelligence picture was garbled, to say the least. Thirteen armed Guatemalans in civilian clothes had been spotted some four miles from Punta Gorda; ten more had been seen near San Antonio; and 200 more were said to be marching on San Antonio from the

village of Pueblo Viejo, near the frontier. Much of this was speculation based on wild rumour and a flight over the Pueblo Viejo
area revealed nothing abnormal. At the diplomatic level, too,
the Guatemalan government disclaimed all knowledge of these
extraordinary developments.

Following a rough passage, Support Platoon reached Punta
Gorda at 11:15 on 22 January. Two sections, commanded respectively by Second Lieutenant Wigmore and Corporal Feeney, were
sent to check on the locations near the town where some of the
invaders had been seen, but found nothing. Wigmore was then
ordered to leave Corporal Feeney's section in Punta Gorda and
take the rest of the platoon to San Antonio, from whence he was
to proceed with a section into Pueblo Viejo. During the evening
Captain Dickenson set ambushes on all probable routes leading
into Punta Gorda, including the waterfront.

At 22:30 a telephone call was received from the priest at
San Antonio, who had just returned on horse-back from visiting
parishioners at Pueblo Viejo. He confirmed that twenty armed
men had crossed the frontier, of whom nine had thought better
of the idea and retraced their steps. The remainder had stolen
shot-gun cartridges and food from the village, burned the Union
Flag, together with portraits of The Queen and the Duke of Edinburgh, and hoisted the flag of the imaginary Central American
Union.

The invaders, in fact, called themselves "The Belize Liberation Army," and they were led by one Francisco Sagastume, a
Guatemalan hot-head whose burning ambition was to liberate
"the lost province of Belize," no matter what agreements had
been reached between his own government and that of Queen
Victoria. The eleven-strong invasion force had then made its way
to San Antonio, where Sagustume harangued a small crowd in
memorable style.

"This country belongs to you and to me! We have come to
kill the British and drive them from our country! We mean no
harm to you niggers!"

Such a speech was unlikely to win friends among his audience, nor did it. They declined to supply him with food, but when
he proudly announced that he was on his way to "hoist our flag in
the capital," they handed over a truck to speed him on his way
towards Punta Gorda.

Next morning a patrol consisting of Captain Dickenson,

152

Corporal Feeney and several men of the latter's section found tracks leading through thick bush to the saddle of a hill. There was a brief exchange of fire as the patrol came into contact with the invaders near the summit. One of the Guatemalans, armed with a .22 rifle, was captured and the rest fled, abandoning their packs, which were found to contain, as well as personal kit, a portable radiogram, a record of the Guatemalan National Anthem, and another flag. Captain Dickenson's shouted warning that anyone remaining should come out or be shot resulted in some shuffling in the bushes and the discovery of Sagustume himself. At first he adopted the haughty posture considered appropriate to a noble liberator, but since his deeds amounted to little more than illegal entry, petty theft and an assortment of public order offences, this did not last very long.

Unfortunately, the element of "opera bouffe" was present on both sides. The armed police patrol which should have been guarding the road reported that five of the invaders had escaped across it. When asked what they had done about it, they replied that they had blown their whistles loudly!

The next thirty-six hours were spent either tracking the fugitives or responding to sightings of them, without result. On the morning of 25 January two Guatemalans in possession of .22 automatic rifles were apprehended by forestry workers armed with shot-guns near Milestone 15. That evening 7 Platoon, commanded by Second Lieutenant R.Ashenden, reached Punta Gorda by boat from Stann Creek and by 27 January had relieved Support Platoon, who received a rapturous send-off from the townspeople.

At 21:30 that night a logger informed Captain Dickenson that two men had taken possession of his campsite, situated in a remote spot off the Moho river, some six miles south-west of Punta Gorda. He drew a sketch map and agreed to guide the patrol, which set off at 03:20 on 28 January, consisting of Captain Dickenson, Corporal Grist, Privates Ford and Wallis, and three armed policemen. The camp was successfully surprised and its starving occupants offered no resistance. One, Sagustume's Second-in-Command, was armed with a pearl-handled .22 revolver and the other had a .22 automatic pistol. One of the pair, evidently anticipating elevation to Cabinet status after the Liberation, had gone to war in a natty blue suit which was now in tatters and minus a trouser leg.

So ended the active phase of the informal war between Y Company and the Belize Liberation Army, the remaining members of which simply vanished without trace.

Hardly had the echoes of this episode died away than the Battalion found itself confronted with another violent situation. In British Guiana the first few weeks of 1962 kept A Company, now commanded by Major M.F.A.Wilson, extremely busy. First came a visit from Brigadier Lister. This was followed by a visit to the colony by the Duke of Edinburgh, for whom a Guard of Honour, commanded by Captain T.de C.Luckham, was provided, as well as guards for the Royal aircraft. After His Royal Highness had left Colonel Warren and the Colonel of the Regiment arrived. A successful guest night was held in the Officers' Mess, memorable for the British Guiana Police Band's essentially Caribbean rendering of *The Farmer's Boy.* Unfortunately, these visits were overshadowed by the deteriorating political situation within British Guiana itself.

Once again, Dr Jagan's doctrinaire government was in trouble. Its budget raised howls of protest from the opposition, which formed the majority of the electorate in the Georgetown area. Protest meetings resulted in a call for a General Strike, commencing on 13 February. The Colonel of the Regiment departed on the last aircraft to leave before the strike, but Colonel Warren remained behind. In fact, trouble in one form or another had been anticipated for some time and A Company had been reinforced with a third platoon early in February as well as being supplied with a high powered radio set with which to maintain communications with Jamaica.

On Wednesday 14 February the government itself aggravated the situation, first by issuing an unenforceable proclamation to the effect that the area surrounding the Legislative Assembly was out of bounds to public demonstrations, and then by announcing modifications to some of its budget proposals. This had a contrary effect to that intended in that it merely encouraged the strikers to press their demands all the harder.

By the following day the crowds were becoming increasingly aggressive. One police officer was shot dead and rumour had it that the police themselves were about to strike, as were the magistrates. A Company was placed on ten minutes' notice to move. As Cable and Wireless were on strike, an Operations Room had already been set up in which Captain Luckham, Corporal

Stonehouse and the signallers maintained communications with Kingston, where Battalion Tactical Headquarters and one platoon of B Company were placed on immediate stand-by, with the rest of B Company at short notice to move. HMS 'Troubridge', too, lay in the offing.

The morning of Friday 16 February passed without incident and Major Wilson attended a conference in town. At about noon the situation began to worsen dramatically. Riots, accompanied by wholesale looting, broke out at about 13:00 and at 13:25 the Police Commissioner came through on his own net to say that the situation was beyond his control and that troops were needed in Georgetown. Within seven minutes of the bugler blowing "Fall-in" A Company was leaving the camp in battle order. The convoy was met by Major Wilson, who led it into Georgetown, reaching the Police Training School at 14:50. The course of the subsequent action is described by the then Lieutenant Bob Long, who had been commissioned into the Regiment during his National Service in 1956 and re-joined with a Regular Commission in April 1961.

"Sandy Wilson called an O Group. Long had prepared himself for this day, the first action he had ever experienced. His notebook was prepared with appropriate headings. With sharpened pencil, he was poised to take down detailed orders. Sandy Wilson spoke. His orders were short:

'Situation - crowds are rioting in Georgetown. Mission - to clear the street. Execution - 1 Platoon (Lieutenant Hastings Neville) to guard Dr Jagan's house; 2 Platoon (Lieutenant Bob Long) to clear Camp Street; 3 Platoon (Lieutenant Evan Ozanne) to guard vital points along the waterfront and act as reserve. Move now. Any questions?'

"Long asked, 'Are we getting support from the police or magistrates?' 'No,' came the reply. 'Off you go.' Long put his notebook away. The School of Infantry, Warminster, had been much more complicated

"Off they went. Immediately. All the practice of formation drills from 'Keeping the Peace Parts 1 and 2' were to be validated in reality. With fixed bayonets, steel helmets on and live rounds in the magazine, 2 Platoon marched up Camp Street towards a noisy and animated crowd. The system worked! The crowd were unwilling to debate matters with grim-faced soldiers. 'Go home now - the party's over!' said the Platoon Commander over the loud hailer, without a smile. The crowd began to disperse. Marching in strict step up the street, still in open formation, the Platoon was obliged to run past the intense heat of intermittent burning buildings. One hour later (or was it two?) the Platoon Commander reported to Sandy Wilson, 'Camp Street clear - over.' 'Keep it clear - out,' came the reply.

"The rest of the day passed in a flash. Half-sections were sent to block road junctions and prevent the crowds from returning. Long borrowed a bicycle to get round his extended area of responsibility. Colour Sergeant Cardey, the CQMS, Sergeant Herbert, the Platoon Sergeant, and the Salvation Army produced much-needed refreshment. Across the city smoke arose from blazing buildings, but there was little tension.

"The situation changed after dark. Unruly and rum-fortified crowds returned to loot. It was necessary to shoot a persistent looter; the crowd dispersed like magic. The crowds did not return immediately. When they did, it was more in sorrow and amazement than in anger. It had been a strange and rather exhilarating experience."

Meanwhile, Lieutenant Hastings Neville's 1 Platoon had taken up position around Dr Jagan's house, which was rumoured to contain a small arsenal, although that had nothing to do with the business in hand. Nothing happened, largely because the rioters were more interested in looting or burning the premises of Indian shopkeepers, and in due course Mrs Jagan appeared with cups of tea for everyone. After the platoon had been in this position for approximately an hour and a half the police assumed responsibility for the Prime Minister's security and Major Wilson re-deployed it to clear Booker Square, where its experience was similar to that of 1 Platoon. So many looters were arrested and made to lie face down under guard on the grass in the centre of the square that they began to resemble sardines packed in a tin. Even this did not discourage the more persistent among the criminal element and it became necessary to open fire on several occasions.

By now all aspects of the contingency plan for unrest in British Guiana had been activated under the codename of Operation Windsor II. Battalion Tactical HQ and one platoon of B Company flew into Atkinson Field at 16:00, being driven into Georgetown on the back of flat Public Works Department Trucks because of the critical shortage of transport. The former took over command responsibilities from A Company and the latter joined a landing party from HMS *Troubridge,* which had been equipped by their Master at Arms with a variety of weapons, including Lanchester sub-machine guns and Lee Enfield No 4 rifles. The seamen's approach to riot control was vigorously informal. They commandeered bicycles and pedalled off furiously to wherever they had been sent; they mounted police horses and bundled the mob along as though it was a bad-tempered football crowd; and they took immense pleasure in driving brand-new cars out of burning showrooms at speed.

On Saturday 17 February the rest of B Company arrived. If any of the rioters retained doubts that the authorities meant business these were dispelled the following week by the arrival of HQ 2nd Brigade, the 1st Battalion The East Anglian Regiment and one company of The Duke of Edinburgh's Royal Regiment. A Company was inclined to view the build-up a little indulgently, claiming, with some justice, that they had "sorted" the problem long before anyone else turned up.

It was indeed true that after the events of 16 February the real heat went out of the situation, so that from then onwards it was simply a question of patrolling and guarding key points. Against this, there were elements within Georgetown's volatile population who were still in an emotional state and who clearly regarded the chance to loot as being one of life's occasional blessings. Lieutenant Mike Martin and a platoon were given the task of clearing looters from a wrecked liquor warehouse known as the Robb Stelling. The looters were enjoying themselves far too much for simple persuasion to be effective. With bayonets fixed the platoon advanced on them in quick time, then double time, at which they scattered in every direction, vanishing over walls, round corners or diving acrobatically into the sea. Martin's further instructions were to smash the bottle stock, officially on medical grounds, in fact to remove a dangerous temptation from the rioters' path. While so engaged, he received an order from Battalion Tactical HQ, which wished to verify the condition of the stock for itself, but considerately restricted its demands to the choicer vintages!

By the end of the month tension had eased considerably. On 7 March the Chief of Defence Staff, Admiral of the Fleet Earl Mountbatten of Burma, paid a visit to the Battalion and, having returned to Trinidad, wrote to Colonel Warren the following day.

"My dear Warren,

"I am writing to thank you for the interesting briefing you gave me in Georgetown on Tuesday, and for the arrangements you made for me to see some of the men of your B Company in Georgetown and A Company at Atkinson. The Guard of Honour was very smart and the demonstration of riot drill most interesting. Please express my appreciation to all concerned.

"As a Hampshire man I feel very proud of the splendid show the Royal Hampshires put up during the recent troubles in British Guiana."

After recent events the rest of the Battalion's tour was comparatively quiet, although A Company managed an interesting adventure training exercise to King George VI Falls in April. C Company had already returned from Nassau and been disbanded on 27 January and shortly after order had been restored in British Guiana the Battalion was informed that it would be returning to the United Kingdom in stages by air between May and August 1962. It was with great pleasure that the Battalion learned from the Birthday Honours List that Major Barry Matthews and Captain Robin Tillard had been awarded the MBE for their work during Hurricane Hattie, in addition to the BEMs awarded to Clayforth and Clarke.

On 2 June 1962 the Queen's Birthday Parade was held at Up Park Camp, Kingston. The Colours, carried by Lieutenant R.C.J.Brasher and Lieutenant H.D.H.Keatinge, were marched in quick time past the Captain General and Commander-in-Chief, Sir Kenneth Blackburne, GBE, KCMG, and then trooped in slow time through the ranks of the Jamaica Constabulary and the 1st Battalion The West India Regiment to the strains of *Auld Lang Syne* before being marched off parade. That evening a ceremonial Changing the Guard took place at King's House, during which the Battalion handed over to the 1st Battalion The West India Regiment.

Perhaps the Battalion's achievements during its tour in the Caribbean are best summarised in a letter written by Sir Kenneth Blackburne two days after the above events.

"Dear Colonel Warren,

"Now that the sad time has come for The Royal Hampshire

Regiment to leave Jamaica, I should like to send to you, and to all Officers, Non-Commissioned Officers and Other Ranks, the most grateful thanks of everyone in Jamaica for all that the Regiment has done to help us during the past period of just over two years.

"You have had as difficult a time as any British unit in the West Indies in recent years. You have had to send troops at short notice to the Bahamas, British Guiana and British Honduras; and I know from the reports received from my fellow Governors that on each occasion the Regiment has acquitted itself magnificently. You have also suffered two grievous casualties in Jamaica when serving in support of the Government in catching and eliminating the Henry Gang in 1960, very shortly after your arrival.

"Throughout your stay in Jamaica the Regiment has established many friendly contacts with the people of this Island in sport and through the performances of the Regimental Band. The extent to which your departure is regretted is shown by the record attendance of 15,000 people at the Queen's Birthday Parade on 2 June, and by the reception given to the Guard and Band by the 3000 guests at King's House on the same evening.

"The Royal Hampshire Regiment is the last unit of the British Army to serve in Jamaica. For the first time in 307 years, this Island will have no British garrison. Although we accept that Jamaican Independence makes this change necessary, it is with sad hearts that we see this break in tradition; but we will always be grateful that the Royal Hampshire Regiment was in Jamaica in 1962. Your high standards will long remain in the memory of Jamaica and serve as an example for us in the future."

The advance party had already flown home on 21 May and was followed at regular intervals by the rest of the Battalion in June, the last to leave being Y Company from British Honduras in August. Everyone went on four weeks' leave after they landed at Heathrow Airport, then reported back to Haig Lines, Crookham, near Aldershot, where the Battalion reassembled.

* * * * * * * * *

THE HAMPSHIRE TIGERS

WELL DONE THE BAND

EXTRACT OF LETTER FROM COLONEL ALBERTO MONSERRATE PEREZ, VENEZUELAN ARMY, TO THE BRITISH MILITARY ATTACHE IN CARACAS, FORWARDED TO HQ CARIBBEAN AREA AND THENCE TO LIEUTENANT COLONEL D.J.WARREN, DSO, MC, COMMANDING 1st BATTALION THE ROYAL HAMPSHIRE REGIMENT, REGARDING THE BAND'S PARTICIPATION IN THE PARADE HELD TO CELEBRATE THE 150th ANNIVERSARY OF VENEZUELAN INDEPENDENCE, AND FINALLY COMMUNICATED TO MAJOR ROGER MAY, BANDMASTER PLANT, THE DRUM MAJOR AND THE MEMBERS OF THE BAND AND DRUMS

"I have been charged by the Constitutional President of the Republic, Romulo Betancoirt, with the pleasant and honourable duty of appraising each and every one of the senior officers, non-commissioned officers, cadets, men and students who took part in the Military Parade of 5th July of this year, of the warmest congratulations on the smartness and discipline displayed before the Highest Authorities of the Nation, the honourable Diplomatic Corps and the high Military, Civilian and Ecclesiastical authorities and the general public, who in a tremendous gathering which was probably the most numerous ever seen on a similar occasion, fervently cheered the March Past of your soldiers whilst the members of the Bands were playing the epic marches of the Venezuelan Armed Forces.

"On this memorable occasion fraternal delegations from countries closely united to our own by blood, creed, culture and common struggles for the forging of Liberty condescended to accompany us. Columbia, Ecuador, Peru, Argentine and Mexico are the peoples who throughout history have lent their monolithic shoulders, broad minds and generous hearts in favour of the Venezuelan cause. And also the noble Albion, whose gallant British Legion knew how to give their quota of courage and sacrifice under the sun at Carabobo to seal, with the triumph of Venezuelan Liberty, an eternal compact of inter-continental fraternity.* To these ancestral deeds, engraved with indelible marks on the heart of Venezuela, are united now the warmth, the harmony and the bearing of the distinguished soldiers who, drawing the purest emotions from the soul of our people, came to lend their courage and to honour this Homeland on such an

160

extraordinary day . . . . Caracas, July 6th 1961 "

* The British Legion referred to by Colonel Perez was not, of course, the modern ex-servicemen's organisation. Commencing in 1807, Spain's Central and South American colonies initiated a series of Wars of Independence, lasting until 1825. Following the defeat of Napoleon, many of Wellington's discharged veterans, unable to obtain work at home but possessing some knowledge of Spanish, enlisted with the colonists, and it would be surprising if there were not some former soldiers of the 37th and 67th among them. The most famous of these units was the British Legion, upon which Simon Bolivar, Liberator of Venezuela, Colombia, Ecuador and Peru, relied heavily, and which was largely responsible for winning the Battle of Carabobo on 25 June 1821.

Experience during the Peninsular War had taught these men to march far harder than the standard 120 paces to the minute. They sang a lot on the march, usually to tunes with a fast, steady rhythm like *Green Grow The Rushes, Oh!*.   It is believed that the constant repetition of this phrase led to them being collectively named Gringos by the colonists. Although they have largely been forgotten at home, these men created an enormous fund of goodwill for the United Kingdom which persists to this day.

* * * * * * * * *

TYPICAL AGENDA OF THE DISASTER RELIEF COMMITTEE IN BELIZE FOLLOWING HURRICANE HATTIE

Working of the Holden Hospital
Relief stores for Stann Creek
Purity of water supply
Red Cross Organisation - military assistance
Transport availability
Fire risk in Belize
Refrigeration space for meat arrivals
Disposal of dead
Public Works Department - impressed labour
Wesley Hall - Relief and Food Centre
Retail trading - when to return to normal
Dumping of bad rice and corn
Sibun river - state of flood
Sunday working for population
Mobile cinema
Kerosene distribution to civilians
Rehabilitation of port
Readiness of Fire Service

* * * * * * * * *

THE HAMPSHIRE TIGERS

ASPECTS OF LIFE IN CARIBBEAN AREA

Each place where the Battalion was stationed had a Governor and Commander-in-Chief (a combined function), to whom Company Commanders were responsible. The Senior Naval Officer West Indies was a Commodore based in Bermuda. He normally had two frigates under command, one being hurricane guard ship during the season. The Battalion worked closely with the Navy and officers, soldiers and the Band were frequently at sea. There was less day-to-day contact with the RAF, but in emergency 42 Squadron RAF with their Shackletons did splendid service, flying reinforcement to British Honduras after Hurricane Hattie and to British Guiana during the troubles there. Local forces included The West India Regiment, which was based in Jamaica and available for operations there, thereby releasing the Hampshires for operations elsewhere if required; the British Honduras Volunteer Guard, which was deployed after Hurricane Hattie; and the British Guiana Volunteer Force, which was embodied during Operation Windsor II and guarded vital points.

Numerous guards and duties made Jamaica the least attractive of the stations. Indeed, one Outstation Company Commander recalls that the threat of being returned to Jamaica was in itself sufficient to maintain good order and military discipline for most people.

Administration of all kinds was a major problem as the efforts of those responsible were spread over four widely dispersed locations. The Quartermaster, Captain Harry Plummer, worked a succession of miracles, assisted by his RQMS WOII Peter Waterman. During the troubles in British Guiana, Waterman was sent there as Garrison QM and became temporarily responsible for looking after a brigade HQ, a battalion and a detached company, as well as the Hampshires' own Battalion HQ and two companies!

The Orderly Room, run initially by ORQMS F.Welch, MBE, (Glosters) was taken over by Sergeant Peter Kirby, a highly effective Chief Clerk. Their problems, like the Quartermaster's, were legion, not least in operating over such a vast area and trying to keep Record Offices in the UK happy while explaining to them the difficulties of administering soldiers who were 600 miles distant. The Pay Team under Major Douglas Stimpson and WOII Hale, RAPC, also achieved miracles in keeping track of the Imprest Account at long range. The feeling that these difficulties were imperfectly understood by those at home was compounded by the latter's signals, which sometimes lost touch with reality.

One such gem, which must surely be included in any future history of bureaucratic lunacy, was received in the aftermath of Hurricane Hattie - it indignantly enquired why troops had been flown from Jamaica to British Honduras when railway travel would have been cheaper!

Whenever possible, sport of every kind played an important part in the Battalion's daily life. Tutored by WOII Hanna, Z Company in British Honduras entered the Army Rifle Association Non-Central Small Bore Competition, firing on a range which they built themselves. They came second.

In Jamaica on 23 May 1962 there was a floodlit World Cup qualifying soccer match between Jamaica and Haiti at Sabina Park. Immediately prior to this match the Regiment played the Jamaica Second XI. The expectation, led by *The Daily Gleaner,* was that the Regiment would be thrashed - in the event it won 1 - 0 thanks to a goal by Private Eric Coysh from a corner by Private Attrill. The remainder of the team were Privates Greetham and Leach, Lance Corporal Riglin, Private Iles, Lance Corporal Hellard (Captain), Privates Curtin and Cabell, Corporal Williams and Private Hennessy. Between the two matches the Band and Drums Beat Retreat. Drum Major Bryant's throwing of the mace and Bandmaster Plant's arrangement of *Jamaica Farewell* and *Auld Lang Syne* provided indelible memories of an unforgettable evening.

The Battalion was instrumental in bringing rugby football to the fore in Jamaica. Prior to its arrival a number of expatriates used to meet once a week with a rugby ball in the grounds of King's House. Captain Tim Wellings reformed the Battalion team and the expatriates formed a club called the Arawaks. A pitch was hewn out of nothing and watered copiously by RSM Harry Barnard. We were all sponsored by the Red Stripe Brewery and played each other once a week. In November/December 1960 a Jamaica Rugby Football Union Touring Side, half Arawaks and half Tigers, toured Trinidad and British Guiana. Later on Nassau toured Jamaica, as did Trinidad, though the latter tour was disrupted by the rapid departure for British Honduras after Hurricane Hattie. Others prominent in the rugby world were RQMS Peter Waterman, Captain Gerald Anthony, Lieutenant Edward Churcher, Lance Corporals West and Mordaunt, Captain David Protheroe, on the Staff in Jamaica, Privates Grant, Tanner, Satterley, Pearce and Allen, who had played for Gloucester, Sergeant Baines and many others, so that by 1961 a Second XV was being run.

Sport in general suffered from the Battalion being so dispersed but in 1960 the hockey team won the Jamaica Knockout Cup and much inter-platoon sport was enjoyed. It proved almost impossible to beat the West India Regiment at cricket. However, on one occasion the Team believed that it was on the point of beating the NAAFI Staff Team when the Numbers 10 and 11 of the latter put on almost 100 to win the match. Captain Buster Russell and Lieutenant Richard Brasher played for British Honduras against the MCC Touring Side.

Some mention has been made of distinguished visitors to the Battalion in Jamaica and elsewhere. Many such visits took place during February, giving rise to the cynical view that raw, grey, winter London had less to offer than a week in the Caribbean. In British Honduras, the problem was that if the weekly flight out was cancelled for any reason the visitor stayed another week. One such was Colonel Scarisbrick, Director of the Army Catering Corps, who made the best of it by borrowing some cook's "whites" and taking over the cookhouse for a week!

Frequent mention, too, has been made of the jungle. Curiously, neither jungle greens nor jungle boots were issued in the Caribbean Area, where normal working and operational dress was khaki drill.

This was the last operational tour in which National Servicemen formed part of the Battalion. As always, the Regulars regarded them very highly indeed and in the outstations the tradesmen among them were especially valued.

CHAPTER 8

GERMANY 1962 — 1965

Reorganisation as a mechanised infantry battalion - the Mobat - the Pig APC - Cpl Kimberley's success at the US 7th Army Academy - Presentation of Colours by Lord Mountbatten - the 1963 Defence White Paper - aspects of contemporary service in BAOR - changes in dress - 1st Battalion placed on standby - Lieutenant Colonel T.S.W.Reeve-Tucker succeeds Lieutenant Colonel D.J.Warren in Command - presentation of Victoria Cross won by Ensign Chaplin at the Taku Forts - Major General R.H.Batten succeeds Brigadier G.D.Browne as Colonel of the Regiment - KAPE Tour of Hampshire 1964 - success of 1st Battalion Shooting Team in the Prix Le Clerc and CENTO Rifle Meetings - Lieutenant C.B.Winchester killed during Exercise Treble Chance - Private Sanderson's Commendation - Inter-Allied Exercise Left Foot - 1st Battalion wins the Army Cookery Competition and Army Squash Cups - ceremonies to mark the 50th Anniversary of the Gallipoli Landings - Friendship Day at Wolbeck - Training in Bavaria - the 1965 Nijmegen Marches - Exercise High Reach - Sergeant John Wheeler becomes the Army's Champion Shot - the 1st Battalion leaves Germany

By the end of September 1962 the 1st Battalion had assembled again at Haig Lines, Crookham, a typical wooden-hutted camp complete with choking fumes generated by numerous coke-fired boilers and stoves. The camp's saving grace was that it was in Hampshire, and this enabled everyone to get home easily.

Earlier in the month the Battalion had sent a 120-strong KAPE team, including the Band and Drums, mortar, anti-tank, pioneer and signal detachments, under Captains Jim Kellie and Robin Tillard, around the County, where it received a friendly welcome from the press and public alike.

Internally, some reorganisation was necessary in order to conform with the Battalion's new role as a component of an infantry brigade group in BAOR. This involved the formation of a Reconnaissance Platoon under Captain F.D.J.Dickenson, as well as organic Support Platoons, consisting of two 3-inch mortars and two 120mm Mobat anti-tank guns, for each rifle company. As mentioned in an earlier chapter, the increasing thickness and ballistic configuration of tank armour had begun to pose serious problems for battalion anti-tank gunners relying on kinetic energy weapons as early as 1946. In theory, there was no limit to the size of the conventional anti-tank gun. In practice, handling anything larger than a 17-pdr in the field was a physical impossibility, and the 17-pdr lacked the penetrative power necessary to deal with the modern generation of Soviet tanks. An interim solution was provided by the class of weapons known as recoilless rifles, of which the Mobat was one, firing chemical energy shaped-charge rounds capable of penetrating any known armour. There were, however, two major disadvantages to the Mobat. The first was that its effective range was limited to 800 metres. The second was that the back-blast from the venturi would instantly reveal the weapon's position. Most Mobat gunners took the realistic view that they would be lucky to fire more than one round against a first-class opponent. Nevertheless, there were to be many more interesting twists and turns in the continuing contest between projectile and armour.

Following this reorganisation, the rifle companies spent a week at Sennybridge, South Wales, where field firing of personal and support weapons was carried out. On 19 October the Battalion exercised the Regimental right as Freemen of the the Borough of Aldershot to march through the town with Colours flying, drums beating and bayonets fixed, the salute being taken by the Mayor, Councillor S.C.H.Gibbs. That night a successful Ball was held in the Officers' Mess, a large contingent from the 4th/5th Battalion being among those who attended.

On 31 October 1962 the Battalion held a Farewell Parade for the last of its National Servicemen and thus, for the first time since 1939, became an all-Regular unit. Air-trooping had now replaced the somewhat Victorian means of movement by train and ship between the United Kingdom and Germany, so that during November it was flown from Gatwick to various airfields in the British Zone, from which it travelled by coach to Münster. There it relieved the 1st Battalion The York and Lancaster Regiment at Waterloo Barracks, Gremmendorf, just to the south of the city. Its role would once again be that of a mechanised infantry battalion, forming part of the 2nd Division's 6th Infantry Brigade Group. In practical terms this meant that each of the brigade's three infantry battalions would have the support of an armoured squadron, the proportion of infantry to armour being the inverse of that which had applied during the Hampshires' last tour in BAOR, when they had formed part of an armoured brigade group. This time, however, manpower was a problem due to the ending of National Service and building up the Battalion's strength was a long-term process. Rifle companies consisted of two platoons, each about twenty strong, and a support platoon with a twelve-strong 3-inch mortar section and a ten-strong anti-tank section armed with Mobats. One of the biggest headaches was the training of drivers and on the first practice call-out, almost anybody of any rank who could drive anything was pressed into service.

Settling into Waterloo Barracks alongside the 22nd (Cheshire) Regiment and the 15th/19th King's Royal Hussars, the Corps armoured car regiment, took place during a winter so hard that most sporting activities had to be called off. The skiers were delighted and made full use of the Battalion ski hut at Girkhausen. CSM Hanna coached the small bore team to such good effect that it won the Brigade's Major Units Competition and came fourth in the BAOR finals. Later in the year he attended the RAF Germany Rifle Meeting, winning the No 4 Rifle and SMG competitions and coming second with the pistol.

During this tour HQ Company was commanded by Major S.G.B. Matthews, MBE, (HQ); A Company by Major M.F.A.Wilson, followed by Major R.J.Freeman-Wallace and then Major P.K.Essame from the Devon and Dorsets; B Company by Major P.Branwell, who handed over to Major George Schneider, US Army, who was doing a year's exchange, succeeded by Major D.C. Munn of The Duke of Edinburgh's Royal Regiment; Y Company by Major C.D. Darroch, who handed over to Major G.C.Phipps on becoming the Battalion's Second-in-Command. The Adjutant during the early part of the tour was Major R.J.Freeman-Wallace, who was succeeded by Captain J.E.Horton. Captain L.B.Edmonds, who had been RQMS in Malaya during his last tour with the Battalion, took over as Quartermaster from Captain Harry Plummer.

Bandmaster J.Plant had moved to the Depot and handed over to WOI (BM) G.E.Gregory. The Company Sergeant Majors, a very experienced group, included WOIIs J.Wiles, H.Robinson, J.Cheesely, R.Brown, R.W.Sargent and W.J.Hanna, and they were admirably supported by Colour Sergeants R.Cardey, W.Sumner, D.Henderson, F.Crockford, H.W.Perkins and Joe Turner. In the Signals Platoon Colour Sergeant F.Wellington was faced with a mass of communications equipment which inevitably came with the BAOR role.

In January 1963 individual training commenced, including driving and maintainance courses for the 120 drivers needed for the Battalion's APCs, the War Office having finally been convinced by experience that APC crews perform most efficiently if they are an organic element of a mechanised infantry battalion. In this case the APC was the FV1611 Truck 1-ton Armoured 4 x 4 Humber, otherwise known as The Pig, for no better reason than it looked like one. The vehicle had been brought into service hurriedly in the early 1950s because insufficient Saracens were available; ironically, it remained in service until the mid-1990s, long after the Saracen was but a memory. The Pig's crew consisted of commander and driver, plus six (at a squeeze, eight) riflemen, and it was fitted for radio. For many, the years in the Caribbean had meant that their all-arms battlegroup drills had become a little rusty and some mental adjustment was required before they became used to working with armour, gunners and sappers again; the term Car Commander, for example, displaced that of Section Commander.

In March, following platoon 100-mile route marches completed in five days, section and platoon training commenced at Haltern, where the 3-inch mortars had a shoot and individuals fired the 2-inch mortar and the 3.5-inch close-range anti-tank rocket launcher. During this period the Battalion received a visit from the Commander of I BR Corps, Lieutenant General Sir Kenneth Darling, KCB, CBE, DSO.

In the meantime, Corporal E.C.Kimberley had been selected to attend an NCOs' Course at the Seventh US Army's Academy at Bad Tolz. No more was heard until Colonel David Warren received a telephone call asking him to attend the Course's Graduation Parade, as Corporal Kimberley had passed out top of 150 students, winning the General George Patton Award for Excellence. The award was presented by Brigadier General Francis Hill, Commanding US V Corps Artillery. In addition, Corporal Kimberley was presented with an engraved cigarette lighter and swagger stick. He was promoted to sergeant shortly after his return to Münster.

Following Easter, the Battalion moved to Sennelager for three weeks' field firing. On the morning of the visit of the Divisional Commander, Major General M.A.H.Butler, CBE, DSO, MC, the Mobats were to lay on a demonstration for him, to be followed later by one for the whole Battalion. The day dawned with a thick mist, the tank hulk targets being barely visible. The Mobats' commander, Captain Bob Long, was therefore surprised to find a beflagged and bestarred Land Rover approaching the firing point earlier than expected. General Butler alighted.

"I didn't hear much firing," he said.

"No, sir," came the indulgent reply. "There's not much point in firing unless you can see the targets properly."

"Nonsense!" the General retorted. "The Russians aren't going to wait for a lovely day! Carry on!"

Seconds later, with a stupendous noise, the 120mm round vanished into the mist, making a satisfactory noise the other end.

"There - you can do it if you try!" responded the satisfied General.

The demonstration to the whole Battalion later that day proved to be a great success, with excellent visibility and targets, enhanced by filling them with combustible material which erupted dramatically when hit.

In May A Company went to Soltau for infantry/tank training with the 13th/18th Royal Hussars. The following month the rifle platoons were involved in a series of demanding test exercises set by Brigade HQ, while the mortars and Mobats went to Putlos on the Baltic for field firing; the latter then briefly relieved their opposite numbers of the 1st Battalion The King's Regiment in Berlin while they went to Putlos. For the mortar crews there was the consolation that the Battalion had been selected to perform the temperate zone troop trials on the new Anglo-Canadian 81mm mortar. Over 5000 bombs were made available for these, as opposed to the usual annual allocation of 1100 or so, and the weapon created an excellent impression. Early in July the Battalion went to the Belgian training area of Vogelsang, situated in pleasant, rolling country, to carry out a week's infantry/tank training with its affiliated armour, C Squadron 4th/7th Royal Dragoon Guards, with whom it quickly established a friendly and efficient working relationship.

The thought now uppermost in everyone's mind was the Colour Parade to be held on Minden Day, 1st August 1963, during which the 1st Battalion was to be presented with new Colours. It will be recalled that when the old 1st and 2nd Battalions amalgamated the new 1st Battalion had inherited the Colours of both. Those of the old 1st Battalion had been presented by HRH Princess Henry of Battenberg, Governor of the Isle of Wight, on 29 June 1907 at Portsmouth, and those of the old 2nd Battalion by Field Marshal HRH The Duke of Cambridge on 2 October 1889 at Chatham. Given that the usual active life of Colours is considered to be twenty to twenty-five years, renewal was long overdue, but within the Regiment itself generations of men had spent their lives serving under the old Colours and because of this the respect and affection in which they were held was all the greater. As with all such occasions, therefore, sadness would mingle with pride.

The parade was planned to take place during the morning at Waterloo Barracks. Under a committee chaired by Major Peter Branwell, much preparation was undertaken. Numerous colour-coded invitations and instructions were despatched. Car parks were identified and designated accordingly. Nothing was forgotten, from the provision of press packs to the conversion of lavatories suitable for lady guests. The Sovereign's choice of Lord Mountbatten, Chief of the Defence Staff, to present new Colours was a particularly happy one. With his home at Broadlands, Romsey, in the heart of the County, his recent visit to the Battalion on operations in the Caribbean, and his Honorary Colonelcy of the 4th/5th Battalion, he was the ideal figure. The parade was to be commanded by Colonel Warren those performing the major roles being as follows:

COLOUR PARTIES - THE OLD COLOURS

1st Battalion	2nd Battalion
Lt J.G.T.Southwood	Lt R.Ashenden
2/Lt B.J.Willing	Lt R.D.Langrishe

Sgt J.Grace   Sgt P.Smith
Sgt A.R.Withers   Sgt J.Lemmon

COLOUR PARTY - THE NEW COLOURS
Lt R.C.J.Brasher
Lt H.D.H.Keatinge
RQMS P.Waterman
C/Sgt F.Crockford
C/Sgt K.Winearls

No 1 Guard and Escort   **No 2 Guard**
to the Old Colours
Major C.D.Darroch   Capt H.D.Canning
Capt R.J.Russell   Lt P.Anthony
CSM R.W.Sargent   2/Lt R.L.Glyn
Sgt R.W.Coleman   CSM W.J.Hanna
Sgt J.Palmer   Sgt A.A.Cripps
Sgt A.J.Rumbold   Sgt K.Price
                                     Sgt J.Wheeler

No 3 Guard   **No 4 Guard**

Major A.J.Imrie   Major M.F.A.Wilson
Lt M.J.Martin   Lt P.E.Keen
Lt B.T.Wigmore   2/Lt J.Martindale
CSM H.Robinson   CSM J.Wiles
C/Sgt J.Cheesley   C/Sgt W.Sumner
Sgt R.Smith   Sgt P.Hogan
Sgt R.Page   Sgt E.Kimberley

Staff Officer to Admiral of the Fleet,
The Earl Mountbatten of Burma: Major R.J.Freeman-Wallace

Regimental Sergeant Major: WOI (RSM) R.C.Daws

     With only a day or so to go, the blow fell. Princess
Alexandra, due to take the Sovereign's Parade at the Rotal Military Academy Sandhurst that day, had become indisposed. The
time of the Colours Parade was therefore changed from the morning to the afternoon. Apart from the chore of having to send out
amended invitations to all the guests, arrangements for guests'

meals had to be changed and travel arrangements altered for everybody. It would be wrong to say that the change was taken in an imperturbable spirit, but in true Regimental style all involved got on willingly with the extra work, and all arrangements were remade.

In so far as any great parade is standard, this one followed the normal pattern. The Battalion noted with great pleasure that as Lord Mountbatten received the General Salute to the strains of *Rule Britannia,* he was wearing a Minden Rose in his naval hat. In his address, Lord Mountbatten referred to the fact that Princess Henry of Battenberg, who presented the old 1st Battalion Colours, had been both his aunt and great aunt, and emphasised his County connections. He ended, "I entrust these new Colours to you in confidence that, in peace and war, their honour will be defended."

Colonel Warren thanked Lord Mountbatten, expressing confidence that should the need arise, and despite whatever perils faced the Battalion in the future, the spirit shown by the 37th at Minden would burn as brightly as ever. "On this Presentation of new Colours," he continued, "we re-dedicate ourselves to the task of maintaining, in the future, the great traditions of the Regiment both in war and peace, and to the destruction of The Queen's enemies wherever they may be. God save The Queen!" The applause which followed was more heartfelt than was usual on such occasions.

After the Battalion had re-formed line, to the centre of which the Colours were marched to the National Anthem, it marched past in slow and quick time. The parade ended with an "advance in review order" and a "present", after which Lord Mountbatten left.

In addition to those already mentioned, the distinguished guests present included Lieutenant General Sir Kenneth Darling, KCB, CBE, DSO, Commander of I (BR) Corps; Major General R.H.Batten, CB, CBE, DSO, Chief of Staff, Northern Army Group; Major General D.E.B.Talbot, CB, CBE, DSO, MC, Chief of Staff, BAOR, who had commanded the 7th Battalion in Normandy and North West Europe 1944-45; Major General M.A.H.Butler, CBE, DSO, MC, GOC 2nd Division; Brigadier C.W.Dunbar, MBE, Commander 6th Infantry Brigade Group; the Mayor of Winchester, Councillor Mrs Richards; Generalmajor Hans Ulrich Kranz, representing the Commander I (GE) Corps; the

Oberburgermeister (Lord Mayor) of Münster, Dr Peus, and other German dignitaries from the city of Münster and the surrounding area, for whom receptions were held in the Officers' and Sergeants' Messes. Unfortunately, duties elsewhere demanded that the British general officers should leave in their helicopters shortly after the ceremony had ended, but during the next few days the Battalion received a flood of congratulatory messages. Of these, perhaps the most highly valued was the following signal despatched by Lord Mountbatten immediately on his return to London.

> From: Ministry of Defence
> To: CO 1 R Hamps
>
> Personal from Chief of Defence Staff(.) Many congratulations for an absolutely outstanding parade which compared favourably with the best Sovereign's Parade which has been seen at R.M.A.S. for some time.

The year 1963 had also witnessed the publication of Mr Peter Thorneycroft's White Paper on Defence, under the terms of which the functions previously carried out by the Admiralty, the War Office and the Air Ministry were to be consolidated within a centralised Ministry of Defence. Superficially, the idea had its logical attractions, since it implied a reduction in the number of administrators required. Unfortunately, the huge outgrowth in Civil Service numbers had not been taken into account. The organisation would have as its headquarters the Whitehall Gardens office block, conceived in 1933 with the object of housing no fewer than eight ministries, yet thirty years later it was incapable of housing more than one-eighth of the new centralised defence ministry's staff. The strength of this was put at 25,000; or, as David Divine expressed it in his book *The Blunted Sword*, one administrator for every sixteen servicemen, one for every six members of the teeth arms, and almost exactly the number of men then serving aboard the Royal Navy's operational ships. Nor could Mr Thorneycroft promise any reduction in the short term; quite the reverse, in fact, despite sustained pressure for further reductions in the armed services themselves.

Fortunately, there were those in the Ministry who recognised that with the ending of National Service it would be necessary to offer greatly improved pay and conditions of service if suffi-cient recruits of the right calibre were to be attracted to a Service career. Emphasis was placed upon the Regular Army's profes-sional status and rates of pay were reviewed regularly. For those in BAOR this was particularly important as the cost of living had risen proportionally with the booming German economy and, since the Deutsch Mark had become more attractive in financial circles than the Pound Sterling, the rate of exchange was steadily tilting against them. There therefore remained no reason why Sterling should be protected by scrip and BAFVs were withdrawn, pay being drawn in Deutsch Marks. A determined effort was also made to eliminate the image of mindless "bull" endured by count-less Regulars and National Servicemen. Battledress was replaced by the smarter No 2 Dress for ceremonial occasions and weather-proof combat kit, initially drawn from central holdings, was worn on exercise. Barrack Dress evolved a little more slowly, beginning with Regimental pattern stable belts worn with shirt-sleeve order in summer, followed by heavy-duty uniform sweaters in the cooler seasons. A black heavy-duty sweater was favoured by the Regi-ment, being worn by officers and warrant officers, who made private purchase, and the heavy-duty khaki pullover eventually became a "personal" issue to sergeants and below. Only a few years earlier such an idea would have been greeted with incredu-lous outrage, yet the overall effect was brisk and businesslike. There was, however, one aspect of the Battalion's current tour in BAOR which gave fewer grounds for satisfaction, namely a short-age of married quarters so acute that some families could only be accommodated far from Münster, with the result that their men-folk only saw them at weekends.

During the autumn of 1963 the Battalion took part in an unusual exercise, driving 1000 miles to the Larzac training area, near Marseilles. For those penned in the back of the Pigs it was an ordeal, but those riding in more civilised vehicles found the journey through southern France delightful. Camp sites en route were near towns, where some Hampshire men learned for the first time that alcoholic value of the Vins du Pays. "You can't drink it by the pint, sir," was one observation made by an ultra-hung-over soldier who had freely indulged the previous evening. The exercise itself was notable for its extremely cold night tem-perature, all the more unexpected in the south of France, and its moonscape rocky formations. The after-exercise recovery camp on the beach near Agde was memorable for its proximity to a nudist beach. The Military Police had put up a barbed wire barrier between the Royal Hampshires and their neighbours, but ingenious soldiers were said to have overcome all obstacles to favour the naturists with their presence and were, by all accounts, well received. In October a successful exchange took place between 8 Platoon, under Lieutenant J.Martindale and Sergeant R.W.Coleman, and a platoon of Panzergrenadier Battalion 322 from Bremen.

On 4 January 1964 the Battalion received a signal placing it on a week's standby for internal security duties anywhere in the world, prompted by the outbreak of civil war between the Greek and Turkish communities in Cyprus. This led to wholesale inoculations, vaccinations and preparations for movement by air which continued into February, when emplaning and deplaning drills for personnel, stores and vehicles were practised at RAF Gutersloh. By then the standby period had been reduced to seventy-two hours, but in the event the Battalion was not needed.

Colonel David Warren's period of command ended on 9 January 1964, when he left to take up a new appointment. "During his tenure as Commanding Officer," noted the Journal, "his firm and capable handling of the Battalion in the many and varied crises of the Caribbean, and his experienced guidance in all aspects of training during the first year in BAOR, has further enhanced the reputation of the Battalion and the Regiment." He was succeeded by Lieutenant Colonel T.S.W.Reeve-Tucker, who had originally been commissioned into The Gloucestershire Regiment and, it will be recalled, had served with the 1st Battalion The Royal Hampshire Regiment as Second-in-Command in the Caribbean and remained with it ever since. Upon the change in command, Major C.D.Darroch became the Battalion's new Second-in-Command. In January there was also a change of RSM when WOI R.C.Daws handed over to WOI G.House, a Hampshire man who had joined the Regiment in 1946.

On 18 March there took place one of the most interesting and unusual parades in the Battalion's history. The parade had two objects, the first of which was to bid Farewell to Brigadier G.D.Browne, who, after ten years as Colonel of the Regiment, was about to hand over his appointment; and the second was to honour an event which had taken place almost 104 years earlier. On 21 August 1860 the 67th Regiment, together with the 44th (later) The Essex Regiment and a contingent of French troops, had stormed the formidable defences of the Taku Forts, at the mouth of the Pei-ho river in China, winning four Victoria Crosses in the process. Three of these were already in the Regiment's possession and now the fourth, that won by Ensign (later Colonel) John Worthy Chaplin, was to be presented to the Regiment by his grandson, Mr J.R.Chaplin, accompanied by another grandson, Major A.C.Swetenham.

With the Colours on parade, the Battalion was inspected by the Colonel of the Regiment and then formed square while the Adjutant, Captain J.E.Horton, read Ensign Chaplin's citation:

"For gallantry at the North Taku Forts. This Officer was carrying the Queen's Colour of the Regiment, and first planted the Colours on the breach made by the storming party, assisted by Private Lane of the 67th Regiment (also awarded the VC), and subsequently on the cavalier of the Fort which he was the first to mount. In doing this he was severely wounded."

Major Swetenham passed the Victoria Cross to Mr Chaplin who made a short speech before presenting it to Brigadier Browne. After thanking Mr Chaplin on behalf of the Regiment, Brigadier Browne handed the medal to Sergeant E.Kimberley, and then made his own Farewell speech, stressing that young soldiers could be every bit as good as old ones, provided they had three things - good leaders, good training and good team spirit. It was, he concluded, up to every man on parade to see that the last was maintained.

Colonel Reeve-Tucker called for three cheers for Mr Chaplin and the medal, on its cushion, was marched to its place with the Colour Party. The Battalion then reformed line and marched past, the salute being taken by Brigadier Browne and Mr Chaplin. Ensign Chaplin's Victoria Cross was later displayed in the Guard Room and the rest of the day was declared a Regimental holiday, with a free bottle of beer for each man.

The new Colonel of the Regiment was Major General R.H.Batten, CB, CBE, DSO, whose appointment was effective from 19 March 1964. General Batten had been commissioned into the Middlesex Regiment in 1929 and, having been given accelerated promotion, joined the 1st Battalion The Hampshire Regiment in 1936, serving in India, Palestine and Egypt until selected for the first Staff Course at Haifa in 1940. During World War II he held numerous Staff appointments, being Mentioned in Despatches on three occasions, awarded the DSO in 1943 and the OBE two years later. It will be recalled that, between further Staff appointments, he had commanded the 1st Battalion 1950-51, and then gone on to serve in the Korean War. His more recent appointments included command of 5 Infantry Brigade in BAOR, Chief of Staff HQ Eastern Command and, latterly, Chief of Staff HQ Northern Army Group until his retirement in December 1963.

It is worth mentioning that during this period senior members of the Regiment occupied a number of important positions throughout the Army. On 7 November 1963, for example, Major General P.H.Man, CBE, DSO, MC, had been appointed GOC Aldershot District and on 18 December 1963 Major General R.G.F.Frisby, CB, CBE, DSO, MC, having relinquished command of the 53rd (Welsh) Division (TA) the previous month, was appointed Chief of Staff to the Commander-in-Chief Allied Forces Northern Europe.

Although it was placed on standby at various periods, this did not prevent the Battalion entering its second annual BAOR training cycle. In April it used the ranges at Sennelager to full effect, and in June was at Soltau, where a series of Company exercises were held in very dusty conditions, gaining the approval of the Brigade commander.

On 27 June the Old Colours of the 1st, 2nd, 4th and 5th Battalions were marched through the streets of Winchester led by the Band and Drums of the 4th/5th (TA) Battalion prior to their being laid up at Serle's House, the salute being taken by the Mayor of Winchester and the Colonel of the Regiment at the Guildhall.

In July the 1st Battalion went on block leave. Simultaneously, a KAPE Team under Captain J.G.T.Southwood toured Hampshire and the Isle of Wight, visiting Portsmouth, Gosport, Bournemouth, Christchurch, Southampton, Andover, Cowes, Newport and other towns. The team produced some thirty potential recruits, which in itself was very satisfactory, but, as it commented on its return, "The interest shown by young and old alike, and the obvious pleasure it gave people to see the Regiment represented in their own town, was reward enough."

During the previous autumn a Battalion Shooting Team, consisting of twelve riflemen, five LMG pairs and two pistol shots, had won an extremely hard match against the 1st Battalion The Cheshire Regiment for the honour of representing BAOR in the

the Prix Le Clerc competition, shot for annually by selected units representing each NATO army serving in Germany, including those of the United States, France, Belgium, Holland, Germany, Canada and Great Britain. The competition rules demanded that each team should consist predominantly of young soldiers with less than three years' service. CSM Hanna selected the team, which was captained by Captain Gerald Anthony, and, together with QMSI R.Dickens, SASC, put it through an exhaustive training programme.

The 1964 competition was held on 31 July at Hagenau in eastern France. During practice sessions it quickly became apparent that questions of national prestige tended to obscure purely sporting considerations, to the extent that other teams were interpreting the rules with obvious flexibility. Some had been shooting together for as much as seven years and, while the Hampshire riflemen used the SLR's standard back-sight, others employed much superior competition sights, including such aids as different sized apertures and even wind gauges. Notwithanding these obvious handicaps, the team finished in overall fifth position.

That, however, was not quite the end of the story. By qualifying for the Prix le Clerc competition, the Battalion Team had automatically won the British place in the CENTO Rifle Meeting, held in Tehran in September. There it shot against teams from Iran, the United States, Turkey, India and Pakistan, winning the LMG event while Captain R.W.Dobin, Duke of Edinburgh's Royal Regiment (DERR) attached to the 1st Battalion, came first in the individual pistol competition, and finished third overall.

On 18 September the Band and Drums took part in the spectacular Berlin Military Tattoo, staged in the city's Olympic Stadium. Over six hundred musicians were present, watched by 95,000 Berliners, who sang them off as they marched away to the strains of the city's own march, *Berliner Luft*.

It was a sad fact of life in BAOR that major exercises always seemed to produce their crop of vehicle accidents, and by no means all of these were the fault of the troops involved. On 29 September, during Exercise Treble Chance, involving the defence of a river line and subsequent counter-attack, Lieutenant Colin Winchester, who had married only two months previously, was killed in one such tragic incident. As a result of his actions during another, four days later, Private E. Sanderson received the following commendation from the Commander-in-Chief BAOR:

"On the night of 2nd/3rd October 1964, Private Sanderson was driving a 3-ton truck in a convoy of the 1st Battalion The Royal Hampshire Regiment on Exercise Treble Chance.

"At 22:30 hours the leading vehicle of the convoy was involved in a head-on collision with a civilian vehicle. Private Sanderson was second in the convoy, about 100 yards behind the leading vehicle. As he drove up to help, the civilian vehicle, in which there were two people lying unconscious, burst into flames. He quickly drove his vehicle forward, past the fire, and then ran towards the scene of the accident with his fire extinguisher, calling upon other drivers in the convoy to do the same.

"Private Sanderson thus took charge of the situation and personally rescued the unconscious passenger from the driving seat. He co-ordinated the fire fighting effort, which was successful, and simultaneously helped others in the rescue of the driver, who had been thrown into the back seat of this 2-door car by the impact of the accident.

"The driver of the civilian vehicle subsequently died in hospital of the injuries he received in the accident. Nevertheless, by his initiative, leadership and complete disregard of his own safety, Private Sanderson undoubtedly saved the life of the passenger and prevented the driver from being burned to death."

After Treble Chance the Battalion was required to provide umpires for Exercise Lowland Fling, fought between 12 Infantry Brigade, commanded by Brigadier W.B.Thomas, DSO, MC, and the 1st Panzergrenadier Brigade.

At the end of the exercise season the Battalion ran an NCOs' cadre at Haltern until December, and then began preparing for the Annual Administrative Inspection, as a result of which a good report was received.

After the usual Christmas celebrations the Battalion went on block leave in January 1965, returning to what was to be the busiest and final year of its current tour in BAOR. First, it was required to organise Exercise Left Foot, designed to practise co-operation with other nations' forces and learn something about their equipment. On this occasion the elements involved were drawn from US and French forces in Germany and the Hampshires rode in fully-tracked M113 APCs, enjoyed K rations and, to the annoyance of the Quartermaster, Captain L.B.Edmonds, swapped their berets wholesale for American "bunny hats." The French caused some confusion with their completely symmetrical Panhard EBR armoured cars, as these had drivers fore and aft and no one was quite certain in which direction they were about to move off. At the end of the first day the Band and Drums beat Retreat and played the Evening Hymn as the three National Flags were lowered, followed by the three National Anthems. This had clearly not been expected by the visitors, who not only appreciated the ceremony but also found it very moving. The natural outcome of a cocktail party hosted by the Royal Hampshires was that the exercise *had* to last three days so that the French and the Americans could reciprocate! Somehow, Colonel Reeve-Tucker managed to persuade the French Medical Officer, who seemed puzzled by some of the words in his own language, to issue a certificate verifying the severe conditions in which Left Foot was being held, thereby obtaining release of the Battalion's rum ration. Initially, few people had thought that the exercise would produce worthwhile results, but it did and everyone left feeling that everyone else had something useful to contribute.

One group of men, generally taken for granted by regimental historians save in the most desperate situations, are the cooks. Yet, as 1965 opened, the Battalion's cooks, including WOII B.Dyson, Sergeant G.Toyne, Corporal Bishop (Ration NCO), Lance Corporal Charman and Private Strugnell, were carrying all before them in the Army Cookery Competition, winning first the Brigade and Divisional rounds and then the final itself, returning in triumph to Münster with a magnificent silver rose bowl and individual trophies. The competition was judged not only on the excellence of the meal itself, which included soup, fish, entrée and pudding, but also on such matters as carving, silver and table decoration, and storekeeping and accounting.

On 3 April 1965 the Battalion Squash Rackets team, consisting of Captain M.G.P.Chignell, who had won the BAOR Individual Championship the previous year, Captain R.N.Tillard, Second Lieutenants R.L.Glyn and A.W.Freemantle and Major D.C.Munn, DERR attached to the 1st Battalion, provided a Regimental "double" by winning the Army Cup, having beaten the 4th/7th Royal Dragoon Guards in the Divisional Final, the Queen's Royal Irish Hussars in the BAOR Semi-Final, 1 RHA in the BAOR Final and the School of Artillery in the Army Final.

The 25 April 1965 marked the 50th Anniversary of the initial landings at Gallipoli, during which so many members of the

Regiment had displayed the highest qualities of heroism and self-sacrifice. That heroism, and the terrible losses endured, were now commemorated by the Regiment in three places - in Münster, in Winchester and at Cape Helles itself.

In Münster the 1st Battalion held a drum-head service on the square at Waterloo Barracks, during which an account of the day's events, including the landing from the *River Clyde*, was read by the Adjutant, Captain Ted Horton. As an act of remembrance there was a minute's silence. The lesson was then read by Brigadier Sandy Thomas, Commander of 12 Infantry Brigade, a New Zealander who had joined the Regiment after World War II. During his address the garrison chaplain, the Rev F.W.H.White, emphasised the importance of maintaining traditions such as Gallipoli Day as an inspiration to further efforts in the present and future. After the service the salute was taken by the Colonel of the Regiment as the Battalion marched past.

In Winchester the 4th/5th Battalion exercised its Freedom Rights, marching past the Guildhall where the salute was taken by the Mayor, Councillor S.G.Steel and Major General P.H.Man, representing the Colonel of the Regiment. This was followed by a service of commemoration in the Memorial Garden at Serle's House, during which Major W.R.Dugmore also read a citation dealing with the events of 25 April 1915.

Though the smallest of the three, the commemoration at Cape Helles was, in its way, the most moving. It was attended by a party from the 1st Battalion, including Captain Jim Kellie, Captain Edward Churcher, CSM Spencer Turner and Corporals Peter Hawker, John Turpin and Adrian Barnett, who had driven 2000 miles in the unit minibus to participate.

The ceremonies began at sunrise when the British Ambassador, Sir Dennis Allan, anchored his yacht, *Four Winds*, close to the spot where the *River Clyde* had beached and cast a wreath of poppies onto the water. A small group, consisting of Sir Dennis and Lady Allan, Brigadier Molyneux Carter, OBE, MC, the British Military Attaché to Turkey, six veterans of the landings, the 1st Battalion party and Consular staff, then left V Beach for a short service of commemoration in the now ruined Sedd el Bahr fort, after which they walked across to the Cape Helles monument. Here, several wreaths were laid, including one in memory of the 1200 men of the 2nd, 8th and 10th Battalions of The Hampshire Regiment whose names are carved on the memorial panels of the monument but have no known graves; among the names were those of the uncles of Captain Churcher and CSM Turner.

Later in the day, a larger gathering of British, ANZAC, French and Turkish veterans of the campaign assembled at the Turkish memorial. On the day after the landing a Hampshire had picked up a Turkish trumpet near V Beach. Now, it was returned by Captain Kellie and WOII Turner to a retired Turkish senior officer, General Selatlin Selaœik, together with the gift of a Regimental plaque. Thanking Captain Kellie, General Selaœik said that the trumpet would be placed in the Turkish Army Museum and, in exchange, presented him with a large red pennant on behalf of the Turkish Old Comrades' Association. This, together with some battlefield souvenirs found by the party, is now in the Regimental Museum.

The party returned to Münster on 4 May. For everyone, it had been a humbling experience to listen to the veterans' tales, recounted with a vividness which gave no indication of the passing of fifty years, and to remember that as young soldiers those same veterans, laden with 80 pounds of equipment, had waded without hesitation to the shore through the bullet-flayed shallows of V Beach, losing half their comrades in the process.

Training, as usual, took place at Sennelager and Soltau. At the latter the Battalion gave a demonstration for the French Ecole Superieure de Guerre, taking the form of an advance to contact, air strikes and a helicopter-borne company assault. The Support Platoons then went to Putlos, where training consisted of a competition for all the support platoons in BAOR. In this the anti-tank gunners came third, with Corporal Martin's gun crew producing the second highest individual score of all.

It will be recalled that at this time a shortage of married quarters led to soldiers seeking accommodation for their families outside Münster. Some found it in Wolbeck, a pleasant, friendly village some four miles from Waterloo Barracks, where they were quickly made to feel at home. The principal figure in Wolbeck mythology is the He Goat, to whom a bronze statue has been erected, and who is honoured annually on He Goat Monday, which falls on the first Monday in February. In 1963 the villagers' request that the Band should participate in the celebrations was granted, the result being that not only was it booked for the next two years, but was also so hospitably entertained as to be non-operational the following morning.

GERMANY 1962 — 1965

The friendship between Wolbeck and the Battalion developed to the extent that when it was learned in March 1965 that the latter was expected to leave Germany towards the end of the year, the Burgermeister approached Colonel Reeve-Tucker to request a final performance, and the date of Saturday 29 May was agreed. At first the villagers proposed nothing less than a full scale Freedom March with the Colours and fixed bayonets, but as this would have raised all sorts of diplomatic questions an alternative programme was devised. There would be a football match in the afternoon, then the Band and Drums, replendent in scarlet, would give a concert at the church. Following this, there would be a march past with the Salute being taken by the Burgermeister, a reception, presentations and finally a floodlit display by the Band and Drums.

All went exactly according to plan. The Burgermeister presented Colonel Reeve-Tucker with a beautifully embroidered banner with the arms of Wolbeck on one side and 1st Battalion The Royal Hampshire Regiment inscribed on the other, together with a sealed parchment scroll recording the event. To RSM Jack House he presented an oak fruit bowl with the arms of Wolbeck for the Sergeants' Mess. The Bandmaster, WOI Gregory, was given a lovely old hunting horn and delighted everyone present by blowing a German hunting call. To the pleasure of the villagers, Colonel Reeve-Tucker responded on behalf of the Battalion in German, presenting the Burgermeister with a Regimental flag mounted ready for hanging with drummers' dress cords. The floodlit display by the Band and Drums was greeted with terrific applause. Afterwards, with a genial disregard for the stiffer aspects of protocol, the Freedom of the Village was extended to the Battalion anyway, and the revelry continued well into the early hours of Sunday morning. The day had provided a wonderful example of mutual goodwill, and happily it had coincided with the visit of The Queen to BAOR.

In July the Battalion entered two teams, led respectively by Captain R.N.Tillard, MBE, and Lieutenant J.Martindale, for Exercise Roadmaster II, organised by HQ 1st Division in accordance with the rules of the British Army Motoring Association. Each team consisted of one quarter-ton Land Rover and two three-ton lorries, each with a crew of three, and covered a 1200-mile route during which road, cross-country driving and manoeuvring skills, navigating ability, physical fitness and shooting were all tested. The event lasted five days at the end of which the Battalion teams, by now extremely tired, were rewarded with the Infantry Trophy.

July also saw the Battalion training in Bavaria as a result of an idea conceived by Major John Darroch during his period as Second-in-Command and followed through by his successor, Major A.D.Rouse, MBE, The Devonshire and Dorset Regiment. The companies camped along the Konigstrasse, a forest track connecting Oberammergau with Füssen, and were set a programme of map-reading exercises, route marches and simple hikes. It rained often, the hills were steep and the rocks were hard, but the air was pure and the scenery was the best in Germany. There were, too, days off when it was possible to visit the Passionplatz in Oberammergau or the eccentric King Ludwig's fairytale castle at Füssen, or simply make merry in the numerous hospitable Weinstubes.

Simultaneously, the Assault Pioneer Platoon under Sergeant Winearls were practising their watermanship on the Forgensee, on the shores of which the Battalion had also set up an Adventure Training Camp under Captain J.E.Horton. This ran two four-day courses, each company supplying ten men for each course. Throughout the courses the students administered themselves and, for safety reasons, alcohol was strictly prohibited save on specific occasions. Each day began at 06:30 with a thirty-minute run, followed by a dip in the lake. During the first two days of each course Lieutenant Martindale and Sergeant Rumbold instructed the students on basic canoeing techniques and capsize drills, ending with a short expedition on the lake. Two days of mountaineering followed, in which the tuition in basic principles, ropes and knots was given by Lieutenant Neville, Sergeant Edwards, Corporal Waterworth, Lance Corporal Jamieson and Lance Corporal Barnett. The party then set off to climb the Hochplatte, moving on to a cave 6000 feet above sea level where they spent the night before tackling the Geiselstein and returning to camp next day.

As visitors to the US Zone the Battalion was under some obligation to its hosts and this was discharged by providing the cordon for an escape and evasion exercise involving German and American Rangers as well as "shot down" Luftwaffe pilots. Of the forty-five would-be evaders, thirty-three were captured and conveyed in their underpants to a POW cage where they provided a feast for a colony of vicious horse flies. By the end of the first day the German directing staff had begun expressing serious concern — not because of the prisoners' treatment, which was modest enough compared to what they might expect in reality, but because during a previous exercise only seventeen out of sixty evaders had been captured! Next day a further four prisoners were taken when the Battalion cleared an area of dense, broken woodland.

Training in Bavaria finished with a half-platoon exercise consisting of 45 miles of map-reading in the hills, carried out in continuous rain. This was won by Lieutenant J.K. West of B Company, but up among the leaders was Sergeant Graham Toyne, ACC, the Cook Sergeant, and a party from HQ Company, who were placed fourth and would have come in higher if they had not lost a man through sickness.

While this was going on, A Company, which had entered three teams for the Nijmegen Marches, carried out a 70-mile route march to Blenheim as part of its training programme. The battlefield itself, on which the Regiment won the first of its Battle Honours - Blenheim 1704 - has not attracted the scale of commercial activity present at Waterloo, or, more recently, at Austerlitz, and it proved to be something of a disappointment as the only record of Marlborough's epic victory was a small monument.

Nevertheless, the training in Bavaria had provided the Company with the fitness and confidence to tackle Nijmegen, where its three teams, commanded respectively by Lieutenant E.H.Ozanne and Second Lieutenants D.R.Southwood and R.J.Horton, reported on 26 July. Each eleven-strong team, every member which of carried 22 pounds of equipment including rifle, was required to march a distance of 100 miles in four days. The effort involved was considerable, but this was balanced by the carnival atmosphere in which the marches took place. There were approximately 12,000 participants, including male and female teams from armies all over the Free World, and numerous civilian entries which included teams of London policemen and coal miners from the Ruhr. On the last day the Hampshire teams led their group through the enthusiastic crowds into the centre of Nijmegen, the presence of their own Band putting the spring back into aching feet and tired limbs. No one had fallen out, so each team was awarded a gilded bronze medal and each participant received a commemorative medal.

On the last day of July the Battalion's climbers, including

Lieutenant D.H.Neville, Sergeant Rumbold, Corporal Waterworth, Lance Corporals Chard, Jamieson and Barnett, and Privates Pepper, Willcox, Lambert and Bardwell, set off on Exercise High Reach, during which they were attached to 13th Battalion Chasseurs Alpins, the famous *Diables Bleus*. Drawing kit from the Battalion's depot at Chambery in the French Alps, the party then joined its 2nd Company in a tented camp at 6800 feet. After a period of acclimatisation, it received instruction in the use of crampons and ice axes and was taught how to escape from a crevasse. It then undertook several climbs with the Chasseurs' A1 Echelon, during which it had the opportunity of observing professionals at work. Climbs, for example, began no later than 03:00 so that the ascent and descent could be completed before the sun rendered the snow soft and dangerous. During the next week the party climbed Albaron (11,181 feet), Grande Motte (11,668 feet) and Mont Brevent (8275 feet). The last four days of the exercise were spent at the French Army's High Mountain School at Chamonix. Rescue duties meant that the French were unable to provide a guide necessary for the ascent of Mont Blanc, but the party contented itself by climbing the Aiguille du Midi (12,602 feet). During the farewell party at Chambery a Regimental plaque was presented to the Chasseurs in recognition of their kindness and hospitality.

However monotonous the North German Plain might be, and however humdrum the repetitious training cycles of Sennelager, Soltau and Putlos were, the events of 1965 demonstrated without doubt that, with a little imagination and energy, service in BAOR could be stimulating, challenging and rewarding. The year also provided the Regiment as a whole cause for great pride when Sergeant John Wheeler, MM, a veteran of Malaya serving extra-regimentally as a weapon training instructor at the Royal Military Academy, Sandhurst, was chaired off the range at Bisley having become the Army's Champion Shot with a score of 634 points out of a possible 750. Sergeant Wheeler had joined the Army as a Junior Leader in 1952 and was the first member of the Regiment to win this coveted title.

In August B Company, commanded by Major D.C.Munn, trained with the Danish Army for ten days at Aalborg. In October the Battalion took part in Exercise Double Deal, which was to be its last major exercise of the year and indeed of its current tour in BAOR. This involved a river crossing of the Weser at

Nienburg, following which it exploited its success so rapidly that the exercise had to be stopped on three separate occasions so that the enemy could take up new positions.

Following its return to Münster, four weeks of hectic activity ensued during which it handed over Waterloo Barracks to its successors, the 1st Battalion The Devonshire and Dorset Regiment. In December the Battalion left Germany by air for the UK, where it would be based briefly in Aldershot prior to flying to the Far East for operational duties.

* * * * * * * * *

MINDEN ROSES

EXTRACT OF LETTER DATED 24 AUGUST 1964 FROM N.M.HALLET, ESQ, HM CONSUL IN KANSAS CITY, MISSOURI,TO LIEUTENANT COLONEL T.S.W.REEVE-TUCKER, COMMANDING 1st BATTALION THE ROYAL HAMPSHIRE REGIMENT

"On arrival at this consular post less than a year ago, I was told that for many successive years the Consulate had received on 1st August, Minden Day, an anonymous gift of six red roses in memory of the fallen of the six British Regiments which took part in the Battle of Minden in 1759. In 1958 some publicity had been given to this in the local newspaper, when an attempt to identify the sender revealed that he had subscribed the florist's order card cryptically as 'M.Day, 1759 Albion.'

"This year the roses arrived as usual on 1st August, accompanied by a card which merely listed the six Regiments. Both the British Liaison Officer at Fort Leavenworth and the Secretary of the British Defence Staff in Washington have been interested in hearing of this, and it is to the former that I am indebted for the suggestion that I should write to the Commanding Officers of the Regiments concerned to let them know of this rather moving and constant memorial tribute to the 'Minden Regiments.'

"It gives me great pleasure, therefore, to let you know that someone in so distant a place as the heart of the Middle West remembers regularly the anniversary of the Battle of Minden and marks his remembrance with such a gift."

THE HAMPSHIRE TIGERS

"The sender obviously wishes his anonymity to be respected, but I should like to let him (or her) know, by courtesy of your columns, that Her Majesty's consul and his staff are deeply appreciative of this gift of roses in tribute to the Minden Regiments and in memory of the soldiers who fell in that battle.

"Whoever he may be - whether an American citizen or a former member of one of the British regiments - we hope he will see this expression of our thanks and appreciation."

So far as is known, the identity of the donor has never been discovered.

KHYBER TO CARIBBEAN

(Extract from the May 1963 issue of the Regimental Journal)

If you go up the Khyber Pass towards the Afghan border you will come to a cliff face covered with Regimental crests. One of them is ours, placed there by the 1st Battalion just before World War II. In Kuala Lumpur you will see in the garrison church a plaque to commemorate the Battalion's tour in Malaya 1953-56. Indeed, wherever we have been we have left our mark and the Regiment's name is inscribed in some way in practically every corner of the world. Our last such installations were in Jamaica and British Honduras. In Jamaica, up in the hills of Newcastle, we carved our crest on the battlements there - the last crest of the many regiments who have garrisoned Jamaica for 300 years. In British Honduras we left behind an inscribed bell (cliffs being at a premium in BH!) just before Major John Darroch with Y Company flew out from this remarkable little Central American colony in mid '62. These are but tangible records of our sojourn invarious parts of the world, and we can properly take an interest in them. Thet are, of course, no substitute for the more lasting record of good behaviour and duty well done which is the hallmark of the Regiment's service everywhere.

GERMANY 1962 — 1965

THE SWORDSMAN

After leaving the Regiment, Lieutenant Peter Jacobs, a National Service Officer who went on to study at Queen's College, Cambridge, won international renown during 1963 for his skill with the épée. At the 1963 Empire Games he was part of the English épée team which won the Gold Medal, personally defeating a taller, heavier and more experienced opponent in the process, and also won the Bronze Medal in the individual event. In the Paris Challenge Picon he beat all comers and won the De Gaulle personal cup. At the World University Games in Porto Allegro, Brazil, he gained a further Gold Medal by winning the individual épée title.

* * * * * * * * *

EXERCISE TREBLE CHANCE

(A "sideways view" expressed in the May 1965 issue of the Regimental Journal)

Exercise Treble Chance was divided into three distinctive phases. Phases 1A and 1B were small one-day exercises, notable for the variety of mushroom fields that the Company passed through, and Phase 2 was the main exercise.

1B was the attack in which the Company was to trundle along the road on a one-vehicle front meeting various forms of opposition. This went reasonably well until after lunch. Support Platoon and Company Headquarters were motoring along through a German village in their usual position at the rear of the column when suddenly, up from behind fences and walls, sprouted many members of the Bundeswehr, pointing weapons in our direction. As the Germans are, however, our NATO friends and allies, much fraternisation and waving of greetings took place. This idyllic scene was shattered by the arrival of the Brigadier who announced that in *this* exercise the Germans were the enemy and that therefore everyone was dead for two hours. Everyone then staggered dying into a Gasthaus and waited comfortably there for the Resurrection.

Treble Chance 2 started at three o'clock in the morning with the occupation of a defensive position. When it became light and people were still digging in, a man in running kit was seen running round the Company's position. He was obviously a Canadian spy and was therefore chased and caught by two fit

189

Hampshiremen who brought him back for interrogation. It was some time later that the badly frightened man was able to convince his ruthless captors that he really was a German civilian!

Later on, Canadian OPs appeared on the far side of the river and were mortared out of existence every few minutes. Nobody told them this so they stayed where they were. When the Canadians appeared in strength and attempted to cross the river in front of B Company, they had the misfortune to be on the same radio frequency as the B Company mortars. The Support Platoon Commander and Corporal Freyer, assuming Canadian accents, then spent the night having conversations with an amiable Canadian assault platoon commander who insisted on sending frequent sitreps. When, the next morning, Lieutenant Willing captured several Canadians complete with a marked map, certain pieces fitted together.

The next morning the Canadians announced in clear that they were going to "Take out a company of the enemy." When we consulted our maps this was seen to be us. However, A Company lent us a platoon under Lieutenant Curtis to assist in the battle, and the Canadian take-over bid failed, but not before the operator of a 4th/7th Dragoon Guards' tank in our position, appreciating that the situation was tricky, had bravely eaten his Griddle to prevent it falling into enemy hands. The next day, after a worthwhile attack across a river, a worthwhile exercise came to an end.

* * * * * * * * *

CHAPTER 9

EMERGENCY TOUR IN BORNEO AND A FURTHER FREEDOM — 1966

The 1st Battalion leaves for the Far East - nature of Confrontation between Malaysia and Indonesia - Jungle Warfare School at Ulu Tiram - Hong Kong - Battalion responsibility in Borneo - A Company at Ulu - B Company at Serudong Laut - Y Company at Kalabakan - Z Company and the Tawau Assault Group - the end of the Confrontation - Indonesian incursions and Operation Timber Top - capture of armed intruders - 4th/5th Battalion and the Freedom of Basingstoke

After block leave the 1st Battalion reassembled in Montgomery Lines, Aldershot, at the beginning of January 1966. Its stay, however, would be a matter of weeks only, during which the major social event was a large luncheon party held in the Officers' Club, attended by Lord Louis Mountbatten, Major General Pat Man, GOC Aldershot District, and several generations of the Regiment's Officers, both Regular and Territorial.

Meanwhile, preparations continued apace for the Battalion's departure on an unaccompanied emergency tour of duty in the Far East. Z Company, which had been absent from its order of battle since 1962, was re-formed, jungle greens were issued and everyone received a civilian passport in which the bearer's occupation was inscribed as Government Servant, this precaution being considered necessary to avoid diplomatic incidents in the event of an aircraft having to make an emergency landing in one of several potentially unfriendly countries that would be overflown. No such incident is known to have taken place; had it done so, the presence of so many fit Government Servants of military age, for all their wearing of civilian clothes, might just have lit a bulb within the dimmest head of the potentially unfriendly immigration service.

The reason for the Battalion's departure was the Confrontation which had existed for some time between Malaysia and Indonesia, "Confronation" being a 1960s Newspeak word used to describe a situation in which wars could be fought without their being declared, and thus ignored by everyone else. The proximate cause of the conflict lay in the desire of Ahmed Sukarno, the ageing President of Indonesia, to generate a little popularity for himself by creating a Greater Indonesia, incorporating the Malay Peninsula, Singapore and the three territories of British Borneo - Sarawak, Brunei and North Borneo or Sabah. Well aware of his neighbour's ambitions, Tunku Abdul Rahman, Prime Minister of the Malayan Federation since Independence, recognised that to survive his country must expand into a larger and more viable political unit that would itself absorb the Borneo territories into the Federation of Malaysia, brought into existence on 16 September 1963. Brunei did not join the Federation but of course had parallel interests in the developing situation.

Sukarno, who had already tried unsuccessfully to engineer a rising in Brunei and was regularly inserting subversive elements across the frontier, now announced that the Confrontation had begun. In fact, the British and Malaysians were ready for him. In December 1962 Major General Walter Walker was appointed Commander British Troops Borneo and since then he had established the infrastructure that would enable him to meet the threat, setting up a joint headquarters to co-ordinate the activities of the three services, the police and the intelligence-gathering agencies. His command was steadily expanded until, by March 1965, it consisted of thirteen infantry battalions, about half of which were British and the rest Gurkha, Malaysian, Australian and New Zealand. The ground troops included a composite British/ANZAC SAS Regiment, the 1550-strong Border Scouts, recruited from indigenous tribes, two battalions of the Police Field Force, and two regiments each of armoured cars, artillery and engineers. In addition there were eighty helicopters and some forty fixed-wing aircraft including Javelin jet fighters capable of giving ground support. Offshore and on the rivers, the Royal Navy maintained a fleet of coastal minesweepers and patrol craft.

Initially, British strategy was simply to defend the 900-mile frontier separating Sarawak and Sabah from Kalimantan, as Indonesian Borneo was called. For the most part, this ran through wild mountain ranges covered in thick jungle and was in places so inaccessible that it remained unmapped. This terrain, of course, was just as difficult for the enemy, whose only approach lay along established trails that could be watched, or in longboats on the rivers which formed the principal highways of the area. The likely crossing places were defended by a series of fortified bases, a mile or so inside Malaysian territory. These were usually held in company or platoon strength and were surrounded by a perimeter of barbed wire or bamboo panjis. The vegetation around the forts was cleared to give a good field of fire and the probable avenues of attack covered by Claymore mines, capable of blasting a horizontal hail of ball bearings through anything in their path. The use of sensitive seismic detectors registering footsteps provided the defenders with advanced listening posts. Within, bunkers and trenches protected the garrison and emplacements were constructed for one or more 81mm mortars or light 105mm howitzers, which were lifted into position by Belvedere helicopters. Whenever possible, forts were situated so that they could provide each other with mutual artillery support.

The bulk of Walker's troops, however, were stationed in camps further back and were employed as a rapid reaction force capable of deployment by helicopter into a threatened sector. Thus, when the Indonesians did achieve a minor success or two in overrunning a small outpost or attacking a village, very few of them lived to tell the tale, as rapid reaction forces were quickly lifted by helicopter into ambush positions along the raiders' line of retreat to the frontier.

By March 1964 Sukharno had replaced his "volunteers," whatever that meant, with regular army units and the tempo of operations increased. By September it had become clear that the Indonesians had established bases of their own beyond the frontier. At first, the British government was reluctant to permit cross-border strikes to eliminate these, but relented when the enemy began inserting parties onto the Malayan mainland, all of whom were quickly rounded up. Forays into Indonesian territory were generally made in company strength against objectives which had been carefully reconnoitred by the SAS, with artillery but normally without air support. Initially, such raids were sanctioned to a depth of 2000 metres, later raised to 10,000 metres and, in special circumstances, to 20,000 metres. These actions were cloaked in secrecy but were fiercely contested and proved the efficiency of the light anti-tank rocket launcher (LAW) when employed against machine gun posts and buildings.

This offensive policy was maintained by Major General George Lea when he took over from General Walker in 1965. In addition to guarding the frontier, the security forces also had to maintain watch on the Clandestine Communist Organisation, political cousins of those who had been defeated during the Malayan Emergency, who drew most of their strength from the urban Chinese population but were too weak and scattered to achieve much.

Such, then, was the state of play when the 1st Battalion The Royal Hampshire Regiment flew out of England at the end of January 1966. One party, consisting of the Second-in-Command, the Company Commanders, the Platoon Commanders and the Platoon Sergeants of every platoon in the Battalion, flew direct to Singapore and then, after a weekend at Nee Soon Transit Camp, travelled to the Jungle Warfare School at Ulu Tiram on the Johore Bahru-Kota Tinggi Road, where they commenced a two month cadre course which would enable them to instruct the rest of the Battalion when it arrived. This was broadly similar to the training described in the chapter on the Malayan Emergency, save that the American M16 Armalite rifle was gaining approval as a tool of jungle warfare in preference to the SLR, being both shorter and lighter; the 7.62mm Bren, on the other hand, remained the preferred light machine gun.

The rest of the Battalion flew to Hong Kong, this being the usual induction route for units on their way to the Borneo Confrontation. Here it was accommodated in Fan Gardens Camp, 20 miles north of Kowloon, with A, B and Y Companies some two miles away and close to the border with Red China at Dodwells Ridge Camp. Those based at the latter inevitably became known as The Diddy Dodwell Men; lest future generations find this completely incomprehensible, it is a reference to the comedian Ken Dodd's famous Diddy Men: small, jovial, colourfully dressed characters who mined treacle for a living!

Most of the time in Hong Kong was spent getting fit, improving snap-shooting techniques, or practising internal security

194

and riot control drills. With exquisite timing, Murphy's Law swung into action to produce a real riot in Kowloon and a composite company of Royal Hampshires and Green Howards was called out to restore order during their handover/takeover period. At the end of March the companies began leaving for Singapore by Landing Ships Tank, the flat bottoms of which did not make for a comfortable passage of the South China Sea. Before leaving, the following message was received from Lieutenant General Sir Dennis O'Connor, KBE, CBE:

> "Now that your Battalion is about to leave Hong Kong for an operational tour in Borneo please convey to all ranks my very best wishes for the future. It has been a particular pleasure and privilege for me to have had your Battalion under my command as a motor battalion in 6 Armd. Div in BAOR in 57/58 and again in Hong Kong. I have been most impressed with the high standards of your Battalion and know that in Borneo you will acquit yourselves in the highest traditions of your Regiment. Good luck to you all."

Ironically, during this period Sukharno was stripped of power by his generals and the leaders of the new Indonesian government, having reached the conclusion that the policy of Confrontation was leading nowhere, decided to end it. Talks began in Bangkok between their representatives and those of the Tunku to discuss a mutually agreeable formula. In the meantime, nothing had changed and nothing could therefore be taken for granted.

The Battalion's own jungle warfare course at Ulu Tiram involved everyone in six weeks' intense training and culminated in eight-day company exercises. Despite this, there was time for an inter-company football tournament and chances to visit Singapore, Kuala Lumpur, Malacca and Mersing. On leaving Ulu Tiram the companies flew or sailed aboard LSLs or LSTs from Singapore to Tawau on the eastern coast of Sabah. On 17 June 1966 the Battalion assumed responsibility for 60 miles of border, taking over from the 2nd Battalion The Royal Green Jackets, where it found itself in the unique position of forming part of a Malaysian brigade. At first, this seemed to cause outsiders a little confusion, for someone, on learning that the Hampshires were now in charge, wrote a letter to "I.R.Hamps, Esq, Officer Commanding 2nd Royal Green Jackets!"

At the Jungle Warfare School Colonel Bill Reeve-Tucker handed over command of the 1st Battalion to Lieutenant Colonel M.F.A.Wilson on taking up a staff appointment in Hong Kong. Of Colonel Reeve-Tucker the Journal records, "It is sufficient to say that he was respected and liked by all who served under him, and will be remembered as a fine soldier and an understanding Commanding Officer."

Operationally, the Battalion was dispersed across a very wide area, with Battalion HQ and Y Company at Kalabakan, a logging centre, A Company at Ulu, B Company at Serudong Laut, and Z Company at Wallace Bay with the Reconnaissance Platoon up-river at a fortified base named Point 281 under Captain Hastings Neville and Sergeant Withers, thus giving three companies forward and one in reserve. Each rifle company had its Iban trackers, just as it had during the Malayan Emergency, and a mortar section. In addition, the Battalion had an Air Platoon equipped with two Sioux helicopters, and a boat platoon. Artillery support was provided by 38 (Seringapatam) Battery, 40 Light Regiment RA, also known as The Tigers.

Fortunately, each company has left a record of life in its outpost. A Company was commanded by Major Peter Essame, Devonshire and Dorset Regiment, and its first impressions of Ulu were depressing:

"Set in the middle of nowhere, surrounded by miles of jungle and a double perimeter of wire, two hundred yards long and fifty wide, Ulu was a product of the times, being completely dependent on the helicopter. A shanty town bunkerland, the first impressions from the air were dismal, these being confirmed on the ground.

"Facing outwards the parapets of the bunkers were ready to be manned by the people living in them at dawn and dusk stand-tos and that single fact was the only one we never really liked. Stumbling around in the dark every morning before dawn to get stood-to can get tedious after the first thirty or forty times. Apart from that, however, the whole Company was surprised to find that the first impressions were false impressions and that life was not only bearable, but thoroughly satisfying. Everybody seemed to enjoy living at Ulu.

"Basically we were responsible for patrolling the large section of the border nearby. There was always a platoon on patrol so that we got to know the area well. Everybody arrived where they had intended to and this in itself was no small achievement in a virtually unmapped area. The jungle was primary and pig-ridden and no mystery at all, especially to our Ibans. At the end of two months at Ulu everybody was fit. The constant physical exercise and the lack of clothes worn around the base camp combined to bring out some permanent looking tans, more black than brown. In retrospect the advantages and disadvantages of Ulu were negative ones - no mosquitos, but no lights; no drink and no women, but no big bills, and everybody saved." In such a place good administration is vital and Private "Archie" Moore, the medical orderly, Private Gibson, responsible for water, Private Brown in the canteen and Corporal Ted Hayward, with Privates Devine, Vanstone and Joynes, the cooks, were among the more important members of the Company.

B Company was commanded by Major David Munn, The Duke of Edinburgh's Royal Regiment. Its fort on the Serudong river was slightly less isolated in that boats could be used in addition to helicopters to maintain contact with the outside world. "The fort was some 4000 yards from the Indonesian border and provided a secure base for mounting jungle patrols going out on border surveillance. This was to be our home for four months during the Confrontation. Command posts, barbed wire obstacles, DF tasks, fixed lines and dugouts are terms more in keeping with trench warfare than jungle operations, although we soon became accustomed to our new way of life under the watchful eye of the Company's Second-in-Command, Captain Buster Russell, and CSM Spence Turner."

At Kalabakan, in addition to holding the main base camp, Y Company, commanded by Major Alan Imrie, was also responsible for holding three advanced positions, the Upper and Lower Necks, a thousand yards distant, and a hill named Tempilat, ten minutes away by helicopter, where a rifle section guarded the Battalion rebroadcast station.

"The Company quietly slipped into a routine of one week on the Necks, one week patrolling and one week camp fatigues, which included loading and unloading the supply ships from Tawau, and the helicopters. Whilst the amenities in Kalabakan were undoubtedly better than those of A and B Companies, the Company, because of its proximity to Battalion HQ, undoubtedly had an extra load of duties to shoulder and could not have quite the same relaxed atmosphere as the other three companies.

The Company mounted four quarter guards, all trained by CSM Tony Cripps, including those for the visit of Mr Healey, Secretary of State for Defence, and Lieutenant General Sir Michael Carver, C-in-C FARELF.

"The Company, as it was in reserve, patrolled well back from the Indonesian frontier. Much of its area had been logged a few years back which made going difficult. Each platoon developed and practised its jungle skills and soon found that the base camps on top of hills were good but for the problem of water. As there was none immediately available, water bags had to be carried several hundred yards and each man had either two or three water bottles of his own.

"The Necks overlooked the Kalabakan river and were miniature defensive positions with dug-outs and Claymore mines laid on the approaches. In both positions, living conditions were primitive, but constant maintenance of the positions helped pass the time. Also, over-friendly wild pigs gave a chance of 'big game hunting,' but they all escaped. Rumour also had it that ghosts from a Muslim cemetery adjacent to the Lower Neck used to pay social calls but they never left their visiting cards. Corporal Preston and others of 8 Platoon claimed they saw crocodiles basking on the other side of the river to the Lower Neck, but none were ever shot and brought back to prove the point.

"On Tempilat, the altitude of 3000 feet made life very pleasant, and the Company virtually used the camp as its change of air station. On a fine day there was an excellent view southwards over the Indonesian frontier. Plenty of wild life was around the camp, such as Orang Utang, wild bear and cat, and of course the odd snake - Lieutenant A.W.Freemantle's platoon actually killed and curried a 21-foot python near Kalabakan."

When, towards the end of the Confrontation, A Company was withdrawn to Tawau, blowing up its fort at Ulu, Y Company's patrol area was extended right up to the Indonesian border.

For its part, Z Company, commanded by Major Tim Wellings, formed the lynchpin of the Tawau Assault Group (TAG), a joint military and naval group whose purpose was to maintain watch on a force of Indonesian Marines partly based on Nanukan Island and partly on the Indonesian portion of Sebatik Island.

"The area contained the main sea approach to Tawau past the Wallace Bay timber firm's headquarters on Sebatik, and four main river approaches leading into the interior and to B Company and Battalion HQ. It is totally tidal throughout and the mangrove swamp between the main rivers is intersected by a maze of channels and creeks, some impassable, some navigable only at certain states of the tide. In the channel and rivers there is a 5-7 knot tide with a rise and fall of 15 feet. The waters are littered with submerged logs, floating palm trees, and the deadly 'sinkers' - half waterlogged logs with their ends at an angle of 45 degrees just below the surface. To this must be added treacherous currents, eddies and sandbanks. Altogether not normal country for infantry soldiers!"

The Officer Commanding Z Company was, by virtue of his office, also Senior Officer TAG or SOTAG. The Company carried out foot patrols in its few "dry" areas, but the bulk of its work took place in powered assault boats operating from LCPs of the Royal Malaysian Navy. The location of boat observation posts and patrol areas were intentionally varied to prevent the enemy detecting any sort of pattern. In the event of trouble the patrols could call on artillery support and invoke the intervention of guardships or piquet vessels belonging to the Royal Navy, the Royal Australian Navy and the Royal Malaysian Navy, several of which lay back in the river complex by day and replaced the boat patrols at night. Efficient inter-service VHF radio communications were maintained by 517 Troop Royal Signals, whose operators spent an average of 247 hours on their sets during the tour, which ended with the disbandment of TAG in September.

At this period in the war the official policy was not to seek out the enemy and provoke an engagement with him; on the other hand, if he crossed the border he was to be given a bloody nose, and cross-border fire was to be returned in kind. Late one evening, the Border Observation Boat, manned by a team from the Reconnaissance Platoon, and anchored in the channel on "our" side of the border, was fired on from an Indonesian island on which an enemy brigade HQ was known to be located. It just so happened that at that precise moment Captain Hastings Neville, commanding the Reconnaissance Platoon, was on board the Australian mine hunter HMAS *Snipe*. Fortunately there were no casualties but the Captain and Captain Neville estimated that some 40 rounds of 20mm ammunition had been used by the Indonesians. The Captain stood-to his 40mm gun crew and, turning to Captain Neville, said, "40 rounds of 20mm equals 20 rounds of 40mm in my book, do you agree?" Targets were selected and engaged.

As the Royal Navy and Special Forces had built up a very accurate location map of the enemy's buildings and distances to them, first round hits were virtually guaranteed. Several rounds were directed with great accuracy into the enemy Officers' Mess. For the rest of the tour the Indonesians showed no interest in repeating the incident!

HQ Company was based at Imam Camp, Tawau, where the Company Commander, Major Tony Luckham, and the Quartermasters, Captain Les Edmonds and Lieutenant Harry Barnard, MBE, were responsible for supplying the Battalion with everything it needed. Here supply ships had to be unloaded and small boats and helicopters were loaded and sent forward by the Company Resupply NCOs, respectively Corporal Austin (A), Corporal Evans (B), Sergeant Barton (Y) and Corporal Grist (Z). At Kalabakan the Battalion had its own airstrip, managed by Corporal Moss with Corporal Griffin of the Signal Platoon serving as a very professional air traffic controller. The monthly lift to A Company could be as much as 12,000lbs and in one record month the airstrip handled 3221 passengers and 212,355-lbs of freight.

In parallel with the regular logisticians worked the Battalion Contractor, Mohammed Ibrahim, who had also worked for the Battalion during the Malayan Emergency. He would provide almost anything that was needed from a twenty-four-hour refreshment service to the most unlikely items requested by soldiers marooned in jungle bases. Contractors were well-informed people and Regimental legend has it that Mohammed Ibrahim wrote to Colonel Reeve-Tucker in Germany to tell him that the Battalion was going to the Far East long before the military authorities did so!

Given the difficult terrain in which the Battalion was required to operate, the Signal Platoon, commanded by Captain Edward Churcher with Sergeant Rose as radio sergeant, played an indispensable role with great efficiency, including establishing a rebroadcast station on Mt Tempilat, which was run chiefly by Corporal Crawley. The Paymaster, Major Douglas Stimpson, also worked in difficult conditions, albeit of a different kind, as within a period of twelve months the Battalion served in Münster, Aldershot, Hong Kong, Malaya, Sabah, Singapore and Netheravon!

On 11 August 1966 the representatives of Malaysia and Indonesia signed an accord bringing the state of Confrontation to an end. During its operations the Battalion had sustained one tragic death, that of Private Malcolm Reeder of B Company, while on patrol. Its grip on its own sector of the border had been so complete that the enemy had not even bothered to try conclusions, and this made what followed all the more inexplicable.

On 25 August the Battalion was informed that the Indonesians had mounted an operation against Kalabakan. As one of their few successes during the Confrontation had been an attack on the village three years earlier, coupled with a raid on the food store at the nearby 12 Mile Village, the report was taken very seriously.

The Battalion's response, codenamed Operation Timber Top, was undertaken by Y Company under Major Alan Imrie with a platoon of A Company under command. Coming to grips with the intruders was a slow, painstaking business. A cordon-and-search operation at 12 Mile Village produced a store of rice in the house of a known Indonesian sympathiser. The enemy, however, remained elusive. Various sightings suggested that they consisted of a four-strong party, well armed but hungry and probably lost. Patrols, ambushes and, on two occasions, the searching of an area with 81mm mortar fire, failed to induce a contact. As the operational area involved was too large to search with the troops available a change of tactics was devised. On 20 September all logging vehicles were given "shotgun" escorts as they made their regular runs up and down the dusty tracks. This quickly produced the required result for at about 15:00 a vehicle with Lance Corporal Munday and Private Cook aboard came across the intruders standing beside a track near 12 Mile Village. Although each was armed with an FN rifle and 200 rounds of ammunition and they had six grenades between them, they all surrendered promptly. Just what they intended to achieve by their jungle wanderings, forty days after the end of the Confrontation, remained unclear. It seems, however, to have been part of a high-level policy, for the following month another member of the Regiment, Major J.R.E.Laird, serving with the Royal Brunei Malay Regiment, was awarded a Brunei decoration, the Bintang Perwira Agong Negara Brunei, for the part he played in the capture of four more armed infiltrators in Temburong, leading two platoons in dangerous sweeps to flush them out.

The satisfactory conclusion of Operation Timber Top marked the end of the 1st Battalion's part in the Confrontation and in fact its withdrawal had already been scheduled before the

Indonesian incursion. After handing over to the 7th Battalion Royal Malay Regiment some flew to Singapore from Tawau and the remainder sailed aboard the MV *Auby* on 12 October. On reaching Singapore a week was spent at Nee Soon Transit Camp, where tropical kit was handed in. On 28 October the Battalion flew back to the United Kingdom, departing for six weeks' disembarkation leave on landing.

While the 1st Battalion was in Borneo the Honorary Freedom of the Borough of Basingstoke had been conferred on the Regiment during a parade held at the War Memorial Park, Basingstoke, on 16 July 1966. The Regiment was represented by the 4th/5th (TA) Battalion and the Bands of the 1st and 4th/5th Battalions, the former playing from the bandstand before and after the parade, some seventy members of the Comrades' Association and the local detachment of the Army Cadet Force. Commanding the parade was Major G.J.Fulford, TD; the Colour Party of the 4th/5th (TA) Battalion consisted of Lieutenant A.R.Oakley (Queen's Colour), Lieutenant T.P.Lowden (Regimental Colour), WOII Browning, Colour Sergeants Dear and Cleary (Escort), and the Comrades' Association Contingent was led by the Vice-Lord Lieutenant of Hampshire, Colonel the Rt Hon the Earl of Malmesbury, TD. The parade was attended by Admiral of the Fleet The Earl Mountbatten of Burma, KG, Chief of the Defence Staff, in his capacity as Honorary Colonel of the 4th/5th (TA) Battalion, and the Colonel of the Regiment, both of whom were received with their respective General Salutes.

On handing the Freedom scroll and its casket to the Colonel of the Regiment, the Mayor of Basingstoke, Councillor Harold Redstall, said that, "The words on the scroll do little justice to our warmth of feeling for the Regiment; its history of valour and distinguished service make it an honour to give them the Freedom of Basingstoke."

In reply, General Dick Batten thanked the Mayor for the honour which had been conferred upon the Regiment and said that a direct connection existed through the old Militia with the Hampshire archers who had fought at Agincourt in 1415 and whose skills and gallantry won the award by King Henry V of the red rose which still formed part of the Regiment's badge. (The wyvern had never been adopted as a cap badge by the Regiment's Territorial battalions.)

After the ceremony the 4th/5th (TA) Battalion and its Band

exercised their Freedom rights with a march through the decorated streets of the town. The Regiment was then entertained to tea in marquees in the War Memorial Park and later that evening the officers held a cocktail party for representatives of the Borough in the Town Hall. The parade, held on a wonderful summer day, had been a tremendous success for the Regiment and the townspeople alike. While it was regretted that, for obvious reasons, the 1st Battalion could not be present, it was felt fitting in many ways that the 4th/5th Battalion, now in its final year of service, should have represented the Regiment on this stirring occasion.

* * * * * * * * *

THE HAMPSHIRE GRENADIER

On 12 May 1764, Thomas Thetcher, a twenty-six-year old Grenadier of the North Hampshire Militia, died of a violent fever contracted, it was said, by drinking small (i.e. weak) beer when hot. He was evidently a very popular man, for his comrades paid for a memorial stone to be erected in the precincts of Winchester Cathedral, inscribed with the words:

> *Here sleeps in peace a Hampshire Grenadier,*
> *Who caught his death by drinking cold small Beer,*
> *Soldiers be wise from his untimely fall,*
> *And when ye're hot drink Strong or none at all.*

Seventeen years later the stone, having decayed, was replaced by the Officers of the Winchester garrison, who added the following lines:

> *An honest Soldier never is forgot,*
> *Whether he died by Musket or by Pot.*

Somehow the replacement stone was irreparably damaged and was itself replaced by the North Hampshire Militia when that unit disbanded in 1802. This time it survived until 1966, when a survey indicated that it was in danger of collapsing. Thanks to two former members of the Regiment, Mr A. E. Edmonds and Mr W. W. Powell, who made the necessary arrangements and contributed half the cost, the Cathedral authorities granted the Regiment permission to replace it, which was duly done. Both Mr Edmonds and Mr Powell insisted that their generosity should be concealed within the additional inscription

And again replaced by The Royal Hampshire Regiment 1966

but it is entirely appropriate that it should be recorded in these pages.

CHAPTER 10

STRATEGIC RESERVE :
NETHERAVON AND CYPRUS
1966 — 1969

Reorganisation and training for airportable role - the Torrey Canyon disaster - the Squash Rackets team win the Army Cup for the second time - training at Otterburn and in Cyprus - Exercise Unison - the Winchester Trophy - Freedom Marches through Aldershot, Winchester, Basingstoke, Southampton and Portsmouth - night training - running the Infantry Display at the Aldershot Show - KAPE Tour 1968 - announcement of amalgamation with The Gloucestershire Regiment and related discussions - Regimental plaque for tigress Rose - Exercise Iron Duke - Freedom Marches through Bournemouth and Romsey - Lieutenant Colonel Wilson succeeded in Command by Lieutenant Colonel W.R.B.May, MC - posting to Cyprus as part of UNFICYP - 1st Battalion's role and duties - founding of *Tiger Rag* - distinguished visitors - UN Medal Parade - return to Netheravon - D Day Commemoration Parades in Normandy - contingent supplied for the funeral of Field Marshal Earl Alexander of Tunis - reversion to Regimental cap badge on Minden Day 1969

In December 1966 the 1st Battalion returned from disembarkation leave to Airfield Camp at Netheravon in Wiltshire. The camp itself was comfortable enough, but the feeling of many, as the winter winds howled in off Salisbury Plain, was that there was rather too much air about the place, and there were definite twinges of nostalgia for the tropical warmth of Sabah. Here the Battalion said farewell to RSM Jack House, who had kept it up to the mark despite its numerous moves and fragmented postings.

He was succeeded by RSM G.S.Thomas, a former member of the Regiment who on this occasion rejoined from the Glosters.

The Battalion now formed part of 5 Infantry Brigade, 3rd Division, the Army's Strategic Reserve, and after the Christmas and New Year celebrations were over, it began 1967 training for its airportable role, which could take it to any part of the world at short notice. Once again, Z Company ceased to be a rifle company, its new role being broadly similar to that of the old Support Company in that it administered the specialist Mortar, Anti-Tank, Assault Pioneer and Reconnaissance Platoons, as well as the Battalion Training Wing. The need for a Machine Gun Platoon had disappeared with the issue of the General Purpose Machine Gun (GPMG), which took the place of both the Bren LMG and the Vickers MMG. The GPMG was a belt-fed weapon which could either perform the LMG role within sections and platoons, or, using a heavy duty barrel and mounting, the sustained fire role. At this point it is worth mentioning that the erratic Sten submachine gun carried by platoon and section commanders had already been replaced in 1959 by the more robust and reliable Sterling SMG. To this day, legend has it that each Sten cost 7/6d (37p) to manufacture; in fact, the figure was about £2.50, still well within the Woolworth's price range.

Colonel Wilson had been informed that the Battalion would be exercised in its new role early in March and in preparation for this two Command Post and Air Documentation exercises were held. Exercise Stardust itself had been set jointly by the HQ 3rd Division and 38 Group RAF to test the use of helicopters in the tactical and logistical support of a brigade. After passing through a Movement Control checkpoint at Tidworth the Battalion was moved to a notional "forward" airfield at RAF Odiham in coaches instead of aircraft. The companies were then lifted by helicopter to the "trouble spot" and immediately became involved in counter-insurgency operations. During the later phases of the exercise these were escalated to a limited war scenario, involving a Battalion attack across the Avon towards Airfield Camp.

Easter leave began on 23 March 1967 and was abruptly terminated two days later by the wrecking of the tanker *Torrey Canyon* off the Cornish coast, as a result of which thousands of gallons of crude oil were disgorged into the sea and washed ashore. Such was the scale of the disaster that the civil authorities requested immediate military assistance. As a result of this the

Battalion quickly reassembled in response to Adjutant Captain John Southwood's despatch of 450 recall telegrams and 50 telephone calls and on the morning of 27 March was on its way to Cornwall by train. In the meantime, Colonel Wilson had been flown around the Cornish coastline and attended the first of many conferences with civil and military representatives in Penzance, where Battalion HQ was established. The Battalion's area of responsibility extended from Falmouth in the south and thence westwards round Lands End and north to St Ives. On arrival, the companies were accommodated in TA drill halls - Major John Morrish's A Company at Porthleven, Major Buster Russell's B Company at Camborne and Major Tim Wellings' Y Company at St Ives.

After two days of instruction in the use of detergent, the great clean-up began. Those using the detergent equipment were dressed in protective clothing consisting of black oilskin-type jackets and trousers, foul weather boots, goggles and gloves. The 40-gallon drums of detergent were taken as close to the areas of pollution as possible. When they could not be transported by vehicle to the site they were flown in by RN and RAF helicopters and then carried down or lowered over cliffs to the coves and rocks, the pilots' performance in getting to spectacularly inaccessible places being greatly admired. From the drums the detergent was manually pumped through 4-inch diameter pipes and sprayed onto the pools or slicks of oil, the object being to break up the oil which would tend to solidify and could then be hosed away by the Fire Service into the sea or carried off by the tide and break up and sink. This method was found to succeed although it might have to be repeated several times as new slicks were washed up by incoming tides. Priority was given to beaches and harbours, then to coves and rocky shores. It is estimated that the Battalion sprayed in excess of 100 drums each day and, concurrently, some platoons helped construct improvised booms across harbour entrances and the seaward approaches of beaches. Ironically, scientists subsequently claimed that the detergent did more damage than the oil.

It was hard, tiring, filthy, frustrating and sometimes dangerous work, as the detergent could raise blisters or damage eyesight; several men, in fact, required hospital treatment. There were, however, compensations. The local people were extremely hospitable and the young ladies in particular seemed to find the "tar babies" from the shoreline very attractive. The WVS were generally about to supply free tea and wads; those working at Porthleven were given supplies of fresh vegetables; and at St Ives the Round Table and the Town Council provided crates of beer. St Ives, always a centre for artists, also had its hippy colony, which could confuse those seeking feminine company; heads of shoulder-length blonde hair, for example, were sometimes found to sprout beards. Y Company rather liked the man who, determined to make some contribution, emptied two packets of domestic washing powder into the sea!

On 7 April the Battalion handed over to the 1st Battalion The Royal Ulster Rifles and returned to Netheravon, where it began preparing for Exercise Staghunter, a company test exercise to be held on the Otterburn training area, Northumberland, in May. In the meantime the Squash Rackets team had won the Army Cup for the second time in three years, beating 5 Field Regiment RA in the Army final at Reindahlen. Major Mike Ferro, Major David Munn, Captain Mike Chignell, Lieutenant Andrew Freemantle, Lieutenant Patrick Keen, Second Lieutenant John Hooley and Second Lieutenant James Dewar all played in the team at some stage.

Otterburn proved to be something of a disappointment. The training area consisted of cold, bleak, windswept moorland so soggy that the mortars sank into the peaty soil unless fired from a hard track, and poor flying weather restricted helicopter participation to the extent that the point of the exercise was somewhat lost. As A Company put it: "We were left to prove just how fit we were - we did this alright but fast deployment was not possible over the ground we were required to move over."

In the middle of June the Battalion, augmented by attached Ever Ready reservists, flew to Cyprus. It will be recalled that, with the exception of two British sovereign bases at Dhekelia and Akrotiri on the south coast, plus a number of "retained sites," the island had been granted its Independence in 1960. Since then, however, the ancient racial and religious hatreds between the Greek majority and the Turkish minority had erupted into such violence that a United Nations force (UNFICYP), including a British contingent, had been forced to intervene in 1964 and was still present. On this occasion, nevertheless, the Hampshires had not been despatched to Cyprus as part of UNFICYP, but were engaged on a deployment and acclimatisation exercise. One point of interest during the fly-out was that from the flight deck of aircraft approaching RAF Akrotiri it was possible to see, far below, Israeli fighters on their way to attack Egypt.

The deployment aspect was concluded satisfactorily, but it was also proved beyond any reasonable doubt that a unit cannot be moved directly from Salisbury Plain to a climate where the temperature is 90 degrees in the shade and expected to operate at 100 per cent efficiency. The Ever Readies, coming straight from civilian life, were worst affected, while the fittest members of the Battalion suffered least. Battalion HQ and Y Company were encamped at Evdhimou near Episcopi, and A and Y Companies at Dhekelia near the sea.

"The companies went straight into training on a circuit spread round the island," recorded the Journal. "The training was organised by the Battalion's Second-in-Command, Major Richard Freeman-Wallace, who was gifted with both an eye for detail and innovative ideas. The SLR and SMG shoots on homemade jungle lanes were voted the best, possibly because they were located at Akamas on the north-east coast, the furthest area from Battalion HQ. At the opposite end of the island the mortar sections under the Mortar Officer, Lieutenant Bruce Willing, and Lieutenant Andrew Burgess were put through their paces, despite the need for an 03:00 start to ensure range clearance. The GPMG teams under Lieutenant David Southwood and WOII Bob Hogan were perched on a hill in the central Mesouria Plain, one of the hottest parts of the island with temperatures frequently exceeding 110 degrees. The heat and the use of tracer led to fires which of course built up half a mile from the firing point. Nearer the coast the companies practised Carl Gustav and 94 Energa grenade shooting. (The 84mm Carl Gustav, a shoulder-fired recoilless anti-tank weapon of Swedish design adopted by NATO, had an effective range of 350 yards and, although it was also capable of firing HE and smoke to greater distances, some questioned whether this justified its weight of 32 pounds.) Section field firing and normal range practices behind Dhekelia completed the circuit.

"On Sunday 2nd July the final exercise began. The aim was to test B Company in their stealth, and A and Y Companies in their stopping power. By 18:00 both defending companies were in position in the area around Evdhimou and B Company had 24 hours in which to get to a 'pick-up point' on the coast via two checkpoints. The commanders were 'killed off' early on to allow those seasoned soldiers Lieutenant Freemantle and Captain Hanscomb to exercise their will. However, even this shrewd move did not prevent B Company flitting through the defence like ghosts in the night with the loss of only one section, and pushing on to the checkpoints with amazing stamina in such a climate."

This exercise concluded the Battalion's training programme in Cyprus, which had taken place in the turbulent diplomatic aftermath of the Arab-Israeli Six Day War (5-10 June). Shaken as they were by the scale of their defeat, the Arab nations were adopting a hostile attitude to the West, one consequence of which was a dramatic increase in the price of crude oil that was to cause serious economic dislocation. It was also feared that Nasser would encourage escalation of the terrorist campaign which had troubled Aden and its hinterland since 1963 and, although the base was to be abandoned in November 1967 in pursuance of the Wilson government's stated aim of disengagement east of Suez, it was decided to evacuate the remaining families at short notice. This strained the resources of RAF Transport Command to the extent that the Battalion's return to the United Kingdom was delayed for a week. It had, however, enjoyed its training period in Cyprus, during which it received visits from two very distinguished senior officers: Major General Anthony Deane-Drummond, DSO, MC and Bar, GOC 3rd Division, an Arnhem veteran who had also served with the SAS in Malaya and Oman; and Major General David Lloyd-Owen, DSO, OBE, MC, GOC Cyprus District, who had commanded the Long Range Desert Group 1943-45.

Many members of the Regiment recall this period as epitomising the tremendous family spirit which always existed within the *'Appy 'Amps*. It could have been a difficult time with bored soldiers confined to temporary camps because of the Six Day War, but it was not. In fact, everyone threw themselves into making the best of the situation. A sea sports festival was organised with swimming and assault boat races and even an inter-company sand castle building competition, and the evenings witnessed some of the best company parties ever held.

Following block leave the Battalion began preparing for Exercise Unison, which took place on Salisbury Plain in August. This was intended to demonstrate British equipment to representatives of Commonwealth armies and no expense was spared — the Anti-Tank Platoon, for example, received three years' entitlement of ammunition with which to practise, plus more for the demonstration itself, while the 81mm mortars were kept so busy that four of the six tubes exceeded their barrel lives. The emphasis was on the spectacular, with displays of live firing and bombing, air mobility and helicopter assaults. The demonstration, again organised by Major Richard Freeman-Wallace, received high praise for its originality and scope.

26 September saw the award of the Winchester Trophy, subscribed to by both the Officers' and Sergeants' Messes in memory of Lieutenant Colin Winchester, who, it will be recalled, had been killed in an accident while training in September 1964. The Trophy was an annual award, usually for the platoon which demonstrated the highest standard of training and tactics. On this occasion, however, due to the very full battalion programme it was awarded for the best annual classification score and was presented on this occasion by Brigadier H.R.S.Pain, MC, Commanding 5 Infantry Brigade, to Second Lieutenant Peter Miller's 7 Platoon. Peter Miller subsequently joined the US Marine Corps and in 1995 became a full colonel commanding a Marine Regiment.

Although the Battalion was required to provide umpires for exercises in Germany and at Otterburn, the undoubted high point of the autumn of 1967 was the series of Freedom Marches it carried out in its own County. These took place on 6 November in Aldershot, 10 November in Winchester, 11 November in Basingstoke, 14 November in Southampton and 17 November in Portsmouth. On each occasion the parade consisted of the Band and Drums; No 1 Guard in sixes, 150 strong; the Colour Party; No 2 Guard in sixes, 150 strong; and twenty-four Land Rover with heavy support weapons; a total, including Regimental Police, Guidon Bearers and Parade Orderlies, of 477. Everywhere the Battalion was greeted with friendliness by the watching crowds and welcomed by the civic authorities, who also provided generous hospitality. The parade at Portsmouth was particularly memorable.

"The march through the city to the Guildhall was witnessed by thousands of people. All the schools in the area lined the route and the business houses and shops flew bunting. A tremendous crowd at the Guildhall Square and on the steps watched the march past. This was the first time since it was awarded in 1950 that the Battalion had exercised its Freedom rights. Also present were two Chelsea Pensioners - Old Soldiers of the Regiment. The whole

Battalion was treated to a sit-down lunch - 400 at Kimbells with 60 All Ranks, including 20 Privates, at the Guildhall in the Lord Mayor's Banquetting Room. The Lord Mayor's speech of welcome made us feel even more proud of our Regiment."

After what had been an extremely busy and diverse year the Battalion began 1968 with its Administrative Inspection on 25 January. During the following week it received visits from the Secretary of State for Defence, Mr Denis Healey, and the retiring Chief of General Staff, General Sir James Cassels, GCB, KBE, DSO. Individual training was followed by platoon training at Sennybridge and the Brecon Beacons, conceived and organised by the platoon commanders themselves in preparation for the Winchester Trophy, which was won by Second Lieutenant James Dewar and 8 Platoon.

Good sport was enjoyed throughout the Battalion's time at Netheravon, but the winter of 1967/68 was notable for a particularly good boxing team run by Captain Harry Barnard. Privates McAllister and "Bert" Thornhill both won their weight at the Southern Command Novices, while Private Hoare was runner-up in his weight. In the Army Cup, 16 Light Air Defence Regiment RA, the previous year's Singapore champions, were beaten 7-4, and the 15th/19th Hussars, the previous year's BAOR runners-up, only won, after a drawn match, by virtue of winning the 1st String Welter. Colours were awarded to Lance Corporal Power and Privates Jones 56, Harden, Davies, Hoare, McAllister and Thornhill. Another who distinguished himself was Lieutenant Peter Martin, the MTO, who shot for the Army small bore team.

In April the Brigade Commander, Brigadier E.N.W.Bramall, OBE, MC, directed that his troops would spend a fortnight operating solely at night. Colonel Wilson decided that the first week, commencing on 29 April, would be spent at Netheravon and the second on Dartmoor. During the first week the normal barrack and training routine was simply inverted. There were, perhaps, some who entered into the spirit of the thing with more enthusiasm than judgement, as when the Corps of Drums struck up on the square at 03:00, provoking a sudden display of bedroom lights in the nearby RAF married quarters, notably in the Group Captain's house! By the third night, however, most people had begun to accept the new regime as normal. The exceptions were the management and the Quartermaster's staff who worked a near twenty-four-hour day because the rest of the Army inconsiderately stuck to its usual routine! The Dartmoor phase of the exercise, involving the defence of Yes Tor by Y Company against the rest of the Battalion, was marred by continuous torrential rain that saturated clothing and flooded trenches. Towards the end of the week some men were beginning to suffer from the effects of exposure and the exercise was terminated a day early.

In June the Battalion was given responsibility for the Infantry Display at the Aldershot Show. The terse instruction received from the Directorate of Infantry was that the display had "got to be better than last year." The questions facing Major John Morrish, therefore, were what did the public want to see and how best could it be exhibited? His answer was to provide a series of sideshows in a comparatively small area, with a timed programme of working displays and permanently open static displays. Lieutenant Richard Warren's 2 Platoon ran a house-clearing demonstration, with numerous thunderflash explosions to draw the crowds; there was an assault course competition; and 3 Platoon showed the public how to "bash up" in the jungle. Static displays were provided by Captain Hugh Keatinge and his signallers, complete with airborne TV camera, the Parachute Regiment's jumping towers and death slide, shooting galleries, Wombat and 81mm mortar pits, a dug-in command post and a stand where the public could try its hand at cooking lightweight rations under the supervision of WOII Frank Blake; this last proved to be so popular that it had to be forcibly closed at 8 pm each eveing. Also present were a Vigilant training simulator (the Vigilant was a first-generation shaped-charge Anti-Tank Guided Weapon (ATGW) with a range well in excess of the Wombat) and an FV432 fully-tracked APC. The public clearly loved the display, and congratulatory letters were received from the C-in-C Army Strategic Command, the C-in-C Southern Command and the Director of Infantry.

June also saw most of Y and Z Companies, the Band and Drums and most of the Signals and MT Platoons engaged on a KAPE Tour which visited Portsmouth, Havant, Gosport, Southampton, Christchurch and Bournemouth with a small party attending the Carisbrooke Tattoo. During the tour successful visits were made to ACF detachments and youth clubs, both of which continued to be a valuable source of recruits for the Regiment. Adventure training during the summer months included sailing on the Norfolk Broads, canoeing in Belgium and orienteering in Scotland.

In July 1968 the event which the Regiment had feared for many years took place. The Wilson government's poor economic housekeeping, which had resulted in the drastic reduction of the Territorial Army the previous year, had not improved. The understanding behind the re-organisation of the reserve forces had been that it would obviate the necessity of cutting any deeper into the Regular establishment. This was brushed aside on a that-was-then-and-this-is-now basis, and indeed the government could argue that the ending of the Confrontation with Indonesia, the departure from the Gulf and the evacuation of Aden would enable it to complete disengagement east of Suez (notwithstanding a bitter secret war being waged by the SAS in the Dhofar region of Oman) and concentrate on its commitments in Europe. That being the case, it argued, fewer troops would be needed. The Royal Armoured Corps and the Royal Artillery would each lose four regiments, the infantry eight battalions, and the Royal Engineers four squadrons.

Within the infantry this was to be achieved in two ways. First, the Fusiliers, Light Infantry and the remaining Irish regiments would each form a "Large Regiment." Secondly, each infantry brigade, the term being used in its administrative rather than tactical sense, would lose one battalion. Some regiments, notably the Cameronians (Scottish Rifles) and the York and Lancaster Regiment, opted for disbandment rather than amalgamation. Within the Wessex Brigade it was deemed more appropriate that the two hitherto-unaffected regiments, The Royal Hampshire Regiment and The Gloucestershire Regiment, should amalgamate. As Colonel of the former, General Batten issued an Order of the Day to that effect, and on 8 July Colonel Wilson announced to the assembled 1st Battalion that the amalgamation would take place at some time between 1970 and 1972.

During discussions between the two Regiments agreement was reached on a number of matters which are of some historical interest. The new Regiment would be known as The Royal Regiment of Gloucestershire and Hampshire; its cap badge would be a silver sphynx superimposed on the centre portion of the Hampshire Rose, this mounted on a silver eight-pointed star surmounted by a gold crown; the collar badges would be the Royal Bengal Tiger surmounted by the word "India" in a scroll; buttons would be marked with a sphynx superimposed on a rose; the Gloucestershire Regiment's unique "back badge" would be worn by all members of the new Regiment, but the Presidential Citation flash won at the Imjin only on the shoulders of those actually serving with the 1st Battalion; the new Regiment's quick march would be *The Highland Piper,* formerly played by the 1st Battalion The Royal Hampshire Regiment and the 2nd Battalion The Gloucestershire Regiment; and the Headquarters of the New Regiment would be at Serle's House, with a Regimental Office in Gloucester. So advanced were these negotiations that the November 1969 issue of the Journal contained an addendum slip announcing that the Amalgamation Ceremony would take place on 5 September 1970 at Portsmouth. All of this, however, lay in the future and the story was to take a number of unexpected twists and turns.

In the meantime, after the initial shock had been absorbed there was nothing to be done but soldier on, although July 1968 could hardly be said to have been a pleasant month. Despite this, on the 25th Captain (QM) Harry Barnard, MBE, visited Rose, the survivor of the two tiger cubs temporarily adopted by the Regiment in Malaya, who had been moved from London to Paignton Zoological Gardens some years earlier, to present a new Regimental plaque recording her history. Possibly Rose retained some distant memory of the former Colour Sergeant who had hand-fed her all those years ago; certainly, she approved of him sufficiently to allow him to tickle her ears through the wire of her enclosure.

The celebration of Minden Day had to be curtailed because the major brigade exercise of the year, Iron Duke, began on 2 August.

This involved working with armour, airmobile deployments and helicopter assaults. During the initial phase the Battalion was given the tasks of delaying the enemy advance and defending a river line, followed by a prearranged withdrawal, first on foot and then by helicopter, to the main defensive position. In the second phase it formed part of the counter-attack force and secured bridgeheads across the River Avon after long night approach marches.

After block leave the Battalion returned to Netheravon to prepare for a six months' tour of duty with UNFICYP in Cyprus. During the ensuing pause Colonel Wilson was able to fulfil an ambition by completing the Regiment's cycle of Freedom Marches within a year. On 19 September the Battalion marched through the streets of Bournemouth before large crowds, and the following day repeated the performance at Romsey, unfortunately in heavy rain. On both occasions the reception was enthusiastic and the civic hospitality, as always, generous.

In October Colonel Sandy Wilson relinquished Command on taking up an appointment at the School of Infantry. His unstinting work on behalf of the Regiment was to earn him an OBE in the New Year's Honours List. He was succeeded by Lieutenant Colonel W.R.B.May, MC, whose first task was to take the Battalion to Cyprus almost immediately and assume the responsibilities of UNFICYP's British contingent.

The 3500-strong UNFICYP was commanded by a Finnish officer, Lieutenant General A.E.Martola, whose headquarters were located in Nicosia. With the exception of the British sovereign bases and "retained areas," Cyprus was divided into a number of civil Districts and each national contingent was responsible for one or more Districts. Thus, the north of the island was controlled by the Irish, Canadian and Finnish battalions, the east coast by the Swedes, the central sector by the Danes and the south and west by the British. The 1st Battalion The Royal Hampshire Regiment was responsible for the Limassol Zone, containing the Paphos, Limassol and Kophinou Districts, its role within UNFICYP being defined by UN Security Council Resolution No 186 of March 1964 in the following terms: "in the best interests of preserving international peace and security, to use its best efforts to prevent a recurrence of fighting and, as necessary, to contribute to the maintenance of and restoration of law and order and a return to normal conditions."

As Commanding Officer, Colonel May was also Zone Commander, his Zone Headquarters being at Polemidhia Camp, overlooking Limassol. The Battalion's task would require nine platoons, rotating within and between the three Districts on a fortnightly basis, and for this reason some internal reorganisation was necessary. To achieve this, B Company HQ was temporarily disbanded and static District Headquarters were established with A Company HQ at Kophinou, Y Company HQ at Paphos and Z Company HQ at Limassol. The District Commanders were Major John Morrish at Kophinou, Major Robin Laird at Paphos and, first, Major Ted Horton, succeeded by Major Mike Draper of The Duke of Edinburgh's Royal Regiment at Limassol.

Because the Battalion was so widely dispersed in outposts, the Signals Platoon, commanded by Captain Hugh Keatinge until

December and thereafter by Captain R.J.Shrimpton, was required to establish and maintain a very large and busy communications network. "Every outpost had radio, often backed by line, which meant 58 radios and 78 telephones from four exchanges. Radio stations varied from our Rear Link on the UNFICYP net, Zone and District Control stations and, of course, the manpack OP sets manned by rifle platoon soldiers. The Battalion (or Zone) net depended upon a rebroadcast station atop Troodos (6015 feet); it was backed by C11 sets on which morse was frequently used."

Another group of extremely busy people was the Band under Bandmaster WOI Gregory and Band Sergeant Major Bill Bailey. As the only band serving with UNFICYP it provided music for seven or eight national contingents, requiring a multilingual knowledge of words of command. Its main task, however, was to entertain the soldiers manning outposts in Kophinou, Paphos and Limassol Districts. More often than not, lack of space in the outposts made it impossible to use the full Band, so a ten-piece Dance Band Concert Group was formed. This toured the outposts giving concerts of pop music, traditional jazz, and musical and comedy sketches, its visits providing an incalculable boost to morale at these lonely locations with their achingly boring routine. Sometimes, too, the Band would play for the Greek and Turkish communities, distracting them temporarily from their mutual antipathy.

Another aid to morale was the Regimental magazine *Tiger Rag,* which was the brainchild of Private Barnie Thompson, the Orderly Room Despatch Clerk. Private Thompson had submitted detailed plans for the magazine to Colonel May, who gave them his whole-hearted approval and support. The magazine appeared monthly and contained articles on recent events and personalities, humour, cartoons and competitions. It was an immediate success, its arrival being eagerly awaited in the outposts. In addition to circulating throughout the Battalion, copies were sent sent to Old Comrades as far away as Canada, Australia and New Zealand, to the Glosters and the relieving unit, the Worcesters, to the Regimental Museum, the Imperial War Museum and the Portsmouth Museum.

The three Districts under the Battalion's control were very different in character. Paphos contained a higher proportion of Turkish villages than elsewhere, was relatively prosperous, and life there had more or less settled down, albeit with scant love lost between Greek and Turkish neighbours, who were separated by a Green Line in the towns of Ktima and Polis. In Limassol, the second largest town in Cyprus, the two communities had also been physically separated by a Green Line where armed Turkish Fighters confronted Greek National Guardsmen, but there was little or no trouble during the Battalion's tour of duty. Kophinou, lying astride a strategically important junction on the Nicosia-Limassol road, was the smallest of the three Districts but potentially the most explosive, having witnessed serious inter-communal fighting in 1967. Then, the Turks had physically prevented the Cypriot Police from exercising jurisdiction within the village. The issue was resolved by force when Colonel George Grivas, better remembered as the controller of the EOKA terrorist campaign of the 1950s, mounted an attack in battalion strength with the Greek National Guard. As a result of this the Turks were ejected with the loss of twenty-five killed, Greek casualties amounting to two dead and two wounded. Several UN posts, then manned by the 1st Battalion Royal Green Jackets, had come under mortar and small-arms fire, and in one, surrounded by National Guardsmen with cocked weapons, two Riflemen were forcibly disarmed. Understandably, the affair had rankled and because of it additional security precautions were taken at District HQ, which subsequently became known as The Compound or Stalag III because of its barbed wire perimeter fences. Its occupants had a love/hate relationship with the place and those who spent the whole six months there designed and produced a Kophinou tie in UN blue with white barbed wire stripes, the barbs being in the form of a letter K. Happily, the worst incident to occur there was the accidental destruction by fire of a huge stores marquee in which Private Harker continued to slumber peacefully until he was rudely propelled to safety.

In all three Districts the officers' time was often taken up with interminable meetings with the civil representatives of the two communities. The agenda could range from the resolution of potentially serious disputes to Turks who declined to pay water and electricity bills issued by a government they refused to recognise. Entrenched attitudes meant that even Solomonic judgements were rarely acceptable; in the final analysis, both sides had to be persuaded where their best interests lay, and that took time. Probably the most potentially dangerous incident of the tour occurred in Polis, where a Turk murdered a Greek civilian whom he suspected of seducing his daughter. The Greek National Guard surrounded the Turk's house for twenty-four hours to seek justice and it was only the intervention of Captain Alan Withers, a platoon of B Company and three British UNFICYP armoured cars which calmed down the situation. The Turk was disarmed by Corporal Mort, who was given a GOC's Commendation for the incident, and handed over to the Turkish authorities for trial.

Activity in the outposts became a "corporals' war." Incoming sentries were briefed on the local communities' normal daily round of life in their sector and told what was and what was not acceptable activity. Hours of acute observation through binoculars would follow. Irregularities would be reported to District HQ, who would then negotiate with community leaders with a view to stopping trouble before it started. In the more serious cases, reports would be passed to Zone and, if necessary, to UNFICYP HQs for the appropriate action to be taken. Most of the time was spent in dull, routine surveillance in remote locations. Each Company did its best to improve OPs and off-duty facilities; there being little to spend pay on, credit balances began to mount. Opportunities for sport and swimming were eagerly taken and Battalion players represented Army Cyprus in soccer, rugby, hockey, cross-country and squash events as well as winning the Inter-Contingent darts competition. One notable highlight was provided by Lieutenant Andrew Freemantle, who rounded up a group of a dozen motley donkeys and staged an enjoyable inter-company Donkey Derby.

Considering the short duration of the tour, the Battalion received a remarkable number of distinguished visitors, whose arrival provided a welcome break from routine. They included Lieutenant General Martola and his Deputy Chief of Staff and Commander of the British Contingent, Colonel D.B.Riddell-Webster, OBE, on several occasions; Marshal of the Royal Air Force Sir Charles Elworthy, GCB, CBE, DSO, MVO, DFC, AFC, Chief of the UK Defence Staff and Major General Lloyd-Owen, GOC NEARELF on 29 October 1968, and the latter again on 3 December, accompanied by Colonel H.A.Decker, ACC, Inspector Army Catering Corps, Mr A.Smith and Mr E.Brett, respectively News Editors of the *Southern Evening Echo* and the *Portsmouth Evening News*; Mr John Morris, MP, Minister of Defence for Equipment, on 16 January 1969; Colonel C.A.Morris, CBE and Lieutenant Colonel C.H.Jaeger, OBE, from the Royal Military School of Music, Kneller Hall, the following day; Major General J.H.Gibbon, OBE, Director of Army Staff Duties, and Brigadier P.C.S.Heidenstam, CBE, Colonel of the Gloucestershire Regiment, on 4 February; Mr George Hogan, Assistant Editor of *Soldier* magazine, on 7 February; Major General M.Forrester, CB, CBE, DSO, MS, Director of Infantry, on 19 February; and General Sir Geoffrey H.Baker, GCB, CMG, CBE, MC, ADC(Gen), Chief of General Staff, on 29 March.

In addition, there was a continual stream of visitors from every UN contingent in Cyprus, including the Australian policemen serving with UNCIVPOL, whose task was to assist in police matters when problems arose between the Greek and Turkish Cypriot police. Equally popular were the officers of the Irish Battalion, who would start a party at the slightest excuse.

On 7 March 1969 the 1st Battalion paraded to receive the United Nations Medal in the Service of Peace. Four guards were on parade with the Colours and the Band and Drums. General Martola presented medals to twenty specially selected officers and men representing all elements of the Battalion, including the personnel of attached Corps, and then made a speech congratulating the Battalion on the skill and firmness with which it had handled all the difficult situations it had encountered. The parade ended with a marching display given by the Band and Drums to a large and appreciative audience, including the doctors from an Austrian medical unit ordered by their commanding officer to attend and see how a parade should be done!

At the end of April the Battalion was relieved by the 1st Battalion The Worcestershire Regiment, flying home by company groups and then going on three weeks' leave. If there had been times when the UN peacekeeping role had seemed dull, few doubted that it had been worthwhile and the very fact that there had been no serious incidents in its Zone proved that the job had been done effectively. Alas, in the long term only the Greeks and Turks themselves could resolve their differences, and they did not choose to do so. In 1974 the Greek National Guard engineered a *coup d'état* as a result of which a former EOKA terrorist and convicted murderer was created President. This was too much for the government of Turkey, which promptly mounted an invasion and occupied the north-eastern third of the island, creating a state of partition that still exists.

Hardly had the first men returned to Netheravon from leave than the Battalion became heavily involved in the preparations for Exercise Normandy Landings, the codename for the British part in the celebrations to mark the 25th Anniversary of the D Day Landings in Normandy on 6 June 1944. It was given the dual tasks of erecting and running the tented camp for the British contingent at Ouistreham and providing the major element of troops parading, participating in the American ceremony on Utah Beach on 5 June, the British ceremony at Ouistreham on 6 June followed by the Beating of Retreat at Bayeux later that day, and French ceremonies at Saint Lo on 7 June and at Mont Saint Michel the following day. As ever, the Battalion's Second-in-Command, Major Basil Hobbs, and the Quartermaster, Captain Harry Barnard, were due great credit for their efforts.

"Two particular ceremonies deserve special mention," recorded the Journal. "These were the two torch-light ceremonies at the 3rd Division Memorial at Hermanville and at the 239 Brigade Memorial at Le Hamel, which initiated the start of the celebrations. In both, the Battalion provided a Guard of Honour and an officer torch bearer. The ceremony at Le Hamel was attended by the Mayor, Madame d'Anselme, who was present on D Day when the Regiment came ashore and whose chateau was used as a casualty clearing station, where many members of the Regiment probably received treatment."

After being involved in the Ouistreham parade, Y Company was sent to Avranches, where even the hospitable French excelled themselves. It made a fitting finish to the Normandy parades when the Colour Party and the Company, led by the Band and Drums, marched through Avranches early on the final Sunday morning. The marching, the drill and the music could not have been better; indeed, an English voice was heard to comment, "Forget about the others - here come the real soldiers!" The Parade Commander was Colonel Roger May, the Adjutant Captain Mike Martin, the Parade RSM WOI George Thomas and the Drum Major Lofty Ferris. The parade, which also involved French and American contingents, was short but moving and the quietness of the early morning was broken only by the crack of 150 rifles in the final movement of the "Present Arms." Afterwards, the participants were treated to lunch by the townspeople, being pressed to eat and drink as much as they could.

Back in England, the following weeks were devoted to

individual training, with A and Y Companies spending a fortnight at St Martin's Plain Camp, just outside Folkestone, where, not having fired their weapons for a year, they took full advantage of the facilities provided by the Hythe-Lydd range complex.

At the end of June the Battalion was required to provide a detachment of ninety-six officers and men for the funeral of Field Marshal Earl Alexander of Tunis. This was a considerable honour as the contingent, commanded by Major Robin Laird, was the only one to be drawn from outside the Household Brigade. The funeral, attended by the Field Marshal's family, statesmen, senior officers and the military attachés of many nations, was held in Windsor. As the junior unit on parade, the Royal Hampshires led the cortège in slow time from Victoria Barracks through the packed but hushed streets to St George's Chapel in Windsor Castle while, from Windsor Great Park, a troop of the Royal Horse Artillery boomed out a measured nineteen-gun salute.

A limited amount of training was carried out on Dartmoor in July but perhaps the most radical event to take place since the Battalion's return from Cyprus was the formation of Command Company under Captain Bob Long. This consisted of the Orderly Room personnel, the Intelligence Section, the Regimental Police, the Signals Platoon, the Drums Platoon and the Reconnaissance Platoon. In camp the Company was concerned primarily with administrative matters, but in an active service scenario many of its personnel had their own specialist tasks to perform while the OC and his immediate staff manned the Battalion Operations Room.

The period at Netheravon saw the departure from Regimental Duty for the last time of several notable people. Major Tim Wellings, a fine soldier and a typically cheerful Hampshire, moved on to command the Depot. WOII Peter Kirby, Chief Clerk for six years, also left for the Depot. After many years as Drum Major and latterly as Company Sergeant Major, WOII Butch Bryant departed on receiving promotion to WOI, and WOII Peter Waterman was posted on being commissioned.

By now, the functions of the Wessex Brigade Depot had been absorbed by the Depot of The Prince of Wales's Division at Lichfield, Staffordshire, the responsibilities of which extended across a wide area stretching from Cheshire to Devon. The term "division" was used in an administrative connotation only and the Ministry of Defence gave permission for infantry regiments to revert to wearing their own rather than brigade cap badges. There was no marked dislike of the Wyvern but the feeling within the Regiment was that if its independent life was to end the following year, it would prefer to wear its own time-honoured insignia. The re-badging ceremony took place during the Minden Day parade, Royal Hampshire Regiment badges being presented to representatives from all Companies by Colonel May, prior to the distribution of Minden Roses by Company Commanders. A special Minden Day lunch was provided and during the evening the Officers' and Sergeants' Messes combined to hold a very successful Minden Ball in the Tidworth Officers' Club. Everyone then departed on three weeks' block leave, believing that when they returned the Regiment's independent life would have but a year to run.

They were wrong. Their leave would be cut short, the Army as a whole was about to enter a new phase in its history, and there would be no amalgamation with The Gloucestershire Regiment.

* * * * * * * * *

CHAPTER 11

FIRST ULSTER TOUR
AND REDUCTION

Background to the Ulster Troubles - 1st Battalion recalled from leave - deployment to Belfast - aid to the civil power and good relationship with both communities - IRA strategy - Public Duties in London - Fit for Role Inspection - Exercise Soleil - Ceremonial Parade at St Cross - need for infantry in Ulster - amalgamation replaced by reduction - formation of Minden Company and dispersion of 1st Battalion

In 1920 the British government concluded a Treaty with those factions in Ireland which demanded home rule, and as part of this six counties of the Province of Ulster, containing as they did a majority who did not wish to be governed by Dublin, were also granted their own legislature. In the aftermath of this a savage civil war was fought between, on the one hand, the security forces in Ulster and those of the Irish government, and, on the other, the Irish Republican Army, which, together with Sinn Fein, was violently opposed to the Treaty. Following its defeat the IRA became a clandestine organisation which persistently maintained that its aims remained the removal of British influence from Ulster and ultimately the reunifaction of the island under a single Irish government. As the years passed the Dublin government itself began to have second thoughts about partition and in 1937 it abrogated several clauses of the Treaty, declaring that "The National territory consists of the whole island of Ireland." Having thus been suitably if unintentionally encouraged, in 1939 the IRA embarked on a campaign of violence, mounting attacks on barracks and police stations throughout

Ulster, stealing arms and blowing up public utilities. This was curtailed when American troops were stationed in Ulster during World War II, as the terrorists had no wish to alienate their supporters among the influential Irish-American community in the United States. In 1956, after years of sporadic activity, the IRA mounted a fresh campaign of terror in Ulster, terminated in 1962 as a result of vigorous anti-terrorist measures which included closing all but fourteen border crossings to prevent hit-and-run raids, heavy penalties imposed by Special Criminal Courts, and the internment of IRA members on both sides of the border. By 1969 the IRA, while retaining a certain nuisance value, was in what appeared to be terminal decline, its ageing members being regarded as local curiosities who, for a drink or two, would retail stories of "the old days."

In Ulster itself the majority of the population were fiercely defensive of their Protestant faith and their links with the Crown. They were, and remain, fully aware that in a united Ireland they would become a minority and subject to the rule of a Dublin government which they believed to be heavily influenced by the Catholic Church. The long, sad history of Ireland, littered with atrocities committed by Catholic against Protestant and vice versa, the events of the Irish Civil War and the subsequent activities of the IRA had done nothing to diminish their fears. They saw their own Catholic minority as a potential threat, although it was a travesty of the truth to suggest that every Catholic was also a republican nationalist and a supporter of terrorist activity. The safeguard chosen by the Protestants was repression, which, as history repeatedly confirms, offers only a short-term solution. In elections, blatant gerrymandering ensured that Protestant interests were preserved; and in matters such as employment and housing, Protestants always received preferential consideration. Mutual hatreds and fears existed in both communities, especially in the poorer areas, which could least afford them. In the cities, Catholics and Protestants lived together yet apart, each in their own neighbourhoods, maintaining an uneasy peace that could be blown apart by the smallest spark.

That spark was provided in 1969. The sixties had witnessed two major and very important social changes, namely the evolution of television as the primary means of mass communication, and the creation of numerous new universities for the provision of further education. In both areas the growth was so rapid that, inevitably, unsuitable candidates were sometimes appointed to positions of great influence and importance. As a result, instant idealism often replaced mature consideration in matters of general concern, every aspect of authority was derided, personal rights were idealised in preference to public duty, and protest in the form of rowdy and sometimes violent demonstrations was considered to be a valid alternative to the democratic process. The irony was that in Ulster the Catholic minority, treated as second-class citizens, had genuine grievances. What the student politicians and their media supporters tragically failed to understand was the effect that such demonstrations would have on extremist elements within the Protestant community. Civil Rights marches were stoned, ambushed and harassed, but the Stormont government did promise social and political reform and a General Election was called in March 1969. When the result of this was declared it became clear that extreme elements would not permit the passage of the necessary measures. There was rioting in Londonderry and Belfast, followed by acts of sabotage. By now, hatred and fear on both sides had been raised to fever pitch. On 14 August the annual Protestant Apprentice Boys March in Londonderry was attacked by a Catholic mob from the Bogside. Mass violence ensued and quickly spread to Belfast. People on both sides were killed, families were turned out of their homes, buildings were set ablaze and looted, barricades were erected, and the police were attacked with petrol bombs, stones and clubs. The sheer scale of the trouble placed it beyond the capacity of the over-extended Royal Ulster Constabulary to contain, with the result that it called out its B Reserve. The "B men," as they were known, were detested by the Catholics, for the very good reasons that they were an almost exclusively Protestant force, they were armed and they were far from impartial. Again, as their discipline did not match that of the regular RUC, a real possibility existed that they would get dangerously out of hand in difficult circumstances. With Ulster on the brink of civil war, the authorities had no alternative but to call the Army to the aid of the civil power.

"I was sitting in my married quarter watching the BBC's 9 o'clock evening news, which featured the first major rioting in Ulster," recalled the then Captain Hastings Neville, commanding the 1st Battalion's rear party at Netheravon. "I said to my wife that I wouldn't mind betting that we will be called out to go over and help restore law and order. Literally, as the signature tune was dying away the phone rang. It was the Brigade Commander, Brigadier (later Field Marshal) Edwin Bramall, who asked if I was the rear party commander. Having confirmed that I was, he asked if I could come immediately to Brigade Headquarters. I explained that I was in scruff order and in my carpet slippers. 'Never mind, come as you are,' he said. At Brigade HQ we discussed the problems of recalling the Battalion from leave in case reinforcements were needed in Ulster. The next morning, Friday 15 August, the recall was confirmed. The Battalion was to be mustered at Airfield Camp by noon on Sunday 17 August with a view to flying to Ulster within the next 48 hours. Major Basil Hobbs, the Battalion's Second-in-Command, happened to be in his quarter so the two of us went into camp to put the necessary action in hand. We were not allowed to use national radio or television, which would have been an enormous help, but we were permitted to request the Automobile Association to put up roadside messages for key individuals such as the Quartermaster (Captain Harry Barnard) and the Paymaster (Major Douglas Stimpson). Colonel May, just starting a holiday in Switzerland, was located through the Military Attaché's office in Berne. Messages were put through the letter boxes of all who were living in married quarters, but the bulk of the Battalion were to be recalled by telegram. As we were part of Strategic Command everyone had to write out a telegram to himself before going on leave. Standing instructions indicated that the 300-plus telegrams should be despatched via the local Post Office. The Postmaster in Netheravon village nearly had apoplexy when I presented him with the task. He politely explained that he would have to phone each one through and would still be at it the following week! We needed to think again. I phoned HQ Strategic Command to tell them that their instructions regarding telegrams were simply not practicable. After much discussion, and as the contents of each telegram was identical, we were asked if we could type out all names and addresses and group them in telegram code lists which they would give us. The military Comcen would then get them out in a matter of a few hours. We drafted in everyone who could use a typewriter, including several volunteer wives, and by 14:00 the job was done. Throughout the weekend people were steadily pouring into camp, vehicles and trailers were being loaded, lashed down and weighed in preparation for an airlift."

FIRST ULSTER TOUR AND REDUCTION

By the time the deadline was reached fewer than a dozen soldiers were unaccounted for. The Adjutant, Captain Mike Martin, when asked by a senior staff officer of HQ Strategic Command what the Battalion thought, was mollified with the memorable words, "Don't worry - the RUC are having a spot of bother. It will all be over in a couple of weeks!"

The advance party flew from RAF Brize Norton to Aldergrove airport, north of Belfast, during the afternoon of 18 August, followed by the main body next day. From Aldergrove the Battalion was transported to the temporarily unoccupied Abercorn Barracks at Ballykinler (the normal occupants of which were on exercise in Kenya), where it spent two days sorting out and learned that it was now part of 39 Brigade, which was responsible for Belfast and the counties of Down and Antrim. It then moved to West Central Belfast, scene of some of the most vicious rioting, where it relieved the Royal Regiment of Wales.

Operationally, the Battalion was organised into six composite groups - A Company (Major Charles Chandler), Y Company (Major Mike Draper, The Duke of Edinburgh's Royal Regiment), Z Company (Major Robert Bewell, The Gloucestershire Regiment) acting as a rifle company, Tactical HQ, Echelon and Base. A Company established themselves in Proctor and Gamble's warehouse in Cupar Street. Apart from the strong smell of soap powder and detergent it was an adequate building but lacked heating and sufficient ablutions, although it enjoyed the facilities of a brand new kitchen belonging to a local school. Y Company was somewhat dispersed with Company HQ and one platoon in a large house belonging to a doctor, another platoon in a disused primary school and the third platoon in a recently vacated police station. Z Company occupied a basement of the Royal Victoria Hospital, with one platoon two streets away in Roden Street Police Station. Tactical HQ was set up in the half-completed Springfield Police Station and the Echelon was based in the TA Centre at Sunnyside under the Quartermasters, Captain Harry Barnard and Captain Bob Bate-Jones.

A Company was deployed first, arriving in its area on 20 August. It was clear at once that, whatever historical wrongs the English were said to have committed against the Irish, these did not begin to approach the horrors Irishmen were capable of inflicting on each other. "It was a terrible sight; rows of gutted houses, ruined factories, still smouldering, littered streets, tense

229

frightened people confronting each other across the Orange-Green line of Cupar Street, peering from behind barricades of burnt-out cars; fear and suspicion walked the streets. Was this really the United Kingdom? We settled into a routine of patrols, negotiations, pacification and attempts to lower tension. We became a mixture of Marriage Guidance Bureau, Public Utilities Agency, Policemen, Welfare Centre, removal firm, King Solomon and Dutch Uncle. We made ourselves popular. The people brought us food, even fully-laden breakfast trays with boiled eggs, toast and coffee. One indignant couple even came to inspect our cookhouse, saying that our soldiers always appeared hungry! The job required tact, patience, understanding, firmness, politeness, alertness and toughness when necessary."

The experiences of Y and Z Companies were very similar. Protestant and Catholic alike welcomed the troops as saviours, generously plying patrols and picquets with cups of tea, sandwiches and cake at all hours of the day and night. Once in position, the first task was to mark maps with the boundaries of Protestant, Catholic and mixed areas, thereby enabling a patrolling, vehicle checkpoint and picquetting plan to be drawn up.

The Battalion was to remain in West Central Belfast until 28 November, with occasional rest periods at Ballykinler, and was gradually able to create an intelligence picture of personalities in the area, which was sub-divided into four districts. To control these effectively Colonel May was given a fourth company, first from the 3rd Battalion The Light Infantry, then from 1st Battalion Grenadier Guards and then from 41 Commando Royal Marines, plus one of the Brigade reserve companies retained permanently in the area.

Great pains were taken to impress on the population that the Army was completely impartial. Unfortunately, the very concept of impartiality was meaningless in Ulster, where one was either for or against a particular group of people. Thus, a platoon commander striving to stop a Protestant mob from attacking a Catholic area would be stridently accused of treachery, since he was English and quite possibly a Protestant himself; yet the same subaltern, preventing a Catholic mob from assailing Protestants, would be roundly denounced for favouring the latter. At first, such events could be unsettling, not only because the angry men on both sides preferred bellowed invective to reasoned argument, but also because, for the first time, the troops were operating under the eye of the world's television cameras, which would show everything and explain nothing. More often than not, the very presence of the cameras would inflame the hot-heads into displays of exhibitionism that could lead to a full-scale riot, a situation which seemed to suit the media folk very well - after all, scenes of violence, stone-throwing and burning vehicles are the lifeblood of every news editor, whereas quiet, peaceful steets are not. The demands made on the patience, understanding and forbearance of every soldier were enormous, but were amply fulfilled.

The Journal provides an excellent summary of the Battalion's activities during this, its first tour of duty in the Province:

"In the middle of September it was decided that a Peace Line should be built to separate the two factions and with a lot of discussion and a certain amount of misgivings by everyone it went up. As it turned out the building of the Peace Line was the first of four significant chapters that led to the general quietening down of the situation.

"The Peace Line is a rather terrifying wall of corrugated iron, barbed wire and searchlights which creates a No Man's Land between the two sides. It caused an enormous amount of world comment and it was at this time we were faced with the might of the World Press. Although they had been around the whole time, with the Peace Line they were on the ground as it was being planned and as it went up. One found that a discussion on policy at 15:30 hours on the ground tended to be World TV news at 17:50 that evening.

"It was at this time we made the headlines in a big way by using CS gas. It was a quiet autumn Sunday afternoon and everyone seemed to be minding their own business when an instant riot happened. By instant, we mean that the local population lived up to their promise of being able to produce four thousand people on either side in four minutes. As a result, two soldiers from Y Company found themselves back to back keeping the masses apart. The use of CS gas to disperse the crowd was necessary if the soldiers on the ground were to prevent loss of life. The Company Commander, accepting command responsibility for the incident, was temporarily suspended from duty pending an enquiry and was replaced by the newly appointed Adjutant, Captain Bruce Willing. The enquiry completely exonerated anyone of taking an unwise decision and also brought out the fact that the use of a non-toxic gas was infinitely preferable to the use of force of arms in the exercise of minimum force. Thus chapter two was entered.

"Once the Irish had learned to respect the use of CS gas and to know what it meant when a soldier donned his respirator a certain amount of steam went out of the situation. However, as in all situations there is always a man who wants to chance his arm and, whether through drink and thus Dutch courage, or just bone-headed stupidity, decides to push further than was previously thought necessary. Therefore, it was decided that we would have to show that we were there in the cause of law and order with the result that the famous arrest squad (later known as the snatch squad) was born.

"Each company had an arrest squad and they were used as fast policemen who sorted out trouble on the spot and, if necessary, gave chase. They did not wear equipment and carried a truncheon instead of a firearm. After the initial impression, when, among other things, a bus full of drunkards was quietened down in front of BBC News, a bank robber was caught by Lance Corporal Lawless, a 100-metre sprint champion, and the local yob found he wasn't as fast as he or his girlfriend thought, it was accepted and undoubtedly helped the Battalion to control its area without the use of firearms. A third and very significant chapter had been reached and there was one more to come.

"The Shankill Road, although our northern boundary, was exclusive to us. On the night of 11-12 October the Protestants decided that for one reason or another they had had enough and that they would have an illegal gathering of a couple of thousand militants, and if we (the Army) threw gas, they would retaliate with small arms fire. However, they made a serious misappreciation in that they thought the much-maligned RUC would get out of the way. It was a mistake that led to tragedy, deaths on both sides and a tenth battalion being flown into Northern Ireland.

"The RUC did not get out of the way, the militants did not wait for the gas to be thrown, an RUC constable was shot and killed, and in the resulting exchange of fire between the militants and the Army, three Irishmen lost their lives and many more people on both sides were wounded. Having tried everything the militant Irishmen at last realised the Army was there for business. Chapter four was closed and now we could look for normality.

"In the meantime the conditions under which the soldiers were living had come in for a lot of publicity. An enormous amount of work was undertaken by the Ministry of Public Buildings and Works and soon the Company locations were almost habitable. The finer touches were provided by our Quartermasters and it was not just good luck that our soldiers had their heaters, beds, blankets and sheets before anyone else!

"During the whole time we were in Belfast, one of our main problems was to help in getting the RUC back into Catholic areas. Some of these areas had not been patrolled regularly by the RUC for years. It took hours of patient negotiation before the joint Army and RUC patrols went into these areas. At the same time each company took on community relations programmes, armed patrols were reduced, and the situation returned to as near normal as it ever can be in Northern Ireland."

The Hampshires had made many friends on both sides during their stay in Belfast - so many that, as their tour drew to a close, petitions were presented to the various headquarters requesting that they remain in the city. In addition to the official messages of appreciation received by Colonel May, there were numerous private letters of thanks. Extracts from one very moving example, written by a Catholic lady, are quoted below:

"Sir, politicians may argue and extremists may fight and murder and troops seem to bear the full brunt of everything but if they think of the so many women, children and old people to whom their presence here in N.Ireland has brought so much peace and freedom from the anguish and dread of recent months then maybe it will make their efforts seem worthwhile. While they stand on guard at street corners with so many people passing, your lads may think these people don't give them a single thought. So many of us do. For their cheerfulness and civility I wish now to give my deepest thanks. . . I am no one important, just a widowed mother with children, praying and hoping for an end to all this nightmare. . ."

So far, very little has been said about the IRA, for the simple reason that it had played a very minor role in the inter-communal strife. For years it had prided itself on being the protector of the Catholic areas, but when the Protestant mobs came it was shown to be powerless. Its few remaining gunmen had dug out their weapons and fired a few rounds into the crowd, then disappeared. Now, it stood discredited among the Catholics. Its upper echelons in Dublin, in fact, were keener to engage in Marxist politics than in terrorism, and in December 1969 they announced that Sinn Fein would recognise the Westminster, Stormont and Dublin governments and contest elections for all three. This was too much for the hardliners from Ulster, who were all for a renewed campaign of terror against the British security forces and the Protestants. As a result the IRA was split down the middle into the Official IRA, consisting of the older, more politically-minded leadership, and the Provisional IRA, containing the Northern hardliners. The two hated each other as cordially as they hated the British and the Ulster Protestants, and a protracted campaign of mutual assassination ensued, during which the Provisionals gained the upper hand. From this point onwards their strategy became clear. Support for their cause within the Catholic community would be restored in two ways: first, by terror and intimidation, thereby proving they were still a force to be reckoned with; and secondly, by engineering riots, sniping and other incidents within those areas that would provoke a strong military reaction, so alienating Catholic support for the Army. Thereafter, the campaign would generate its own momentum.

Meanwhile, back at Netheravon, the 1st Battalion was preparing for its sixth major change of role in a year, proving that it was nothing if not versatile! In October Colonel May had been informed that the Battalion would be required to perform Public Duties in London during the New Year because of Household Division commitments in Ulster and elsewhere. This was a great honour, albeit that the idea was a little intimidating at first. However, the Hampshires' neighbours in Belfast, the 1st Battalion The Parachute Regiment, had performed the role the previous year and from the details supplied by them it was apparent that the difficulties were not insurmountable.

Public Duties consisted of mounting a guard at St James's Palace, Buckingham Palace, the Tower of London and the Bank of England, requiring five officers and 124 soldiers, plus the Band and Drums for the Changing of the Guard Ceremony at Buckingham Palace. Dress for all guards would consist of greatcoats, No 2 Dress, No 1 Dress hat with chinstrap down, best DMS boots and black webbing with the Wilson buckle, a buckle bearing the Regimental badge on a silver coloured plate, instituted by Colonel Sandy Wilson during his time as Commanding Officer. The mention of greatcoats raised some eyebrows, for although such things were still issued they had largely been replaced by the combat jacket and were rarely worn. Moreover, unlike its counterpart in several Continental armies, which had been designed for visual effect, the British greatcoat was intended for hard usage and consisted of thick, inflexible cloth upon which the domestic iron made little or no impression. Happily, the Household Brigade wore greatcoats as a matter of course throughout the winter and possessed enormous steam presses that would prove more than equal to the problem.

The square at Airfield Camp was marked out by the recently appointed RSM, WOI George Thomas, an ex-Gloster soldier who had fought at the Battle of the Imjin and who had been posted in as a part of the preparations for amalgamation. His challenge was to re-create the dimensions of the square in Chelsea Barracks and the forecourt of Buckingham Palace, while the Officers' Mess car park doubled for St James's Palace and the Tower of London. Several senior Guards NCOs arrived to advise on the detailed aspects of the ceremonial and a Regimental Drill Sergeant, WOII Colin Burnett, was appointed. Drill, in fact, became a continuous daily round, punctuated by such traditional Guards reprimands as "You're in bad order!" and "You've lost your name!"

"It was decided that rather than turning everyone into a 'jack of all trades,' we would practise the policy of maximum specialisation. Thus the soldier at the Tower of London did the same duty for his complete tour. A, Y and Z Companies formed duty teams from their own manpower resources, augmented by HQ Company. Each duty team would go to London for ten days at a time, stay in Chelsea Barracks for the whole period and thus do day on and day off with one of the Guards Regiments. The only people who stayed in Chelsea Barracks for the whole of the Public Duties period were the Band and Drums and the administrative party."

The tour of Public Duties lasted from 15 January to 10 February 1970. All went well, the high standard of drill being remarked upon by experts in the subject. For most of the time the Queen was not in residence, and in these circumstances single sentries only were posted, while at the Tower there was no Guard Mounting or Dismounting Ceremony. At St James's Palace and the Tower sentries were in direct contact with the general public and could find themselves draped in admiring tourists until the police intervened. The Band (WOI (BM) G.E.Gregory) and Drums (Drum Major Ferris) were particular favourites of the female staff in the BOAC Terminal in Victoria, who would fling open their windows and lean out whenever they passed and even submitted requests for *Those Magnificent Men in Their Flying Machines* and *Hello Dolly*, which were duly played in their honour. Earl Mountbatten of Burma paid an informal visit to Chelsea Barracks, inspecting a Guard under Major M.G.P.Chignell prior to their going on duty, and later called in at the Sergeants' Mess. Equally welcome, albeit for different reasons, was the actress Miss Alexandra Bastedo, who had been elected "Miss Royal Hampshire".

On 10 February Colonel May, acting as Captain of The Queen's Guard dismounting on the day of an investiture, was presented to The Queen, who noted in conversation that this was the last Guard to be provided by the Regiment and showed great interest in the Regiment's recent activities and the projected amalgamation.

As Colonel of the Regiment, Major General Batten had watched the performance of the 1st Battalion's duties very closely, as had many of the Regiment's senior officers, including Brigadier H.W.Le Patourel, VC, and Brigadier P.H.Cadoux-Hudson, MC, DL. All wrote to Colonel May expressing pride in the high standard of discipline, drill, turnout, bearing and music that had been achieved. Similar letters were received from a senior police officer involved in the civil aspects of Public Duties, and from members of the public whose offices lay along the route. Major General The Hon Michael Fitzalan Howard, CB, CBE, MVO, MC, Commanding the Household Division, wrote to thank the Battalion for the presentation of a silver cigarette box commemorating the tour, commenting, "I very often noticed the sentries myself and have yet to find anything wrong with them. They are producing a very high standard and I do congratulate you all."

Once the entire Battalion was back at Netheravon it commenced individual training and prepared for what had formerly been known as the Annual Adminstrative Inspection but was now known as the Fit for Role Inspection, since it included a considerable tactical element. As part of the Inspection the Battalion was required to:

provide a Quarter Guard;

move a Company together with all its vehicles and stores by air;

236

move a Company by helicopter to a location where a company group defensive position was dug;

fire mortar defensive fire tasks in support of the Company position using live ammunition;

fire the Battalion anti-tank guns at night, using live ammunition against tank targets illuminated by the Battalion mortars;

mount a reconnaissance patrol and a platoon strength fighting patrol;

and lay a minefield.

The Divisional Commander, having spent much of the night with the Battalion in the field, commented in his report, "Throughout the exercise the morale was of the highest order and the self-confidence of the junior NCOs was particularly impressive."

At the end of May 1970 the 1st Royal Hampshires battalion group, including a Light Battery RA, a Field Troop RE, a Drowned Vehicle Park Team from Infantry Workshops and a Forward Air Control Section RAF, took part in a major amphibious exercise, codenamed Soleil, at Saunton Sands on the North Devon coast. The ships participating were the RFA *Sir Geraint* and the LCTs *Aachen* and *Audemer* and the actual landings involved two LCMs and an Amphibious Beach Unit from HMS *Intrepid*, three Wessex helicopters, three hovercraft and twelve DUKWs, the last being six-wheeled, 2-ton amphibious trucks manned by the RASC and used to transport supplies from anchored ships to the beach. A and Y Companies came ashore by a combination of DUKWs, hovercraft and helicopters, with the vehicles and guns being landed from the LCTs at Instow. The landings were not without incident, particularly for the Commanding Officer and his radio operator who found themselves cast adrift on the orders of the Captain of the RFA *Sir Geraint* as he was concerned that the Mexefloat, being used by troops for transfer onto the hovercraft, was damaging his ship. Fortunately the Adjutant was also at the stern and therefore able to plead for the return of his Commanding Officer. The Mexefloat came back and the exercise continued. The various designated objectives were captured, care being taken not to invade an adjacent nature reserve that was home to an extremely rare snail. Re-embarkation was carried out without incident the following day. The Brigade Commander expressed himself well pleased with the result, commenting to Colonel May that his headquarters had gained a valuable understanding of the problems that might be encountered in similar situations.

With the shadow of the proposed amalgamation looming

ever closer, it had already been decided to hold a final ceremonial parade. This took place on 13 June in the beautiful surroundings of the Green Jackets Cricket Club at St Cross and was witnessed by some 2000 spectators. For what was expected to be the last time, the Colonel of the Regiment inspected the 400 officers and men of the 1st Battalion. The Colours, carried by the oldest and youngest serving officers, respectively Captain H.L.Barnard, MBE, and Second Lieutenant P.W.L.Hughes, were then trooped along the ranks, after which the Battalion marched past in slow and quick time, followed by the Comrades. The perfect weather could not conceal the nostalgia of the occasion, yet the sadness expressed by participants and spectators mingling afterwards in the tea area was to prove unexpectedly premature.

There were a number of reasons for this. The public had been angered not only by the latest round of defence cuts, but also by the way the Army had apparently been forced to fight with one arm tied behind its back during the latter days in Aden. The politicians, it seemed, had their own definition of minimum force, and the words "necessary" or "appropriate" did not form part of it. Anger had boiled over when, following the ambush and murder of a number of British soldiers in Crater by the mutinous Aden Armed Police, the authorities had apparently prohibited any form of retaliation. The Army's honour had been restored when Lieutenant Colonel Colin Mitchell re-occupied Crater with the 1st Battalion The Argyll and Sutherland Highlanders, giving short shrift to any terrorists who attempted to operate in the area. When awards were made for the campaign, Mitchell received a mere Mention in Despatches, which the public regarded as a vindictive insult, the more so as the Argylls remained on the list of regiments due to lose their separate identity. Mitchell, having left the Army and been elected to a seat in Parliament, became the most prominent figure in the Save the Argylls Campaign, which received enormous public support. With memories of the Battle of the Imjin still comparatively fresh, a similar campaign to Save the Glosters also won immense support. The extent to which these measures alone would have influenced the government, even after Edward Heath's Conservative administration came to power in June 1970, remains a moot point, but they did create a climate in which the public would respond favourably to an abatement in the proposed cuts.

Such an abatement was rendered inevitable by the deterio-

238

rating situation in Ulster, where the IRA, after its shaky start, was now engaged in a full-scale terrorist campaign. "Without infantry," Field Marshal Montgomery had once said, "one can achieve absolutely nothing - nothing." In a counter-insurgency situation the demand for infantrymen on the ground is extremely heavy, and suddenly the Army found itself so short of infantry battalions to deploy in Ulster that artillerymen and dismounted tank crews would be brought in to operate in the infantry role. In these circumstances, therefore, the Treasury was forced to concede the preservation of some infantry assets that would otherwise have vanished in the drive for economy. The Royal Hampshire Regiment (37th/67th) was to be offered the alternatives of either amalgamation with The Gloucestershire Regiment (28th/61st) as planned; or reduction to a single independent Company, while the Glosters, because of their seniority, remained at full strength; the Argylls (91st/93rd), too, would be reduced to a single independent Company. While still painful, the decision took due note of seniorities and at least it permitted regiments to preserve their separate identities.

Such was the need for haste, with the Amalgamation Parade planned for 5 September, that the first intimation of these decisions to be received by Colonel May was a telephone call from the Chief of the General Staff on 5 August, followed the next day by a formal letter delivered by hand. Colonel May immediately joined the Colonel of the Regiment, who was watching the Regimental XI play cricket against the Lord Lieutenant's XI at Winchester. The two repaired to Serle's House where they decided that the second option was preferable since it permitted the possibility of future expansion. This decision was ratified four days later at a meeting attended by the Colonels, Commanding Officers and Regimental Secretaries of both Regiments, the Ministry being notified accordingly.

Preparations for the amalgamation, including the presentation of a jewelled brooch to the Duchess of Gloucester, who was to have been Colonel-in-Chief of the new Regiment, negotiations with the civic authorities in Portsmouth, where the Amalgamation Parade was to have taken place, and even the issue of a commemorative postal cover, were at a very advanced stage and had to be thrown into sharp reverse immediately.

Thus, at the eleventh hour, was the Regiment's identity preserved. Major General R.H.Batten, CB, CBE, DSO, DL, would remain as Colonel of the Regiment, the active element of which, for the moment, would consist of one independent company named The Minden Company, The Royal Hampshire Regiment (37th/67th Foot), commanded initially by Major B.R.Hobbs, The Duke of Edinburgh's Royal Regiment, who was Second-in-Command of the 1st Battalion. The Ministry's instructions were that Minden Company should be activated at once and on 25 August 1970 it paraded for the first time. In the meantime, having received the thanks of Colonel May for maintaining the Regiment's high standards to the end, the remainder of the 1st Battalion dispersed, the majority to The Glosters, some to The Duke of Edinburgh's Royal Regiment, some to extra-Regimental employment and some to civilian life on retirement. The sorrow at the parting of old comrades-in-arms requires no further emphasis.

* * * * * * * *

CHAPTER 12

MINDEN COMPANY 1970 — 1972

Establishment and roles - Public Duties at the funeral of Field Marshal Lord Slim - KAPE Tours in Hampshire - troop trials with Puma helicopter - move to Colchester - jungle warfare training in Malaysia - Major General Richard Batten succeeded as Colonel of the Regiment by Brigadier D.J.Warren - announcement that the 1st Battalion to be restored to full strength - the deteriorating situation in Ulster - the Company in Gibraltar - training and sport - success of the Rugby Football team - the Inter-Section Rock Race - return home and disbandment

On 4 September 1970 the Colonel of the Regiment inspected Minden Company, commanded by Major B.R. Hobbs, The Duke of Edinburgh's Royal Regiment, for the first time. Intentionally, the 120-strong Company represented the 1st Battalion in a reduced form, its platoons being lettered A, B, Y and Z, plus Company HQ and a small transport echelon. In due course Z Platoon acquired a section each of Wombats and 81mm mortars and provided a small Corps of Drums. Throughout its lifetime the Company emphasised that it was the heart of the Regiment and therefore home to any of the now dispersed Hampshires who cared to visit it. Shortly after its formation, Major Hobbs was succeeded in command by Major D.A.Protheroe and in December 1970 the unit's title was formally amended by the Army Board of the Defence Council to The 1st Battalion The Royal Hampshire Regiment Minden Company.

Selection of the Company's personnel had lasted three days and great efforts had been made to pick the best men available with due consideration being given to individual career and promotion factors. Of those selected only half a dozen had declined the offer, all for good reasons.

Given that the battalion was the fundamental infantry unit, there were some who doubted whether an independent company was a viable proposition and, in the light of recent developments, there were suggestions that the concept owed much to political expediency. In fact, Minden Company had a number of clearly defined roles to perform within its Brigade. These were:

to seize and hold ground for the Brigade Commander;

to carry out important Brigade patrol tasks that would otherwise have to be centralised;

to act as Brigade Airmobile Reserve;

to reinforce other units in Ulster if required;

and to similarly meet any world-wide requirement for a company-sized force.

On 22 December the Company performed its first public ceremonial duty, providing three half-companies, each consisting of one officer and twenty soldiers, for street-lining during the funeral of Field Marshal Lord Slim, KG, GCB, GCMG, GCVO, GBE, DSO, MC, in Windsor. The half-companies were trained by CSM A.J.Rumbold and commanded by Lieutenant J.P.D.Hooley and Sergeant M.Gibson; Second Lieutenant P.W.L.Hughes and Corporal P.Copping; and Second Lieutenant P.A.Davis and Sergeant J.Le Gallou.

Visitors to the Company included Lord Balniel, Minister of State for Defence, on 22 February 1971, accompanied by Major General G.C.A. Gilbert, MC, GOC 3rd Division, and the Colonel of the Regiment, who attended a number of training sessions, including one devoted to the unarmed combat disciplines of Akaido, those taking part having been trained by Lance Corporal Ashton.

Reduction to Company strength made it even more important to demonstrate to the people of Hampshire that their County Regiment was alive and well. Two KAPE Teams under Second Lieutenants Mike Reeve-Tucker and Paul Davis were despatched on a fortnight's tour, demonstrating respectively two aspects of the Company's work, namely Airportability and Jungle Warfare. Audiences varied between a dozen bikers and their girlfriends who turned up expecting a dance but enjoyed the lectures anyway, through small groups of serious-minded Army Cadets, to over 300 wildly-excited schoolchildren. As always, the Teams were well received and thoroughly enjoyed themselves, returning convinced that they had each secured a number of potential recruits.

Minden Company was next required to participate in troop trials with the new Puma helicopter. This was capable of carrying sixteen fully-armed soldiers, was fast, offered excellent visibility and good communication between the troop commander and the pilot, and in these latter respects represented a vast improvement on the Wessex. The principal task was to establish drills for mounting and dismounting in the shortest possible time. It is pleasing to record that these problems, which confounded the experts for several hours, were solved by the soldiers after a few minutes' talk among themselves!

Shortly before Easter, Minden Company moved from Netheravon to Roman Way Camp, Colchester, Essex, where it came under the command of 19 Airportable Brigade, commanded by Brigadier G.L.C.Cooper, MC. After settling in, it took part in an air mobility exercise, Sky Warrior, on the Stanford Training Area, and on 10 May travelled to the Hythe/Lydd range complex, where the annual range classification was fired.

Major David Protheroe had already been informed that the Company would be undergoing training at the Jungle Warfare School in Malaysia. The next few weeks were therefore spent in reaching the necessary standard of fitness and learning the basic drills. The Company landed at Singapore on 12 June and during the ensuing two months took part in an exercise with the 1st Battalion The King's Own Royal Border Regiment, honed up its patrolling and ambush skills against an enemy provided by the WRAC, competed for the Winchester Trophy, which was won by A Platoon, celebrated Minden Day in the traditional manner, enjoyed periods of rest and recuperation in Singapore, and held an adventure training exercise on three islands off Mersing, on the east coast of the Malayan Peninsula.

During this period events of great importance to the Regiment took place. On 30 June 1971 Major General Batten relinquished his Colonelcy of the Regiment and was succeeded by Brigadier D.J.Warren, DSO, OBE, MC. It was General Dick Batten who had decided upon reduction to a single company rather than amalgamation on the basis of "While there is life there is hope," and now the wisdom of this was to be amply demonstrated. In October Brigadier Warren travelled out to Malaya to visit Minden Company for the first time in his capacity as Colonel of the Regiment. Shortly after his arrival he was shown a signal which Major Protheroe had just received from the Ministry of Defence. The 1st Battalion The Royal Hampshire Regiment was to be restored to full strength and this would be announced by Lord Carrington, Secretary of State for Defence, the following day. Little time was lost in advising the rest of the Company of this excellent news, which was appropriately celebrated.

The background to this development was complex and contained political strands as well as consideration of low manning levels in some regiments. In Scotland, where preservation of regiments was a greater political issue than in England, the Save the Argylls campaign had attracted enormous support and, prior to the 1970 General Election, Lord Balniel, then Opposition Spokeman on Defence, had spoken publicly of finding a "meaningful role" for the Argylls. This placed his colleagues in something of a dilemma since the Argylls (91st/93rd Foot), however distinguished, were still a junior regiment, and if something was done for them it would also have to be done for threatened regiments with greater seniority. When the General Election produced a Conservative victory it was, therefore, necessary to address the problem. Prime Minister Edward Heath was opposed to the cadre system but had agreed to the formation of representative companies in the case of regiments whose manning levels had shown a recent improvement, of which the Royal Hampshire Regiment was one; hence Minden Company. Now, because of the continuing deterioration of the situation in Ulster the government was forced to restore the representative companies to full battalion strength.

By various means, including intimidation, the Provisional IRA had turned round large sections of the Catholic community. It orchestrated violent riots, the images of which were shown on television screens around the world. In the United States these were used by Provisional agents as evidence of brutal British repression in Ireland, and the large Irish-American community, with its strong inherited folk-memory of famine, absentee landlords, eviction and mass emigration, willingly provided ample funds for the terrorists in the belief that the money would be used for relief work. A partial answer was found by commandeering the television crews' lighting systems. This removed much of the incentive to riot, as there would be little television coverage, and fewer riots took place. The Provisionals also began sniping and bombing, the reponse of the security forces being to mount weapon searches in the Catholic areas. These produced some results but could be counter-productive if they were carried out in a heavy-handed fashion, as wrecked homes further alienated the Catholics and provided recruits for the terrorists. Their success in re-establishing their authority in the nationalist areas led the Provisionals to embark upon what they called their Aden Strategy. Aden, it had been said at the height of the terrorist campaign there, was not worth the life of a single British soldier, and now the Provisionals tried to create similar conditions in Ulster, making special targets of the Army and the RUC, reasoning that public opinion in mainland Britain would be outraged by the loss of life and demand that the troops be withdrawn. In fact, there was a consensus of opinion between the politicians and the public that a surrender to violence was out of the question not only on political grounds but also because it would merely encourage any crackpot with an axe to grind and access to firearms or explosives. A further complication was that extreme "loyalists" had started terror gangs of their own. For its part the Army, having initially been called to the aid of the civil power, now found itself having to wage a counter-insurgency campaign without an adequate intelligence infrastructure, save for information supplied by the RUC's Special Branch, which was of limited value since it had little or no sympathy among the nationalist community. The Army was slowly building up a network of contacts and informers as well as developing its own surveillance techniques, but time was needed for it to become effective. Meanwhile, the figures told their own grisly story. One police officer had been killed in 1969 and two more in 1970, but in 1971 the death toll would rise dramatically and include forty-three soldiers, five members of the Ulster Defence Regiment, a partly regular and partly part-time force recruited from Protestants and Catholics with the intention that it should replace the hated "B" Specials, and eleven policemen. There were 213 terrorist shooting and 170 bombing incidents in 1970, but for 1971 the respective figures would be 1756 and 1515. In 1970 324 weapons and half a ton of explosives had been found; in 1971 the figures were 717 weapons and two-and-a-half tons of explosives. Over the period of the Emergency to date, 61 republican terrorists had been killed (of whom 52 died in 1971), plus two "loyalist" gunmen. All the indications were that things would get much worse before they started to improve, and that the Army, because of its commitments in Germany and elsewhere, would be stretched to contain the situation.

On Minden Company's return from the Far East it enjoyed a week's leave and then began to prepare for an emergency tour in Gibraltar as Frontier Company. Such frequent comings and goings led someone to suggest that its unofficial motto should be "Have Gun, Will Travel," the title of a current television series. The Company flew into Gibraltar on 10 November and was accommodated in Devil's Tower Barracks. Its duties included patrols along the frontier wire, manning three observation posts and a Guard Room, undertaken by one platoon on a weekly rotation. A ceremonial guard was mounted outside the Guard Room, both the Guard Changing and the sentries being a popular tourist attraction. In the observation posts any event of note on the Spanish side of the frontier was duly logged, as well as items of purely passing interest, such as the Guardia Civil (known to A Platoon as the Guard of Seville) disappearing to relieve themselves. One entry, timed at 00:01 on 25 December, reported three old men leaving the Eastern Beach, apparently following a star!

A Junior NCOs Cadre course was held and all members of the rifle platoons attended introductory lectures on support weapons. Close co-operation with the other services was maintained during exercises for the defence of the Rock and many friends were made with members of the Royal Navy and RAF, who were often encountered socially in Gibraltar's numerous pubs and bars, of which there were no fewer than 188 in an area measuring just three-and-a-half square miles. As a result, the Company was drawn into the local craze for "zapping," a zap being a sticky, luminous piece of paper in the shape of a crest that could be slapped on other people's property, conferring prestige in proportion to the difficulty involved in reaching the target. Z Platoon, having adopted a Tiger zap, proved to be experts in the art, zapping the Captain's table on HMS *Bacchante*, the boot of the Governor's car, the mascot of a Fusilier regiment, and Miss Gibraltar. Others in the Company took great pleasure in slapping Regimental zaps on the RAF's closely guarded Hunters.

Sport of every kind was considered to be of primary importance in Minden Company. In Gibraltar most afternoons were given over to physical exercise. Soccer, hockey, basketball and squash were all played. Dinghy sailing was also available, two courses run by the Company producing eight qualified helmsmen. Rugby football was something the Company excelled at. In Colchester its seven-a-side team, consisting of Lance Corporal Donaldson, Private Batty, Corporal Unsworth, Second Lieutenant Reeve-Tucker, Lieutenant Davis, Lieutenant Hughes and Lance Corporal Lawless, shocked the opposition's supporters into silence by fighting their way through to the final of the 3rd Division competition. Proving that this was no fluke, the full team also inflicted convincing defeats on 3 RHA, a local civilian club called The Affairs, and the 1st Battalion King's Own Border Regiment. In Gibraltar, because of the hardness of the ground, the game was restricted to the "tag" variety, resulting in some very fast matches.

When Major Protheroe returned to the UK in preparation for the expansion to full battalion strength, command of the Company passed to Major Bob Hanscomb, who until then had been its Second-in-Command. Major Hanscomb instituted a competitive Inter-Section Rock Race, the prize for the winning section being two days' extra leave when the Company returned home. Scoring was on the basis of time, recorded on a ladder, so that any section could improve its placing by further runs within a given period. Each section made its run in combat kit with skeleton order and section weapons, starting and finishing at the Moorish Castle, and going round the flagpole at the 1392 feet high summit of the Rock on the way. The first week's efforts were understandably exhausting and resulted in an average time of 37 minutes, but they generated a great deal of enthusiasm. During the second week the average time had fallen to 34 minutes. In the end 1 Section of Y Platoon won with a time of 30 minutes 7 seconds. Lance Corporal Turner achieved the fastest individual time for the course with 26 minutes. Gibraltarians watching the runs thought them insane, but were inclined to view the Royal Hampshires with renewed respect. Since then, Rock Racing seems to have caught the collective imagination of the Gibraltar garrison and the crews of visiting RN ships.

Minden Company returned to the United Kingdom at the end of January 1972. In fact, it had technically ceased to exist on the 15th of that month, the date that the 1st Battalion The Royal Hampshire Regiment was officially re-formed. A significant number of those who had served in the Company went on to achieve greater things in the years to come. CSM Rumbold later became the Battalion's RSM; in due course, Sergeant Crawley, one of several Crawleys in the Regiment, became the Battalion's Chief Clerk; Corporal M.R.Power, the Signals NCO, became a major; and many others, including Colour Sergeant Restall, Sergeant Jesty, Corporal Scott of the MT, and Corporals Copping, Lawless and Link, all enjoyed full and successful careers in the Regiment.

In his introduction to the May 1972 issue of the Journal, the Commanding Officer, Lieutenant Colonel L.J.P.Morrish, paid the members of Minden Company the following tribute:

"They have guarded and even enhanced the reputation of the Regiment in the course of their short existence. They have proved to be an excellent foundation for the expansion. The Colonel of the Regiment, with the agreement of the Regimental Committee, has directed that this period in our history is to be marked, on any future occasion when the 1st Battalion Troops the Colour, by the Escort to the Colour being referred to, throughout the parade, as "The Minden Company." This, it is felt, is a suitable and unique manner in which to pay tribute to those who, for 17 months of our 270 years' history, maintained the Regiment's standing."

* * * * * * * * *

CHAPTER 13

RE-FORMING AND ULSTER
1972 —1974

The 1st Battalion re-forms at Colchester under Lieutenant Colonel L.J.P.Morrish - composition and organisation - Cadet NCOs Leadership Course - symbolic return of Colours by Minden Company at Winchester - burglary at the Regimental Museum - consolidation training in Canada - pre-Ulster training - 2nd Ulster Tour 1972/73 - location of Companies - operational tasks - IRA "come-ons" - urban operations in Newry - Major Wright wounded - deaths of Corporal Leahy and Private King - equipment and visitors - return to Colchester - Z Company re-formed - Bisley results - KAPE Tour and Service - recruiting - improvements in pre-Ulster training - 3rd Ulster Tour 1973/74 - location of Companies - comparisons with previous tour - "come-on" at Donaghmore Bridge - the Estate Specialist - reflections on 3rd Tour - preparations for Hong Kong

T he problems of expansion are not as familiar in the Infantry as those of contraction," wrote A Company's correspondent in the May 1972 issue of the Journal. "There can be no doubt about which set of problems is the more congenial. Constructing instead of destroying is marvellous for the morale of all involved."

Officially, the 1st Battalion was re-formed at Roman Barracks, Colchester, on 15 January 1972. On that date, in fact, it amounted to little more than a skeleton organisation as Minden Company had yet to complete its tour in Gibraltar, return from leave and move from its home base in the nearby Roman Way Camp and only key personnel were present.

THE HAMPSHIRE TIGERS

The Commanding Officer, Lieutenant Colonel L.J.P.Morrish, had joined the Army as a National Serviceman in 1951 and, having decided that he wished to become a Regular, he entered the RMA Sandhurst and was commissioned into the Regiment in 1954. He had served with the 1st Battalion during the Malayan emergency and then in Germany. Following Staff College and his Staff appointment, he had returned to the 1st Battalion in 1967, commanding A Company until the end of the UN tour of duty in Cyprus. He was then posted to the Directorate of Army Staff Duties and the Ministry of Defence, where he was involved in the decision to form Minden Company. He was appointed Second-in-Command of the 1st Battalion The Gloucestershire Regiment in 1971.

Colonel Morrish was able to brief the nucleus of the Battalion on the probable form events would take during the next year. Re-forming would involve three phases. Phase 1, to be completed by 1 June, would bring the Battalion up to an approximate strength of 450, achieved by attracting volunteers from every regiment in the Prince of Wales's Division, of whom the majority were expected to be former members of the Battalion. Phase 2, to be completed during the summer, would see 150 more men posted to the Battalion, some of whom would be volunteers and the rest directed. Phase 3 would involve an internal reorganisation aimed at forming Support (Z) Company early the following year. For the moment, emphasis would be placed on section training until the end of June, after which company training culminating in a Battalion exercise would be carried out in Canada. On its return from this the Battalion would be trained for Ulster, where it could expect to be deployed towards the end of the year.

Not all of those who had previously served with the old 1st Battalion volunteered to return. Some were making excellent progress with their careers elsewhere, while others had embarked on financial or other commitments that prevented them from up-rooting themselves for a second time. Nevertheless, as expected, the great majority of the volunteers were former Royal Hampshires, this being particularly so in the case of the Warrant Officers and Sergeants, led by RSM R.W.Coleman. In other respects, drafts of varying size arrived from regiments within the Prince of Wales's Division and from the Wessex, Mercian and Welsh training depots. Naturally, some of these men were very young soldiers, yet also present was a wealth of experience from every operational theatre in which the Army had been engaged in recent years, and, individually, all believed that their future lay with The Royal Hampshire Regiment. The presence of so many Welshmen produced an interesting situation. They were good soldiers, and there were enough of them to avoid feeling swamped by the Hampshires; rather, the effect was to stimulate healthy competition.

The professional aspects of re-formation - the reception, administration, interviewing and internal postings - presented all those involved with unaccustomed but welcome challenges and also much hard work, particularly for the Adjutant, Captain B.J.Willing, and the Orderly Room staff under ORQMS Crawley. Captain Willing was well placed to carry out this pivotal role as he had been Adjutant during the run-down of the Battalion in 1970.

The families and their welfare were seen as an important part in achieving a successful re-formation and the Battalion was fortunate in having Major B.J.Lambert of the Staffordshire Regiment posted in as Families Officer. He was subsequently to be made an MBE for his work - probably the first Families Officer in the infantry to be recognised in this way. The Battalion was also fortunate in having Padre Jim Shewan, who gained the respect and affection of all ranks and became an influential member of the Welfare team. The Quartermaster's Department inevitably faced a considerable workload but, again, the Battalion was well served, initially by the acting Quartermaster, Captain F.Thomas, Royal Welch Fusiliers, and subsequently, on his return from the Gloucesters, by Captain R.J.Bate Jones, MBE.

During these early months, the Battalion was concentrating on internal tasks but there were also outside commitments including, on 28 March 1972, a Freedom March through Aldershot as part of the Borough's 50th Anniversary celebrations. An unscheduled task arose from the operational deployment of another battalion at short notice, the result being that the Battalion became responsible for running the UK Land Forces Cadet NCO Leadership Course at Stanford Training Area from 4th to 20th April. While much of the outline planning had already been done, there was still a considerable amount of detailed work to be undertaken and it fell to Major D.A.Protheroe, the Second-in-Command, and Captain F.Thomas, who carried the main burden. Although the Battalion's initial reaction at being given such a high-profile task was not enthusiastic, the undoubted success of the course, coupled with the quality of the 200 or so cadets who attended, made it a thoroughly rewarding and enjoyable break from the serious business of re-forming.

The Battalion's most notable visitor at Roman Barracks during this period was the Chief of General Staff, General Sir Michael Carver, GCB, CBE, DSO, MC, ADC, who arrived on 17 April. On 2 May a party of trainee journalists from Harlow Technical College visited the Battalion as part of their public relations course and were shown various aspects of service life, including weapon training.

Undoubtedly, the most significant and symbolic occasion since the 1st Battalion was re-formed took place during the Comrades' Association Reunion in Winchester on 10 June. This event had been chosen by the Colonel of the Regiment for the formal return of the Colours from safe keeping with the Minden Company to the 1st Battalion. The parade began in the Memorial Garden at Serles' House where, before the assembled Comrades and their Branch Standards, the Colours were handed over by the Minden Company Colour Party to the Colonel of the Regiment and passed to Colonel Morrish, who in turn handed them to Lieutenants Paul Davis and Mike Reeve-Tucker of the 1st Battalion's Colour Party. Following a short drum-head memorial service, the 1st Battalion marched through Winchester behind its own Corps of Drums and the Hampshire and Dorset Band of the Wessex Regiment, the Salute being taken at the Guildhall by the Mayor, Councillor David Sermon. Marching with the Comrades' column, over 300 strong and led by Brigadier H.W.Le Patourel, VC, were Corporal William Halsey, aged 78, and Private Reginald Head, aged 67, of the Royal Hospital, Chelsea, both of the Isle of Wight and former members of the 1st Battalion.

After the parade, over 300 members of the Battalion, Comrades and guests gathered in the Guildhall for the annual reunion dinner of the Comrades' Association. During his speech, Brigadier Warren described the re-forming of the 1st Battalion as "perhaps the most important single event in the 270 years of our history." Proposing a toast to the City of Winchester, Colonel Peter Sawyer, OBE, MC, TD, JP, DL, Chairman of the Association's Executive Committee, stressed that Winchester was the Regiment's home and announced that the Association would be presenting the 1st Battalion with six marker flags for use on ceremonial occasions. Replying, the Mayor said that the city treasured its very close connections with the military, continuing, "On behalf of the citizens, I can say we are absolutely delighted at the re-formation of the 1st Battalion The Royal Hampshire Regiment."

Among those present was Major General Dick Batten, whose wise counsels had resulted in the preservation of the Regiment's separate identity and whose wish to see a re-formed 1st Battalion return to Winchester had now been given substance. Already seriously ill, General Batten died five days later.

On 12 June a two-day air movement administration exercise was held in preparation for the Battalion being placed on the Spearhead Roster - a commitment demanding readiness to move by air at short notice to any part of the world. This was followed at the end of the month by a Battalion Skill-at-Arms Meeting on Colchester ranges, including a Platoon Rifle Match, a GPMG Match, a Falling Plate Competition, a Pistol Match, a Section March and an Assault Course Competition.

June also witnessed a burglary at the Regimental Museum, during which 162 medals, three uniforms and two epaulettes were stolen. Within twenty-four hours two of the uniforms were offered to the Museum by a London dealer, who, on learning what had taken place, supplied the police with a description of the would-be vendor. Thanks to this, together with the detailed records maintained by the Museum and the circulation of dealers, a week later the Museum staff were able to identify every single item among those displayed on several tables at Winchester Police Headquarters. A man was subsequently charged and sentenced to a term of imprisonment at Winchester Crown Court. The police work had been exemplary and the Colonel of the Regiment wrote a letter of appreciation to the Chief Constable.

Between 19 and 22 July the Battalion flew to Canada for Exercise Pond Jump (East) 1972. The objects of this were, first, to practice the Battalion in an air move and in setting up a tented base, and, secondly, to complete Phase 1 of the re-formation process by carrying out individual, sub-unit and unit training, designed to produce a co-ordinated unit, fit and well trained in infantry skills.

This took place at the Canadian Forces' Base, Gagetown, New Brunswick, the largest such base in the Commonwealth, which possessed 428 square miles of training area, incorporating every possible form of military terrain save desert. Because of the large spaces available, field firing presented few problems, but was always well controlled by a centralised Range Control. The base itself supplied administrative support and recreational facilities, including a magnificent swimming pool and a CANEX, the Canadian equivalent of the NAAFI.

The Battalion established itself in Hibernia Camp, already set up by the Advance Party under Major D.A.Protheroe, over-looking the valley of the St John river. Mosquitos were a nuisance and at night indigenous neighbours, including racoons, skunks, porcupines, deer and moose, would drop in to look the Hampshires over. One sentry, spotting a burly figure near the officers' lines in the grey half-light of dawn, wished it a cheery "Good morning!" It proved to be a bear, who neither returned the greeting nor responded to other attempts at conversation; instead, after regarding the startled sentry impassively, it sham-bled off into the woods.

There was, however, little breathing space before tackling the training programme prepared by the Company Command-ers. The training itself at company level was divided into three main categories: map reading, field firing and practising jungle techniques. Starting with individuals, training graduated until each section attained a good measure of expertise in each of these fields. During the navigational exercises, some people learned the hard way that reliance on the compass is essential, and that the map is more accurate than instinct. Beginning with basic range shooting, the field firing exercise progressed through the indi-vidual jungle lanes to full section firing exercises. The latter proved to be particularly valuable in terms of providing operational real-ism with the result that not only did the shooting improve and fieldcraft become noticeably more proficient, but also because the younger soldiers gained enormously in professional confi-dence. Those new to the jungle soon learned now to make them-selves as comfortable as possible in platoon bases, how to lay ambushes, and how to react when ambushed themselves.

One surprise was provided by the startling contrasts in the Canadian climate. Temperatures varied between 97°F at noon and 46°F at night, giving the Medical Officer, Captain J.Ryan, RAMC, heat exhaustion cases to deal with one day and exposure cases the next. A short break in the exercises enabled Minden Day to be celebrated with a parade during which Brigadier Gen-eral S.V.Radley-Walters, DSO, MC, CD, Commander of CFB

Gagetown, took the salute and presented roses imported from Nova Scotia.

A week's rest and recreation was permitted between 12 and 19 August, during which some members of the Battalion covered remarkable distances across the North American continent. One group of twenty-eight travelled 200 miles down the St John river in canoes provided by the Canadian Armed Forces. Colonel Morrish, Captain Willing and RSM Coleman paid a visit to the Regiment's affiliated unit, 49th (Sault Ste Marie) Field Regiment, RCA, at its Armoury in Sault Ste Marie, a steel town in Ontario.

The final phase of Pond Jump (East) consisted of a Battalion exercise codenamed Tiger Jump. A counter-revolutionary warfare situation was set with Y Company, reinforced with members of 2nd Royal Canadian Regiment, providing the enemy who had infiltrated across the border. The exercise included rioting, shooting and grenade attacks, patrols, ambushes and road blocks, culminating in a two-pronged attack on the terrorists' camps. At the conclusion of the Battalion's time in Canada, Colonel Morrish was satisfied that, having arrived with a uniy comprised of soldiers from different backgrounds and with widely different levels of experience and training, he would take home a well-trained and cohesive battalion.

Having returned to Colchester at the end of August, the Battalion went on block leave until 2 October. Its collective mind was now focussed firmly on preparing for the forthcoming tour in Ulster. The first phase of preparation consisted of week's visit from the Northern Ireland Training Team (NITAT), which instructed officers and senior NCOs in the skills, tactics and operational techniques required. During the following week those who had attended the NITAT briefing instructed the rest of the Battalion. The next two weeks were spent in the specially constructed Northern Ireland Training Area at Lydd, Kent, where the lessons received a practical form, including the dispersion of 200 rioters in a convincingly ugly mood.

Having received a most complimentary report following its Fit for Role Inspection, the Battalion celebrated its impending departure with a series of guest nights, parties and social events in its various Messes. The guest night held in the Officers' Mess on 9 October was notable in that it marked the first public performance of the Band since re-formation under the baton of Bandmaster French.

Throughout 1972 the Provisional IRA had pursued its "Aden Strategy" vigorously, with the result that this was the most violent year of the present Troubles. There were, in total, 1853 bombings and no fewer than 10,628 shooting incidents. As a result of these 103 Regular soldiers, 26 members of the Ulster Defence Regiment, 17 policemen and 223 civilians had lost their lives. The cost to the Provisionals, however, was 95 killed, and this was an unacceptably high rate of attrition in a terrorist organisation of which comparatively few members belonged to so-called "active service units." Furthermore, as the intelligence gathering resources of the security forces improved, 531 terrorists, republican and loyalist, had been charged and many were serving terms of imprisonment, arms finds rose to 1264 and no less than 27 tons of explosive were discovered. The Provisionals had also made a serious error of judgement in ostentatiously declaring that certain parts of Londonderry and Belfast were "No Go Areas" as far the security forces were concerned. They lost much face when, having been suitably warned that the Army was coming to evict them during Operation Motorman, which took place on 31 July 1972, their gunmen fled.

The Battalion's Advance Party left Colchester on 22 November, travelling by road and rail to Liverpool and thence by sea to Belfast.

"We arrived a few hours late, to be met by the Battalion Second-in-Command, Major C.W.E.Coppen Gardner, MC, and a grimly flak-jacketed escort of the 1st Battalion The Argyll and Sutherland Highlanders, which had also been re-formed from company strength early in the year, and the armoured cars of the 17th/21st Lancers. As we had brought all our own vehicles, it was a large convoy that set off through Belfast, headlights blazing, our way smoothed by the RMP and RUC through traffic lights and difficult junctions. We headed for Bessbrook, the location of Battalion HQ and Y Company, where we split into packets to make for our final destinations. It was a strange feeling, driving through the apparently peaceful countryside knowing that at any moment a landmine might explode or an ambush might be sprung."

The main body of the Battalion moved to Ulster on 27 November and by mid-afternoon the following day had relieved the Argylls, assuming operational responsibility for some 500 square miles of South Armagh. This had become known as Bandit Country, partly because it lay on that portion of the border which offered the terrorists the most direct route between their hideouts in the Republic and Belfast, partly because many of the local population were republican sympathisers willing to provide support for them, and partly because the terrain was so ideally suited to ambushes. The roads had become so dangerous that in the worst areas helicopters were often used for personnel and supply movements; even the Lancers' Ferret scout cars were vulnerable to mine damage, although their Saladin armoured cars offered better protection.

Battalion HQ and Y Company were located at Bessbrook, A Company at Crossmaglen with platoon bases at Newtownhamilton and Forkhill, and B Company at Newry. With the exception of Bessbrook Mill (Battalion HQ and the Echelon) and the Technical College (Y Company), bases were located in RUC stations or UDR centres. All were crowded and resembled miniature fortresses, with corrugated iron screens to deter snipers, high wire fences to prevent grenades or petrol bombs being thrown, and sandbagged watchtowers.

That the Battalion was now confronted by a real enemy was emphasised on the afternoon of 28 November, during which the Provisionals launched a series of attacks against police stations along the border. While A Company was still flying in to Crossmaglen the roof of the police station was hit by two rockets while a third exploded harmlessly in a field beyond - these, in fact, were the first RPG-7s to be fired in the Province. Simultaneously, for the next few minutes, the base was raked with small arms fire from a range of 150 yards. Fortunately, no casualties were incurred.

Crossmaglen, with a population of 1500, is located just over a mile from the border and was the heart of Bandit Country. "The people," recalled a member of A Company, "are strongly Republican in sympathy, xenophobic in outlook, uncommunicative and, except for a vociferous minority, politically indifferent. The surrounding countryside is pretty, rolling farmland, dotted with smallholdings and intersected with small roads. Newtownhamilton lies some eight miles to the north and is a mixed Catholic and Protestant village. Forkhill is about six miles due east of Crossmaglen and takes its name from its position between two hills. The population of about 650 is again strongly Republicanand the Forkhill base is the most vulnerable to attack."

THE HAMPSHIRE TIGERS

A Company's notes for the Journal provide an excellent account of its operations in this area. "These are geared to the acquisition of further information, hence intelligence, leading to targeted searches for weapons and explosives, 'lifts' of wanted men, and general hindrance of IRA activities. Lack of communication with the local population - their choice, not ours - made information hard to come by. Route clearing was an almost daily task. This involved moving on foot along a road, spread out in an inverted V formation, looking for wires leading to mines under or close to the roads, car bombs, ambush positions and anything else which might make the road unsafe for vehicles. In difficult country the rate of progress might be less than one mile per hour. Another task was Vehicle Check Points, carried out on foot, from vehicles or even from the air - the last being known as Eagle Patrols - the purpose being to search cars, particularly those coming over the border, for arms, ammunition and explosives, wanted persons and anything and anyone contributing to the IRA campaign. The Company searched an average of 100 cars per day in this manner. The 'Farmer's Daughter' patrols involved moving across country calling at farms and cottages, compiling a survey of who lives where, car ownership, dogs - one can follow the progress of a night patrol by the barking of the dogs - and other information which might lead a patrol to spot anything unusual or suspicious. Then there were 'Black-face' Patrols, night tasks on which men with blackened faces flitted silently through the darkness, watching and listening. Other operations included searches of derelict houses, ambushes, observation posts, visiting possible IRA targets, and air observations. Success was measured by small achievements, such as the first smile from a Crossmaglen resident, the first Eagle Patrol with a policeman at Forkhill, and the successful disposal of a car bomb at Newtownhamilton. One soon lost any ideas of cracking the whole problem in two weeks - the conflict was too nebulous for that. Each platoon had its excitements; all three were attacked in their bases by rockets and small arms fire, and all three found bombs before the bombs found them. We made the odd arrest and added quite a lot to the store of intelligence gathered."

Early in the Battalion's tour of duty, two lorries were left abandoned on an isolated road very close to the border. As this was clearly a plant by the IRA aimed at inflicting casualties either from booby traps, mines or an ambush, or possibly all three, the

258

area was "quarantined" for some weeks. Colonel Morrish decided to clear the obstacle by securing the area with 7 and 9 Platoons from Y Company and then flying in a mine-clearing detachment from the Royal Engineers shortly before last light to clear an approach to the suspect vehicles during the night; the ATO would then be flown in at first light and blow up the vehicles. The operation was completed successfully without major incident though two sections of 7 Platoon under Lieutenant P.A.Davis came under small arms fire from across the border; this attack was silenced by several controlled bursts from a GPMG.

In January 1973, halfway through the tour, Y Company replaced A Company as the border company. Y Company already knew the area well, having carried out surveillance patrols throughout the previous two months. Such patrol activity now increased. Each day at first light the high ground south of Crossmaglen was occupied by sections of 7 and 9 Platoons led by Lieutenant Davis and Colour Sergeant Dicker. This activity had both a moral and practical advantage in that it allowed the Company to dominate a particularly active section of the border. Night patrols, normally consisting of eight men including a sniper and a thermal imaging night sight device, were also carried out. On one occasion, after many nights of observation, a small ambush patrol succeeded in arresting a suspected terrorist visiting his girlfriend! The use of Saladin armoured cars by day was increased, sometimes in the role of decoy. At least one bomb exploded under a Saladin but apart from a badly grazed face little damage was caused and the vehicle commander carried on.

Further discoveries included a wire concealed in a wall. This led to a 500-pound bomb concealed in a home-made culvert under a road 1000 yards distant, and a booby-trapped stolen car in a barn some thirty yards from the border. The bomb was defused and the barn was blown up by the ATO.

The experience of B Company at Newry was slightly different in that operations took place partly within an urban environment. Patrolling, manning VCPs and observation posts were a daily routine. Major improvements were made to the O'Meath Road VCP which, on takeover, had consisted of a small tent permanently wet with water running off the high ground behind the position. Bearing in mind that the VCP was manned round the clock, the Quartermaster, Captain Bob Bate Jones, provided an airfield trailer for living purposes within a day and shortly after

259

Colour Sergeant Jesty provided all the other essentials as well as building a sandbag protective wall. These improvements meant that the soldiers manning the VCP were more efficient and their morale was much improved.

During the first two weeks the Company was faced with three days of rioting when several individuals were "lifted" from the town's housing estates. One such estate, Derrybeg, though small, was known to be the home of several gunmen, and patrols entering this were regularly subjected to a barrage of bricks, bottles and abuse from the women and children. On one occasion a demonstration mounted by the People's Democracy marched on the UDR Centre. "They ended up about 600 strong and decided to throw stones, paving stones and bricks into the Company base. They were dispersed by Corporal Stroud and his section, ably assisted by some baton rounds from No 1 Sangar, water from the MT compound, and Sergeant Henry with a section from No 6 Platoon, who apprehended a Japanese photographer carrying a Chinese Red Flag who was egging on an Irish riot!"

Despite this sort of behaviour among the die-hard republican element, most of the townspeople, in contrast to the sullen atmosphere existing in Crossmaglen, were happy to talk to the Company's foot patrols, albeit a little guardedly. The relationship between the inhabitants and the Company was further improved by the latter providing practical assistance when parts of the town were flooded during the winter. The Provisionals clearly resented B Company's grip on the town and in March 1973 bombing and shooting incidents increased. "A favourite ploy of the IRA was to set up a bomb or hoax bomb in some part of the town. This meant that we had to deploy one or more sections to clear the streets and help the RUC to divert traffic. Whilst this was happening the IRA would either deploy their gunmen and shoot at us while we were clearing the area or they would set up an ambush for us on our return. It was during such an incident that the Company Commander and his escorts were shot at. The two Land Rovers were returning from a bomb hoax when they were fired upon from at least two different positions. Major Wright was hit in the head; the remainder of the escort were lucky to escape injury, as both Land Rovers were like a couple of pepper pots after the event."

Major Wright's skull, in fact, had been creased by a .22 round and while he made a quick recovery he was unfit for the rest of the tour. His parent regiment was the The Worcestershire and Sherwood Foresters but he had volunteered to join the Battalion on completion of his Staff College course. He was a popular officer and his Company were understandably angered by the incident, so much so that they found it hard to exercise restraint, and Colonel Morrish decided that the Battalion's Second-in-Command, Major Coppen Gardner, should take over the Company for the rest of the tour. It is, of course, an article of faith in counter-insurgency warfare that the security forces must act within the law, even if this limits what can be achieved. The terrorists, by their very nature, subject themselves to no such restrictions. They were, for example, quite capable of opening fire on a patrol from behind the cover of women and children, who would then cover their escape.

In Bessbrook, a pretty village with a friendly mixed community, the tasks were much the same but the atmosphere was totally different. The centre of the village was barriered off from the outside world at the request of the villagers themselves to prevent car bombs and robberies. Although the companies stationed at Bessbrook constituted the Battalion's operational reserve and maintained a high state of readiness, the immediate area remained comparatively quiet.

Short, sharp gun battles between elements of the Battalion and IRA gangs occurred regularly throughout the tour. Most of these took place close to the border, enabling the "bhoyos" to escape when they had had enough; seldom, if ever, did the Gardai appear until long after the shooting had stopped. During these incidents the Hampshires killed one terrorist and had three hits confirmed out of five claimed. The professional opinion of Y Company was that, "As far as the gunmen operating in our area were concerned, they were not so good when one weighs up all the points they had in their favour, especially the safe sanctuary of the border. Their explosives men, on the other hand, were well trained and determined."

It was the bomb makers who caused the Battalion's two fatal casualties of the tour. On 8 March 1973, Corporal Joe Leahy led a patrol to an abandoned farm which a telephone call reported as being the scene of suspicious activity. This was an IRA "come on" and the building was booby-trapped. When Corporal Leahy kicked in the door there was a tremendous explosion and he sustained injuries which proved fatal despite speedy evacuation

261

by air. Five days later a series of bombs were detonated by radio control as a Y Company patrol crossed Coolderry Bridge, south of Crossmaglen, killing Private John King, wounding Corporal Donaldson so severely that he was later invalided out of the service, and injuring Privates Clarke and Murphy. The bombs had been placed at intervals which corresponded with the distance maintained between patrol members, the bomber's intention being to kill the entire patrol. This was the first occasion on which the terrorists had employed radio-controlled bombs and it verified the fears of intelligence sources which had been aware for some time of the sale of equipment used in radio-controlled model aircraft to known activists. There were lessons to be learned from both incidents.

Captain Andrew Freemantle sustained a minor wound in the thigh when, carrying out an air reconnaissance of the border shortly before Christmas, his Sioux helicopter was engaged with rocket and small arms fire. This was the second time he had been wounded within a year, having recently returned to the British Army after service with the Australian SAS in Vietnam.

Throughout the tour, common dangers, a sense of purpose and good results produced self-confidence, high morale and a strong esprit de corps throughout the Battalion, mirrored in the recently re-introduced *Tiger Rag*, under the editorship of its creator, Lance Corporal Thompson. Active service, with a strong presence of danger, was preferable to barrack routine and the training cycle. Again, instead of the parsimony associated with exercises, there was plenty of the latest equipment available, including armoured cars, helicopters, night vision devices and good communications. Much responsibility had devolved upon the junior NCOs, but Colonel Morrish had anticipated this and had placed particular emphasis on their training throughout the reformation.

Based as it was in one of the most dangerous areas in Ulster, it was also encouraging for the Battalion to know that not only was it fully appreciated by senior officers, but also that it was in the minds of those at home. Distinguished visitors included General Sir Michael Carver, Chief of the General Staff, General Sir William Jackson, the Quartermaster-General, Mr Ian Gilmour, Under Secretary of State for the Army, Lieutenant General Sir Harry Tuzo, GOC Northern Ireland, who commented that the Royal Hampshires were "a well-ordered battalion with a light touch," and his successor, Lieutenant General Sir Frank King. At Christmas the Battalion received hundreds of cards from well-wishers in Hampshire, and local people baked cakes galore for consumption in the various locations. At the end of January the comedian Frankie Howerd and supporting cast visited Bessbrook. Another visit greatly appreciated was that of Miss Marilyn Ward, holder of the title Miss United Kingdom and runner-up to Miss World in 1971, who toured the bases. In anticipation of her arrival at Crossmaglen, where the helicopter pad had been reduced to an acre of mud, a sedan chair was constructed. Miss Ward made many friends during her visit, as did her minder, a female corporal of the RMP; inevitably, the injection of such glamour into the lives of men living a close-packed monastic existence was simultaneously pleasurable and not a little disturbing!

During the last week of March 1973 the Battalion handed over its area of responsibility to the 2nd Battalion The Parachute Regiment, veterans of Belfast. The Royal Hampshires were able to look back on their first tour since re-formation with a quiet sense of satisfaction. By their commitment and professionalism they had done much to contain the terrorist threat in a difficult area where the enemy had practically all the advantages. Some details of the Battalion's operational successes are recorded at the end of this chapter but statistics can never tell the whole story.

By 29 March the whole Battalion had arrived back in Colchester. Such tours naturally generate anxiety among soldiers' wives, although they strive not to show it and are mutually supportive. On this occasion they had formed a concert party named the Tiger Lilies, which gave the troops a show on their return.

This was followed by three weeks' block leave. The Battalion already knew that it would be posted to Hong Kong early in 1974 and now it heard that it was to undertake a further tour in Ulster in five months' time. The understandable question, "Why us?" was indicative of bewilderment rather than reluctance, but underlined how thinly the infantry as a whole were being stretched. On 2 April Z Company, consisting of the Mortar Platoon, Anti-Tank Platoon, Assault Pioneer Platoon and the Drums Platoon, was formed under Major H.D.H.Keatinge, thereby completing the last phase of the the Battalion's re-formation.

May and June were devoted to platoon and company training and a cadre course was run for section commanders and their seconds-in-command. On 16 May General Sir Michael Carver,

Chief of the General Staff, presented RSM Roger Coleman with his Long Service and Good Conduct Medal during a visit to Roman Barracks. On 22 May the Battalion furnished the Colour Party and the majority of the Guard of Honour, formed from units with the Borough's Freedom, for a visit by the Duke of Edinburgh to Aldershot.

Of necessity, sport had suffered in Ulster although, whenever possible, RSM Coleman had collected a soccer team with which to play other units. A return to a more normal routine enabled many afternoons to be devoted to sport and soccer, swimming, orienteering and athletics competitions were held. At Bisley the Shooting Team achieved 15th place out of 60 in the Major Units Competition, came 5th in the LMG match, and Lance Corporal Potter gained 40th place in the Army Hundred.

The last week of May found Y Company departing for a KAPE Tour of Bournemouth, Southampton and Portsmouth, hoping to attract recruits with details of the forthcoming tour in Hong Kong. In fact, all three services were experiencing difficulties in recruiting at this time, and the figures for the Army were down by almost 50 per cent on the previous year. Various reasons were put forward in explanation, including full employment; the raising of the school-leaving age, which reduced the flow of junior entrants; the expansion of further education; poor career prospects because of continued reduction in the armed services; pressure from parents and girlfriends not to join because of continued heavy commitment and casualties in Ulster; and basic pay which offered no improvement on semi-skilled civilian rates. Some of these problems would solve themselves, but others needed careful examination and appropriate action. Furthermore, with six major units recruiting in the County, plus the Royal Navy, Hampshire was in danger of becoming over-recruited.

In July the Battalion began preparing for its third tour in Northern Ireland. "Training was now getting better," recalls Brigadier Bruce Willing. "There were formal courses for intelligence gatherers, photographers, search teams and drivers. The equipment was becoming more specialised and with it the requirement to adapt our counter-terrorism procedures. *Keeping the Peace Part 3* had long been forgotten; we were, and are today, dealing with a terrorist who had become very sophisticated, one who is invisible within the community, has the support of his community and the education, ability and experience to improvise and make use of technology to kill and maim."

During the first week of September 1973 the Battalion deployed to North Armagh, with Battalion HQ, A, Z and HQ Companies based in Gough Barracks, Armagh, responsible for Armagh City and a stretch of the border, B Company at Lurgan and Y Company at Dungannon with outstations at Coalisland and Stewartstown; later, the Anti-Tank Platoon established a permanent patrol base at Aughnacloy. Frequently, a company of the Province Reserve and an armoured car squadron, based at Gosford Castle, were placed under command for operations.

There were marked contrasts between this and the previous tour. First, the terrorists were less active in North Armagh. This enabled the Battalion to get on much better with both elements of the mixed community and an additional military resource existed in the locally-recruited UDR, who were most active at night and at weekends. The RUC were also under less pressure than was the case further south and in the companies' tactical area of responsibility the chain of operational responsibility answered directly to the local RUC Sub-Divisional Commander, a Superintendent. On the other hand, in the larger, equally-balanced urban communities (Armagh 15,000 and Lurgan 24,000) there was a potential for sectarian strife which had not existed in the largely Catholic South Armagh. Again, in the south the hostility of large sections of the population was a constant factor that could be allowed for in operational planning; in North Armagh, one was never quite certain where one stood. Finally, the accommodation in North Armagh, both in the purpose-built Gough Barracks and in the outstations, was far superior.

The operational routine was much as before - patrols of various sorts, route clearing, VCPs, house clearing, searches, surveillance, establishing community relations and "lifting" suspects. Patrolling the tortuous, unmarked border was never easy; unless map reading was exact a patrol could find itself being led back into Ulster by friendly Gardai. Bombs, hoax bombs, sniping and "come ons" remained a fact of life, but occurred less frequently than during the previous tour. In October, thanks to good intelligence work, arms, ammunition and bomb-making equipment were found in Armagh City and a number of useful arrests were made. On 26/27 October the Provisionals responded by hijacking 100 vehicles with which to set up sixteen road-blocks across the Battalion area, the intention probably being to demonstrate that they remained a force to be reckoned with. It was undeniably cheeky, but was counter-productive in that it caused more inconvenience and nuisance to their fellow countrymen than it did to the security forces. While returning from one of these incidents Colonel Morrish and RSM Coleman came under fire but drove through the ambush unharmed.

A good example of a complex but potentially dangerous "come on" occurred on 13 November 1973. At 19:40 hours a call was received from the police that a milk churn had been discovered by the Mother Superior outside the main door of the convent school at Donaghmore, a village some two miles from Dungannon. The school housed some 160 girl boarders and the milk churn was estimated to contain some 200-300 pounds of explosives. Quite clearly this was an occasion when a quick reaction was required in order to clear the area and to evacuate the children and nuns.

At about 20:00 hours a section from 8 Platoon, travelling in two armoured vehicles, was sent by a devious route to clear the convent and secure the building in order that the ATO could defuse the bomb in comparative safety. Having negotiated a minor road, the section turned north onto the main street of the village. Immediately it had done so, the bridge over which it had just passed blew up. The rear doors of the second vehicle were forced open and the section commander suffered a bruised knee. The bomb was later estimated to have been 300 pounds and it completely blocked the road with a crater some five feet deep and five yards across. The section continued on its way to the convent.

Because of the clear presence of the enemy in the area, Major John Southwood, commanding Y Company, decided to reinforce the securing party by helicopter, followed by the ATO, using one Scout and a Sioux, the latter fitted with a Nite-Sun. This was a high-powered searchlight which was usually used for night illumination but which Y Company preferred to use as a deception device. Fortunately, the night was clear.

The first group, consisting of 7 Platoon Commander and three soldiers in the Scout, left the Company base at the same time as the Sioux, and very soon the Scout returned for the second group. The task of these two groups, in addition to securing the area, was to ensure that the helicopters were not engaged by the IRA. While the Scout was depositing its load the Sioux carried out diversionary runs away from the selected LZ. The last stick, consisting of Major Southwood, the ATO and two escorts, left after the ground party had reported that all was secure.

Meanwhile a small patrol of the UDR, under operational control, had also succeeded in reaching the convent on foot from the north and the work of evacuating the girls had begun.

The ATO set about the milk churn which had about it an ominous look and a strong smell of diesel. "This must have been about our fiftieth bomb or hoax," recalled Major Southwood, "but nevertheless one did not feel any more confident that pieces of convent would not soon be joining the helicopters in the cold night air. In what seemed very quick time, however, the milk churn was knocked over and some 200-300 pounds of sand, heavily impregnated with diesel oil, spilled out onto the gravel drive of the school. Yet another hoax, but that pile of sand nearly caused half a section of our soldiers to lose their lives on the bridge. There was also a chance, of course, that snipers had been lying in wait for us in the grounds of the convent as well. The recovery, by helicopter, went as smoothly as the insertion and the Mother Superior began the task of re-housing the girls."

A few days later Major Southwood was involved in a very similar incident. He and his escort were returning in two Land Rovers from a meeting with an SDLP politician when a large culvert bomb was exploded by remote control between the vehicles. The second Land Rover plunged into the crater and Corporal Downes sustained a ruptured liver which was to keep him in hospital for a considerable time. On 15 November the terrorists mounted a bomb attack on the RUC Station at Keady, causing extensive damage and injuring the sergeant and constable within. After this, Z Company assumed responsibility for the security of the station.

Another complex task carried out at this time was the recovery of the body of a former RUC Officer who had been kidnapped, tortured and then shot. His body had been dumped in a hedgerow on the border. The operation took several hours because the area had to be cleared to ensure that the body was not booby-trapped. The media representatives, attending in strength, complained that they would miss their deadlines - neither Colonel Morrish nor RSM Coleman was particularly sympathetic.

One procedure which was refined as time went by was the gathering of low-level intelligence. In Armagh, for instance, soldiers were individually selected, on the basis of their affability, powers of observation and ability to draw conclusions, to become Estate Specialists. The tasking of patrols was refined as a result of their work. Some of these specialist soldiers became well known, but paradoxically they were not often themselves the target for physical and verbal abuse, possibly because they were able to identify their assailants and name names, thus demonstrating sufficient knowledge to threaten subsequent prosecution. The tiny and apparently trivial pieces of information they gathered could assume great importance when put together. Local people understandably resented the compilation of this data bank but perversely respected it.

Needless to say, the neighbourhood IRA men were seriously worried by the activities of the Estate Specialists and did everything they could to discredit them. For example, the local chairman of Sinn Fein, which described itself as the "political wing" of the IRA, although dual membership was common enough, launched a personal attack in the local press on one who had become a particular favourite with the children, claiming that he harassed and intimidated them!

The remainder of the tour passed with numerous minor but no major incidents. Mercifully, the Battalion incurred no fatal casualties although a number of soldiers sustained injuries, including four men of Z Company travelling in a Scout helicopter which stalled shortly after taking off and crash-landed on the square in Gough Barracks. Most memories of the tour are of the sheer hard work involved, with eighteen-hour days merging into 126-hour weeks.

When the tour ended in January 1974 the Battalion could claim to have kept the peace and, once again, it was praised for its community relations. A number of thoughtful articles were contributed to the Journal. One, by WOII P.Hawker, with three Ulster tours to his credit, pointed out that the Army had been active in the Province for almost five years, commenting of the two communities that "both sides will have to make sacrifices and see each other's point of view. But if they cannot see this after five years, will they ever see it? Or is this trouble going to drag on for another five years?" Captain Tim Glass, the Battalion Operations Officer, put it another way: "Even a full awareness of the problems of Ireland provides no clue to their solution." Ancestral hatreds, be they Arab and Jewish, Greek and Turkish, or

Ulster Protestant and Roman Catholic, provide the stoniest soil in which reason can take root. Thus, although the Battalion was looking forward keenly to its tour in Hong Kong, it knew instinctively that it had by no means seen the last of Ulster.

Yet, in the overall context, there were definite successes to record. During 1973 fatal casualties among the security forces amounted to fifty-eight Regular soldiers, eight members of the UDR and thirteen policemen, a fall of almost half on the previous year's figures, and as far as the Army was concerned this trend would be maintained. Gunmen killed included thirty-eight republicans and four "loyalists," which again represented a considerable reduction on the previous year. Against this, no fewer than 1414 terrorists had been charged. Likewise, finds of arms and explosives had reached record levels and the intelligence-gathering network was improving all the time. By July 1974 it had become possible to reduce troop levels in the Province from the 21,000 present two years earlier to 15,000. The Provisionals' Aden Strategy had failed.

On its return from Ulster, the Battalion was kept extremely busy handing in stores and fitting tropical uniforms before dispersing on block leave until 21 January 1974. Following this, there was just time for an Inter-Company Rugby Competition, a Platoon Soccer Competition and a further KAPE tour while final plans for departure to the Far East were implemented.

* * * * * * * * *

RECORD OF INCIDENTS, etc,
28 NOVEMBER 1972 to 26 MARCH 1973

INCIDENTS

Shootings	70
Rocket attacks	8 - 9 rockets fired
Explosions	42 - 638 lbs used
Bombs found	11 - 903 lbs
Bomb hoaxes	24
Arson	28
Robberies	53
Hijackings	15
Baton rounds fired	34
Petrol bombs	30
Shots fired at Battalion	537
Shots returned	377
Hits claimed	5
Hits confirmed	3
Terrorists killed	1

ARRESTS

Total	75
Detained	2
Charged	22 - 6 in custody
Imprisoned	3
Released	48

FINDS

Weapons	17 - 1 RPG-7 launcher
Ammunition	250 rounds - 1 rocket
Explosives	1 lb gelignite

SEARCHES

Occupied houses	39
Unoccupied houses	104
Waste ground	23
Ships	2
Cars	74,051

Total number of incidents 362 in 119 days

CHAPTER 14

HONG KONG 1974 —1976

Arrival in Hong Kong and first impressions - overland party - Queen's Birthday Parade and flag march - establishment of Training Wing - difficulties involved in support weapons training - border duties - Colonel Morrish succeeded in command by Lieutenant Colonel F.D.J.Dickenson - Y Company training in Brunei - Brigade rifle platoon exercise - first Korean Honour Guard contingent - Trooping the Colour 31 January 1975 - training in Hong Kong - B Company training in Brunei - end of the Vietnam War and refugee crisis - second Korean Honour Guard contingent - A Company training in Fiji - Minden Day 1975 - final activities and departure for the UK

By the middle of March 1974 the 1st Battalion had flown into Hong Kong aboard RAF VC10s and was established with Battalion HQ, B, Y, Command and Admin Companies in Gun Club Hill Barracks, Kowloon, and A and Z Companies some ten miles distant at Erskine Camp in the New Territories, having taken over from the 1st Battalion The Black Watch. Together with the 1st Battalion The King's Regiment and 1st/ 2nd Gurkha Rifles, it now formed part of 51 Infantry Brigade, commanded by Brigadier P.F.A.Sibbald, OBE.

First impressions of the colony were mixed, for in the eight years since the Battalion's last visit Hong Kong had changed enormously. Population growth had been spectacular - there were now 750,000 people living in the three square miles of Kowloon alone - and the immense pressure on the limited amount of building land available meant that the city was becoming high-rise in the manner of Manhattan. In the urban areas it was, in fact, difficult to escape the sound of the piledriver and the pneumatic drill. Some of the quarters allocated around Kowloon were of a better standard than those at home, but others produced justifiable grounds for complaint. Furthermore, Hong Kong's emergence as one of the Orient's most important trading, financial and entrepreneurial centres had not prevented the local economy inflating at the rate of 30 per cent in a little over a year, so that whereas once bargains had been commonplace, shopping around was now essential. Families could manage, but bachelors hoping to entertain ladies in any sort of style were to find their resources stretched.

Professionally, too, the rapid transition from an active theatre of operations and a degree of autonomy to a peacetime spit-and-polish colonial garrison, in which the minutiae of the Battalion's daily life were visible to numerous senior officers, required some mental adjustment. Equally, everyone was aware that, after having concentrated on the specific requirements of Ulster for so long, an opportunity now existed for the Battalion to further consolidate its standard infantry training, with appropriate emphasis on developing the skills of section commanders and those manning support weapons. In addition, from time to time the Battalion would be required to undertake routine garrison duties which included patrolling the Chinese border and providing the Force Guard for Government House and Flagstaff House, respectively the residences of the Governor and Commander-in-Chief, Sir Murray MacLehose, KCMG, MBE, and the Commander British Forces Hong Kong, Lieutenant General Sir Edwin Bramall, KCB, OBE, MC, plus, from time to time, one platoon for duty with the UN Korean Honour Guard in Seoul.

The last members of the Battalion to reach Hong Kong were the participants in an ambitious adventure training exercise named Heavenly Tiger, including Lieutenants Nigel Alderman and Paul Davis, Lance Corporals R.Passingham and S.Richards, and Privates J.Greco, D.Livie, K.Sullivan, R.Bayston and R.St John. The party travelled overland in two Land Rovers, passing through Holland, Germany, Austria, Italy, Yugoslavia, Greece, Turkey, where a visit was paid to the Gallipoli beaches, Iran, Afghanistan, Pakistan, India, by ferry to Malaysia, Singapore and thence by air to Hong Kong, arriving on 16 April. The cost, amounting to £3500, was met partly by Adventurous Training funds, partly by the Regiment, and partly by the members of the expedition themselves. Detailed advance planning paid off, the only unforeseen incident being the confiscation of some of the expedition's funds by Afghan border officials, a matter which the Embassy in Kabul was left to sort out.

The first major duty performed by the Battalion was to provide two companies, B (Major Peter Matthews) and Y (Major John Southwood), for the Queen's Birthday Parade, held on 25 April. For this occasion HQ Land Forces Hong Kong produced a terrifying document, sixteen pages long, containing symbols, maps, arrows and interlinked musical timetables. Pre-1914, it would have earned the highest marks for a candidate to the German Grosser Generalstab, but most people found it quite incomprehensible. Not so RSM Coleman, who reduced it to two-and-a-half pages of logical progression.

Altogether, there were 1200 men on parade, made up of contingents from all three services and the police. On their arrival the Commander British Forces and the Governor were respectively accorded a General and a Royal Salute. The parade was inspected by the Governor, after which the bands performed and the contingents marched past. Three cheers were then given for The Queen, followed by a twenty-one-gun salute and a *feu de joie*, and the Governor departed. B and Y Companies, six abreast, marched back to Gun Club Hill Barracks along Nathan Road, with Colours uncased but furled. The impression created was excellent, as demonstrated by the comment of Major General E.J.S.Burnett, DSO, OBE, MC, Deputy Commander Land Forces Hong Kong: "The Royal Hampshires' standard was very high, and the effort and hard work put in was highly commendable." Had they looked hard enough, some of the spectators might have noticed that both ensigns, Second Lieutenants A.J.B.Edwards and T.S.Finklaire, were sporting signs of the previous night's revelry, gained during after-dinner sports while guests of The King's Regiment, thus achieving something of a statistical improbability!

April also saw the Battalion coming third in the Land Forces Hong Kong Rifle Meeting and winning the Brigade Athletics Meeting, as well as performing creditably in the Colony Athletics Championships, during which Lieutenant Andrew Edwards broke the colony's 400 metres record.

In May a number of junior officers and NCOs, mainly from

Y Company, left for a month's Jungle Warfare Course in Malaysia. Colonel Morrish had already established a Training Wing under Captain Andrew Freemantle, who, it will be recalled, had served with the Australian SAS in Vietnam. On 5 June Captain Freemantle gave a presentation on the subject of fighting through a jungle position held by the Viet Cong or North Vietnamese Army. This coincided with a visit to the Battalion by Lieutenant General Sir Edwin Bramall, who was greatly interested in the subject and very keen that the lessons arising should be communicated to a much wider audience. During his visit General Bramall also presented Sergeant Hall and Private Jackson with GOC's Commendations for services in Ulster. At about the same time it was learned that five members of the Battalion - Colonel John Morrish, Major John Southwood, Lieutenant Nigel Alderman, Colour Sergeant A.J.Dicker and Lance Corporal R.St John - had been Mentioned in Despatches, and that Major A.P.Wright, formerly B Company Commander, had been awarded an MBE. Later in the month Captain Freemantle ran an arduous inter-section competitive exercise in the New Territories, won by an A Company section under Corporal Sutton.

Training for Z Company's support weapons crews was complicated by Hong Kong's steep, rugged terrain and the heat and humidity which made the manhandling of mortars and anti-tank guns an unpleasant task. Clearly, these factors had not been allowed for when the School of Infantry formulated its theories on the subject and they provided Major Hugh Keatinge, the Company Commander, with much food for thought. There were few suitable positions where all six 81mm mortars could be deployed together, and of these some were not accessible by road. This in turn raised the problem of an ammunition resupply system adequate enough to maintain a high rate of fire. In a European landscape resupply would be undertaken by wheeled or tracked vehicles, but in Hong Kong the terrain prevented this. The only alternatives were helicopters, manpacking or mules. Helicopter support could not be relied on because of unpredictable weather and operational considerations. Manpacking, in which members of the rifle companies delivered one round apiece, was more reliable but would make heavy demands on manpower. Mules provided a more satisfactory answer and in due course a Royal Corps of Transport mule detachment from the garrison's animal transport company was attached for exercise purposes. Logistics, however, like economics, can be a gloomy science, and the logisticians' dismal prediction was that for every bomb delivered each mule would consume one bulky bale of fodder, which sounded suspiciously like an excuse for doing nothing!

The problems facing the anti-tank gunners were very similar. The standard anti-tank gun was now the Conbat, a development of the Mobat fitted with a 12.7mm ballistically-matched ranging machine gun; it used the same 120mm ammunition and had the same limited maximum range of 800 yards. Its weight meant that it could only be moved by road or slung beneath a large helicopter and in the latter case the same consideration applied to the anti-tank guns as did to the mortars, although the demand for ammunition would be less pressing. Again, the terrain severely restricted the number of positions to which the guns could be deployed and, given these factors, Major Keatinge's view was that better results could be obtained by reorganising the Anti-Tank Platoon, in part at least, into tank-hunting teams armed with the 84mm Carl Gustav. Range facilities for live firing with the 81mm mortars and the Conbats were inevitably restricted but adequate.

Hong Kong provided facilities for sport of every kind. Martial arts, including Judo and Kung-Fu, were practised under trained instructors on the Drill Square and, as the Battalion owned a launch named *Cheetah* and a speedboat run by Colour Sergeant Cox and his Assault Pioneers, water-skiing quickly became a popular pastime. Teams were also entered for the famous Dragon Boat races. On the whole, life was enjoyable, if rather less so for those living in Erskine Camp, a collection of World War II tin huts dubbed The Country Club by their inhabitants. In fact, Gun Club Hill Barracks was already being extended to absorb the occupants of the camp, but would not be completed during the Royal Hampshires' period of tenure.

On 28 June the Battalion commenced its first tour of duty on the Chinese border, lasting six weeks and involving two companies which were regularly rotated. This coincided with the Force Guard commitment at Government House and Flagstaff House, so that there were times when the lines seemed strangely deserted. The border was divided into Eastern and Western Sectors. On the Eastern Sector it ran down the main street of the coastal village of Sha Tau Kok, so that patrols on both sides were on nodding terms with their opposite numbers. A few hundred yards inland was another platoon post on Lone Tree Hill, where the resident platoon lived in comfortable air-conditioned bunkers. Twelve miles off Sha Tau Kok was the tiny Ping Chau Island, a popular weekend picnic site, where another platoon was based. Control of the Western Sector was exercised from Man Kam To police post, sited on top of a hill overlooking the Sham Chun river and its road bridge. One platoon manned an observation post on an adjacent feature and acted as a reserve to the police post at Lo Wu, the railway crossing point into China. For most of the border's length, the higher ground lay on the Hong Kong side, permitting observation through high-powered binoculars deep into China. Duties of the border companies included manning observation posts and regular patrols to prevent incursions by the many who sought to desert the iron rule of communism for the freedom of Hong Kong. Just how determined these would-be escapers were is shown by the experience of the platoon on Ping Chau Island, where, daily, half a dozen Chinese risked sharks and their own patrol boats to brave the crossing, only to be picked up and repatriated. The best they could expect was to be beaten up and subjected to a painful process of "re-education," but they never stopped coming.

On 26 July 1974 Colonel John Morrish departed to take up the appointment of Military Assistant to the Military Secretary, Lieutenant General Sir Patrick J.Howard-Dobson, KCB, in London, handing over Command to Lieutenant Colonel F.D.J.Dickenson after two eventful and successful years which had seen the 1st Battalion re-formed, two tours in Ulster and the Battalion firmly established as a welcome element of Hong Kong garrison. All were sad to see him go.

Colonel David Dickenson had previously served with the 1st Battalion in Malaya and the West Indies, and it will be recalled that during the latter period he had rounded up a force of Guatemalan guerrillas who had invaded British Honduras. Since then, he had served as an instructor at the School of Infantry and attended Staff College. In 1968, following Staff appointments, he joined the 1st Battalion The Gloucestershire Regiment in Berlin, spending the next two years as a company commander. Subsequently, he had served as DAAG (Recruiting) at HQ The Prince of Wales's Division, attended a course of instruction at the National Defence College, and in 1971 was posted to the RMA Sandhurst as a company commander.

In August Y Company, supplemented by twenty soldiers from other units in 51 Brigade, flew to Brunei for Exercise Nuptial Feast. The five-week exercise enabled the platoon and section commanders to put into practice the lessons learned in Malaysia in May. It was an excellent training package overseen by 1st/2nd Gurkha Rifles and proved beyond any doubt that the British soldier in general, and the Royal Hampshire in particular, adapts very quickly to whatever environment he is asked to operate in. The training started at individual level and climaxed with a very demanding final exercise. The Company's performance clearly impressed its Gurkha hosts, 8 Platoon's final attack educing the compliment from Major Lalbahadur Pun, MC, "You have all made me very happy!" This was high praise indeed. During off-duty moments it was possible to fish or become proficient in dinghy sailing. During the exercise visits were received from Brigadier Peter Sibbald, the Brigade Commander, and Lieutenant General Sir Edwin Bramall, who clearly liked what they had seen.

The rest of the Battalion's training was disrupted by the typhoon season, but at the end of October 51 Brigade held a competitive rifle platoon exercise in the Castle Peak area, during which the composite Recce/Drums Platoon under Captain Peter Hughes scored the highest marks in the Battalion and in consequence were awarded the Winchester Trophy. The following month the Battalion was engaged in Exercise Long Hop, a four-day rural counter-insurgency exercise against an enemy provided by the Royal Brunei Malay Regiment and the 1st/2nd Gurkha Rifles. This was notable for a remarkable feat by the pilot of a casevac helicopter summoned to pick up Private Warwick of 5 Platoon, who had sustained a serious back injury. The entire area was shrouded in cloud and he was talked down by radio, landing on a hillside so steep that the rest of the platoon had to physically hold the aircraft in place until the casualty was loaded. In lighter vein, a perfect ambush set by Second Lieutenant Simon Frere-Cook resulted in the rout of twenty Chinese back-packers, who fled into the darkness when engaged!

The first UN Honour Guard detachment, consisting of Captain Peter Hughes, WOII Norman Jesty and twenty-three single soldiers, departed by air for Korea. The Honour Guard, the official title of which was the Eighth US Army Honor Guard Company, also contained Thai, Filipino and Korean elements, but as the Americans were in a clear majority their drill manual was to be used. Much to the RSM's disgust, the Royal Hampshire detachment had to be schooled in its mysteries before it left, learning what a "Right Guide" was and how to "hep" and "ho" with the best of them. American hospitality in Korea was overwhelming, but duties, including the manning of static sentry posts and ceremonial parades, were frequent and constant. At the end of each two-month tour a Rotation Parade was held during which the departing national contingent paraded ahead of the rest of the Honour Guard, using its own drill. Needless to say, after due preparation the Royal Hampshires used the occasion to show off a little.

Numerous social events were organised over the Christmas period, the first some families had spent together for four years, and a week's break was enjoyed. January 1975 began with the Inter-Company Drill Competition, judged by officers of the newly-arrived 2nd Battalion The Grenadier Guards. The Rifle Company Drill Shield was won by B Company, and with it the honour of being Minden Company on the forthcoming Trooping the Colour parade, while the Support Company Drill Shield was won by Admin Company.

The Trooping the Colour parade was held at the Boundary Street football ground on 31 January. The Regimental Colour was trooped; initially in the keeping of Sergeant Highmore, it was handed over by the RSM to the ensign, Second Lieutenant Rory Steevenson. Rehearsals gave rise to serious alarm. It rained regularly, turning the pitch to mud; extraneous noise, including that of local traffic, jet airliners on their final approach to Kai Tak Airport and the deafening public address system at a nearby athletics track, drowned words of command; the Band and Drums were echoed by the surrounding high buildings, with confusing results; and there were days when the drill was awful. The final dress rehearsal, attended by the Colonel of the Regiment, Brigadier Warren, who had flown out specially for the occasion, was universally regarded as a disaster.

Yet, the parade itself, performed in No 2 Dress and black belts with Regimental buckles, passed off perfectly. The ground had dried out, the turnout was excellent, the steadiness, including that of the ground markers with the flags donated by the Comrades' Association, was remarked upon, and the drill and dressing were faultless. Satisfying murmurs of approval could even be heard from Grenadier Guards officers, who, as world leaders in such matters, might have been expected to be sparing with their praise. The Governor, who took the Salute, and numerous guests, including Major General Burnett, Brigadier Boorman, senior officers of the Royal Navy and RAF and the US Military Liaison Officer, were all clearly impressed and during the next few days Colonel Dickenson received a large number of congratulatory letters.

The parade was followed by a champagne reception and lunch in the Officers' Mess. During the evening the Sergeants' Mess held a very successful ball to which several officers and other guests were invited. The ball marked a major turning point in RSM Roger Coleman's career, as he was to be commissioned the following day; having begun the evening as a WOI, at midnight he became Lieutenant Coleman, and thus a guest in what until a minute earlier had been his own Mess. Following a distinguished tour as RSM he was awarded the MBE in The Queen's Birthday Honours List. Another change at this time was the departure of the outstanding Families' Officer, Major Bernard Lambert, The Staffordshire Regiment. Never an easy job, his tour had been particularly arduous. Not only had the Battalion been away from Colchester on a long exercise in Canada and two Northern Ireland tours, but he had also overseen the move of the families to Hong Kong and coped with all the problems of settling into such an alien environment. His award of an MBE was richly deserved and widely applauded.

A Battalion Rifle Meeting was held in February, during which the individual rifle competition was won by Captain Tim Glass, that for the SMG by Corporal Paul Hallam, and that for the GPMG pairs by Privates Jones 87 and Crowley. At home, February saw the closure of the Wessex Brigade Depot and the transfer of its training functions to the Prince of Wales's Division Depot at Lichfield.

Distinguished visitors to the Battalion during this period included Major General Anthony Farrar-Hockley, DSO, MBE, MC, Colonel Commandant of the Prince of Wales's Division, and, in March, Field Marshal Sir Michael Carver, Chief of the Defence Staff.

The training season was now well under way, involving the Battalion in Exercise Iron Fist, a rural internal security exercise with an amphibious element, run by HQ 51 Brigade on Lantau Island, and, later, Exercise Gatefold on the Tolo Peninsula,

practising companies and platoons in attack, defence and withdrawal, followed by an escape-and-evasion exercise in which Z
Company acted as illegal immigrants.

On 14 March B Company, plus the Mortar and Anti-Tank
Platoons, departed for Brunei on Exercise Nymph's Delight. This
lasted until 18 April and followed the same jungle warfare training programme as that undertaken by Y Company the previous
year.

Events elsewhere now suddenly intruded on the routine of
the Hong Kong garrison. The United States had withdrawn the
last of its forces from South Vietnam in 1973. The following year
Congressional appropriations for the military assistance of the
South Vietnamese government were severely cut back, with the
result that the latter's aircraft, tanks, APCs and heavy weapons
soon became inoperable for want of spares, ammunition and fuel.
For a while the ARVN soldiered bravely on, and even inflicted
several reverses on the North Vietnamese Army. It was, however,
clearly apparent to the communist leadership in Hanoi that the
South was nearing the end of its resources. In March 1975 it
launched a major conventional offensive in the face of which the
ARVN simply collapsed. By 30 April the communists had taken
Saigon and the war was over.

The immediate effect was that over 50,000 people sought
to escape their new overlords by sea, using any craft at their disposal, in the hope that ultimately they would be allowed to settle
in non-communist countries, particularly the United States,
Canada and France. One such ship, the *Truang Xuam*, with 3700
refugees aboard, began to founder when only two days out of
Saigon. In response to her distress calls the Danish freighter *Clara
Maersk* picked up those aboard and headed for Hong Kong, arriving on 14 May.

Despite being given little warning, the civil government activated its disaster contingency plans and the situation in the already over-crowded colony remained under control. Many of the
refugees went to a tented camp pitched by the garrison in the
New Territories. The rest went to Sai Kung Camp, also in the
New Territories, or to Harcourt Road Camp on Hong Kong Island. The latter was reserved for single men and former members of the ARVN, some of whom, it was suspected, might have
retained personal weapons. It was necessary for the occupants of
all the camps to be contained within perimeter fences, firstly to

prevent them vanishing into the teeming civil population, and secondly to protect them from elements only too willing to take advantage of their plight, namely pimps on the lookout for girls and sharp characters hoping to strip the refugees of their few remaining valuables for a fraction of their worth. The civil authorities were responsible for running the camps, but the Battalion provided companies to guard Sai Kung and Harcourt Road Camps for three or four days at a time. Duties included constant perimeter patrols as well as searching all vehicles entering and leaving the camps. As some of the refugees had converted their wealth into gold wafers which they now sought to exchange for hard currency, it was also necessary to provide them with protection against illegal gold traders from Kowloon, and the biggest, toughest and meanest-looking soldiers were assigned to the task; during three days' trading it was estimated that almost £100,000 changed hands. There was little direct contact with the Vietnamese, save for one small group which attempted to break out of Harcourt Road Camp, hoping to sample the pleasures of the Wan Chai red light district. Heat and humidity dehydrated those involved in these duties to the extent that Support Company alone consumed no fewer than 700 bottles of soft drinks in a single day. Although Vietnamese refugees would continue to reach Hong Kong by various means, by the middle of May some of the original arrivals were being flown onwards to their new homes in the West, and some four months later almost half of them had left.

These unexpected events occurred at an extremely busy time in the Battalion's programme. On 21 May the second Korean Honour Guard contingent, commanded by Lieutenant T.S.Finklaire and Colour Sergeant V.T.West, left for Seoul. On arrival it was soon apparent that the Battalion's first Honour Guard contingent had left a most favourable impression with Americans and Koreans alike. Parades and guards were more frequent, but two range days were held, during which a number of American weapons were fired, including the Colt .45, the M19, the L1A1 automatic pistol and the Remington shot-gun, and there were opportunities for sport. There were, too, a number of lighter moments. During rehearsals for the parade held to commemorate American Independence Day, for example, the Royal Hampshire soldiers made a tongue-in-cheek threat to wear black armbands, causing a number of senior jaws to drop in alarm. The contingent were spectators at the US Army's Bicentennial

Celebration Parade, during which the Honour Guard's American platoon, suitably uniformed, formed nine Colour Party teams depicting various campaigns and the development of the Stars and Stripes. An artillery battery then fired one round for each State, after which a huge birthday cake was marched ceremoniously onto the parade ground and cut with a sabre by General Stillwell, the Commander-in-Chief. On The Queen's Birthday the entire Royal Hampshire contingent were invited to a cocktail party at the British Embassy in Seoul, having been ceremonially employed there during a lunchtime reception, and subsequently beat the Embassy staff in a darts match. Several excursions were made to places of local interest, including a battlefield tour of Solma-Ri, where the Glosters had made their epic stand. On 27 July the contingent returned to Hong Kong.

Meanwhile, A Company (Major Hastings Neville), supplemented by the Drums Platoon under Drum Major Barnes, two sections of mortars, assault pioneers, administrative elements and attachments from minor units within 51 Brigade, had left by air for Viti Levu, the largest of the Fiji Islands, on 31 May, having already despatched their vehicles, assault boats and tentage by sea some time earlier. The objects of the exercise, named Sinon, were to carry out platoon training in mountainous, jungle-type terrain, show the flag, and learn as much as possible about the country in the time available. On Viti Levu the mountains rise rapidly from the coastal plain to a height of about 4000 feet. They are precipitous and broken up by numerous valleys, re-entrants and ridges. Open grass-land gives way to jungle 20-30 miles inland. The Company's main base was at Lautoka, but a training base was set up off a logging track deep in the jungle.

This was the objective of a three-day navigation exercise involving 1, 2 and 3 Platoons and the mortars. On the second day, in defiance of the official "dry" season, it began to rain heavily and continued to do so for the next week. Some local people blamed the French and their nuclear tests, while others blamed the government for planting too many pine trees. Whatever the reason, the hillsides became slippery, while streams and rivers turned into raging torrents. This, however, did not prevent the platoons completing the exercise, after which, as individuals and platoons, they spent the next four days on a training circuit involving ambush drills, jungle lane firing, a search-and-destroy operation and the destruction of an enemy camp by fire. At the end of this phase the Company was invited to an open-air dance by the Nausori Highland Women's Club and learned about grog, a drink made from the Waka root which, while non-alcoholic, induces great conviviality.

The Company then travelled the 120 miles to the islands' capital, Suva, where, together with the Fijian Regulars, Territorials and police, it prepared to take part in The Queen's Birthday Parade. Unfortunately, the rains continued and for only the second time in thirty years the parade was cancelled. This was especially disappointing since the Colours were to have been paraded, but at least it was gratifying that so many Fijians recalled their happy association with the Battalion during the Malayan Emergency. Colonel Dickenson joined the Company in Suva and on its last night there the officers gave a reception for 150 guests, including the Governor General and leading figures from Fiji's civil, military and diplomatic communities. The highlight of this was provided by the Drums Platoon, who, immaculate in tropical full dress, gave a superb floodlit display of drumming, bugle and flute music.

A final exercise, understandably named Waka Route, took place in the Upper Nandi valley between 16 and 21 June, after which the Company enjoyed eight days of rest and recuperation. Much of this was spent on Beachcomber Island, where the assault boats were used for waterskiing, fishing, island hopping, and reef exploration. One of the island's catamarans was used for sub-aqua diving and, elsewhere, two pig shoots were held; no pigs were seen, but a great deal of fun was had by everyone, not least the local villagers. At the beginning of July the Company returned to Hong Kong.

The 1975 Minden Day Parade was a little different from that of previous years in that 20 Light Regiment, Royal Artillery, had recently arrived in the colony and one of its batteries was 12 (Minden) Battery. It therefore seemed a good idea to hold a combined parade with 12 Battery, although this created a number of problems for RSM Terry. The first was that 12 Battery usually celebrated the occasion by driving past with gleaming guns and vehicles. The square at Gun Club Hill was too small for this, so it was decided to hold the parade on the football field. The second was that until the last minute, garrison duties, including B Company being required to provide guards for the Vietnamese refugees in Sai Kung Camp, made it uncertain just how many of the Battalion's soldiers would be on parade. The third was rain, which softened the ground and created a nightmare prospect of vehicles bogging down during the parade itself, to say nothing of the wrath this would generate in the Public Works Department. Once again, however, all went well on the day, notwithstanding a steady drizzle. Distribution of roses to the Battalion was made by Mrs Dickenson, and to the soldiers of 12 Battery by Mrs Heaney, the wife of the Battery Commander, Major J.G.A.Heaney, RA. Colonel Dickenson addressed the parade and then presented Major Heaney with a suitably mounted silver model of a tiger to commemorate the occasion. The parade ended with a drive off and march past by the Battery and the Battalion. During the evening a very successful All Ranks Ball was held on the square at Gun Club Hill Barracks. Minden Day was also celebrated by the Reconnaissance Platoon in Brunei, whence it had gone in late July for three weeks' jungle training.

By now, increases in pay and overseas allowances had some-what ameliorated the financial aspects of life in Hong Kong. Against this, everyone knew that the tour was coming to an end and Colonel Dickenson had already been informed that early in 1976 the Battalion would be returning to Ulster for an eighteen-month tour as part of the resident garrison, together with fami-lies. During the autumn the NITAT advisers arrived to provide briefings on the up-to-date situation in Northern Ireland. On Remembrance Sunday the Battalion was heavily involved in the Parade at the Memorial on Hong Kong Island. At the Hampshire Society of Hong Kong's annual dinner, held at the Repulse Bay Hotel on 15 November, the Band played during the evening and several officers and their ladies attended the function. The Of-ficers' Mess held a farewell cocktail party at the end of the month, preceded by the Band and Drums Beating Retreat on the square.

A Battalion Concert, organised and produced by Major Nigel Woodward, ably helped by WOII Norman Jesty and Band-master Bruce French, was held in the gymnasium on 10 and 11 December. Together, all ranks, the Band and the Wives' Club produced a total of thirty-one acts and the show was such a suc-cess that it played to full houses on both evenings. December also saw the competition for the Winchester Trophy, with strong em-phasis on Ulster, being won by Lieutenant Adrian Pryce's 3 Pla-toon, A Company, and a Battalion Rifle Meeting. In the latter Z Company won both SLR Team Matches, HQ Company the SMG and GPMG Matches, and B Company the Pistol and Counter-Terrorist Matches. In the Inter-Company events, Z Company won the Rifle Match, A Company LMG Match and HQ Company the SMG Match; the Inter-Platoon Falling Plate Competition was won by 8 Platoon. The Rifle Meeting was the last major event to be held before Christmas leave, and indeed of the Hong Kong tour.

On 7 January 1976 the first of the advance party flights left Hong Kong. The rest of the Battalion left between then and the middle of February. As with other places in which it had served, the Battalion left its mark, in this case a way-marked trail on Lantau Island, the start and finish of which were marked by cairns, each embellished with a large brass plaque with the Regimental crest engraved into it. The work was carried out in January by Z Company under Major Alan Withers and the route was opened ceremonially with a bottle of beer by the District Officer (Islands), the Deputy Director of the Hong Kong Tourist Association, and Colonel Dickenson.

The tour was effectively a two-year break from Northern Ireland. It was immensely busy with training both in Hong Kong and in other places. Although an accompanied posting, the men were away from home a great deal, including the tours on the border, while the families found themselves living in flats in the chaotic ant heap that was Kowloon. The men, meanwhile, found peace and quiet on the border and in the Borneo jungle. Militarily, there was always something going on - usually several things at once. The climate could be stiflingly hot and sticky or cold, wet and grey, apart from that short time at the end of summer when skies were blue, there was little humidity and it was neither too hot nor too cold. The families and the single men in particular were probably glad to return home after a never-to-be-forgotten but claustrophobic experience which all looked back on with some nostalgia.

* * * * * * * * *

THE HAMPSHIRE TIGERS

NAVAL AFFILIATIONS

On 29 March 1976 a farewell ceremony was held on the South-ampton dockside to mark the last visit of HMS *Hampshire*, which was due to be scrapped. Because of the ship's long and happy association with the Regiment, the Band and Drums were asked to participate and, by coincidence, the ship's Guard of Honour was inspected by the Rt Hon The Earl of Malmesbury, TD, Lord Lieutenant of the County. During the ceremony, the Colonel of the Regiment received back the ship's silver tiger for safe keep-ing. Subsequently, the Captain and ship's company presented the Regimental Museum with the ship's bell 1963-1976; name board in chrome letters; battle honours board; two 4.5-inch gun tampions; brass deck plate (starboard); the ship's crest from the bridge; and a lifebelt.

To perpetuate the Regiment's long association with the Royal Navy, a fresh affiliation was formed, fittingly with the cruiser HMS *Tiger*, then serving as flagship of the 7th Frigate Squadron. This was formalised on 11 January 1977 when Captain S.A.C.Cassels, RN, welcomed on board a representative group, led by the Colonel of the Regiment, and plaques were exchanged.

CHAPTER 15

NORTHERN IRELAND 1976-1977

Complexity of move from Hong Kong to Ulster - Shackleton Barracks, Ballykelly - economic aspects - Provisional IRA strategy and presence - the 1st Battalion's deployment - extracts from Operational Diary March/July 1976 - successes - murder of Private Watkins - accidental deaths of Sergeant Unsworth and Private Fallows - co-operation with RUC and intelligence considerations - Minden Day 1976 - sporting successes - the Dog Section - Band engagements in Ulster - further successes - Colonel Dickenson hands over command to Lieutenant Colonel R.G.Long, MC - terrorist offensive in South Derry and counter-measures - the Protestant General Strike of 1977 - the Queen's visit to Ulster and Silver Jubilee Celebrations - restructuring within the infantry Battalion - Minden Day 1977 - community relations - congratulatory messages

The 1st Battalion's move from Hong Kong to Ulster was an extremely complicated business carried out in stages to allow for advance parties, leave, training at Lydd under NITAT direction and re-establishing families in Northern Ireland; so complicated, in fact, that in December 1975 Battalion Movement Cells were set up at Brize Norton and Gatwick airfields, Lydd Training Camp, St Martin's Plain Camp and Liverpool. Some families flew direct from Hong Kong to Belfast but this experiment was less than successful and was never repeated.

The Battalion's new base was Shackleton Barracks, Ballykelly, in County Londonderry, situated on an old RAF

airfield on the southern shore of Lough Foyle. The base was suf-
ficiently large to house additional units from Royal Engineers,
REME, RCT and 5 UDR. Internally, it was divided into the Lower
Camp, containing the 1st Battalion HQ, Headquarters Company,
the Officers' Mess and service support units; and the Upper
Camp, containing accommodation for the rifle companies, the
cookhouse, the Sergeants' Mess, the NAAFI, better known as the
Crossed Keys Club, the garrison church and the medical centre.
In-camp facilities included a two-lane bowling alley, an indoor
swimming pool and a gymnasium complete with sauna and two
squash courts. Entertainment included three films a week, discos
in the Crossed Keys Club and sometimes visiting CSE shows. In
November 1976 a pub, known as the Rose and Crown, was opened
in the barracks for the use of private soldiers and their wives, and
was both well used and popular. Security gave rise to considerable concern as the perimeter fence stretched for over three miles
and was regularly penetrated by cattle.

The married quarters were grouped in estates along the
main Limavady-Londonderry road, approximately half a mile west
of the camp. The families' club was known as The White Hart
and used for films, Bingo sessions and other social events. The
Wives' Club organised numerous activities, although restrictions
placed on movement beyond the protected areas obviously limited these.

Arriving in Ulster from Hong Kong was a culture shock in
itself, but by far the worst aspect of the move was the discovery
that inflation had sent the cost of living in the United Kingdom
through the roof. This stemmed directly from the Arab defeat
during the Yom Kippur War of 1973. Many Arab governments
decided to punish the Western nations for supporting Israel by
attempting to dislocate their economies with draconian increases
in the price of oil. This was reflected in the cost of manufactur-
ing and distributing every conceivable item, and therefore pro-
voked claims for higher wages and salaries to keep pace with rapidly rising prices. This spiral would continue until the West found
alternative sources of oil in the North Sea and elsewhere. These
inflationary pressures aggravated the financial difficulties of soldiers and their families returning to the United Kingdom from
Hong Kong, where Local Overseas Allowance was paid, and in
some cases this resulted in real hardship. There was, however,
plenty of land available on the old airfield and Colonel Dickenson

decided to use some of it to produce a potato crop which could be issued at minimal cost; likewise, as the old control tower still possessed its glass, it was used to grow tomatoes. Later, a chicken farm was added to the list of productive projects. At Christmas, too, a visit was made direct to a manufacturer in Manchester to purchase a consignment of toys at wholesale price so that the children would not go short.

There had been important changes in the Ulster situation since the Battalion's last tour. Direct rule of the Province from Westminster had been instituted and every effort had been made to deal with the Catholic community's grievances, but for the Provisional IRA the Troubles remained an end in themselves, for without them it had no purpose. It had embarked upon a long-term strategy intended to inflict economic damage by detonating large bombs in Ulster's town and city centres, knowing that the British taxpayer would foot the very considerable bill in every case. It would gladly kill British soldiers whenever the opportunity arose, but since Prime Minister Harold Wilson's announcement on 7 January 1976 that special forces were being officially deployed to Ulster for the first time, it had become decidedly less chipper; it had, in any event, become less than keen on direct confrontation with Regular troops, preferring instead to murder off-duty UDR men and police officers. Its activities required heavy funding, not least to provide some sort of financial support for the dependants of the growing number of its members imprisoned for their terrorist crimes, and, as the contributions made by sentimental Irish-Americans fell short of the actual expenditure, it resorted to a variety of criminal activities, including protection rackets, bank robberies and extortion to make good the difference. The Provisional IRA, in fact, had become something of a business and every aspect of its altered strategy would become apparent during the Battalion's tour.

On 27 March 1976 the Battalion formally took over from the 1st Battalion The Worcestershire and Sherwood Foresters Regiment when Colonel Dickenson signed an AF G.1033 Issue and Receipt Voucher for the following:

"Two RUC Divisions consisting of 1360 square miles
and 221,000 people;
Five RUC Stations located at Magherafelt, Toome, Kilrea,
Dungiven and Maghera;

HM Prison Magilligan, consisting of 450 staff
and 633 prisoners;
Three Mayors;
Four Chairmen of District Councils;
And two Chief Superintendents (in full working order)."

Active enemy within the County included a well organised Provisional gang and some members of the INLA in the Magherafelt area, and a less organised Provisional gang in the Kilrea area.

Operationally, the Battalion formed part of 8 Infantry Brigade (Brigadier B.C.Webster) and was initially deployed with two companies forward, based respectively on Kilrea and Magherafelt, rotated on a six-weekly basis. Thus A and B Companies (the North Derry Companies) were based with Company HQ and one or two platoons at Kilrea and one platoon at Dungiven, across the Sperrin Mountains; and Y and Z Companies (the South Derry Companies) had their headquarters and one platoon at Magherafelt, one platoon at Maghera, a small, predominantly Protestant town in the foothills of the Sperrins, and one platoon at Toome Bridge, a strongly republican village with a long tradition of anti-British violence, situated on Lough Neagh. Accommodation, based on police stations, was adequate for eating, sleeping and recuperating, but the general feeling was that it was good to get out on patrol. Of the two companies remaining in Ballykelly, one formed the Brigade Reserve Company, with a minimum stand-by time of ten minutes, and the other was required to provide the married quarters guard, gate sentries, watchkeepers and duty policemen, as well as perform routine guards and duties. Once the Battalion routine had become firmly established it became possible to organise a leave rota, leave being taken in blocks of two or three weeks, by companies.

Much of the time was spent performing the same roles undertaken in previous tours and to repeat these would be tedious. However, terrorist pressure remained constant and this is reflected in the Battalion diary for the first four months of the tour.

27 March	6 incendiary devices were placed in four shops in Maghera causing considerable damage. Devices were of a cassette type.
29 March	Armed bank robbery in Swatragh by 4 armed men who stole £1000 and held the manager hostage.

	During the follow-up 3 of the robbers were arrested.
30 March.	5 arrests by RUC with military support in the Bellaghy area.
1 April.	The murder of Pte McCutcheon, an off-duty 5 UDR soldier, west of Toome. He was killed by two bullets from an Armalite and a .308-in Winchester rifle. A booby-trapped poster was defused by the ATO. 21 lbs of explosive and a detonator were recovered.
2 April.	The murder of S-Sgt Lennox, an off-duty 5 UDR soldier, west of Toome. He was also the local postman and was shot 10 times by an Armalite. Area search recovered one .303-in rifle, 10 lbs of Anfo and 1200 assorted rounds. Arrest of a terrorist on the Brigade wanted list at a VCP.
6 April.	A small bomb was thrown into a Protestant-owned shop in Kilrea, device causing minimal damage.
8 April.	A parcel bomb exploded in Hawthorne's Bar in Ballyroanan, its size estimated at 5-10 lbs of explosive.
14 April.	6 arrests by RUC with military support in connection with UDR murders. 100-lb landmine exploded prematurely NE of Bellaghy. No casualties.
15 April.	Find of 20 lbs of Anfo. Gas cylinder bomb exploded near Randalstown.
17 April.	Find of Armalite and 42 rounds of ammunition by 5 UDR patrol.
27 April.	2 arrests by RUC with military support.
29 April.	6 arrests by RUC with military support.
30 April.	Area search and subsequent find of 50 lbs of mixed explosives, a No 6 detonator, 200 metres of wire and a 6-volt battery.
1 May.	9 arrests by RUC with military support. Area search and subsequent finds in three different hides of a .303-in Lee-Enfield, a .38-in revolver, a 7.62mm Springfield rifle, 1380 assorted rounds of ammunition, 7.5 lbs of explosive, safety fuse, Cordtex, 28 detonators, 2 "walkie-talkie" radios and a radio control device.
2 May	3 arrests were made after a shooting incident at a house south of Ballykelly. A .22-in rifle was recovered. During an area search SE of Castledawson 10 lbs of explosives, 28 detonators and 10 rounds of ammunition were recovered.
4 May.	4 arrests by RUC with military support. Routine search north of Portglenone uncovered 20 lbs of explosive
5 May.	A planned search west of Dungiven recovered a .45-in pistol and 35 rounds of ammunition.

6 May.	20 houses were entered in a head check operation, mounted in support helicopters, in search for escapees from the Maze Prison. 3 of these prisoners were from the Glenullin area and were members of the IRSP. They were hard-core terrorists. The operation was negative.
13 May.	2 arrests by RUC with military support.
14 May.	6 shots were fired at an RUC foot patrol in Kilrea. RUC returned 13 shots. No casualties or hits recorded. The follow-up produced Armalite empty cases.
19 May.	A 10-lb duffle bag bomb was thrown through a window of the Roost Bar in Coleraine. A booby-trap device was located behind a closed door of an out-house. The device was neutralised by the ATO and consisted of 5 lbs of explosives with a clothes peg ignition system.
31 May.	100-lb milk churn bomb exploded outside a garage on the east side of Maghera. No casualties, but two persons treated for shock.
1 June.	5 persons arrested by RUC with military support.
8 June.	A follow-up to shots heard the previous night recovered 80 rounds of mixed ammunition.
29 June.	£3900 was stolen from the Draperstown Bank by two masked men, one of whom was armed with a hand-gun.
3 July.	An "aggro" incident occurred outside the Marion Hall (Roman Catholic) and Orange Hall (Protestant) in Kilrea after the local Saturday night dances. Two crowds totalling 700 persons threw stones and bricks at the Army and RUC. 12 baton rounds were fired and 1 arrest was made.
10 July.	A bomb exploded in the Elver Inn, a Catholic bar in Monevnick. 2 youths and an 8-year-old child were severely injured. A 110-lb proxy car bomb was placed outside Pollock's garage in Ballymoney. The ATO cleared the bomb after only the detonator had exploded.
11 July.	An RUC constable was wounded in the hip after a shooting attack east of Randalstown. An Armalite and a Garrand were used.
12 July.	The anniversary of the Battle of the Boyne was celebrated by the Orange Lodges at 7 major parades in Ballymena, Randalstown, Magherafelt, Armoy and Broughshane. A clearance patrol prior to the Randalstown parade uncovered a 6-lb bomb which was defused by the ATO.

16 July.	2 car bombs exploded in Castledawson destroying 4 shops. Bombs consisted of between 200 and 500 lbs of home-made explosive.
17 July.	3 incendiary devices exploded in Coleraine destroying 1 shop and damaging 2.
21 July.	700-800-lb proxy car bomb exploded in Maghera Street, Kilrea, destroying 6 shops and damaging 20. 3 arrests by RUC with military support in Portglenone.
30 July.	Cpl McLeanan, an off-duty 5 UDR NCO, was severely injured by a 10-lb booby trap attached to his car. Pte Scott, also an off-duty 5 UDR soldier, was murdered by a similar 10-lb booby trap attached to a gate on a farm where he worked. Both attacks were south of the Loup.

Nevertheless, by the end of August 1976 the Battalion had, in the space of five months, achieved a great deal. The statistics pertaining to terrorist attacks and the security forces' successes in the Battalion's area during this period were as follows:

Shootings	26
Explosive attacks	33
Bomb scares and hoaxes	21
Arson	29
Armed robberies	11
Hijackings	13
Weapons recovered	14
Explosives recovered	1728 lbs
Detonators recovered	68
Ammunition recovered	4988 assorted rounds
Arrests	120
Arrested and charged	38

Clearly the terrorists were not defeated, but their capacity to operate had been curtailed and their strength continued to be eroded. Of the explosives recovered in the period quoted, over 900 lbs were found in August; the same month also witnessed the Battalion's first fatal casualty of the tour.

On 3 August Private Alan Watkins formed part of an A Company foot patrol in Dungiven. The Provisionals, aware that the patrol's route would take it along Main Street, set an ambush in an unoccupied house, the windows of which had been white-washed to give the impression that interior decorating was in progress. A small hole in the whitewash of a downstairs window had been left for their gunman, believed to have been a Maze escaper, to see his target. The gunman was also kept informed of the patrol's progress by an outside observer, so that when Private Watkins drew level with the window he was shot in the neck with a 12-bore double-barrelled shotgun from a range of three feet. The gunman then escaped through the back of the house to a getaway car, leaving behind an explosive booby trap in the hope of killing some at least of those following up the incident. Good procedures identified the booby trap quickly but such was its construction that it could not be safely dismantled and had to be detonated by the ATO. This brought down the front of the house, rendering it uninhabitable. Whether or not the Provisionals and their sympathisers in Dungiven regarded the demolition as an Army reprisal - which it was not - or simply an operational hazard, is not recorded; the curious fact was that terrorism in the area, like the house itself, simply collapsed. One especially tragic aspect of Private Watkins's pointless murder was that he had been married for less than five months and left behind a sixteen-year-old widow.

Private Watkins was the only soldier of the Battalion to die as a direct result of enemy action during the tour, but two more of its members, Sergeant Michael Unsworth and Private Frank Fallows, both tragically lost their lives as a result of injuries sustained in separate accidents.

The Battalion worked closely with the RUC on the basis that the latter would, sooner or later, resume their traditional role as the civil guardians of law and order throughout the Province, fully a year before this policy was formalised by the then Chief Constable, Sir Kenneth Newman, in his paper *The Way Ahead.* As always, the key to successful operations lay in intelligence gathering. On arrival in Ulster, the Battalion's Intelligence Section had been considerably expanded, with cells at Kilrea, Dungiven, Magherafelt, Maghera and Toome Bridge. Because of the nature of their work, these cells remained where they were and did not rotate when the companies did. The Battalion's operational area covered two RUC Divisions and some felt that even more could have been achieved in intelligence matters if those divisions had co-operated more closely. The need-to-know principle was not in question, but as intelligence was transmitted vertically rather than horizontally, by the time it had been assessed by senior officers and reached the neighbouring division it might have little or no value. Yet, the need for caution was understandable, for even in a force such as the RUC, which had so much to lose, there could be found rotten apples. One such case involved a Special Branch officer who possessed two houses, a large car, a wife and a mistress, and was obviously living well beyond his known means. He was running an informer who, as well as being a Provo, was also a professional criminal, and he was taking a cut from the latter's robberies. Ultimately, the two were charged and convicted, but not before an RUC sergeant who had voiced his suspicions was murdered. In such circumstances, the calculation of risk had to be very fine indeed.

Despite the pressures, morale rose during the tour. The soldiers were happy to be doing a real job, and the people in the community were happy to see them, to talk with them and to be seen to do so. After they had settled in, the families, despite financial burdens and security restrictions, found that life in an Ulster quarter was actually pleasanter than life in a high-rise Kowloon flat. Again, everyone of note seemed intent on visiting the Battalion and receiving a personal briefing. Whenever time permitted, sport included soccer, hockey, rugby, cricket, squash, volleyball and basketball. Sailing also became popular and a neglected nine-hole golf course within the perimeter was restored and re-opened by Colonel Dickenson on 21 June 1976. Sporting successes included the Rugby Seven reaching the Army semi-finals in Aldershot, and Private Ken Burchell becoming the individual European light-heavyweight Hapkido champion as well as captaining the winning Great Britain team in the European championships. The following year he led the British team to victory in the World championships and became World Champion himself.

There were, too, several incidents which brought an unintended humour to the daily routine. An inexperienced attached subaltern from a support service, leading a night patrol in the Sperrin Mountains, flayed a valley with 76 rounds of GPMG in response to what he believed was a shot. The "enemy" proved to be a crow scarer and the subaltern was spoken to sharply; as was the patrol's senior NCO for not minding him properly. A confession made by a terrorist arrested in Dungiven resulted in the recovery of a .22-in rifle, two sawn-off shotguns and an air rifle from the roof space of a gentlemen's lavatory in a local shirt factory; all were rusty and his story was that he intended cleaning them at his own convenience! For their own safety, personnel travelling as individuals in private cars between bases did so in civilian clothes. In the case of one of the Battalion's visitors, a staff officer, civilian clothes meant a British Warm and a Herbert Johnson trilby; somehow, he survived, perhaps because the Provos thought he was part of an elaborate set-up!

Whatever was happening operationally, two constant requirements of Battalion life, namely the need to maintain professional skills and recruiting, were not neglected. Career courses and potential NCO cadres were run at frequent intervals, and during the summer a well-planned two-week KAPE tour of Hampshire, involving the Band, half the Reconnaissance Platoon, the Regimental Recruiting Team and the Wessex Display Team, resulted in thirty-five serious enquiries from potential recruits.

One of the hardest worked elements of the Battalion during this tour was the Dog Section, run by RSM Ted Kimberley. As manpower was not available to patrol the extensive perimeter of Shackleton Barracks, the role of the handlers and their dogs was vital. They were mainly responsible for the security of the Lower Camp, the Battalion Arms Kote and the Ammunition Compound. The average handler covered between 60 and 70 miles a week on patrol and put in some 333 working hours per month, exclusive of normal routine work. The Dog Section always attracted the interest of visiting VIPs and brought great credit to the Battalion when Lance Corporal Bullin with Major, and Lance Corporal Wickham with Roxy, took second and third places respectively in the Northern Ireland Dog Trials of 1976, then went on to repeat the performance at the UK Trials. These were no mean achievements after only four months' experience.

When the Band was not engaged in Regimental work or employed on guard duties in Shackleton Barracks it performed an important community relations role, entertaining local people in churches and schools and at village fêtes and fairs throughout Ulster. In its travels it played in very varied surroundings; for example, one evening it was performing in a tent for the villagers of Eglinton, and the next day at the City Hall in Belfast for the Lord Mayor's inaugural dinner. Whatever differences the Irish have among themselves, they are great lovers of music and wherever the Band played it was met with genuine friendliness and appreciation. It regretted that it saw little of the Drums, since the latter were so heavily engaged elsewhere, but in September 1976 the two got together and, with the pipers of 5 UDR, Beat Retreat at Ballykelly, Sergeant Highmore having taken over as Drum Major from Sergeant Barnes.

Elsewhere, life in the Battalion's area continued much as before. On 21 August, an exceptionally low tide at Balls Point uncovered a cache of terrorist ammunition. Aboard the Belfast - Liverpool ferry a soldier of Z Company going on leave spotted a man on the Brigade's Wanted List; the Special Branch in Liverpool were promptly alerted and arrested the man as soon as the ship docked. Another wanted man was picked up by the Anti-Tank Platoon early one Sunday morning at his parents' home near Toome, complaining loudly about such "unfair" use of the Sabbath. In the Dungiven area B Company's successes included discovering a large hide constructed from corrugated iron in a roadside bank. The contents included 250 lbs of explosives and two incendiary devices complete with typed instructions for use. Z Company had a particularly busy time. In Maghera quick thinking by two soldiers of the Drums Platoon foiled a terrorist attempt to destroy the town centre with a proxy car bomb containing two dustbins filled with home-made explosive. Three rounds of 84mm Carl Gustav were fired into the vehicle, disrupting the bomb's mechanism. Shortly after, the Mortar Platoon foiled a similar plot to devastate Magherafelt. Near Toom Bridge the Anti-Tank Platoon was ambushed but escaped with three minor wounds. Further afield, 13 explosive devices caused extensive damage to shops in Ballymena. This epidemic ended when a similar bomb went off in a car, injuring the four occupants, who were then able to assist the police with their enquiries. Arrests continued to be made regularly and the terrorists continued to murder, or attempt to murder, off-duty policemen and members of the UDR. Private Smith of 5 UDR had a remarkable escape when the cans of Guinness he was carrying absorbed almost all of the blast from a shotgun, fired at five yards' range.

A welcome visitor during October was the Colonel of the Regiment. On 23 November 1976 Major General D.T.Young, DFC, Commander Land Forces, presented Long Service and Good Conduct Medals to WOII A.J.Rumbold, WOII Green, WOII T.O'Dell, Colour Sergeant J.Harding and Staff Sergeant Brooks, RAPC. Christmas 1976 was celebrated with parties, dances and discos in all the messes, the Cross Keys Club and the Rose and Crown. On 19 December an inter-denominational carol service was held in the cookhouse, otherwise known as the Foyle Grill, and on 20 and 21 December Major Nigel Woodward put on another very successful Battalion Concert in the Disco Room of the Cross Keys Club.

In January 1977, Colonel Dickenson handed over command of the 1st Battalion to Lieutenant Colonel R.G.Long, MC. Colonel David Dickenson's tour had been an extremely active one, marked throughout by quiet efficiency and good humour not only in the operational context, but also in handling the Battalion's current problems, not least the welfare of families, and laying the groundwork for its future. Preceded by the Band, he and his surprised Jack Russell terrier, Josie, left Shackleton Barracks in an armchair mounted on a fork-lift truck with RSM Kimberley at the controls. Josie had become something of a Battalion character in her own right and, like every self-respecting Jack Russell, could exhibit a ferocity quite disproportionate to her size; certainly Private Atkins, the Colonel's driver, thought so when making an unsuccessful attempt to retrieve the Commanding Officer's briefcase from his office! With him, Colonel Dickenson took an unusual souvenir - an Austrian Mannlicher rifle of 1914 vintage, part of a consignment intended to arm the loyalists of that era, which had been discovered, together with a quantity of ammunition, stuffed up a chimney. The weapon was test fired for interest, then neutred, and is now in the Regimental Museum.

Colonel Bob Long had previously served with the Battalion in Germany, the Caribbean and Hong Kong. During the intervening periods had served with the 1st Battalion Malaysia Rangers in Ipoh and Borneo and with the Federation Military College; in 1971, having passed through Staff College, he was posted to the 1st Battalion The Gloucestershire Regiment as a company commander, for his conduct in which capacity in Belfast he was awarded the Military Cross. In 1972 he returned to the Staff College as GSO2 and in October 1975 was posted to the Ministry of Defence as Military Assistant (GSO1) to the Quartermaster General.

He took command at the very moment when the terrorists decided to escalate their level of violence, as a result of which two policemen were shot dead and two more were killed when their cars were booby-trapped. The reason for this was that in

County Londonderry the terrorists had been contained by the security forces to the point that they were beginning to lose credibility. This did not please the Provisional godfathers at all and they ordered the local gangs (known among themselves as Active Service Units or ASUs), reinforced by additional banshees from Belfast and the Republic, to mount a sustained offensive.

During the January incidents it became necessary to reinforce the garrison at Maghera and a section of the Special Patrol Group was introduced to Magherafelt. February was quieter in South Derry and the SPG section was withdrawn early in March. The enemy promptly reacted with a series of shootings as a result of which Battalion Tactical HQ was deployed to Magherafelt and a company from the 1st Battalion The Black Watch was placed under command and moved into Maghera. From 25 March, therefore, deployment within the area involved three companies, i.e. one in Kilrea, one in Maghera and one in Magherafelt.

On 7 April the Mortar Platoon was involved in a gun battle near Mullanstown as a result of which two of the most wanted men in Ulster, one of them seriously wounded, were captured. Next day, however, two SPG constables were murdered in a shooting attack near Moneymore. The subsequent follow-up involved seven companies and every available helicopter in the Province. The terrorists had not allowed for this kind of response and made themselves so scarce that there were few major incidents during the next five months.

Hardly had this operation drawn to a close than some elements of the loyalist community, led by the Rev Ian Paisley, began to give trouble. Dr Paisley, a powerful orator, made clear his view that too many concessions were being made to the nationalists, and that the British government should be adopting a much harder line against the terrorists. The language in which these opinions were expressed varied between the merely immoderate and the loudly intransigent. The Provisionals appeared not to mind, for the fear he generated produced the recruits they sorely needed; the security forces did, as the activities of the Doctor and his supporters sometimes meant a diversion of resources when none should have been necessary.

In this instance Dr Paisley had threatened to bring Ulster to a complete standstill with a general strike unless Mr Roy Mason, the Secretary of State for Northern Ireland, granted his demands. Mr Mason was not impressed and the strike itself was a failure, although numerous roads were blocked for several days with agricultural machinery. The power station workers remained on duty, the Harland and Wolff shipyard stayed open, and the shopkeepers were disinclined to lose business. As far as the Battalion was concerned it involved the temporary movement of Tactical HQ and A Company to Coleraine in support of the RUC. Subsequently, A Company moved on to Limavady and then formed part of the force which moved into Ballymena, where Dr Paisley was arrested by the police and charged with obstruction. Elsewhere, loyalists foolishly attempted to establish a roadblock with their tractors and other equipment on the bridge in fiercely nationalist Toome. The nationalists took umbrage, setting fire to some vehicles and tumbling others into the river. Now seriously alarmed, Dr Paisley's supporters began clamouring for Y Company's assistance. Unfortunately for them, their own road blocks got in the way and it was not until six weeks later that Royal Engineer vehicles from Ballykelly extracted their drowned tractors from the river. The situation possessed a certain quality of black humour.

The year 1977 marked the Silver Jubilee of The Queen's Coronation, celebrated with bonfires, street parties and bunting in cities, towns and villages throughout England, Wales and Scotland, and with lines of blazing beacons the length and breadth of the mainland. Save in staunchly republican areas, the story was the same across much of Ulster and, whatever troubles afflicted the Province, it was unthinkable that they should prevent The Queen visiting this part of her realm on such an occasion. She was to receive an understandably rapturous welcome from most of the community, and even dedicated republican terrorists, recognising the potential damage their cause would sustain if she were harmed, seemed content to display nothing more malignant than studied indifference. There remained, however, the risks posed by die-hard fanatics acting on their own initiative. Indeed, during Her Majesty's visit to Coleraine the Battalion was required to find another rifle company from its own resources, making no fewer than five of its own companies deployed and a further two under command. As well as its involvement with security, the Battalion made a further notable contribution to the success of the royal visit when Colour Sergeant Tim Hamlett and other members of the mess staff served lunch to Her Majesty at the new University of Ulster outside Coleraine.

The Band, under Bandmaster C.J.French, was also kept fully occupied during the summer. Its most important engagement took place on the evenings of 7, 8 and 9 June, involving all nine Bands and Corps of Drums of the Prince of Wales's Division in Beating Retreat on Horse Guards Parade, the Prince himself being present on the last evening. On 10 June the Band, in company with the Bands of The Devonshire and Dorset Regiment and The Duke of Edinburgh's Royal Regiment, performed a similar ceremony in Paignton, Devon. Together, all three Bands next gave a series of concerts and marching displays throughout Devon, Dorset, Wiltshire, Berkshire and Hampshire, including a two-hour concert to a packed house at the Guildhall, Southampton, a march through Romsey, and Beating Retreat at Broadlands, with Lord Mountbatten in attendance. This was followed by participation in the Army Show at Aldershot, where a total of eighteen Bands were massed for the Musical Pageant, after which the Divisional Bands moved on to the Wembley Pageant. After a short break back at Ballykelly the Band took part in the Cardiff Jubilee Tattoo before returning to Ulster in mid-August to fulfil its last engagements of the tour.

Colonel Long was already aware that at the end of its tour the 1st Battalion would be moving to Münster and that this would involve restructuring to conform with the government's latest round of defence cuts. No further amalgamations or disbandments were required; instead, a reduction in the Army's overall manpower was demanded. Of this the infantry's share was to be 8 per cent, involving a decrease in battalion strength to 650 all ranks. HQ Company would absorb the tasks previously carried out by the Admin, Command and Support Companies, including the Mortar and Anti-Tank Platoons, and the Reconnaissance Platoon would disappear. The four rifle companies would remain but within Z Company the Corps of Drums became a platoon "who just happened to be good at drumming," while the Assault Pioneers were split between companies. Another Z Company platoon would assume responsibility for manning the Weapon Training Wing, the Gymnasium and the Officers' and Sergeants' Messes. If the idea gave pleasure to the Treasury's accountants, in that more was supposed to be done with less, professional opinion fell far short of this and from BAOR, where the new policy was already being implemented, the word most commonly heard was "overstretch."

At this particular time the word could also be applied to the 1st Battalion in Northern Ireland. In addition to meeting operational requirements, the tempo of which remained constant, it was also preparing for the move to Germany, coming to terms with the reduced establishment, running NCO cadre and career courses, and maintaining a leave programme, all of which demanded management skills of a very high order. In the absence from Ballykelly of the CO, the administrative burden fell upon Major Jim Hewitt, the Second-in-Command, who dealt with a plethora of difficulties with imperturbable charm and good sense, well supported by the Quartermaster, Major Bob Bate Jones until December 1976 and thereafter Captain Jack Barrow.

The entire thrust of the security forces' strategy remained the creation of conditions in which the RUC could resume responsibility for greater areas of the Province. With this in mind, Colonel Long developed an excellent working relationship with his opposite number in the RUC, Divisional Superintendent Nigel Spears, who had seen wartime service with the RAF as a bomber pilot. As Minden Day 1977 approached it was agreed that the prevailing circumstances would justify holding a commemorative parade in a public place in Magherafelt. The Brigade Commander, Brigadier A.D.Myrtle, expressed concern but gave his blessing when Colonel Long admitted that the Chief Constable had already accepted an invitation to take the salute. Lady Newman, the Chief Constable's wife, who hailed from Brockenhurst, presented the roses, thereby putting an end to some interesting speculative discussions on the subject. One career-minded officer proposed Brigadier Myrtle for the task, but this idea was quickly overtaken when the Adjutant, Captain Paul Davis, a keen student of the turf, suggested Lester Piggott. However, neither the Brigadier nor Mr Piggott offered serious competition for Joanna Lumley, the reigning Miss Royal Hampshire, who was proposed by the Officer Commanding A Company, Major James Dewar. At this point the Public Relations Officer claimed that his office conferred obvious seigneurial rights entitling him to personally escort Miss Lumley throughout the day, a point fiercely contested by the OC A Company. Miss Lumley, herself of Army stock, would have been greatly diverted by this vigorous and by now hypothetical debate, had she been aware of it.

The parade itself was a success. Every one of the one hundred officers and men on parade had live rounds in the

Above: Sergeant John Cox explaining the GPMG to potential recruits at Eastleigh. The Regimental Recruiting Team, which had several titles over the years, formed an important part of the Regiment

WOII Jeff Rumbold, Company Sergeant Major, Minden Company, Colchester, December 1971

Right: Colonial pomp.
The Colonel of the Regiment, Brigadier David Warren, greets the Governor of Hongkong, Sir Murray MacLehose, at the Trooping of the Colour, January 1975.

Right: Minden Day, 1977, Megherafelt, Northern Ireland. Mrs Newman, wife of the Chief Constable, presents a rose to Maj Richard Ashenden. Capt Paul Davis and Sergeant Bill Male look on.

General Sir Edwin Bramall,
an old friend of the Regiment,
inspects the Trooping Parade
at Dover, Minden Day, 1981,
which commemorated
the centenary of the
amalgamation of the
37th (North Hampshire) and
67th (South Hampshire)
Regiments.

The association between the Regiment
and New Forest District, July 1982.
The Colonel of the Regiment receives
a carved Dog Gauge.

The Falklands, 1983.
Pte Roden with
the Prime Minister

South Georgia, 1983.
Cpl Lihou leads Pte Grant
and Pte Beddoe ashore

Pte Howten of the
Drums Platoon on
exercise in Scotland,
1983.

The Mortar Platoon
firing at Hohne.

WOII Allen and Sgt Lloyd with
the Assault Pioneer Platoon,
winners of the Berlin Infantry
Brigade Assault Pioneer Platoon
Concentration, 1984.

The Finest Triumph:
the winning team in the
Northern European Command
Infantry Competition.

The 'Chain Gang'
on parade!
Presentation of silver
fanfare trumpets by the
Lord Mayors, Mayors and
Chairmen of New Forest,
Rushmoor, Portsmouth,
Basingstoke, Bournemouth,
Southampton and
Winchester, 1983.

The Colonel of the
Regiment chats to Harry
Small, aged 97, September
1989. Mr Small survived
to enjoy his 100th birthday.

Granting of the Freedom of
the Borough of Test Valley,
High Street, Andover,
June 1986.

Berlin, 1983.
CO and QM stir the
Christmas Pudding

Cpl Flain, Pte Brown and
Pte Richards on exercise at
Thetford, 1988.

Cpl Tubb and Pte Baxter with
GPMG in the sustained fire role,
1986.

The first visit of the
Colonel-in-Chief to
Serle's House, 1988.
The Regimental Secretary,
Lt Col John Darroch,
explains a technical point.

The Colonel-in-Chief in Londonderry,
January 1990.

Londonderry, 1989.
Pte Moorby with
Tyrone.

Left: Londonderry 1989.
CSM Roberts and small friend

Bottom left: Lt Col Tim Glass presents
the Winchester Trophy to Colour
Sergeant Greenhalgh.

Bottom right: RSM Rodda hands over
to RSM Baker, January 1989.

Londonderry, 1990.
Pte Eardley at
'Free Derry Corner'.

The Royal Hampshires who fought with 1 Staffords in the Gulf:
Sgt Turley, L/Cpl Sampson, L/Cpl Bettesworth, Maj Dennis, L/Cpl Taylor

Training in Kenya, 1991

2/Lts George Churcher
and Chris Parker, 1991

TO THE GLORY OF GOD
AND
IN MEMORY
OF
THE MEN OF
THE HAMPSHIRE REGIMENT
WHO DIED IN THE
TUNISIAN CAMPAIGN
NOVEMBER 1942 — MAY 1943

2ND BN. THE HAMPSHIRE REGIMENT
1ST/4TH (TA) BN. THE HAMPSHIRE REGIMENT
2ND/4TH (TA) BN. THE HAMPSHIRE REGIMENT
5TH (TA) BN. THE HAMPSHIRE REGIMENT

The Memorial
in Tunis —
unveiled in March 1990

magazine of his weapon and Magherafelt was guarded by a further rifle company. The Chief Constable congratulated the Battalion on its excellent working relationship with the RUC and in particular on the efficient operation of the unique and pioneering joint communications room which had been set up. In his reply, Colonel Long thanked the Chief Constable not only for his attendance but also for bearing witness to the fact that the Battalion's task, namely the seeking out and destruction of The Queen's enemies, whenever and wherever they might be found, had not changed since that first Minden Day in 1759.

In conjunction with its operational role the Battalion had, throughout its tour, carried out a community relations campaign, providing assistance to local civilian organisations whenever possible, thereby generating trust and confidence in the Army. Something of the Band's part in this has already been mentioned, but there were many other ways in which goodwill was created. SQMS Green and some of the cooks provided a barbecue for 200 Coleraine children; once a fortnight Sergeant Lyddall and the PT staff entertained more children in Shackleton Barracks, using the trampoline, the gymnasium and the swimming pool; a sponsored swim by the Battalion's own children raised £168 for the benefit of a local youth club; WOII Hawker, Private Hall and Private Clark rescued a sheep from the bottom of a cliff; and RSM Kimberley assisted in judging the final of the Northern Ireland Scottish Pipe Bands Competition. There were more examples, but without any doubt the most important contributory factor in establishing good community relations lay in the daily contacts made between everyone from the Commanding Officer to the private soldier and their civilian counterparts. In such circumstances willingness to help, efficiency and courtesy made deep and lasting impressions among the local people. There were, of course, a few people one could not help, such as the lady who asked for a helicopter to fetch her spare car keys!

Six weeks before the tour ended responsibility for South Derry was handed over to the 2nd Royal Tank Regiment. Battalion Tactical HQ withdrew to Ballykelly, where Colonel Long received the following congratulatory message from Brigadier Myrtle:

"On handing over to 2 RTR in South Derry I congratulate you on the major contribution your Regiment has made to developing Army/RUC co-operation in that area. The comparative peace there during the last four months is due largely to your joint concept of operations and the successful support given to covert operations. Your continued presence in Maghera and your Intelligence personnel in all locations will be of great assistance to 2 RTR. I hope that 2 RTR will dispose of the South Derry ASU by building on the foundations laid by you at Magherafelt. Well done."

The Battalion's last task at Ballykelly was to undergo its Fitness for Role Inspection, following which a further signal was received from Brigadier Myrtle, the Inspecting Officer:

"Today's FFR Inspection confirmed the high opinion I have of your Battalion. I know your Battalion administration is on a sound footing and you have achieved a most creditable programme of individual and junior NCO training. Operationally you have answered all the calls I have made upon you, and you have won for yourselves a fine reputation with the RUC in O Division."

On 4 October 1977 the Battalion formally handed over to the 1st Battalion The Gloucestershire Regiment. It could look back upon a job well done, during which 150 terrorists had been charged, 75 weapons and 7000 rounds of ammunition had been recovered, and large quantities of explosives discovered.

Many of its members had already left for England and four days later the Battalion celebrated its homecoming by exercising its Freedom rights in Winchester. The parade consisted of the Band, the Colour Party, two guards and a contingent from the Comrades' Association. The March itself began at Newburgh House and took the traditional route down High Street to the Broadway, the Salute being taken at the Guildhall by the Mayor, the Colonel of the Regiment and Chief Superintendent Spears, RUC, who remarked that it made a change to see Englishmen marching! Spectators could not fail to notice the fit, professional, self-confident look of the Battalion as it swung past, emphasised by the wearing of combat dress. The day itself was grey, damp and misty, as befitting England in October, but the welcome was warm and sincere. Sadly, the Battalion's visit to its home County was to be very brief and its Advance Party had already arrived in Münster.

* * * * * * * *

CHAPTER 16

MÜNSTER 1977 — 1981

Conditions of service - role - award of BEM to Corporal Turner - 2nd Armoured Division Skill-at-Arms Meeting - sporting successes - KAPE Team and training - Minden Day 1978 - adventure training - Exercise Gryphons Galore - Royal Military Music Show - move to Londonderry and deployment - operations - community relations - return to Münster - Colonel Bob Long hands over to Lieutenant Colonel M.J.Martin - deaths of Earl Mountbatten, Brigadier Le Patourel and Major General Man - the murder of Private Robins - KAPE 1979 - the Band in Full Dress - Exercises Lion Heart 12 and Keystone - Commanding Officer's Days, the Minden Trophy and sporting activity - Field Force Commander's excellent report - GOC's commendations arising from Ulster tour - Tiger Marches and Winchester Trophy 1980 - Terence Cuneo painting of Tebourba - Gallipoli Day 1980 - training in Portugal - Minden Day and dedication of stained glass window - good recruiting and re-engagement figures - issue of MILAN ATGW - visit of Ernie Wise - Exercise Crusader 80 and autumn training - sporting domination of Münster Garrison - Christmas Show - move to Dover 1981 - complimentary messages

B y the end of November 1977 the reduced 1st Battalion was firmly established in Buller Barracks, Münster, having travelled to Germany either by air or in private transport, with WOI Kimberley remaining as RSM, the CSMs being WOIIs Jesty (succeeded by O'Dell), Wolfe, Gibson, Austin and Stroud. Captain Roger Coleman returned as Motor Transport

Officer and Second Quartermaster. In Münster there awaited a number of unpleasant surprises stemming directly from the recently imposed financial restrictions. Barrack services had been cut to the bone so that furniture for the families had to be moved by the Battalion's own soldiers. Civil labour costs had also been slashed with the result that, for the first time for many years, significant numbers of men were employed on cookhouse fatigues, area cleaning and other chores. Secondly, although accompanied married soldiers had received an increase in allowances during the last weeks of the Ulster tour, the cost of living in Germany was even higher than that in the United Kingdom, despite attempts by the NAAFI to contain prices in its shops. Yet the pay of the trained rifleman barely equalled that of a qualified tradesman at home, and whereas the former was, in the nature of things, paid for a twenty-four-hour day, the latter easily boosted his income by working overtime. The worst effects were felt by those with growing families, especially among the vital junior NCO strata. Obviously, the long-term implications for a professional, selectively recruited Army were very serious indeed. During the coming year some forty soldiers of the 1st Battalion would purchase their discharge for financial or other reasons, a situation mirrored throughout the Army and the other services, ironically at a time when their public standing had never been higher. Warned that catastrophe was unavoidable if the trend continued, the government reacted with appropriate pay increases, but not before many good men had been lost.

Münster remained more or less unchanged since the Battalion's last stay. Save in the village of Wolbeck, where, as mentioned in an earlier chapter, the Battalion was always welcome, most Münsterlanders preserved a stolid indifference to its presence, perversely replaced by a genuine enthusiasm reserved for formal occasions.

The Battalion was now performing the role of an non-mechanised infantry battalion within 5 Field Force, commanded by Brigadier R.A.Pascoe, MBE, part of the 2nd Armoured Division. The role meant that, not having APCs to maintain and look after, it could concentrate all its efforts on honing its fitness and skills as professional infantrymen.

As always, the BAOR cycle began with individual training. Platoon Tiger Marches, covering 100 miles in five days, hardened feet and leg muscles. Some general basic skills, such as map reading and trench digging, had become a little rusty during the long tour in Ulster, and others, such as those of the Mortar and Anti-Tank Platoons, needed rebuilding under Captains Nigel Alderman and Trevor Finklaire. In addition, there were regular NCOs Cadres, the MT Platoon ran driving courses, the Signals Platoon carried out a number of exercises to test their equipment, and the QM's Department under Major Jack Barrow began a "self-help" programme of redecorating some parts of the barracks. Specialist training included courses in such subjects as nuclear, biological and chemical warfare, water duties, first aid, methods of instruction and the German language. Simultaneously, Major Jim Hewitt, the Battalion's Second-in-Command, had organised Exercise Snow Queen, hiring a ski hut at Thalkirchdorf in Bavaria where, in batches of thirty-five, students were taught the basics of downhill and "langlauf" skiing techniques during twelve-day courses. As a result of this a large percentage of the Battalion developed a real enthusiasm for the sport.

Christmas and the New Year quickly came and went. On 24 January 1978 a Miss Smith, daughter of Lance Corporal David Smith and his wife Jennifer, caused a sensation by being born in a car parked on the edge of the Battalion square. History does not record the RSM's response, but the day's Part I Orders contained a paragraph reminding babies wishing to be born in barracks that the square was OUT OF BOUNDS and that they should park outside the Medical Centre!

The Tiger Marches took place in March and, following the Easter break, the competition for the Winchester Trophy was held, the winners being 9 Platoon, commanded by Colour Sergeant Bob Garland. March also saw Y Company (Major Richard Ashenden) participating in a multi-national exercise in Denmark, at the end of which it was praised for its professionalism. On 8 April the Colonel of the Regiment, Brigadier D.J.Warren, presented the British Empire Medal to ex-Corporal George Turner on the square at Buller Barracks in front of the assembled Battalion. Corporal Turner, now the owner of a butcher's shop in the Isle of Wight, had left the Army the previous March after twenty-two years' service. Since 1961 he had been the Battalion Ration NCO and, as the citation reads, in performing this task, he had displayed a "devotion to duty, loyalty and ready acceptance of responsibility, well beyond what is normal for his rank and worthy of recognition."

In the meantime, Colonel Long had asked Major Roger Stockton, OC Z Company, to "organise a fairly small-scale day's shooting — quite a simple affair." This turned out to be the 2nd Division's Skill-at-Arms Meeting, for which no instructions existed. The Quartermaster, Major Jack Barrow, flung wide the doors of his Aladdin's Cave, offering a bewildering selection of necessary items, including "70 tents, 28 flagpoles, 17 latrines, 500 fire buckets, 100 stirrup pumps, 200 six-foot tables and 700 chairs folding flat," with the twin caveats that nothing was to be lost and the General liked everything in straight lines. The groundwork having thus been laid, there remained only the thousand or so minor details to clarify, such as the provision of ice for drinks, where the silver was to go, what the Band was to eat, and the fact that ladies did not use latrine buckets. These matters having been resolved, the Meeting itself, held at the end of April, was a resounding success involving eleven major and thirteen minor units. The Battalion Shooting Team came in second, thereby qualifying for Bisley, with Corporal R.Slade becoming the Meeting's Champion Rifle Shot and WOII Balston and Lance Corporal Hack winning the General Purpose Machine Gun Pairs.

There were other sporting successes to record during the year. The Battalion's seven-a-side rugby A Team, coached by Captain Willie Bickett, beat the Royal Scots in the Münster Garrison final. This season was the last for a great stalwart, Corporal Les Harper, who had inhabited the front row for many years. The badminton team finished the season as runners up in the 2nd Armoured Division Inter-Unit Competition, and the hockey team (Majors Hewitt and Ashenden, Captains Hughes, Alderman, Edwards and Finklaire, Second Lieutenant Jones, WOI French, WOIIs Garland and Marston, Colour Sergeants Allen and Glasspool, Sergeants Bevan and Windebank, Lance Corporals Belton and Judd, Private Bond and Bandsman Woods) won the Infantry Cup BAOR, the Münster Garrison Knock-Out and the 2nd Armoured Division League (jointly), as well as reaching the quarter final in the Army Cup. In the wider sphere, Lance Corporal Ken Burchell again led the British Hapkido Team to victory during the World Championship in Canada, going on to Korea to personally win the title of Supreme Champion, which was competed for once every ten years.

On 7 May Lieutenant N.A.Sim left with a fourteen-strong KAPE Team, plus the Band, for a tour of Hampshire. The Team, with a representative display of vehicles, weapons, equipment, uniforms and mounted photographs, visited Romsey, Andover, Fareham, Basingstoke, Winchester, Eastleigh, Portsmouth, Havant and Southsea, and finally the Gosport Military Tattoo on 27 May. During these visits the Band played at local schools during the morning and afternoon as well as giving public performances at lunch time. Many enquiries were received from potential recruits; surprisingly, very few of these young men raised the thorny subject of pay and, in itself, this indicated how well the Team had got its message across.

During June and July the Battalion was engaged in two exercises on the Soltau training area. The first of these, Exercise Rotary Tiger, was designed to test the companies in bridge demolition guards and helicopter drills. The second, Exercise Tiger Mole, involved digging and camouflaging, with limited Royal Engineer assistance, a battalion position incorporating MEXE command post shelters, this being followed by a fighting patrol exercise in which companies tested each other's defences.

After Tiger Mole the Battalion devoted its attention to preparing for the Minden Day parade under the new RSM, WOI Jeff Rumbold, who had succeeded WOI Ted Kimberley upon the latter being commissioned. The setting for the parade was the baroque splendour of the Schloss Münster, once the home of the city's Prince Bishops and now the principal building of its university. The Guest of Honour, who took the salute with the Colonel of the Regiment, was Dr Werner Pierchalla, Oberbürgermeister of Münster. Rolls Royce Cars Ltd provided a German-registered Silver Shadow complete with chauffeur for the Colonel of the Regiment. The chauffeur was somewhat disconcerted when he arrived in the barracks to have his number-plates removed and replaced with English-style 1 R HAMPS plates. His concern about the legality of the enterprise was assuaged when he was assured, rightly, that the car would receive a motorcycle escort from the German police.

It rained mercilessly throughout the parade, during which Frau Pierchalla presented the roses. The Brigade Commander asked the Commanding Officer under what circumstances the wet weather programme, advertised on the tickets, would be undertaken. Prior to the parade he had been assured that the rain would soon stop; it did not. "Regen, Rosen und Rolls Royce" ran the headline of the local newspaper the following day. An unusual feature of the parade was that at noon the Band ceased playing and the Glockenspiel in the bell tower of the Schloss played the old German march *Lippe-Detmold*. In his speech the Oberbürgermeister praised the steadiness of the soldiers taking part and emphasised the friendly links which existed between the city and the Regiment. Replying in German, Colonel Long thanked the Oberbürgermeister and Frau Pierchalla for honouring the Regiment, which had spent the winter of 1758/59 in Münster and had returned there after the Battle of Minden. It was right, he continued, to demonstrate publicly from time to time that the Alliance of 1759 was still valid in 1978. After the parade receptions, notable for the atmosphere and smell of drying service dress, were held by the officers in the Castle and by the sergeants in the Sergeants' Mess.

During August the majority of the Battalion managed to enjoy some form of adventure training. Most platoons organised their own trips, with activities ranging from rock climbing and hill walking in Bavaria to canoeing on the Danube. One of the year's most noteworthy adventure training events took place in October, when a party canoed all the way down the Rhine from Basle, Switzerland, to Duisburg, and thence by means of the Dortmund-Ems waterway to Münster. The party consisted of Captain Barry Baty, Second Lieutenant Ross Jones, Lance Corporal Andy Cull and Privates Sandy Sanderson, Kenny Baker, Lance Greenhalgh, Johnno Johnson and Alan Lloyd, plus a support group including Corporal Terry Jefferies, Lance Corporal Ken Burchell and Privates Des Fuller, David Sylvester and Larry Lawson, which travelled by 4-ton truck and prepared the camp sites along the way. The total distance covered was 530 miles at an average rate of some 60 miles per day. The last leg of the journey brought the party to a stretch of canal close to Buller Barracks, where the Band and the Battalion were waiting to cheer them home.

Serving in BAOR enabled the support weapons platoons to come into their own. The Anti-Tank Platoon attended the 1 (BR) Corps Anti-Tank Concentration at Putlos and put in some useful shooting in realistic battle conditions. This, in fact, was the first time since the Battalion re-formed that all six guns had been together on the firing point. Later in the year the Mortar Platoon, now commanded by Captain Adrian Pryce, attended the 5 Field Force Mortar Concentration at Münsterlager. Given the limited range space and ammunition available, such concentrations were the best way of enhancing the training and experience of the platoons, especially by means of constructive criticism from specialist instructors.

Much of September was taken up with Exercise Gryphons Galore, which was held in the Hameln area and lasted two weeks, involving the whole of 5 Field Force. During the exercise the Battalion was tested in many aspects of its role, especially in rear area security operations and guarding key points. In the later phases of the exercise it mounted an assault river crossing which earned high praise from the Field Force Commander. The next two days were spent marching and fighting in old infantry style until the Echelon caught up, and the last two in defeating various enemy probes, both helicopter-borne and mechanised. The final hours found B Company engaged in heavy street-fighting in the middle of a town against the Battalion's German opponents. As Major Hugh Keatinge, who had taken over as the Battalion's Second-in-Command on 29 April, commented, "This would have caused apoplexy had it happened in Winchester or Romsey, but the locals took it entirely in their stride, watching the proceedings with great interest." One distinguished visitor who dropped in by helicopter during the exercise was General Alexander Haig, Jr, the Supreme Allied Commander Europe. He created a most favourable impression on those of all ranks fortunate enough to meet him and lined up for exercise stew with the most highly polished mess tin in the British Army, complete with four stars. The Commanding Officer caused a ripple of interest in the ranks of the international press, and considerable consternation among their British minders, when he affirmed that he would vote for General Haig as President of the USA!

On 27 October the Band, under Bandmaster French and Drum Major Windebank, combined with the Bands of The Devonshire and Dorset Regiment and The Duke of Edinburgh's Royal Regiment to perform a Beating of Retreat on the Battalion square, held in honour of the 1st Battalion The Wessex Regiment (TA), which was undergoing training in Germany. Lieutenant Colonel J.G.T.Southwood, commanding the 1st Wessex, described the Retreat as being the most impressive he had ever seen.

Having been warned for a further short tour in Ulster, the Battalion now adopted its Northern Ireland orbat. This meant the temporary disbandment of the Mortar and Anti-Tank Platoons, the members of which went to Z Company, the Intelligence Cell or the Close Observation Platoon.

On 19 November the Battalion began a fortnight's field firing at Sennelager, including an inter-section march-and-shoot competition won by Corporal Taylor's section from Z Company. While at Sennelager the Battalion was visited by the Rt Hon Fred Mulley, MP, Secretary of State for Defence, accompanied by Lieutenant General Sir Peter Leng, GOC 1 (BR) Corps.

The year ended with the Band participating in the spectacular Royal Military Music Show, staged at the Halle Münsterland, the local equivalent of Earls Court, in aid of the German Red Cross. Involving as it did musicians, singers and dancers representing thirteen British regiments, two British schools, one German school and a troupe of Morris Men from Sussex, the show provided superb value for money, playing to a packed and thoroughly appreciative audience.

After three weeks' block leave, concentrated training for Ulster began in January 1979. NITAT provided an excellent three-day presentation, after which the Companies carried out intensive training, culminating in a further two weeks at Sennelager in February.

On this occasion the Battalion would be responsible for the security of Londonderry City west of the river Foyle, where it took over from the 1st Battalion The Royal Welch Fusiliers on 7 March 1979. Battalion Tactical HQ was located in the Strand Road RUC Station, HQ, A and Y Companies were based in the Fort George complex, B Company was based in Masonic Camp within the walls of the old city, and Z Company based in Creggan, with Company HQ and 14 Platoon in Creggan Camp, 12 Platoon in the RUC Station at Rosemount and 11 Platoon manning the vehicle checkpoint on the Letterkenny Road.

Londonderry, it will be recalled, was one of the places where the present Troubles had begun ten years earlier. A walled cathedral city surrounded by sprawling housing estates, it was in 1979 a place where the historic grievances of both sides remained as fresh as if they had happened yesterday, an attitude which prompted the author Leon Uris to write the despairing words, "Ireland has no future — merely a past which it regurgitates time and time again."

Nevertheless, despite the scars left by terrorist bombs, there were signs that much of the population simply wanted to put the

Troubles behind them and get on with their lives. To further lighten the atmosphere, Colonel Long had yellow "smiley" stickers printed and introduced cards explaining just what particular groups of soldiers were doing. When the pro-nationalist *Derry Journal* complained bitterly about the permanent vehicle checkpoints covering official crossing points on the border, these were improved with flower boxes, carefully tended gardens and cheerful signs.

In addition to these checkpoints, A Company, commanded by Major Humphrey James, The Devonshire and Dorset Regiment, was responsible for mounting patrols in two industrial estates and the Shantallow, Carnhill and New housing estates, and conducting operations to prevent the movement of arms and explosives in a country area known as the Northern Enclave, which stretched to the border. It recorded numerous successes, one of the best being the red-handed capture of a terrorist visiting a hide to collect a grenade, pistol and ammunition.

B Company, under Major Bruce Willing, was originally responsible for the Bogside, Brandywell and Fountains estates. It manned two observation posts on the city walls and a third on the roof of the Rossville flats, in the Bogside itself. The Fountains, behind its new protective wall, was Protestant territory, but the Bogside and Brandywell were nationalist heartlands. Their inhabitants, nevertheless, had made it clear to the terrorists that they would not allow bomb attacks because of the risk to their children, and the principal risk to patrols was from the one-shot sniper. To counter this, B Company employed the multiple patrol, splitting patrols into four-man sub-patrols, up to five in number, each commanded by a junior NCO, thereby making the sniper unsure of himself. As described in an earlier chapter, patrols were regularly accompanied by intelligence gatherers who quickly became familiar to the local population and suffered threats and harassment in consequence. Their work, however, was vital and their presence not only resulted in the highest number of terrorist sightings on record but also inhibited the enemy's free movement. As always, the underlying ethos of all patrol work was to be polite but firm, and one reason for the Battalion's continued success in this field was that these qualities came quite naturally to Hampshire soldiers.

Towards the end of tour the city centre was added to the Company's area of responsibility. Because of this 7 Platoon from

Y Company and the patrols platoon of 176 Provost Company RMP were added to its strength, creating something of an accommodation problem in Masonic Camp as far as the former was concerned.

The city centre had originally been the responsibility of Y Company, commanded by Major Tim Glass. It measured one mile by half a mile and included the university, the docks, Strand Road, Waterloo Place, the old walled city and the so-called pub triangle, into which last were crammed no fewer than thirty alleged pubs, discos and other establishments, all sufficiently decrepit as to warrant demolition in the Third World. The Company's task was three-fold. First, it was to deter or catch terrorist bombers in the city, entailing a half-platoon presence on foot or by Land Rover round the clock. Secondly, whenever a bomb was planted the problems created had to be sorted out as quickly as possible. Thirdly, good will had to be shown to everyone, to which end the soldiers gave children chocolate eggs at Easter and flowers to mothers on Mother's Day. Altogether, there were eleven bomb attacks, directed mainly at commercial targets, during which many of the bombs were defused or rendered harmless by prompt action, and one attempt to kill a soldier by sniping - the bullet missed Private James by eighteen inches. What the Company noticed first about the city was "dejection and defiance but above all a kind of dumb, irritating indifference. Quite often when a patrol passed through a busy shopping centre people either barely noticed or simply did not acknowledge one's presence." By the end of the tour, however, the author of the Company's Journal notes was able to write, "Much goodwill was created within the city and many people were impressed by and remarked on our cheerful approach."

Z Company, commanded by Major Roger Stockton, Worcestershire and Sherwood Foresters Regiment, was responsible for the Creggan Estate, the Rosemount Estate and the Southern Enclave, which was a belt of rural land stretching some two to three miles to the border with the Republic. The whole area was regularly patrolled and remained relatively peaceful throughout the tour. Lieutenant Peter Emery's 11 Platoon, manning the Letterkenny Road PVCP, lived in crowded and uncomfortable conditions, working eight hours on and eight off. Of the platoon's twenty-six men, sixteen were required to man the checkpoint and the rest acted as a rapid reaction force based at the

RUC's Rosemount Station, one section being rotated between the two every three days. During the four-month period 180,000 vehicles were stopped, of which 12,000 were searched.

As always, there were arrests to make. The terrorists had become adept at concealing weapons so that they could not be associated with a particular individual or household, but their weapons were found just the same. One young man, having attempted to conceal a grenade wrapped in a sock, protested his innocence until the sock's brother was found at his home. During a check on a suspect pub, someone turned off the lights and the customers began throwing bottles, glasses and chairs at the soldiers; the firing of a single baton round led to yells of alarm and hurried departures via the nearest exit. There were a couple of unpleasant surprises, such as dogs which had been trained to chase open, doorless Land Rovers and bite the occupants' legs, and the first "sweetie jar" bombs, fifty-three of which were aimed at the Battalion during the tour. These devices consisted of a gallon-sized sweet jar filled with petrol and pieces of shrapnel, the intention being to drop them into passing patrol vehicles.

In the field of community relations, for which Major Peter Shepherd was responsible, the Battalion made solid progress. Public relations involved both defensive and positive stances. The defensive aspects included dealing with complaints and although the vast majority of these had no justification whatever the complainant still had to be given a sympathetic and friendly hearing, with appropriate action being taken where necessary. In this way the terrorists were deprived of the opportunity to direct unfavourable publicity at the Battalion through the medium of the *Derry Journal* and other papers. The positive side of the job involved holding monthly community relations meetings at Creggan and Masonic Camps where local people could discuss problems with the Army and RUC, entertaining parties of children on Sunday afternoons at Creggan Camp and Fort George, assisting at youth clubs, lending camp beds, sleeping bags and blankets to various organisations, both Catholic and Protestant, and maintaining two "Playbuses" run by the Social Services. There were, sometimes, occasions when one could be just too helpful, as in the case of the "hijacked" car returned to its owner having been cleared by the Ammunition Technical Officer; the man was not pleased to see it as he was short of cash and had just instituted an insurance claim!

Visitors to the Battalion in Londonderry were numerous and included General Sir John Archer, KCB, OBE, Commander-in-Chief UK Land Forces, General Sir Richard Worsley, KCB, OBE, Quartermaster General, General Sir Roland Gibbs, GCB, CBE, DSO, MC, ADC Gen, Chief of the General Staff, Lieutenant General Sir Timothy Creasy, KCB, OBE, GOC Northern Ireland, Major General J.M.Glover, Commander Land Forces, who took part in a B Company patrol, Mr Derek Stephen, CB, Deputy Under-Secretary of State (Army), Councillor Richard Sotnick, Lord Mayor of Portsmouth, and the glamorous Miss Angie Lane, Miss Royal Hampshire.

On 2 July the advance party of the 1st Battalion The Duke of Edinburgh's Royal Regiment arrived and the Battalion commenced a two-phase move to Germany via Moscow Camp in Belfast. By 14 July everyone was back in Münster, going on three weeks' block leave a week later. The tour had been relatively uneventful and, thankfully, there had been no serious casualties as a result of terrorist action.

On 17 August Colonel Bob Long handed over Command of the 1st Battalion to Lieutenant Colonel M.J.Martin, prior to taking up an appointment at the Ministry of Defence. He had commanded the Battalion for two-and-a-half years, during which it served twice in Northern Ireland as well as completing a BAOR training cycle. He was towed out of Buller Barracks by members of the Officers' and Sergeants' Messes, the *Journal* commenting that he would be very sadly missed by all ranks.

Colonel Mike Martin, whose father had commanded the 2nd Battalion in Tunisia and at Salerno during the Second World War, joined the Regiment from Sandhurst in 1958, serving with the 1st Battalion in Lemgo and throughout the entire Caribbean tour. He was seconded to the Malaysian Army during the Confrontation with Indonesia. After a short tour with the Junior Soldiers' Company at the Wessex Depot in Exeter, he served as Adjutant of the 1st Battalion between 1967 and 1969. This was followed by two years as an Instructor at the RMA Sandhurst and a year as a student at the Army Staff College. Returning to Regimental duty, he commanded a rifle company of the 1st Battalion The Duke of Edinburgh's Royal Regiment in Berlin and for eighteen months at Ballykinler in Northern Ireland, being awarded a Mention in Despatches. Between 1975 and 1976 he was GSO 2 (Instructor) at the Junior Division, Staff College, Warminster. He was then appointed Second-in-Command of the 1st Battalion The Devonshire and Dorset Regiment, a mechanised battalion, in Osnabrück. In September 1978 he attended a course at the National Defence College at Latimer.

Despite its successful completion of another tour in Ulster, for the Regiment as a whole the year 1979 was marked by several deeply sad occasions. First came the death of Admiral of the Fleet Earl Mountbatten of Burma, murdered by terrorists while on holiday at his home in the Republic of Ireland. His death deprived the Regiment of a staunch friend who, it will be remembered, had been the Honorary Colonel of 4th/5th (TA) Battalion from 1964 to 1967. On 4 September Brigadier Pat Le Patourel, who had been awarded the Victoria Cross for his gallantry while serving with the 2nd Battalion at the Battle of Tebourba Gap in 1942 and subsequently been appointed to command the 14th Battalion The Parachute Regiment (5th Battalion The Royal Hampshire Regiment) TA, in 1954, died suddenly at the age of sixty-three. On 10 October Major General Pat Man, who, after a distinguished war record, had most successfully led the 1st Battalion during the Malayan Emergency, died quietly at his home in Suffolk, aged sixty-six.

A quite inexplicable tragedy also beset the 1st Battalion during the autumn of the year. At about 10:30 one evening two prowler guards encountered Private Jefferies leaving a barrack block with a bloodstained pick helve. Jefferies was in a disturbed and potentially dangerous state, and he was quickly placed under restraint by one of the guards, Lance Corporal Bean. Shortly after, Private Robins, a storeman, was found in his bunk, so severely battered that he died on the way to hospital. Another storeman, Private Gibson, was found unconscious in his own bunk, but survived his injuries. No motive for these attacks was ever discovered and Private Jefferies was appropriately charged and sentenced to life imprisonment. Lance Corporal Bean received a Commander-in-Chief's Commendation for his capture of the killer and Lance Corporal Clack, the duty medical orderly, received a GOC's Commendation for his efforts on the night.

Having returned from leave in August, the Battalion despatched a KAPE team to Hampshire under Captain Mike Reeve-Tucker. The team visited Romsey, Andover, Fareham, Portsmouth, Havant, Winchester, Eastleigh, Southampton, Ringwood and Lymington. In addition to the usual displays of equipment, soldiers were sent out in pairs to talk to people in shops and pubs, and the Band gave fourteen school concerts as well as a number of public performances. At the end of the fortnight's tour the Band and the Regimental Recruiting Team crossed to the Channel Islands for a shorter but equally enjoyable tour, after which the Band went to London to make a long-playing record, issued under the title of *Tigers at Ease.*

On its return to Münster the Band and the Corps of Drums received, at Regimental expense, scarlet Full Dress tunics, with crown lace where appropriate, plus helmets spiked universal. Needless to say, the full effect was magnificent, prompting the Quartermaster, Captain Roger Coleman, to comment briefly but with evident satisfaction in the Journal, "They are now properly clothed for ceremonial occasions." Bandmaster French, who had re-formed the Band in Colchester and achieved a very high standard, had been posted to the Depot and the Band was now under the direction of Bandmaster WOI D.W.Wood.

The BAOR exercise season was now in full swing. First, in September, came Exercise Lion Heart 12, a command post exercise, held in an area south of Cologne. This involved Battalion Headquarters, A and B Companies. Few had expected to feel the smallest twinges of nostalgia for Northern Ireland, but at the end of the exercise one participant commented that establishing a command post in a wood or friendly farmer's barn compared most unfavourably with the luxury afforded by an RUC police station!

Lion Heart 12 led directly on to Exercise Keystone in October. The first phase of this was devoted entirely to Battalion training, and the second phase, involving much hard digging in cold but bright and dry weather, concentrated on defensive warfare. Brigadier C.J.Airy, commanding 5 Field Force, expressed himself well pleased with the result and sent Colonel Martin a congratulatory note. During the exercise a surprise visit was received from the Chief of The General Staff, General Sir Edwin Bramall, who remembered the Battalion well from its days in Borneo, Netheravon and Hong Kong.

The autumn also saw much useful individual and section training for the Anti-Tank, Mortar, Signals and Drums Platoons as well as NCOs' Cadres. One new aspect of Battalion life introduced by Colonel Martin was the Commanding Officer's Day. Each such day was set aside to test companies on military skills and fitness, very much on the lines of the annual Fitness for Role Inspection, achieving the objective of being simultaneously enjoyable and professionally constructive. Another was the Minden Trophy, a silver rose bowl to be awarded to the company with the best overall sporting performance during the year.

From 25 November until 7 December the Battalion spent two weeks field firing at Sennelager, the inter-platoon march-and-shoot competition being won by 4 Platoon under Lieutenant Roche, on exchange from the Royal Australian Regiment.

Much emphasis was placed on fitness, all companies spending the first two hours of Tuesday and Thursday mornings engaged in physical training, as well as participating in Battalion cross-country runs. The Battalion Boxing Team, trained by Sergeant Gannon, Army Physical Training Corps, and consisting of Sergeant Cockwill, Corporal Graham, Lance Corporals Nelson, Campbell and Harris, and Privates Craggs, Ellis, Sharpe, Kerswell, Hewitt, Tombs, Williams and Bean, did extremely well, reaching the semi-final of the 2nd Armoured Division Knockout Competition, which was lost by five bouts to four with the final bout being the decider. The rugby, soccer, hockey and squash teams also did well in divisional and garrison competitions. In December the first party of soldiers left for two weeks' skiing at the Battalion ski hut at Konstanza in Bavaria, close to the Austrian border. Further parties continued to leave throughout the winter, during which almost 200 soldiers learned to ski at the very modest cost of only £35 each.

Of the Hampshires during this period Brigadier Airy wrote in his Inspection Report: "I have hardly been critical at all because I have found this to be a thoroughly good battalion. There is a sense of family and it is a battalion of good honest countrymen who are full of smiling enthusiasm and endeavour. I have a soft spot for them and a justified admiration, based largely on their willing attitude to have a go at anything and everything, and then organise things thoroughly well. I am very pleased that they are part of 5 Field Force."

It would be wrong to conclude this summary of the events of 1979 without mentioning one of international significance which, ultimately, would have a bearing on the Regiment's future. Since the end of the long war in Vietnam communist influence had been extended steadily across large areas of Asia, the Middle East and Africa. On 24 December 1979 the over-confident

Soviet Union invaded Afghanistan, ignoring every lesson of history from Alexander the Great onwards. Occupying Afghanistan was a simple matter; conquering the country was not. The British experience in three wars was that one did what one had to and left; to stay was militarily uneconomic, and could ultimately result in catastrophe. Yet, it was precisely the latter course of action the Kremlin chose to adopt. Suddenly, the huge but inflexible Soviet Army found itself bogged down in an apparently endless guerrilla war for which its training, structure and temperament were unsuited. In the long term, the Soviet economy, already stretched to breaking point by over-extended world commitments, would collapse under the additional strain imposed. That, however, lay some years ahead and in the meantime the Cold War would continue as before.

During a visit to the Battalion in January 1980 the Colonel of the Regiment presented GOC's Commendations to Sergeant Baker and Corporal Dodd; it was also learned that Major Bruce Willing had been Mentioned in Despatches and that Corporals Purser and Black had also been awarded GOC's Commendations, all for their excellent work in Londonderry.

As the Battalion entered the new training year Major R.D.Hanscomb took over as Second-in-Command from Major Hugh Keatinge. Individual platoons were now training hard for their Tiger Marches, which took place in icy conditions during February 1980. The Winchester Trophy was competed for in March and won by Lieutenant Richard Dennis and 8 Platoon of Y Company. Simultaneously, the Mortar Platoon, where Captain Adrian Pryce had been joined by WOII Bob Le Galloudec, produced excellent results in the 5 Field Force Concentration at Münsterlager. Elsewhere, the Battalion did its share of site guards and border patrols.

At home, the Regiment had commissioned the artist Terence Cuneo to record on canvas the action which resulted in Brigadier (then Major) Le Patourel, 2nd Battalion, winning the Victoria Cross at the Battle of Tebourba Gap in December 1942. The picture was unveiled at Serle's House by Brigadier Le Patourel's widow Babette. Also present were their daughter Julia and the Brigadier's sister, Mrs Edith Le Tocq. Mr Cuneo said that it had been a privilege for him to have recorded the action of a very brave man, adding that while he had produced a horrific painting, he felt that was what had to be portrayed. In his reply the

Colonel of the Regiment agreed that that was exactly what a battlefield was like. Today, the painting can be seen in the Regimental Museum and those who look closely will find, just in front of Major Le Patourel's feet, Terence Cuneo's hallmark, a small mouse.

To celebrate Gallipoli Day 1980 the Lord Mayor of Portsmouth, Councillor Roland Taylor, and the Mayors of Rushmoor and Romsey, respectively Councillors P.R.Lilywhite and P.D.Brans, travelled to Münster. Having paid their respects to the city's Oberbürgermeister in his Parlour at the Rathaus, they spent the afternoon watching platoon and company attacks on the Dorbaum training area and meeting soldiers. In the evening they witnessed the Band and Corps of Drums Beating Retreat, the Salute being taken by the Lord Mayor of Portsmouth in the presence of the GOC 2nd Armoured Division and Brigadier Airy. This fine display was followed by receptions in both the Officers' and Sergeants' Messes.

The pressure on training areas in Germany had long been intense, so much so that for many years German tank battalions had been carrying out their annual gunnery classification at Castlemartin in Pembrokeshire, while British mechanised units exercised in the wide spaces of the Suffield training area in Canada. The search for suitable training areas had become international in its scope and Major General Walsh, Director of Army Training, believed that he had found one at Santa Margarida in Portugal. The Portuguese government was agreeable to the idea and it was decided that the area's potential should be evaluated by the 1st Battalion The Royal Hampshire Regiment in the spring of 1980. Colonel Martin made several preliminary visits as a result of which he was able to report that the area contained too many privately owned olive trees to be of much use for mechanised training, but that it would suffice for dismounted infantry. The project therefore went ahead during April and May as Exercise Night Echo with the three rifle companies travelling to Portugal by sea or air and then carrying out a guerrilla warfare exercise in conjunction with the Portuguese Army. The Portuguese were extremely proud of the ancient alliance which existed between their country and the United Kingdom and their hospitality was overwhelming; indeed, their staple rations of bread and sardines were apparently designed to encourage consumption of "vinho", which was supplied in copious quantities. During training, visits were received from Lieutenant General Sir Peter Leng,

Commander of I (BR) Corps, Major General Walsh and Brigadier Airy. On completion of the exercise, guests and hosts exchanged plaques to commemorate what for both had been an interesting and rewarding experience, and for the Quartermaster, Major Roger Coleman, and his staff had been another nightmare successfully negotiated.

In July the Battalion spent eleven days field firing at Sennelager, producing excellent results. The rifle company attacks with Jaguar aircraft, artillery and mortar support were particularly impressive. Overall levels of fitness were rising, so that at the Battalion Athletics Meeting, held at the end of the month, a large number of existing records were broken. Private Chase of Y Company won the 110 metres hurdles, the long jump and the triple jump, being presented with the Victor Ludorum cup by Mrs Pat Martin.

During the Minden Day celebrations Brigadier Airy presented roses and the Chaplain General, The Venerable Archdeacon W.F.Johnson, dedicated a stained glass window presented by the Battalion to the Münster Garrison Church to commemorate the Battalion's three tours in the city. The window depicts Mother Teresa with an arm round a starving child, with the Regiment's two cap badges below and the Royal Bengal Tiger superscribed "India" between. In passing, it is worth mentioning that a mischievous rumour to the effect that Mother Teresa herself would be present at the ceremony caused considerable fluttering in clerical dovecots! On 2 August the Warrant Officers' and Sergeants' Mess hosted a very impressive Minden Ball run by WOII Colin Burnett.

The summer and autumn of 1980 were marked by three developments that were of benefit to the Battalion. Firstly, strong recruiting coupled with rising unemployment at home produced a continuing rise in strength; in fact, so difficult did the prospect of finding suitable civilian work seem that in one month alone thirty-two valued members of the Battalion, nearing the end of their enlistment term, extended their service, as a result of which Colonel Martin received a congratulatory letter from the Corps Commander. Secondly, Captain Paul Newton's Anti-Tank Platoon said goodbye to its ancient Wombats and received in their place the MILAN (**M**issile d'**I**nfanterie **L**éger **AN**ti-Tank) guided weapon system. The hollow charge missile was wire-guided, using an optical aiming/infra-red tracking system, and had a range of 2000 metres. This meant that, for the first time since World War II, the Battalion's anti-tank gunners had the capacity to engage their opponents on equal terms. Furthermore, while the backblast from the Wombat's first shot had usually unmasked the weapon's position, Milan had no such disadvantage; the opposing tank commander might, just, spot an annulus of flame closing at almost 450 mph, but that left him with no time at all to do anything about it. At this period the Anti-Tank Platoon was issued with sixteen Milan firing posts and its strength rose in consequence to fifty men. The third development which was to raise the Battalion's operational efficiency was the issue of the light, efficient Clansman range of radios in place of the heavy C42 and A41 sets.

On a lighter note, thanks to the good offices of the Variety Club of Great Britain, the comedian Ernie Wise paid a two-day visit to the Battalion, during which he was appointed "honorary commanding officer" and, wearing a Regimental sidecap, took the salute as the Band marched past playing *Bring Me Sunshine.* As a result of the Wives' Club's fund-raising activities, Mrs Pat Martin was able to present Mr Wise with a cheque for the British Kidney Patients Association, this being used to purchase a kidney machine at a hospital in Hampshire.

A Corps exercise, Crusader 80, was held in September. During this the major part of the Battalion provided umpire teams and administered a large umpire control cell, tasks requiring much detailed preparation and training, as well as 150 "battle casualties" and relief guards at various sites.

Following Crusader 80 a full programme of internal training was launched. The Skill-at-Arms Rifle Meeting took place in October, with Private Easen of A Company, who had only been with the Battalion for three weeks, winning the Best Rifle Shot. A number of potential NCO and section commanders' cadres also took place during the autumn. In November the Battalion took part in a short but exacting exercise on local training areas. Each company marched to its initial position, dug in, patrolled and was attacked by an enemy provided by the 2nd Battalion Grenadier Guards. It then moved by helicopter or vehicle to another training area, attacked a position held by enemy from 4 RTR, occupied the position, mounted a series of ambushes, withdrew and marched back to barracks, all in sub-zero temperatures that were a stiff test for any infantryman.

On the sporting front Colonel Martin presented the Minden Trophy for the first time, the winners, by a respectable margin, being Y Company, commanded by Major Tim Glass. Within the Münster Garrison the Battalion now completely dominated the sporting scene, winning outright the football, hockey, cricket, cross-country and squash cups. Considering that the Garrison also contained five major units (17th/21st Lancers, 4th Royal Tank Regiment, 2nd Battalion Grenadier Guards, 1st Battalion The Gloucestershire Regiment and 8th Regiment Royal Corps of Transport) this was no mean achievement. The football team, run by SQMS McCaffery, ACC, reached the semi-finals of the Army Cup (BAOR) from over eighty entries. The boxers, trained by Sergeant Gannon, APTC, reached the divisional semi-finals, losing 4-5 to the 1st Battalion The Duke of Edinburgh's Royal Regiment. From over fifty entries the cross-country runners, with an average age of twenty, reached 6th position in the BAOR event, with Private Flain coming second and Lance Corporal Cripps third in the Junior Championships.

The year ended with an excellent Christmas show staged by Major Barry Baty on 16 December in the gymnasium, with scenery constructed by the Battalion's Pioneers. The good relations which now existed between the Garrison and the local community solved a number of problems, the Halle Münsterland providing lighting and microphones, while the Münster Theatre made their costume store available and supplied a make-up artist. As a result, the performance, of a high standard, was enjoyed by audience and performers alike.

Once again, as many soldiers as possible took advantage of the Battalion ski hut during the winter months, but by now thoughts were concentrated on the Battalion's return to England, where it had not served since 1974. The months of February and March 1981 were therefore dominated by the move to Dover and in handing over to the 1st Battalion The Light Infantry.

Among the farewell messages received by Colonel Martin was one from Lieutenant General Sir Nigel Bagnall, Commander of I (BR) Corps, who knew the Battalion well from the days when he had commanded its affiliated armoured squadron, C Squadron 4th/7th Royal Dragoon Guards, in Münster 1962-64. The General wrote: "I was pleased to see the same mixture of enthusiasm and professionalism which I remember from the days we served together. Your departure will be a loss to the Corps." Also received was a letter from Major General Martin Farndale, Commanding 2nd Armoured Division: "You will be sadly missed from the BAOR scene but you can all be well pleased with your record here in Germany. Wherever I go, I hear complimentary reports about the Hampshires. Whatever you have had to do, you have done with thoroughness, energy and good humour. You leave the 2nd Armoured Division with our very best good wishes for the future."

* * * * * * * * *

CHAPTER 17

DOVER AND ULSTER 1981 — 1982

The 1st Battalion joins 6 Field Force - Freedom Marches in Winchester, Southampton, Rushmoor, Bournemouth, Romsey, Basingstoke and Portsmouth - varied activities Minden Day 1981 - General Sir David Fraser succeeds Brigadier Warren as Colonel of the Regiment - Exercise Amber Express in Denmark - deployment in Fermanagh - tactical situation and tasks - murder of Private Clifford - the Falklands War - return to Dover - Colonel Martin hands over Command to Lieutenant Colonel D.H.Neville - the New Forest District Council honours the Regiment with an Affiliation - Public Duties at Windsor Castle - the 1st Battalion prepares for duties in the South Atlantic

On 21 April 1981, following block leave, the 1st Battalion reported for duty at Connaught Barracks, Dover. The barracks, situated above the town behind the Castle, were relatively modern and the married quarters, a recently constructed, well designed estate named Burgoyne Heights, were only ten minutes' walk away and surrounded by playing fields. The posting was a popular one, being within easy reach of most people's homes at weekends, and the town was both busy and friendly. The Battalion, together with the 1st Battalion The Royal Regiment of Wales and the 2nd Battalion The Parachute Regiment, now formed part of 6 Field Force, commanded by Brigadier E.H.A.Beckett, MBE, which was based at Aldershot and had as its role the reinforcement of NATO's Northern flank, should this prove to be necessary.

As the Battalion had been absent from England for so long, Colonel Martin placed much emphasis on reinforcing the invaluable links which existed between the Regiment and the County. It was decided, therefore, that the Battalion would exercise the Regimental Freedoms with a series of marches in May and June. The project, known as Exercise Tiger Trek, involved RSM L.B.Le-Galloudec, who had recently taken over from RSM Rumbold who had been commissioned and was now the Families' Officer, and WOII C.D.Burnett, the Drill Sergeant Major, in sustained hard work to produce the high standard of drill and turnout required to match the importance of these occasions. The administration was admirably organised by Major Paul Davis.

During Exercise Tiger Trek the Battalion was temporarily accommodated at Browndown Camp in Gosport. The first Freedom March took place at Winchester on 27 May, followed by Southampton on 28 May, Rushmoor (formed by the amalgamation of the Borough of Aldershot and the Urban District of Farnborough in 1972) on 29 May, Bournemouth on 1 June, Romsey on 3 June, Basingstoke on 5 June and Portsmouth on 6 June. It had been a long time since the people of Hampshire had watched their own soldiers march by - the youngest had never seen them at all - and everywhere shops emptied and crowds many deep lined the routes to applaud and cheer. They were rewarded with a memorable and moving experience as the Battalion, now above strength, swung past in sixes, led by the Band under Bandmaster D.W.Wood and the Corps of Drums under Drum Major C.A.Windebank, resplendent in its scarlet, gleaming brass and immaculate pipeclay.

The parades were well covered by all the media and the *Southern Evening Echo* published a souvenir colour supplement to commemorate them. The atmosphere in which they were held is best summarised by the following quotations.

Hampshire Chronicle 29 May: "In Winchester, the lunchtime crowd,[despite]the slight drizzle, cheered and applauded as the soldiers marched down the High Street, led by the Band."

Southern Evening Echo 29 May: "Southampton's City Centre came to a standstill today as thousands packed the pavements to watch the 1st Battalion The Royal Hampshire Regiment march through the Bargate. Office workers and shop assistants left their desks and counters to join the cheering crowds."

Romsey Advertiser 5 June: "The pride in the Regiment was seen in the men's faces, in their bearing, and the way in which they marched with just that little touch of 'swank': the almost indefinable something which transforms a march into one which touches the heart. The whole parade, from the Commanding Officer to the newest Private, looked 'smart as paint,' and there was many an old soldier in the crowd touched to the point of watering eyes as the Regiment went past the saluting base."

Basingstoke Gazette 8 June: "Basingstoke people turned out in their thousands for Friday's March Past of the Royal Hampshire Regiment."

Technically, because of local government boundary changes, Bournemouth no longer formed part of Hampshire, but the people could not have cared less and in his address to the soldiers after the march the Mayor made his feelings very clear: "I congratulate you on your turnout. We are proud of you. You make everyone proud to be British." As recorded in the *Southern Evening Echo* of 6 June, Basingstoke people also made their feelings very clear when a group of "peace campaigners" tried to distribute leaflets during the march: "Demonstrators who protested yesterday are upset at the response they had from spectators...as protesters walked past a school there were angry shouts and fist waving from catering assistants who refused to accept any literature."

As always, civic hospitality was generous in the extreme. At Portsmouth the Freedom March was preceded by a service of thanksgiving and commemoration in the Cathedral and was followed by the Battalion firing a *feu de joie* in the Guildhall Square. Here, the local authority had spared no effort to welcome the Regiment and mark a major event in the City's calendar - so much so that Colonel Martin was heard to murmur, "I now think I know how victorious Roman generals felt entering the Coliseum with their legions!"

Altogether, Exercise Tiger Trek generated fifty-three press articles, including twelve front page stories, nine television slots, and regular coverage of events on local radio stations. Numerous letters of congatulation were received, among them one from Lieutenant General Sir Paul Travers, the GOC South East District, who had witnessed the parade at Portsmouth, to the Colonel of the Regiment. This concluded with the sentence: "They [the 1st Battalion] are great contributors to and, if I may say so, they personify all that is best in the Regimental System and the County regiments - you must be very proud of them."

Exercise Tiger Trek was followed by a short but intensive KAPE tour in which the Battalion regrouped into three company-sized teams covering the County. During this, thirteen schools were visited, four training evenings were conducted for the ACF, two training evenings were held for Territorials, the Band and Drums performed at the Portsmouth Tattoo, and the Band gave numerous concerts. By now, Colonel Martin had become something of a celebrity, to the extent that some of the children requested his autograph.

Having returned to Dover early in July, the Battalion was quickly dispersed on a variety of tasks. The Band played at the Wembley Pageant then left for a tour of Jersey; a small contingent under Captain Nick Sim, with Colour Sergeant Harvey, Sergeant Young and Corporals Barter and Baughan, went to the Hythe/Lydd ranges to assist with the training of forty Italian para-commandos; a demonstration platoon led by Second Lieutenant Matthew Pearce went to St Martin's Camp, Shorncliffe, where 1000 CCF cadets were attending their summer camp; Captain Ross Jones with the ubiquitous Corporals Barter and Baughan plus Lance Corporal Cadet and a small team visited Dulwich College to assist in training the school's CCF contingent; the Shooting Team went to Bisley, finishing 29th overall, an improvement of nineteen places on the previous year; Battalion HQ took part in a two-day 6 Field Force Command Post Exercise at the Battle Group Tactical Trainer in Bovington Camp, Dorset; a Potential NCOs Cadre was completed; two TEWTS down to section commander level were held on Defence and Withdrawal; the Companies each had several days' shooting on the Hythe/Lydd ranges; and many people attended external courses. Following this extremely busy period the Companies went off to a two-week Battle Camp - A Company (Major David Hannah) to Stanford, where they acted as enemy for the 5th(V) Battalion The Queen's Regiment, and B and Y Companies (Majors James Dewar and Andrew Freemantle), plus the Mortar and Anti-Tank Platoons, to Otterburn for live firing.

Hard on the heels of this came Minden Day. It had been 100 years since the Cardwell Reforms had resulted in the formation of the Hampshire Regiment from the old 37th and 67th Regiments of Foot, and Colonel Martin decided that the occasion should be properly marked by the Ceremony of Trooping the Colour. For several reasons, notably lack of adequate space, Connaught Barracks was unsuitable and the parade was held in the grounds of the Duke of York's Royal Military School. This was a happy choice as, while the school itself was on holiday, the stands erected for its Grand Day were still up. The Inspecting Officer was General Sir Edwin Bramall, GCB, OBE, MC, ADC (Gen), Chief of the General Staff, who, after the ceremony, made a relevant and memorable speech which is recorded elsewhere. Some 200 members of the Comrades' Association were present and when they marched past the Battalion, for the first time on such an occasion, came to the Present Arms; the compliment was moving and greatly appreciated. Over 2000 spectators watched the parade, some doubtless drawn by wildly optimistic speculation in the Dover press that they would see "600 men in scarlet uniforms." The general reaction was summed up by one ninety-one-year-old local veteran: "The damnedest fine show I ever saw!" thereby reflecting great credit on RSM Bob Le Galloudec.

The was the last parade attended by Brigadier David Warren in his capacity as Colonel of the Regiment. He had held the appointment for ten years and on 7 September 1981 was succeeded by General Sir David Fraser, GCB, OBE, whose home was at Isington, near Alton, Hampshire. General Fraser had been commissioned into the Grenadier Guards in 1941 and served with his Regiment in North West Europe. He had commanded the 1st Battalion Grenadier Guards from 1960 to 1962 and the 19th Infantry Brigade from 1963 to 1965. After a year at the Imperial Defence College he moved to the Ministry of Defence as Director, Defence Policy. From 1969 to 1971 he was GOC 4th Division, returning thereafter to the Ministry of Defence as Assistant Chief of Defence Staff (Policy), in which post he remained until 1973. From then until 1975 he was Vice-Chief of the General Staff. His last two appointments before retirement in February 1980 were UK Military Representative on the NATO Military Council in Brussels, and Commandant of the Royal College of Defence Studies. At the time of his appointment as Colonel of the Regiment he was working on his incisive study of the British

Army in World War II, *And We Shall Shock Them,* published in 1983.

Shortly after Minden Day the Battalion went on three weeks' block leave. On 1 August it left Dover for Salisbury Plain to take part in a 6 Field Force work-up exercise in preparation for a NATO exercise, Amber Express, that would take place in Denmark the following month. The move to Denmark was made by road, ship and air and owed much to the efforts of Captain Simon Frere-Cook and Captain Peter Hawker, the Unit Emplaning Officer. Exercise Amber Express lasted from 14 - 27 September and during this period the Battalion was based at Hagested, a small village five miles from Holbaek, sharing a muddy tented camp with 5th Queens (V), excellently set up by Captain Len Brown, the Quartermaster, and his team. The first week was devoted to company training and a Force medical exercise. The second week found the Hampshires acting as rear battalion in a defensive position while the forward battalions contained an enemy beach landing. During this period Battalion HQ occupied a comfortable barn; by a happy coincidence, the owner happened to have attended the same Olympic Appeal Dinner as Colonel Martin in Malaya in 1964! A night withdrawal to new positions followed, and from these good shooting by Captain Paul Newton's Milan teams influenced the course of the battle. In the final phase the Battalion took part in a Force counter-attack, securing vital ground as demanded by the exercise plan. The exercise was adjudged to have been a success both militarily and politically. Off duty, visits to Copenhagen were thoroughly enjoyed and there the Band were invited to perform at the Tivoli Gardens' last night of the season, giving a memorable performance in conjunction with the famous Tivoli Guards before an audience of several thousand people.

The Battalion had already been warned that in the New Year it would be carrying out an unaccompanied four-and-a-half month tour in County Fermanagh, Ulster, and as soon as it returned to Dover it began preparing for this. The Winchester Trophy, based upon the theme of Northern Ireland training, was staged on 12-13 November and won by the Milan Platoon. The Battalion Skill at Arms Meeting, again with a strong Ulster emphasis, was held on 16-17 November. The NITAT advisers had already provided briefings the previous month and between 22 November and 4 December the Battalion moved to Lydd to undergo the standard pre-tour training package that covered urban techniques in a mock village, shooting and other skills. There was just time on returning to Dover to stage the final events of the Minden Trophy, which was won by Y Company for the second year running, then it was off to the Stanford training area on 12 December for five days' rural training. These were memorable for their testing conditions, with heavy snowfalls by day and temperatures which plunged to minus 17°C at night.

The Advance Party, 250 strong under the Second-in-Command, Major Bobby Hanscomb, left on 28 and 30 December. The main body followed on 4 January 1982 and at 18:00 on that date operational responsibility for some 700 square miles of southeast Fermanagh was assumed from the 1st Battalion The Royal Anglian Regiment. Battalion HQ, the Echelon (Major Brian Madigan) and B and Z Companies were based on an old wartime airfield at St Angelo near Enniskillen, with A and Y Companies some 12 miles away at Lisnaskea. Internally, as the specialist skills of the Mortar and Milan Platoons were not required, Z Company (Major Harry Doodson) became a fourth rifle company, and a Close Observation Platoon (Captain Nick Sim) was formed, its function being to watch the houses of suspected terrorists from concealed positions, often for protracted periods.

Operating in this part of Ulster presented its own problems, as Brigadier Bruce Willing records. "Fermanagh is hugely different from the rest of Northern Ireland; more than half of it is water and the remainder is sparsely populated with the exception of Enniskillen, a town of 13,000 people, and Lisnaskea, with a population of 4000. Terrorism had affected this evenly mixed community deeply, to the extent that there had been a polarising of the two communities into mono-religious areas, easily defined between and adjacent to large expanses of water. In more peaceful times agricultural and commercial considerations had led to a degree of re-integration. At this period, Protestant farmers south of Lough Erne and close to Fermanagh's 108 miles long border with the Republic had held on, and as cross-border violence increased they called for and gained the re-introduction of border crossing points similar in concept to the VCPs in Londonderry. When the Battalion arrived it therefore inherited 19 such VCPs along the border, each one demanding at least a section and combining to absorb more than sixty per cent of the Battalion's operational effort. The concept of company-sized operations was moribund and the 'war' was waged at section or individual patrol level, relying much on good administrative support by the Quartermaster and his team.

"Again, the Commanding Officer's aim was to make the best use of the Hampshire soldier's firm but fair ethos and the result was a complete absence of complaints from the local community. This in itself was a tribute and a comment on the Regiment's standards and traditions as some of the 'Tigers' still came from the West Midlands and Wales."

The Battalion's primary task was to assist the Royal Ulster Constabulary in maintaining law and order, and it therefore co-operated closely with the police and the 4th (County Fermanagh) Battalion of the Ulster Defence Regiment. The steadiness of the long-term community policemen and their commander, Chief Superintendent Tom McGowan, made a deep impression, as did the commitment of the UDR soldier. The latter, living close to the border as he did, was well aware of the terrorists' stated ambition to drive the Protestant population into an enclave along the north-east coast of Ulster, and he lived in the front line, year in and year out. Whether on duty, at work or at home, his SLR never left his side and he remained in a constant state of readiness to protect himself, his family and his neighbours or to respond to a call-out immediately.

At the VCPs the soldiers, despite living in primitive sandbagged positions reminiscent of World War I, remained ever cheerful, resourceful and efficient. Administering and supplying so many VCPs presented problems and there were frequent discussions as to whether they were all necessary. One, that at Anaghmartin, was closed down but had to be restored shortly after. In addition, endless hours were spent patrolling over the hills and remote areas for which the Battalion was responsible, and visiting numerous farmsteads, some of which were modest and others very small. Movement of troops and stores across country was by means of helicopter so as to avoid possible ambushes and mined roads, and to keep the terrorists uncertain of operational intentions. All of this took place against a background of the heaviest snowfalls ever experienced in Fermanagh in January, followed by the wettest February and the driest March. There were times when it seemed that Irish water perversely flowed uphill to create yet more bogs!

There were comparatively few incidents. On 10 February a

proxy bomb was driven into A Company's area at Newtownbutler and was successfully cleared. On 22 February terrorists engaged B Company's VCP at Mullan Bridge (Sergeant Barter) with gunfire from across the border. Twenty-one rounds were returned but, as had been discovered in earlier tours, the gunmen lacked the stamina for this sort of thing and they sheered off after a few minutes. Elsewhere, members of the Close Observation Platoon were adopted by an Irish setter for five days, at the end of which its owner appeared and, speaking to the bush which concealed the OP, said that he did not mind his house being watched but he wanted his dog back!

The Battalion's only casualties occurred on 30 April. Near Belleek the terrorists placed a 500lb culvert bomb beneath the road, laying a command wire across the border into the Republic. It is believed that their designated target was a police car, but when a foot patrol commanded by Corporal Burrell appeared they decided to murder them instead. The explosion inflicted fatal injuries on Private (Drummer) Colin Clifford, a Jerseyman, and Corporal Burrell sustained lacerations and severe shock, but the rest of the patrol escaped injury. It was especially tragic that this incident should have taken place just three weeks from the end of the tour.

There was another extremely serious matter occupying the Battalion's thoughts at the time. On 1 April 1982 the military junta ruling Argentina launched an invasion of the Falkland Islands and South Georgia. Its reasons for doing so at that time had their roots in certain decisions taken in London by the Ministry of Defence and the Foreign Office. The former announced that the ice patrol ship HMS *Endurance,* the only British naval presence in the area, was to be scrapped and would not be replaced on station. The latter, in its eagerness to please, had already agreed to hold talks with the Argentine government on the future of the islands, although why this should have been necessary has yet to be explained. These decisions were interpreted in Buenos Aires as signs of indifference and weakness. In the junta's view, the United Kingdom no longer possessed the will to react to events 8000 miles from home, and the acquisition of the islands by *coup de main* would restore its own fading popularity. This proved to be a major miscalculation, as Prime Minister Margaret Thatcher was neither indifferent nor weak. Avoiding the mistakes which had proved so disastrous during the 1956 Suez

Crisis, she ensured that the leading elements of a task force were at sea within days, and in this she had the support of a convincing majority of the British people, who, holding their armed services in high regard as they did, had been bitterly angered by photographs of the tiny Royal Marine garrison having to surrender to the troops of a treacherous, third-rate power. South Georgia was recovered on 25 April. On 21 May a beachhead had been secured on East Falkland and on 14 June, having lost all the vital ground surrounding Port Stanley, the Argentine commander, Major General Mario Menendez, surrendered. He and his troops then suffered the further humiliation of being transported home in British ships. In Argentina itself, the emotional reaction to the defeat resulted in the collapse of the junta and the establishment of a more democratic form of government.

The Falklands War laid the ghosts of Suez and reinforced international respect for the professionalism of the British armed services. On the ground, it had been an infantryman's war, involving much hard marching across difficult terrain and attacks pressed home with the bayonet. The enemy, part of a badly-officered conscript army, was incapable of mounting either offensive operations or counter-attacks, but in strong defensive positions, laid out according to the textbook, he fought back, sometimes to the end, and inflicted a toll on the victors. Once his will had been broken, however, nothing would induce him to fight on. Significantly, all save one of the British attacks were made at night.

The war still had some weeks to run when, on 17 May, the Hampshires were relieved by the 1st Battalion The Parachute Regiment, who were understandably feeling frustrated at being given another Ulster tour when their Regiment's 2nd and 3rd Battalions were on the point of winning fresh laurels in the South Atlantic.

Visitors received by the Battalion in Fermanagh included Lieutenant General Sir Richard Lawson, KCB, DSO, OBE, Commander Northern Ireland, and Major General P.I.Chiswell, CBE, Commander Land Forces Northern Ireland, who wrote to Colonel Martin, "It was a tremendous pleasure to meet your splendid battalion; the good humour and spirit of your soldiers brought back many memories for me of what an impressive bunch they are." Other visitors were the Colonel of the Regiment, Brigadier R.T.P.Hume, Commander 2 Infantry Brigade, Brigadier W.K.L.Prosser, MBE, MC, Commander 8 Infantry Brigade, the

Rt Hon James Prior, Secretary of State for Northern Ireland, entertainment celebrities Frank Windsor and Georgina Moon and, by no means least, Miss Debbie Boyland from Southampton, the reigning Miss Royal Hampshire.

The Battalion flew direct from Aldergrove to RAF Manston and, having completed the usual post-Ulster administrative chores, went on four weeks' block leave from which it returned on 21 June. On 25 June Colonel Mike Martin handed over Command to Lieutenant Colonel D.H.Neville and, preceded by the Corps of Drums, was towed out of Connaught Barracks by members of the Officers' and Sergeants' Messes. Colonel Martin had been offered the option of handing over prior to the recent tour in Fermanagh but had declined, and his period of Command, spanning some thirty-four months, was therefore the longest since World War II. Of him, the Journal recorded in appreciation, "Those who served under him in the Battalion will not easily forget him. His enormous frame, forthright leadership and genuine knowledge of all the men under his command immediately come to mind. Perhaps the abiding memory of those who served with him will be that it was a happy Battalion. We worked hard, cheerfully and in harmony. It is a legacy he inherited and has reinforced and passed on."

Colonel Hastings Neville was commissioned into the Regiment in December 1959 and served with the 1st Battalion during its Caribbean tour. He then spent a two-year tour of instructional duties at the Army Outward Bound School in Wales, returning to the 1st Battalion in 1965. He commanded the Reconnaissance Platoon in Borneo before being posted as Adjutant to the Wessex Brigade Depot in Exeter. In May 1969 he again returned to the 1st Battalion and served with them thereafter in Netheravon and Ulster successively as Company Second-in-Command, Operations Officer and OC HQ Company. In October 1970 he left for courses at the Royal Military College of Science and the Staff College and in March 1972 was appointed Assistant Defence Adviser to the British High Commissioner in Singapore. He rejoined the 1st Battalion in Hong Kong in June 1974, taking over A Company, which he continued to command when the Battalion moved to Ballykelly in Northern Ireland. Following this tour he was posted to the Royal Military Academy, Sandhurst, as Chief Instructor at New College, where he remained for over two years until being appointed GSO 2 (SD) at Headquarters UK Land Forces.

During this period, because of the demands of the South Atlantic, the Battalion was called upon at short notice to perform a wide variety of duties within South East District. The Close Observation (now Reconnaissance) Platoon and one platoon of A Company under Lieutenant Pearce, for example, performed the role of demonstration platoon for Cadet Camps at, respectively, Longmoor and Folkestone.

Simultaneously, the New Forest District Council had accorded the Regiment an Affiliation, the highest honour that it could bestow, and the ceremony to commemorate this was held at Appletree Court, Lyndhurst, on 8 July 1982. The parade consisted of the Colour Party, the Band and Corps of Drums, and two Guards, each of forty-eight men. Having inspected the Guards, Councillor John Waddington, Chairman of the Council, presented the Colonel of the Regiment with a carved plaque incorporating the Hampshire Rose and the "dog gauge" which had formed the cap badge of the 4th Volunteer (later 7th) Battalion. In his reply, General Fraser stressed the Regiment's long historical association with and deep roots within the County, then presented the Chairman with a Regimental plate. A march through Lyndhurst followed, and such was the enthusiasm of the crowd that words of command could only just be heard above the cheering. Afterwards, the parade attended a sumptuous reception on the lawns of Appletree Court.

The most important additional commitment given to the Battalion, however, was a period of Public Duties at Windsor Castle. This lasted from 23 July until 30 August and was necessary because the 2nd Battalion Scots Guards and 1st Battalion Welsh Guards were in the Falklands. The task was given to Major Andrew Freemantle's Y Company, in which CSM Sutton had taken over from CSM Garland, reinforced with soldiers from A and B Companies and the Drums Platoon. Preparation began immediately after the Affiliation Parade at Lyndhurst with daily visits from Shorncliffe to Dover by two ferocious drill instructors, CSM Milloy, Scots Guards, and Lance Sergeant Barton, Welsh Guards, who spared no one. Thus, in drill pig language, soldiers who were "things" had some sorting out to do; those who were "gargoyles" had rather more; and the junior officer who used his sword "like a bread knife" was in serious danger of collecting extra duties. Privates Gore and Kennings and Lieutenant Barnes, respectively, had their difficulties.

In Windsor the Company was accommodated in Victoria Barracks. "The Company was divided into three guards working in a rota: doing guard; kit preparation/day off; and standby for anti-terrorist duty at Heathrow airport. Guard duty was for 24 hours, and every day the new guard would march up through Windsor behind the Corps of Drums, to be met by up to 3000 tourists waiting to watch the mounting itself."

Minden Day was celebrated by the Company with a small parade in Victoria Barracks and another in the Castle, where the Colonel of the Regiment, accompanied by Colonel Neville, distributed roses and the Corps of Drums Beat Retreat during the evening. The excellent impression created by the Company as a whole was echoed in a letter from the Dean of Windsor to General Fraser, commenting that they were much smarter than "the usual lot!"

Elsewhere, Major J.G.T.Dewar and a large party left for Bisley to perform range and butt-party duties that would have been carried out by the 1st/7th Gurkha Rifles had they not been in the Falklands; the Milan and Mortar Platoons carried out live firing with their weapons at Otterburn; and Z Company assisted other units with their Northern Ireland training.

Because the Battalion was due to move to Berlin on a two-year tour in December 1983, it was thought that they were "in baulk" and not liable for emergency tours, because of the amount of specialist training to be done before arriving in Berlin. Thus the need to carry out at short notice an emergency tour in the Falklands came as a surprise. Colonel Neville announced that the Battalion would carry out a five-month garrison tour of the Islands and South Georgia from November 1982, inclusive of travelling time. The tour would have been longer, and although this might have been welcomed by single men, Colonel Neville was conscious that the Battalion's continued absences from England, punctuated by periods of leave that did not coincide with school holidays, would in the long term prove detrimental to family life. Already conscious of the over-stretch problem within the Army as a whole, the authorities accepted his point.

There was just time to stage the final events in the contest for the Minden Trophy. The last of these, the Tug of War, coincided with a pre-embarkation visit by the Colonel of the Regiment, and Lady Fraser presented the Trophy to Y Company, winners for the third year in succession, as well as the major trophies for other competitions held during the year.

In late October the Battalion received a briefing on its role and conditions in the Falkands from a team of recently returned officers. Early in November it was joined by the Gurkha Demonstration Company from the RMA Sandhurst, who were to remain under command as a fifth company, plus a small detachment from the 1st Battalion The Royal Welch Fusiliers and a rear-link detachment from the Royal Signals. A two-day exercise, designed to illustrate the sort of operational tasks that would be faced in the Falklands, was held on 10 and 11 November.

The move to the South Atlantic took place over the period 20 November to 4 December, with company groups flying out from RAF Brize Norton. On 23 November the Mayor of Winchester, Councillor A.J.D.Austen, and the Town Mayor of Carterton (Brize Norton), visited the airfield to wish Colonel Neville and his Advance Party a successful tour.

* * * * * * * * *

THE VALUE OF TRADITION

EXTRACT FROM THE ADDRESS BY THE CHIEF OF THE GENERAL STAFF, GENERAL SIR EDWIN BRAMALL, GCB, OBE, MC, ADC (Gen), DELIVERED TO THE 1st BATTALION THE ROYAL HAMPSHIRE REGIMENT ON MINDEN DAY, 1 AUGUST 1981

Today's parade of course recognises two important events in the Regiment's history: Minden Day, which celebrates that splendid infantry action (scarcely ever surpassed) which took place 222 years ago outside the town of Minden in Germany when the British Infantry Brigade, of which the 37th Regiment of Foot formed part, advanced unsupported against mass squadrons of French cavalry and in the process broke up three cavalry charges made against them, as well as turning back the French infantry who tried to take them in the flank; and we are also celebrating the unification, 100 years ago, of the North (37th) and the South (67th) Hampshire Regiments into what is now, as a reward for your performance in World War Two, The Royal Hampshire Regiment.

But some of you may just be wondering why we should be making such a fuss of a battle which happened all that time ago on some foreign field. Well, as an outsider, I would like to give you my views why I would agree with those who have organised this parade and undoubtedly the Colonel of your Regiment (who I might add is attending his last Minden Day in his present appointment after some 42 years' service, including, at the age of 25, commanding the Battalion on D Day and winning a DSO) why I would agree that this annual parade really is an important occasion.

I look at it this way. The event itself, although heroic and important at the time, is just one incident in the glorious history of your Regiment, which reads like the history of the British Army - just one part of the terrific spirit of a Regiment which has been in so many battles, including, in the living experience of some, Gallipoli in the First World War and, in the Second World War, Tebourba Gap, Salerno, Cassino and D Day, to mention just a few; all places where literally the fathers of some of those on parade today gave such a good account of themselves, and where the Regiment gained such honour, to say nothing of three Victoria Crosses. Even in an Army whose stock and esteem could not stand higher in the country, the spirit and performance of your Regiment need fear no comparison with anything or anybody. Whether you fully realise it or not, you have inherited all this.

When you parade as you do once a year, you are really doing two things. You are saluting the gallantry and loyalty of the old 'uns - those who, like you are doing now, served their Queen and country all over the world, and whose place you have now taken; and you are letting it be known that their example is in good hands and that you will not let them down; you never have and we all know that you never will. In the British Army, where pride and self-respect, self-discipline and comradeship are such vital factors in obtaining high morale, I suggest that practically nothing could be more important than this collective act of remembrance and dedication.

THE HAMPSHIRE TIGERS

CHAPTER 18

THE FALKLANDS AND BERLIN
1982 — 1986

Deployment in the Falklands - ceremonial duties - impressions of the battlefields - training and garrison tasks - visit of the Prime Minister - the South Georgia Detachment - return to the UK - Regimental "At Home" at St Cross - 1st Battalion march through Portsmouth - re-organisation and new equipment - Exercise Winged Victory - life in Berlin - Exercise Tiger Strike - shooting successes - Queen's Birthday and Allied Forces Day Parades 1984 - outstanding sporting and other successes - autumn training - Colonel Neville relinquishes Command to Lieutenant Colonel Andrew Freemantle 9 January 1985 - training at Vogelsang - HRH The Princess of Wales becomes Colonel-in-Chief of the Regiment - Queen's Birthday and Allied Forces Day Parades 1985 - field firing and adventure training - visit of the Colonel-in-Chief - 1st Battalion takes the first eleven places in the Brigade Inter-Platoon Competition - Assault Pioneers win the Brigade competition - more sporting successes - handover and departure for the UK

The journey south was made in two stages. First, the Battalion flew in company groups to Ascension Island and then, with the exception of the Advance Party and the South Georgia Detachment, who continued by air bridge, sailed for the Falklands on two ships, the MV *St Edmund*, a converted North Sea Sealink ferry, and RFA *Sir Geraint*.

The Battalion became operational on 5 December 1982 and its initial deployment was with Battalion HQ at Shag Cove, A

Company at Fox Bay, B Company at Roy Cove and D (Gurkha) Company at Port Howard, all on West Falkland, Y Company at Goose Green, Z Company at North Arm, Lafonia, and the Echelon at Port Stanley, all on East Falkland. Later, the Gurkha company moved to Port San Carlos and B Company was redeployed to defend the only airfield at Port Stanley.

The Falklands offered superb training facilities and companies took advantage of the fact, carrying out their own training which ranged from individual to company tactics. The culmination of the company training was a full field firing exercise for each, with mortar, artillery, fighter ground-attack and naval gunfire support, plus a Hercules air-drop resupply. These were carried out during what passed for summer in these southern latitudes, although some people retained vivid impressions of experiencing all four seasons within any given period of twenty-four hours.

The exercises also revealed that the Battalion's new boots left a lot to be desired. During the war itself the Argentines had been equipped with a high boot made from good leather and had suffered less from trench foot than the British, who wore the standard ammunition boot. The recently introduced British equivalent, unfortunately, had suffered from too hasty a trials period. The leather, for example, remained stiff however much one dubbined it, and the design not only gripped the ankle too fiercely but also affected the Achilles tendon.

In addition to training, there were ceremonial duties to perform. On 16 December HQ Company provided a Guard of Honour for the opening of the first session of the Falkland Islands Parliament since the war, and on 20 February 1983 a contingent from B Company took part in the colony's 150th Anniversary Celebrations, the salute at the march past being taken by the Civil Commissioner, Sir Rex Hunt, the Foreign Office having abandoned the title Governor in its anxiety not to further ruffle Latin American feathers.

Major B.D.Madigan, commanding HQ Company, has left an interesting account of life in Port Stanley in the immediate aftermath of the war: "To live in Stanley is also to understand the people. They are of strong character, honest, very independent and very loyal to the Crown; insular, quiet but friendly and approachable. After the experiences of recent months, they have also proved to be a tolerant race of people. Even now the area around Stanley remains littered with the debris and evidence of war. Armoured cars, rusting machine guns and mortars, live artillery shells and Argentinian clothing can still be found in many places. To walk the slopes of Tumbledown is to follow in the footsteps of the Scots Guards who fought for the ground. There are minefields on the western slopes, dominated by defensive positions above. Behind one rock can be found a dozen expended cartridge cases; 70 metres beyond, another rock and more cases, shell dressings and bloodstained bandages. 105mm shells landed here in abundance with devastating effect. Metal objects all round, holed and dented, are a mute testament to the lethality of modern artillery fire. At the highest point is a cross in memory of the Guardsmen who fell in the battle, their names inscribed on a brass plaque at the base. It is a desolate place but we felt proud to be there, to pay our respects to those who died."

It was also possible to trace the course of other actions, and at Goose Green, where Captain Peter Emery, Second-in-Command of Y Company, gave the numerous visitors a carefully researched explanation of the battle as it had developed, it was professionally interesting to note the part played by 2 Para's Milans in neutralising the enemy's bunkers. Yet one could not wander at will, as the Argentines had been prodigal in their use of minefields which, in their scruffy-minded and ill-supervised manner, they had neither marked nor mapped accurately, with the result that people and livestock were still being killed or injured. Periodically, Argentine dead were also being discovered, often without identity disks. A firm of British undertakers had been brought in to handle them and they were finally interred in a proper war cemetery which Y Company helped to prepare. The Company provided a Guard of Honour and a firing party at the dedication ceremony on 19 February 1983.

The Mortar Platoon, commanded by Captain Robert Jordan, carried out trials on an idea put forward by the Royal Military College of Science. This was the Raschen Bag, named after its inventor, Dan Raschen, who came out to supervise the trials, and involved filling a suitably sized bag with any soft material readily to hand, for example, tussock grass. The bag was then positioned beneath the mortar base plate where it absorbed the force of the weapon's recoil. It was found that whereas previously the mortar had tended to bed itself into the soft, peaty soil of the Falklands, as it had in Malaya, it now remained on the surface, and in trials on other sorts of terrain the idea proved equally successful, simultaneously providing quicker target acquisition times and conserving ammunition.

Getting about in the Falklands had never been easy as, outside Port Stanley, the settlements were connected only by primitive good-weather tracks crossing wild moorland terrain. The burden on the Echelon, tasked with supplying the companies' frequently remote out-stations was, therefore, heavy. Major Len Brown, the Quartermaster, worked minor miracles to get the supplies out to the companies.

"Every day has been a test in some way. The Chinook helicopter fleet is overworked, and these beasts of burden should be here in twice the quantity to provide an adequate service. To help out we have also employed small merchant vessels to transport stores by sea; but on arrival at a company location helicopters have been needed to offload from ship to shore. You cannot win!"

In the midst of training and garrison duties, the companies found time for sport and other activities. Some men borrowed local horses on which to explore the country or even ride in races staged as part of the 150th Anniversary celebrations. Fishing, trips by boat, sometimes escorted by a school of porpoises, and visits to penguin colonies were also popular. A Company, at Fox Bay, enjoyed visits by HMS *Liverpool* and *Ariadne;* Y Company's 8 Platoon helped a farmer round up his 100,000 sheep; and in Z Company WOII Allen, Sergeant Lloyd and the Assault Pioneers spent three weeks refurbishing the 150-feet-long pier at North Arm. During the Christmas celebrations Santa Claus (Corporal Belton), who seemed to prefer travelling by Scout helicopter in the Falklands, dropped in with presents at parties given for the local children.

Visitors were legion. Some had good reasons for being in the islands, others merely sought the experience. They included the Chief of the General Staff, the Adjutant General, who presented Corproal Saunderson with his Long Service and Good Conduct Medal at Shag Cove, the Civil Commissioner, a team from the School of Infantry, Lord Shackleton, the Foreign Affairs Select Committee, the House of Commons Defence Committee, assorted Members of Parliament and civil servants, journalists galore, ITV's TV Eye team and the BBC Panorama team. Some whose presence would have been both useful and welcome were denied seats on the air bridge and the ships — even visitors who were prepared to fly RAF to Ascension Island and thence by sea. The Colonel of the Regiment was one casualty of the ban which arose from the hostile threat situation and the cost of helicopter travel while in the islands. "How priorities for these seats are allocated remains a mystery when one sees some of the people who arrive in RAF Stanley," mused the Adjutant, Captain S.A.C.Frere-Cook.

Two visitors were particularly welcome. One, in fact the Battalion's first, was Keith Hamilton of the *Southern Evening Echo,* whose articles were read with great interest throughout the tour. The second, and most important visitor the Battalion was to receive, was Prime Minister Margaret Thatcher, then at the height of her popularity, who visited the islands in January 1983. At Goose Green she was met by a large painted sign saying Y COMPANY TIGERS WELCOME MAGGIE TO GOOSE GREEN and presented with a Y Company sweat shirt by Private Roden. She gave every impression of thoroughly enjoying the cheerful informality and photographs of her with the Company's soldiers appeared in newspapers around the world. In her subsequent letter to Colonel Neville she said:

> "I much enjoyed meeting officers and men of the 1st Battalion of The Royal Hampshire Regiment during my visit to Goose Green, Port San Carlos and Fox Bay East on 10 January. Throughout my visit to the Falkland Islands I found the professionalism and spirit of our Armed Forces most inspiring. The Hampshires demonstrated these qualities splendidly. My best wishes to you all."

Another letter received by Colonel Neville was from Mohammed Yusef, who had been the Battalion Contractor in Malaya and Borneo. He had read of the Prime Minister's visit in the Canadian press and now wrote, "God has provided me with another opportunity to renew my services to the 1st Battalion and I am very keen on coming to Goose Green to serve you." Unfortunately, too little time remained.

The South Georgia detachment, commanded by Captain R.W.Dennis, consisted of the Reconnaissance Platoon, a Milan section and attached sappers and signallers. Captain James Cook had once described the island as being "of such horrible and savage aspect that I have not words to describe," but the reality was that it was a place of outstanding beauty and fascination with a wildlife population consisting of seals, reindeer and twenty-nine species of bird, including millions of King, Gentoo and Chinstrap penguins.

The detachment reached the island aboard the RMS *St Helena* and, having taking over from a detachment of The Queen's Own Highlanders, became the most southerly British garrison in the world. By virtue of his office as Garrison Commander, Captain Dennis also became South Georgia's Postmaster, Harbour Master, Collector of Customs, Receiver of Wrecks, Registrar and Magistrate. The garrison was accommodated in the former quarters of the British Antarctic Survey at King Edward Point, consisting of an accommodation and research block, Shackleton House, stores, cold rooms, a post office, a customs house and a gaol, approximately half a mile from the abandoned whaling station at Grytviken.

In such a remote spot morale is best maintained by constant activity. First, defences were refurbished or redug, a new generator was installed and a workboat, the twenty-seven-foot *Albatross,* restored to full working order. Next, patrols visited every BAS field hut within two days' march of the base to repaint, repair and restock as necessary. Then, they struck deeper into the mountains, following different routes to St Andrew's Bay, where Cindy Buxton and Annie Price filmed *Life Among the Penguins* and remained during the brief Argentine occupation. Finally, there was a week of tactical exercises and live firing.

Between whiles, there were other distractions. "On the night of 22 December, HMS *Hecate,* our Guard Ship, arrived alongside and the next four days saw a continuous stream of joint Christmas activities with the Senior Service. Two football matches, a concert party and a Christmas Eve midnight carol service in Grytviken Church were the major events, but in between there was a continual flow of friendship and hospitality between the ship and the garrison which made Christmas away from home much more bearable. The New Year was seen in in fine fashion. A twenty-foot bonfire was built on the foreshore and an excellent venison barbeque was laid on by Lance Corporal Potts and Private Walls, with a little help from the Platoon snipers and our resident butcher, Corporal Lihou. Expeditions in *Albatross* to Leith not only gave the attached soldiers a chance to see something of the island but also enabled the sappers and signallers to acquire certain handy items from the general stores in the whaling station.

Visits from ships bound for the Antarctic with polar survey teams created one or two interesting diversions, and the fortnightly mail drops by Hercules from RAF Stanley were not only terrific morale boosters but also good training for our boats' crews, for the parachute loads plummeted into Cumberland Bay from 1000 feet."

At the end of March 1983 the Battalion began handing over to the 1st Battalion The Royal Irish Rangers, then boarded the requisitioned cruise liner SS *Uganda* by companies as she sailed round the islands, finally leaving Port Stanley on 3 April. The ten-day voyage to Ascension Island was enjoyable for the most part, although during one period of foul weather the severity of the ship's roll actually surpassed the crew's previous experience. From Ascension the Battalion flew to RAF Brize Norton over a four-day period. The South Georgia detachment, having sailed to Port Stanley aboard the LSL *Sir Percival,* used the air bridge and arrived home on 13 April.

After leave, the Battalion re-assembled at Connaught Barracks on 23 May for another busy summer. Demonstration platoons were again provided for CCF camps and a weapons and equipment demonstration team gave a firepower demonstration at Hythe for the Royal College of Defence Studies. The latter was attended by foreign military attachés from the London Embassies, who departed having expressed themselves suitably impressed. The Band and Drums were also kept extremely busy, their most important engagement being participation in the Ceremony of Beating Retreat staged by the Massed Bands of the Prince of Wales's Division on Horse Guards Parade on 7, 8 and 9 June.

June also saw the Battalion involved in a 2 Infantry Brigade exercise, Second Strike, on the Stanford training area in Norfolk, during which it received visits from General Sir Frank Kitson, Commander-in-Chief UK Land Forces, who presented Corporal Eames with his Long Service and Good Conduct Medal, and Lieutenant General Sir Richard Trant, GOC South East District.

On 16 July, the Saturday of Cricket Week, the Regiment held the annual "At Home" at St Cross, during which the Band was presented with seven new silver fanfare trumpets and banners by the Freedom Cities and Boroughs and the New Forest District. This very generous gift was much appreciated as the existing fanfare trumpets were at least fifty years old and had sustained a battering during their recent trip to the Falklands. Six days later the 1st Battalion's Colour Party, the Band and Drums and two Guards marched through Portsmouth prior to Beating Retreat in the Guildhall Square, where, once again, the response from the public was overwhelming. Early on 1 August, Minden Day, what had been a sweltering few weeks broke with a heavy downpour, but fortunately this ended before the parade took place. The day had been designed as a family occasion and among the guests welcomed by the Battalion were the Colonel of the Regiment and Lady Fraser, Colonel Roger May, MC, Lieutenant Colonel and Mrs Mike Martin, and Colour Sergeant Wood and In-Pensioner McConnell from the Royal Hospital, Chelsea. Roses were presented by Lady Fraser, Mrs Neville and the company commanders' wives. After the Battalion had marched past the Colonel of the Regiment lunch was served in marquees and during the afternoon everyone enjoyed themselves at company sideshows. The Sergeants' Mess Minden Ball, held in the gymnasium, with professional entertainment provided by the comedian Ted Rogers, went on well into the night.

Concurrently with these events, preparations were already in hand for the Battalion's tour of duty in Berlin. These involved re-establishing the Reconnaissance and Assault Pioneer Platoons, expanding the MT Platoon to almost three times its usual size, and a number of important equipment changes. In consequence, over 300 members of the Battalion attended external courses.

The immediate beneficiaries in equipment terms were the Mortar, Anti-Tank and Reconnaissance Platoons. The Mortar Platoon, under Captain Robert Jordan, received the L2A1 Hand-Held Laser Ranger Finder, which could determine the range of targets from 150 to 6000 metres to within ten metres, and their plotter was replaced by the Mortar Fire Data Computer, permitting much faster calculations and electronic storage of target data, the combined effect of both devices being to accelerate response times and save ammunition. The Milans of the Anti-Tank Platoon (Captain Peter Jones) were supplemented by portee-mounted 120mm Wombats, which could still perform a useful function within the confines of built-up areas. Both the Mortar and Anti-Tank Platoons ran recruit cadres which culminated in live firing at Otterburn at the end of September.

The Reconnaissance Platoon (Captain Richard Dennis) underwent the most dramatic change of all, being equipped with eight CVR(W)s (Combat Vehicles Reconnaissance (Wheeled)), better known as Fox armoured cars to those with no ear for regurgitated English, plus four reconnaissance Land Rovers armed with GPMGs. The Fox, armed with a 30mm Rarden cannon and a co-axial machine gun, carried a crew consisting of commander, gunner and driver, and to acquire the appropriate skills members of the Platoon attended intensive courses at the RAC Centre at Bovington and Gunnery School at Lulworth.

In addition, the Battalion would, in Berlin, draw six FV432 APCs, some of which mounted the same turret and armament as the Fox armoured cars. The life expectancy of soft-skinned vehicles in the sort of street-fighting that might be expected in Berlin was clearly very limited, and in such circumstances the role of the APCs would be ammunition resupply, transport for the Assault Pioneers, and casualty evacuation.

The major exercise of the year, Winged Victory, involved the Battalion, less Z Company, being seconded to 5 Infantry Brigade and took place near Stranraer between 3 and 14 October. The scenario envisaged the extraction of British citizens living on an island during the opening hours of an armed insurrection. The exercise itself consisted of four phases: the fly-in to secure an airhead and a beachhead; the extraction of the threatened civilians and securing lines of communication; fix-and-destroy operations against the armed insurgents; and finally the Brigade fly-out. As intended, many lessons were learned concerning the problems which could be encountered in out-of-area operations.

Training for the Battalion Skill-at-Arms Meeting commenced on 24 October on the Hythe range complex. The inter-company competition was won by A Company and the prize for the best young soldier was awarded to Private Degaris. On 2 November, at the invitation of The Queen, Colonel Neville, four officers, two warrant officers and eight soldiers were present at the unveiling of the statue of Earl Mountbatten of Burma on Foreign Office Green. Little time now remained to the Battalion in Dover. The move to Berlin commenced on 16 November and on 5 December the Hampshires assumed responsibility for Wavell Barracks in Spandau, to the west of the city.

Berlin in those days was a uniquely fascinating city. Its status had remained unchanged since 1945 and it was still divided into British, American, French and Russian sectors of occupation, the only major differences being the infamous Wall erected by the East German government to prevent its citizens escaping to the West, and the reduction in the number of crossing points to one, Checkpoint Charlie, near the Brandenburg Gate. West Berlin, that is the British, American and French sectors, was as smart and sophisticated as any Western capital, with bustling shops, thronged pavements and a thriving night life. In sharp contrast, East Berlin, despite being described as the showcase of communist economic and social planning, was grey, dismal and down-at-heel, memorable for its multitude of soul-destroying blocks of flats and depressing food queues. Most of pre-war Berlin's important buildings lay in the Russian sector. Predictably, the Kaiser's Palace had been levelled, its site being a desolate square named after a communist deity, the Cathedral had been allowed to decay to the extent that piles of fallen rococo plasterwork now littered the floor, and the gutted ruins of the Reichstag stood as a memorial to Stalin's finest hour. Yet there were a few good reasons for visiting East Berlin, even if uniform was mandatory for the safety of the wearer. Great pains had been taken to restore the Opera House to its former glory, and the Museum was well worth seeing. Again, if one paid in Deutsch Marks, which had a higher Black Market value than the local Ost Marks, one could acquire a piece of Meissen at an absurdly low price, and the same was true of high-quality optical goods such as cameras and binoculars.

Under the terms of the 1945 convention between the Allied Powers, no armed German troops were permitted in the city. The Russians and East Germans had subsequently chosen to disregard this provision, so that the East German Army had a presence in the Soviet sector. So, too, had another armed organisation, the Volkspolizie. The Vopos, as they were better known, seemed to have been recruited exclusively from thugs with all the instincts of the Allgemein SS and the Hitlerjügend. At Checkpoint Charlie welcoming smirks were rigidly enforced by their superiors, but elsewhere in their sector they loved to throw their jackbooted weight about, their authority enforced with snarling guard dogs and slung sub-machine guns. The East Berliners were clearly terrified of them but, since their presence was not recognised by the Western Powers, the latter's troops were instructed to ignore them and their demands. If the Vopos wished to press a point, British soldiers were issued a card saying, in German, GO AND FETCH AN ENGLISH-SPEAKING RUSSIAN OFFICER,

352

and, as that meant serious trouble, the bully boys invariably faded into the background. For their part, the Russians themselves wasted no opportunity to remind those in the Western sectors that they inhabited a tiny island in a sea of overwhelming force. The firing of tank guns on nearby ranges was clearly audible in Spandau, and during the evening, their MiGs deliberately created sonic bangs in Western airspace. It was all rather pointless as such things became accepted as part of daily life.

Berlin was an intelligence gatherer's paradise. The 1945 convention permitted the troops of all the occupying powers access to each other's sectors, a right formally maintained by the use of Flag Patrols. For many years now these had been routed solely on an east-west axis, for obvious reasons. It was said, with perhaps a germ of truth, that their execution mirrored the attitude of their respective armies. The Russians were unpredictable both as to the number and the frequency of their visits; the Americans, helmeted and armed to the teeth, passed through the checkpoint hourly; the British, usually four men in a Land Rover, crossed once a day with a specific object in mind; and the French sent over an officer and driver once a week, complete with stick loaf, Brie, butter and a decent bottle of wine!

Shortly after arriving the 1st Battalion became the British sector's duty battalion; the tour of duty lasted a month with the role of duty company coming round every fourth day. This involved providing guards for Spandau Prison, for the British Military Train which travelled daily between Berlin and Brunswick in West Germany, cinemas, and bus trips into the Eastern sector. Simultaneously, the Reconnaissance Platoon carried out border patrols along the British sector's outer boundary.

One of the most interesting, if hardly enjoyable, of these duties was the prison guard. Spandau Prison, which once contained several high-ranking war criminals, now held only Rudolf Hess, Hitler's one-time deputy, who was guarded in monthly rotation by all four Powers. It was probable that the Western Powers would have released Hess, now a pathetic old man with a broken mind who presented no threat and was hardly an ideal figurehead for the nascent neo-Nazi movement. The Russians, perhaps for symbolic reasons or maybe because provision of a guard increased their presence in the Western sectors, were adamant that he should remain a prisoner. The changing of national guards was always completed with due ceremony and followed by an inter-Allied lunch. The prison itself was a grim Teutonic pile and, for the Hampshires, one guard post, that at Tower No 2, quickly acquired a most sinister reputation, the reasons for which are discussed at the end of this chapter.

Local training was undertaken in the Grünewald, a belt of woodland stretching down the western outskirts of Berlin, itself bounded on the west by the waters of the Havel, and at Ruhleben ranges, where a specially constructed "village" was used to perfect fighting in built-up area techniques. The 1984 Brigade Inter-Platoon Competition was held there during the first week of March and although the Battalion did not produce the winning platoon it had eight platoons in the first sixteen places from a total of twenty-seven entries, and was over one thousand points ahead of its nearest rival, with B Company winning the Champion Company prize. A Company's No 1 Platoon was the Battalion's highest scorer, taking fifth place, and was awarded the Winchester Trophy by Colonel Neville in consequence. What made these results particularly gratifying was that new arrivals in Berlin were usually considered to be out of the running for the prizes. From 16 March until 5 April the Battalion was involved in Exercise Tiger Strike, which took place near Bad Segeberg in Schleswig-Holstein. This consisted of a Battalion exercise followed by the dispersion of companies to separate villages for specialist training, the final phase being devoted to company exercises in the forests with emphasis on night work and junior leadership. On its return to Berlin the Battalion was tasked with running a Brigade Study Period on the two themes of "The Reserve Bridge Demolition Guard in an Urban Setting" and "Defence of a Key Point in Berlin." This was held at Ruhleben and tackled with such imagination and humour that even blasé veterans of many study periods were heard to murmur, "Best I've ever seen," and "Highly entertaining."

Ruhleben was also the venue for the Brigade Skill-at-Arms Meeting on 18 April. During this the Battalion won the GPMG Team Match and also the following awards:

Champion-at-Arms -	Lance Corporal Begam
Winner, Moving Target Match -	Colour Sergeant Slade
Winners, Falling Plate Match -	Colour Sergeant Slade, Sergeant Hack, Corporal Wright, Lance Corporal Begam

As a result of this, twelve members of the Battalion were selected for the British Garrison Team, captained by Captain Richard Dennis, at the Allied Weapons Meeting on 9 May. Firing against French and American opposition, the British team won the GPMG, SMG and pistol matches outright, as well as all but two of the individual prizes. Hampshire successes were:

Individual Winner, SLR -	Lance Corporal Begam
Winners, GPMG Match -	Corporal Wright,
	Lance Corporal Mears
Winners, GPMG Match (Reserve Firers) -	
	Lance Corporal Ayers,
	Lance Corporal Ridout
Winner, SMG Match (Reserve Firers) -	
	Private Mussell

In preparation for the Queen's Birthday Parade, RSM M.W.Gibson held an inter-platoon drill competition on 14 May, this being won by Lieutenant Mark Parminter's No 9 Platoon. For the parade itself, held on the Maifeld, a large grassed area outside the Olympic Stadium, on 1 June, the Battalion was required to produce a Colour Party, the Band, two guards each of three officers and sixty-six rank and file, four Fox armoured cars, eight Land Rovers, appropriately painted and crewed, six APCs and numerous fatigue parties. The salute was taken by HE Sir Jock Taylor, KCMG, the British Ambassador to West Germany, the highlights of the parade being the twenty-one-gun salute fired by the Chieftain tanks of D Squadron The Queen's Royal Hussars, the infantry's *feu de joie,* and the Army Air Corps' fly-past in Gazelle helicopters.

While preparations for the parade were taking place a composite platoon under Lieutenant Mark Coburn underwent three weeks' training with the 1st Battalion's affiliated American battalion, 5/502nd Parachute Infantry, at Wildflecken in Hessen. The full range of American weapons was fired, night vision equipment was handled and there was a chance to abseil from the new UH-60 Black Hawk helicopter. Sections took part in a 5/502nd Battalion March and Shoot Competition in which Lance Corporal Wells's section (Lance Corporals Wells and Edkin, Privates Cummins, Cook, Sandford and Parfit) distinguished itself by winning.

The annual Allied Forces Day parade, an ever-popular event with Berliners, was held on 16 June. This involved British, American and French contingents in a continuous march along 17 Juni Strasse, led by the dismounted elements, including a Tripartite Colour Guard, with the mechanised elements bringing up the rear. The Battalion provided the Band and Corps of Drums, three guards of four officers and eighty-four rank and file (each marching in six files of fourteen), five Fox armoured cars, six FV432 APCs, and eighteen Milan, Wombat and 81mm mortar vehicles, all suitably crewed. No sterner critic of a unit's performance on parade exists than its own Regimental Sergeant Major, but on this occasion RSM Gibson was delighted. "The parade went without a hitch and was greatly appreciated by the huge Berlin crowd. The exhilaration and pride of marching behind our own Colours to the beat of the Drum brought out the best in all of us. On this day the three guards of the Royal Hampshire Regiment were filled with pride and confidence. They looked good, and they knew they were good."

In Spandau the Battalion had quickly established a good relationship with its German neighbours. The Band played at a mayoral birthday party, at the local "Schützenfest", at the launching ceremony of a new lifeboat on the Havel, at the Whitsun Music Festival, at the opening of the new U-Bahn station, and on many other occasions, becoming a firm favourite of the Spandauers. During Anglo-German Friendship Day, held in the town's market square, the Wives' Club ran an English Tea stand which was enormously popular and in return one of the local stores laid on a fashion show. Such, indeed, was the friendship of the townspeople that some single soldiers spent Christmas with local families.

Visitors during this period included the Colonel of the Regiment and Lady Fraser, General Sir Nigel Bagnall, KCB, CVO, MC, Commander-in-Chief BAOR, HE Sir Jock Taylor, the British Ambassador to West Germany, Major General B.C.Gordon Lennox, GOC Berlin (British Sector), Brigadier A.Makepeace-Warne, MBE, the Brigade Commander and Mr J.P.Stanley, MP, Minister of State for the Armed Forces. Mr C.G.Gould, the Deputy Judge Advocate General, paid a visit in March to inspect the leopard skins worn by the Drums Platoon, which he had presented to the Battalion (then in Cyprus) while serving as Senior Magistrate in Kenya in 1969. In May Captain D.S.Dobson, RN, and five officers and ratings from HMS *Southampton* were entertained and inspected the Battalion's heavy weapons. At the same time fourteen chaplains arrived for the aptly-named Exercise Trinity 84, during which the Battalion was tasked with giving them "a clear and up-to-date insight into the skills, equipment and working life of an infantry soldier."

The Minden Day parade, commemorating the 225th anniversary of the battle, was held in Wavell Barracks. Guests included local German dignitaries, Lieutenant Colonel Cardell Hunter, commanding US 5/502nd Parachute Infantry, and Lieutenant Colonel Philippe de Susbielle, commanding the French 11ème Regiment de Chasseurs, the Battalion's affiliated units in Berlin. To demonstrate that no hard feelings existed regarding the outcome of the battle, Colonel de Susbielle arrived with a boot full of the choicest champagne! Thirty-three members of the Comrades' Association had made the journey from England to take part in the parade, at which the salute was taken by Major General Gordon Lennox, who also presented the Long Service and Good Conduct Medal to WOII H.K.Baker. After the parade the officers entertained 260 guests, the Sergeants 200, and the soldiers' families joined their husbands in company marquees.

Adventure training in many forms had continued throughout the year in venues as widely separated as Bavaria and Norway, and, locally, there was canoeing and windsurfing on the Havel. If the Battalion had already made its mark professionally within the Brigade, on the sports field it achieved almost complete dominance, winning over a period of months the Berlin trophies for swimming, association football, rugby football, hockey, sailing and boxing, as well as the BAOR Infantry Cricket Cup. Likewise, on August Bank Holiday the Assault Pioneer Platoon, now commanded by WOII J.L.Greco, won the Brigade Raft Race in fine style, following up with another win in the Brigade Assault Pioneer Competition, during which it scored 90 per cent on all tasks. These results reflected the Battalion's continued emphasis on physical fitness and sporting activities of every kind. Not to be out-done, the cooks went on to sweep the board in the Berlin Cookery Competition, winning eight first and two second prizes out of sixteen classes, with Corporal Colin Slade and Private Mark Jeffreys, both ACC, winning respectively the titles of Chef and Young Chef of the Year.

A Brigade all-arms exercise, Hungry Bear II, was held at

Soltau during the last days of November. This was not an un-qualified success as the training area had become a quagmire in which tracked vehicles, wheeled reconnaissance and support ve-hicles, and dismounted infantry could only move at different and incompatible speeds. Hungry Bear II, however, was immediately followed by a very successful fortnight's field firing at Sennelager. "The high point of the first week was a company defence exercise organised by the Operations Officer, Captain G.J.Martin. A, B and Y Companies, each with mortar, Wombat and Rarden in sup-port, enjoyed a live-firing bonanza made more realistic by the generous use of plastic explosive by the Assault Pioneer Platoon. In addition (except for Y Company, as weather did not permit), the USAF provided a flight of A10 ground-attack aircraft to liven up proceedings with aerobatics and cannon fire at a mere 4000 rounds a minute."

When the Battalion returned to Berlin little time remained before Christmas. A carol service was held and at the soldiers' Christmas lunch Colonel Neville presented the Minden Trophy to Major Paul Davis of Y Company. This was the fourth occasion in the five-year history of the Trophy that it had been won by Y Company, who had lost it temporarily to HQ Company the previ-ous year.

Visitors during the latter part of the year included the Ad-jutant General, General Sir Roland Guy, KCB, CBE, DSO, and the Military Secretary, Lieutenant General Sir David Mostyn, KCB, CBE, in September; the Mayor of Winchester, Councillor J.Broadway, accompanied by the Regimental Secretary, Lieuten-ant Colonel John Darroch, in November; and the incoming Bri-gade Commander, Brigadier P.P.D.Stone, CBE, in December.

On 9 January 1985 Colonel Hastings Neville relinquished command to Lieutenant Colonel A.W.Freemantle, MBE. Colonel Neville's period in command had been one of the most reward-ing in the Regiment's post-World War II history for, while the 1st Battalion had always shone professionally, it had now also be-come renowned for its sporting victories and successes in other fields - so much so that in the Journal his successor warned against complacency, pointing out that, as the Brigade turned over, newly arrived units would be only too keen to try their luck against the Hampshires. That, however, lay in the future; for the moment the Festive Season lingered on to the extent that Colonel Neville's departure from Wavell Barracks was made in Santa Claus's sledge!

Colonel Andrew Freemantle has been mentioned in previous chapters, and it should also be mentioned that his father had fought as a subaltern with the 2nd Battalion during the Battle of Tebourba Gap, where he had been seriously wounded. Colonel Freemantle had been commissioned into the Regiment in 1965 and served with the 1st Battalion in Germany, Malaya, Cyprus and Borneo. In 1969 he joined the Australian Armed Forces, serving with the Australian SAS for eleven months in Vietnam. He then rejoined the Regiment, accompanying the 1st Battalion on two occasions to Ulster and to Hong Kong. In 1978 he attended the course at the Army Staff College, after which he became Chief of Staff to 22 Armoured Brigade in Germany. He returned to the 1st Battalion in 1980, commanding Y Company in Germany and the United Kingdom before completing a two-year appointment as a member of the Directing Staff at the Staff College.

In January Y Company, now commanded by Major A.J.B.Edwards, provided a Guard of Honour for the recently arrived French GOC Berlin, General de Division Paul C.Cavarott, when he visited British Headquarters. Having inspected the Guard, the General described it as being "very smart and firm."

At the end of March the Battalion moved to the extensive Vogelsang training area, situated in the Eifel, close to the borders of Belgium and Luxembourg, in terrain reminiscent of the English Lake District. Here, perhaps for the first time in its history, the entire Battalion, less officers, was accommodated in a single enormous barrack block. The training area possessed a Belgian permanent staff, but what they did was obscure, as the Hampshires were told on arrival that as the largest unit present they would be responsible not only for administering the other eleven major and minor units there, but also for allocating and controlling the ranges. These unwelcome problems were dealt with admirably by Captain P.Goss (Glosters, QM Tech) and Major P.J.W.Shepherd (OC HQ Company), who were responsible respectively for administration and the ranges. The Battalion's own training programme is described by its Second-in-Command, Major D.A.C.Hannah.

"The first phase was company level training, including a two-day field firing package; the second, a Battalion exercise; and the third, a Berlin Brigade test exercise, Hungry Bear III. The two exercises were punctuated by two days' rest and recuperation.

"For the first phase each company was allocated an area and given a number of training objectives to achieve. Weather conditions can only be described as barely marginal; wind, snow, ice and rain all had to be contended with. Company camp sites after two days looked like the Somme; even Battalion HQ couldn't find a dry spot and suffered equal misery! Activities included preparing a defensive position, reconnaissance and fighting patrols, a daylight quick attack, fighting through a position at night and assault boat training. The field firing came as a welcome break; each company completed a range package which started with the whole company running the gauntlet of the Battle Inoculation Range - a popular activity, despite the wayward firing of the Belgian range staff and the ample mounds of sheep dung liberally spread about the range! The package ended with a section shoot across the lake, for most soldiers the first time they had fired across water.

"The Battalion exercise, Pipe Opener I, followed. The Battalion deployed to a concentration area approximately thirty-five miles from the camp. Orders were issued by the Commanding Officer for an infiltration advance to a forward battalion hide. Many soldiers will remember the long tab on a rather warm day over a distance of some 30 kilometres, not to mention the very steep climbs and descents over some very difficult terrain. Having started at 14:00, most of the companies were safely into the hide by 02:00 the following morning.

"The next day was spent patrolling against an enemy position provided by Z Company. As a result of the information gathered by the patrols, orders were given for a Battalion dawn attack. The Second-in-Command was despatched with a team to secure the start line and was closely followed by the leading companies. All seemed well until the companies discovered that they had to climb a 300-foot cliff to reach the objective! After much puffing, panting and swearing they managed to reach the top, only to find that they had a 400-500 metre fight-through. After the objective was finally taken the exercise ended, one soldier being heard to remark that it had been a 'ballburster!' At the weekend, between exercises, trips were organised to Belgium, Trier and Cologne and a Battalion smoker was held.

"During the final phase the Battalion moved initially into a concentration area from where it advanced clearing two routes forward to a Battalion hide. Companies were challenged en route by isolated pockets of an enemy force provided by a composite Ordnance Company, but these were quickly brushed aside. Orders were then given in the hide for a night assault river crossing followed by an attack. The silent crossing soon became a noisy one as the assault company, Y Company, were bumped. This did not deter them and they soon reached their objective. B Company crossed in phase two and despite an assault vertically down yet another cliff they too captured their objective. The Battalion advance continued. Each Company was then tasked with a support helicopter attack mounted in quick time before congregating in another concentration area prior to a dawn attack on the remnants of the enemy company. The final attack was memorable for the fact that the Commanding Officer acquired from nowhere a troop of Leopard tanks who happened to be exercising in the same area. Their commanders were only too willing to participate, and, much to the consternation of Brigade Headquarters and the enemy, quickly helped the Battalion to mop up the position. At the end of the exercise everyone agreed that they had had a 'knackering' but challenging seventy-two hours."

Back in Berlin, the Battalion celebrated the 70th Anniversary of Gallipoli with a parade at which the salute was taken by Major General Gordon Lennox, who presented Long Service and Good Conduct Medals to WOII (TQMS) D.Sutton, who was shortly to take over as Regimental Sergeant Major from RSM M.W.Gibson, Colour Sergeants Lovell and Taylor, and Sergeant Gray. Once again, the shooting team did extremely well in the Brigade Skill-at-Arms Meeting, from which Sergeant Hack emerged as Champion-at-Arms and Second Lieutenant P.S.O'Sullivan as the best Young Officer. Between 13 and 19 May Y Company provided a fighting in built-up areas demonstration for each of the recently-arrived 1st Battalion Devonshire and Dorsetshire Regiment's companies.

Thoughts were now concentrated on the fast-approaching Queen's Birthday Parade, during which the Battalion would Troop the Queen's Colour before HRH The Prince of Wales. This, in fact, would be the first time in the Battalion's history that it would Troop a Colour for Royalty. In preparation RSM Gibson followed the precedent set the previous year and held a drill competition, this time between companies. Z Company emerged the winners and as a result of this it was decided that on the day elements of the Company together with B Company (2nd) would provide the

Escort to the Colour, and that Y Company (3rd), together with elements of Z Company, would provide No 2 Guard.

While final preparations for the parade were in progress, the Colonel of the Regiment was able to inform Colonel Freemantle that HRH The Princess of Wales had accepted The Queen's invitation to become Colonel-in-Chief of The Royal Hampshire Regiment. When Colonel Freemantle communicated this very popular and quite unexpected news to the 1st Battalion on 3 June 1985 it was received with three spontaneous cheers. To commemorate the event the decision was taken by the Regimental Committee to present the Princess with a gold and jewelled brooch in the form of the Regimental Badge.

The Queen's Birthday Parade took place on 7 June and was once again held on the Maifeld. The Prince of Wales, accompanied by Major General Gordon Lennox and Brigadier Stone, took the salute mounted on horseback, with an escort provided by a mounted troop of the RMP equipped as lancers. The Colonel of the Regiment, Lady Fraser, Colonel R.G.Long and Mrs Long were also present to witness this historic event. What had been a remarkable week for the Regiment as a whole ended on 8 June with the Villa Lemm Ball, one of the highlights of the Berlin social season, for which A Company under Major T.M.Reeve-Tucker had done much of the preparatory work.

The Allied Forces Day Parade was held on 22 June, with Captain R.J.Jordan as the officer commanding the Tri-Partite Colour Guard. On this occasion, the parade differed slightly from previous years in that it was decided to have each battalion's band and corps of drums immediately in front of the marching troops, a change appreciated both by those taking part and by the crowds. From 28 to 30 June the Band and Corps of Drums also took part in the Musical Pageant held at the Waldbühne open air concert theatre. This was held instead of the annual Berlin Tattoo and included twelve bands from BAOR, the US Army Berlin Brigade Band, the French 46th Infantry Band, the Berlin Police Orchestra, the Morriston Orpheus Male Voice Choir from Wales, the Spandau Youth Choir, the Band of the Grenadier Guards and the King's Troop RHA from London. The Senior Director of Music, Lieutenant Colonel Derek Kimberley, brother of the 1st Battalion's Quartermaster, Captain E.C.Kimberley, brought the whole show to a thrilling climax with a performance of Tchaikovsky's 1812 Overture, complete with cannons and fireworks.

Meanwhile the Battalion had moved down to the British Zone for its annual field firing. Battalion HQ, HQ Company and the rifle companies went to Sennelager; Z Company, less the Milan element of the Anti-Tank Platoon, went to Bergen/Hohne ranges, and the Milan teams went to Putlos to participate in the I (BR) Corps Milan Concentration. On its return in mid-July the Battalion spent two weeks fighting mock battles at Ruhleben as part of a Defence Operational Analysis Establishment research exercise on fighting in built-up areas.

During the Minden Day parade roses were presented by Mrs Pat Freemantle and the other officers' wives. The parade was followed by hockey and soccer matches between, on the one hand, officers, WOs and sergeants, and on the other junior NCOs and privates, played to variable rules. Finally, luncheon was served in the Messes and in the Soldiers' Dining Hall for families.

Once again, the year's adventure training programme had included skiing in Bavaria and Norway, plus canoeing, wind-surfing and dinghy sailing on the Havel. In April, however, Captains Nigel Williams and Peter Emery had taken a party of climbers to the snow-covered Taurus Mountains in Turkey and, while the Battalion was at Sennelager, Captain Peter Goss arranged one-day-and-one-jump courses for seventy novice sky-divers at Bad Lippspringe, static line descents being made from a height of 2000 feet. As a result of the latter seventeen novices were accepted on full three-week courses and most of the others decided to travel from Berlin to Sennelager for week-end training. On 8 September a twenty-nine-strong party from the Wives' Club made a 16-kilometre sponsored walk which raised £1200 for the Hampshire Ambulance Service (Portsmouth Branch).

Compared with what had gone before, August and September were comparatively quiet months involving a spell as Duty Battalion and Potential NCOs and Section Commanders' Cadres. Everyone, however, was looking forward to the first official visit of the Regiment's new Colonel-in-Chief in October and much preparation and hard work went into making this a success. As the Princess was new to the Army and its ways, this included a visit by Colonel Freemantle to Kensington Palace in order to brief her on the Regiment and the role of the 1st Battalion.

The Colonel-in-Chief's two-day visit to the 1st Battalion began on the afternoon of Friday 18 October 1985. After flying in to RAF Gatow the Princess paid a brief visit to the Schloss

Charlottenburg to meet Berlin's Governing Mayor, Herr Eberhard Diepgen, and other dignitaries, and to sign the famous Golden Book. Accompanied by Major General Gordon Lennox, the Colonel-in-Chief was met at Battalion Headquarters by the Colonel of the Regiment and Colonel Freemantle, being introduced to the Mayor of Spandau, Herr Werner Salomon, Frau Salomon, Lady Fraser, Mrs Pat Freemantle and Major Hannah. After the Colonel of the Regiment had presented her with her unique Regimental brooch in Colonel Freemantle's office, she emerged for the parade held in her honour.

This took the form of an inspection of the four guards on parade, then a Troop by the Band and the Corps of Drums, a March Past and an Advance in Review Order, followed by the firing of a *feu de joie* and three cheers for the Colonel-in-Chief. After the parade the Princess walked from the Officers' Mess to a Tea Party in the gymnasium and on the way paused to speak to several of the families and was presented with posies by Stephen Spicer, son of Lance Corporal and Mrs Spicer, and Tina Smith, daughter of Corporal and Mrs Smith 04. She also stopped to talk informally with a group of soldiers and show them her Regimental brooch, in which she clearly took the greatest pleasure. The Tea Party gave her a further opportunity to meet a cross-section of the Battalion's families. In the evening she attended a Ladies' Guest Night in the Officers' Mess, meeting all the Battalion's officers and their ladies. After dinner the Band and Corps of Drums gave an excellent and at times humorous concert, which was followed by a disco in the cellar bar.

Next morning the Colonel-in-Chief arrived to see the Battalion at work. She first inspected the Quarter Guard, provided by Z Company and commanded by Captain Philip Hatton, then visited A Company's accommodation, where she was greeted by the Officer Commanding, Major Michael Reeve-Tucker, and WOII Nye. Moving on to the Assault Course she was briefed on the Milan and Wombat by Captain Emery and WOII Kerswell of Z Company. Next, Major Nick Sim's B Company demonstrated the recovery of a casualty while under enemy fire and Major Andrew Edwards's Y Company showed their paces in transporting heavy, awkward objects over the Assault Course. As a finale two teams from A Company free-abseiled from US Huey helicopters, after which they and their American pilots and instructors were presented to the Colonel-in-Chief; to her amused surprise, the

Princess was then herself presented with a red rose and a box of chocolates by Private Baynton and Lance Corporal Clifton, emulating the hero of the Cadbury's Milk Tray advertisement who regularly risked life and limb to provide such things for the lady of his choice! It was now the turn of the Colonel-in-Chief herself to participate and, wearing a Regimental track suit, she took the controls of a Rarden 432 and, under the guidance of Colour Sergeant Jones, the Battalion's chief driving instructor, negotiated a course laid out by the MTO, Captain Bob Le Galloudec.

After another quick change the Princess concluded her visit by meeting the WOs and Sergeants and their wives in their Mess. While there, she presented Long Service and Good Conduct Medals to WOII McLaughlin, WOII Rodda, WOII Andrews and Lance Corporal Ellis. Shortly before 13:00 the Colonel-in-Chief, accompanied by the Colonel of the Regiment and Lady Fraser, left for the return journey to England. Her first visit had been a tremendous success and enjoyed by everyone, not least herself.

The Brigade March-and-Shoot Competition, for which there were forty-two entries, was held a week after the Colonel-in-Chief's visit. The first day involved a 10km road run ending at Ruhleben, followed by an assault course through and over the dummy houses, a grenade throw and a shoot on the ranges. The second day also began with a 10km run, this time through woodland, including an abseil, then an assault boat river crossing and more shooting. The competition was won by the Battalion's Reconnaissance Platoon (Captain Philip Hatton), with A Company's 3 and 2 Platoons, commanded by Second Lieutenants Adam Edmunds and Jonathan Eldridge, in respectively second and third places. Thus far, the Battalion's performance might simply have been regarded as excellent; what made it unique was that Hampshire platoons also took the 4th, 5th, 6th, 7th, 8th, 9th, 10th and 11th places! Capitalising on this remarkable success, the Assault Pioneers won the Brigade Assault Pioneer Competition for the second year running.

In November visits were received from the Mayor and Mayoress of Romsey, Councillor and Mrs Geoff Street, the Lord Mayor of Portsmouth, Councillor Fred Warner, and the Lady Mayoress, and a contingent from HMS *Southampton*. The Minden Trophy was won by A Company for the first time in December, and as 1985 drew to a close the Battalion could once again look back on a year of outstanding sporting achievement, having again won first places in the Berlin Brigade swimming, athletics and cross-country championships and creditable first and sixth places in the 3rd Armoured Division and BAOR cross-country championships respectively.

The Battalion's tour of duty in Berlin was also drawing to a close. Much of January 1986 was spent handing over Wavell Barracks to the 1st Battalion The Gloucestershire Regiment and in February the main body moved to Tidworth.

* * * * * * * * *

THE STRANGE STORY OF TOWER No 2

Shortly after the 1st Battalion arrived in Berlin it provided the Guard for Spandau Prison. One night the sentry manning the guard post at Tower No 2 fired five shots and was subsequently discovered in a severely shaken state. His story was that he had been approached by a figure which gave every impression of being about to launch a violent assault on him. The figure had not responded when challenged and had simply vanished when the fifth shot was fired.

The following day Colonel Neville mentioned the subject to a friend in the Military Governor's office and, to his surprise, was asked if the incident had taken place at Tower No 2. It seemed that similar incidents had taken place there in the past and American, French and Russian sentries were all known to have opened fire in the belief that they were about to be attacked. Tower No 2 was said to have been the scene of an atrocity during the Nazi era. Higher authority had a mind to discipline the Hampshire sentry, suggesting negligent discharge of a weapon as the appropriate charge. However, when Colonel Neville pointed out that each round had been deliberately aimed and fired the matter was dropped. The Battalion experienced no further problems at this particular guard post, although it retained its sinister reputation.

Recurrent manifestations are widespread phenomena for which no explanation exists. One theory suggests that they may be reflected images from a time of extreme emotion, visible only if the mind is attuned to receive them; dogs, cats and horses are credited with a natural ability to receive such "signals," but this is far rarer in humans and much seems to depend upon circumstances. Since they are merely images such manifestations have no awareness, although they can clearly induce an understandable terror.

CHAPTER 19

TIDWORTH AND SOUTH ARMAGH
1986 — 1989

Role and training - the Tidworth Marathon - Freedom of Test Valley - Presentation of New Colours by the Colonel-in-Chief - training in Schleswig-Holstein - threat to Serle's House - General Sir David Fraser relinquishes Colonelcy of the Regiment to Brigadier R.G.Long, OBE, MC - deployment in South Armagh - Operation Bullet - mortar attack on Bessbrook Mill - murder of Lord Chief Justice Gibson - return to Tidworth - Colonel Andrew Freemantle hands over Command of the 1st Battalion to Lieutenant Colonel T.A.L.Glass - ceremonial occasions in London - 1st Battalion team wins the Northern European Command Infantry Competition - firefighting in Wales - Freedom of Christchurch - laying up of Old Colours and Dedication of the *Third Book of Remembrance* at Winchester Cathedral - the SA 80 rifle and Saxon APC - training in Kenya - Freedom Marches at Romsey and Portsmouth - Exercise Bold Grouse - Service of Dedication and departure for Londonderry

Lucknow Barracks, Tidworth, was located on the boundary between Hampshire and Wiltshire so that for the first time in many years part, at least, of the 1st Battalion was based in its home county. It now formed part of 1 Infantry Brigade, commanded by Brigadier J.F.W.Wilsey, CBE, and its role was similar to that which it had carried out at Dover, namely reinforcement of NATO's Northern flank in an emergency.

Having settled in during February, the Battalion began work in earnest the following month with a series of Battle Camps, Z Company (Major M.J.Cornwell, The Duke of Edinburgh's Royal

Regiment) going to Otterburn, A Company (Major A.H.Pryce) to Dartmoor, and B and Y Companies (respectively Major N.A.Sim and Major A.J.B.Edwards) to Sennybridge, South Wales. In April the Battalion prepared for its Spearhead role, which included a NITAT update, Battalion and UK Land Forces test exercises, and the Reconnaissance Platoon under Captain Philip Hatton live-fired its Rarden cannon at Lulworth ranges. Further training, including the South West District and Battalion Skill at Arms Meetings and cadres for Section Commanders and Potential NCOs, continued well into June. On 5 June the Battalion organised the Tidworth Marathon. This included the Marathon itself, a Half Marathon, a 5 x 5-mile Relay and a Fun Run, all to raise money for charity. Second Lieutenant S.R.Jones came second in the Marathon with a time of 3 hours 3 minutes and 20 seconds, while WOII M.J.Mulligan proved to be the fastest warrant officer in the Brigade in 4 hours 2 minutes and 13 seconds, finishing in 30th place out of 52 runners. Over 200 members of the Battalion, including the Commanding Officer, ran in the Half Marathon, with Private Stamp coming second out of 573 finishers in 1 hour 15 minutes and 21 seconds. The Battalion finished third in the 5 x 5-mile Relay from an entry of 21 teams. Well over £4000 was raised for various charities, over £1000 more than the previous year, a remarkable achievement considering that two of the garrison's major units were absent at the time.

In the meantime, at a meeting held on 28 February 1986, the Test Valley Borough Council had resolved to admit the Regiment to the honorary Freedom of the Borough. The ceremony itself took place on 25 June before packed crowds in the High Street of Andover. The parade was commanded by Colonel Andrew Freemantle, leading two guards, each of forty-eight men, commanded by Major A.J.B.Edwards and Major A.H.Pryce. Also on parade were the Colours, the Band and Corps of Drums, Standards from all the Comrades' branches save Guernsey and Jersey, and the Cadets of No 1 (Andover) Platoon, Z Company, 2 Cadet Battalion, Hampshire and Isle of Wight ACF. Invited guests included Sir James Scott, Lord Lieutenant of Hampshire, Major General B.M.Lane, CB, OBE, GOC South West District, Brigadier Wilsey and the Mayors of the Regiment's other Freedom Cities, Districts and Boroughs.

After the inspection the Mayor, Councillor Bryan Beggs, addressed the parade on behalf of the Borough: "We are proudly, formally and ceremonially recognising the strong bonds of loyalty and friendship that have always existed between our population and our Royal Hampshire Regiment." He then asked the Colonel of the Regiment to sign the Roll of Honorary Freemen on behalf of the Regiment and presented him with a framed Freedom Scroll. In return, General Fraser presented the Mayor with a Regimental plate. Having obtained the Mayor's permission to march off, Colonel Freemantle then led the parade through the streets of Andover with Colours flying, Band playing, Drums beating and bayonets fixed. Afterwards, those on parade were entertained to a ploughman's lunch reception given by the Borough at the Westover Sports Centre.

The remainder of June and much of July were devoted to preparations for one of the most important ceremonial events in the 1st Battalion's post-World War II history, the presentation of new Colours by the Colonel-in-Chief on Minden Day. The greater part of the work devolved upon Major Brian Madigan, the Project Officer, and Major Ted Kimberley, the Quartermaster. The parade, watched from stands by some 4000 spectators, almost all of whom were part of the Regimental family, was held in glorious sunny weather on the Tidworth Polo Field, which itself provided a splendid backdrop of trees with the Hampshire hills visible in the distance. Those on parade included:

The Commanding Officer
Lieutenant Colonel A.W.Freemantle, MBE

Colour Party - The Old Colours

Lieutenant J.A.Spooner -	The Queen's Colour
Second Lieutenant S.R.Jones -	The Regimental Colour
WOII M.J.Mulligan	
Sergeant T.T.Moore	Sergeant K.G.Ruston

Colour Party - The New Colours

Lieutenant A.W.Dabell -	The Queen's Colour
Lieuteant C.F.Warren -	The Regimental Colour
WOII K.B.Dodd	
Sergeant D.A.Hayden	Sergeant L.P.Greenhalgh

Custodian of the New Colours
Major (QM) E.C.Kimberley

Minden Company and
Escort to the Old Colours
Major A.J.B.Edwards
Captain I.Passingham
2nd Lieutenant J.J.Eldridge
CSM J.L.Clay
Colour Sergeant C.C.Erickson
Colour Sergeant R.J.Holmes
Sergeant B.Judd
Sergeant R.L.Dutton

No.2 Guard
Major A.H.Pryce
Captain A.M.Barnes
2nd Lieutenant D.A.Wright
CSM P.A.Young

Sergeant D.J.Wright
Sergeant P.P.Lever

No.3 Guard
Major N.A.Sim
Captain J.C.D'E.Phipps
Lieutenant A.M.Prior
CSM S.J.Nye
Colour Sergeant R.H.Mitchell
Colour Sergeant P.M.J.Cain
Sergeant D.R.Havers
Sergeant A.W.Johnson, QGM

No.4 Guard
Major M.J.Cornwell*
Captain F.C.J.Dodd
2nd Lieutenant P.A.Sibeth
CSM B.J.Lane

Sergeant P.F.S.Enfield
Sergeant D.K.Chambers

Escorting Officer to the Colonel of the Regiment
Major D.A.C.Hannah

Regimental Sergeant-Major   WOI RSM D.Sutton

Bandmaster   WOI (BM) D.W.Wood

Drum Major   Sergeant D.R.Beer **

Guidons
WOII J.L.Greco
Colour Sergeant W.Baker
Colour Sergeant M.T.Crowley
Sergeant D.Bryant

Sergeant J.A.Davies
Sergeant T.J.Davis
Sergeant R.J.McDermott

*   Duke of Edinburgh's Royal Regiment
**   Royal Welch Fusiliers

The Colonel-in-Chief arrived promptly at 10:30 in a helicopter of the Queen's Flight and was met by the Colonel of the Regiment, who then accompanied her throughout the visit. She was presented with her Minden Rose by Colour Sergeant R.H.D.Wood, an In-Pensioner of the Royal Hospital, Chelsea, and then walked to the saluting dais where she was received by the parade with a Royal Salute.

The Old Colours were trooped through the ranks of Nos 2, 3 and 4 Guards and slow marched off parade to the strains of *God Bless the Prince of Wales* and *Auld Lang Syne*. The Corps of Drums piled their drums in the centre of the parade ground and the Battalion formed three sides of a hollow square. The new Colours were marched onto parade by the Quartermaster and, having been uncased for the first time, were placed upon the drums ready for the service of consecration and blessing. This was conducted by the Venerable Archdeacon W.F.Johnson, Chaplain to The Queen and to the Armed Forces. Majors Edwards and Pryce then handed the Colours to the Colonel-in-Chief, who in turn presented the Queen's Colour to Lieutenant A.W.Dabell and the Regimental Colour to Lieutenant C.F.Warren. Following the presentation, the Princess addressed the 1st Battalion:

"Royal Hampshires! I am delighted that, as your Colonel-in-Chief, the Queen has invited me to present the 1st Battalion with new Colours on Her Majesty's behalf. The First of August has been observed by the Regiment as a very special day, the anniversary of one of its most historic Battle Honours - and this particular Minden Day will always be remembered by me and, I am sure, by you.

"I have been greatly impressed by your appearance on parade, your drill, turn-out and performance of ceremonial. We have said good-bye, today, to Colours you have carried with distinction in Hong Kong, Malaya, Borneo, Cyprus, at several stations in Germany and, of course, at many posts in England and Northern Ireland. Everywhere you have been true to your Colours and to your own traditions. In entrusting to the Battalion's hands these new Colours I know that, whatever the duties demanded of you, you will perform them as you always have, and bring fresh honour to Colours on which triumphs of the past are already proudly borne."

Colonel Freemantle replied:

"Your Royal Highness, I thank you on behalf of the Officers and Men of the 1st Battalion of your Regiment for the great honour you have bestowed on us today by presenting, on behalf of Her Majesty The Queen, our new Colours. It is a great source of pride to my Battalion and the many past and present members of the Regiment who are watching, that Your Royal Highness has found the time to visit us twice since you became our Colonel-in-Chief just over a year ago. It is also of great significance to us all that so many distinguished civic representatives from our County should be here today, Minden Day, to witness Your Royal Highness entrust the County Regiment with new Colours, for it signifies the close ties kept and the high regard which the Regiment and the County of Hampshire have each for the other. I conclude, Ma'am, by affirming that the 1st Battalion of your Regiment will continue to strive always to live up to the courage and sacrifice of our forebears, whose deeds and heroism are borne on these Colours. With God's help we shall ever follow their magnificent and inspiring example. God Save The Queen!"

With its new Colours, the Battalion then marched past in quick time, followed by the Comrades with their Branch Standards and the Army Cadet Force Guard. Finally, before the Battalion was dismissed, the Princess was cheered off the parade ground. A champagne lunch, attended by the Colonel-in-Chief and a number of distinguished guests, was held in the Officers' Mess while the Battalion and their guests gathered for refreshment in five huge marquees arranged in a semi-circle. After lunch the Colonel-in-Chief spent over an hour meeting members of the Regiment, representative of all ranks, past and present, and their families, giving immense pleasure by so doing. At the end of her visit, the Princess walked slowly to her helicopter through a lane of children waving flags. As well as emphasising the importance of the occasion, photographic records of Minden Day 1986 also show it to have been the happiest of Regimental family days.

After due preparation, the Battalion flew or travelled by ferry to the Bad Segeberg area of Schleswig-Holstein for Exercise Bold Guard, a brigade exercise designed to test the defences of the Baltic approaches. This took place between 11 and 30 September and consisted of holding a defensive position followed by a Brigade counter-attack involving an approach march and a river crossing. The opportunity also presented itself for some exchange training with a Bundesheer unit, Panzergrenadier Battalion 182, during which the latter's G3 rifle was generally deemed to be a better weapon than the SLR; the German MG3 was also admired for its rapid rate of fire, with the same reservation which had been levelled at the Spandau in World War II, namely that far more ammunition had to be humped to maintain it in action. Of even greater interest was the firepower possessed by the Royal Marine enemy armed with SA 80 rifles, which were to be issued to the Battalion in a few months' time.

Back at Tidworth the Battalion received a visit from General Sir John Akehurst, Commander UK Field Army, on 2 October, just as training for its projected roulement tour of duty in South Armagh was getting into full swing. This included a Northern Ireland Commanders' Cadre followed by a preliminary reconnaissance of the operational area carried out by Colonel Freemantle, the Intelligence Officer, Captain M.A.Coburn and the Close Observation Platoon Commander. On 20 October the NITAT presentation team began a two-day visit which brought everyone up to date on the current situation in South Armagh. Northern Ireland also formed the central theme for the Winchester Trophy competition, convincingly won by Captain F.C.J.Dodd's Milan Platoon. On 28 November the Battalion left Tidworth for three weeks' concentrated training at the Hythe/Lydd complex and the Stanford training area. Following block leave the main body returned to Tidworth on 12 January 1987, the advance party having already flown to Ulster.

Elsewhere, developments affecting the Regiment as whole had taken place. For some considerable time one aspect of the government's desire to restrict spending on the armed services had involved the Ministry of Defence selling barracks, buildings and land on the open market to capitalise its assets. The Ministry's eyes were now fixed upon Serle's House, but the Colonel of the Regiment was very concerned that this historic building should remain at the heart of the Regiment's life, as Headquarters, Museum and the centre of its activities in Hampshire. He therefore encouraged at every opportunity its use for functions, dinner parties and all occasions on which the County could associate with its own Regiment. General Fraser continues:

"Also of considerable importance was the future of Serle's House in any plans to develop Peninsula Barracks and many discussions took place. It was, obviously, important to involve not only the County but also the City authorities in considering the right solution for so notable a building and so prime a site. Equally, it was important that the Ministry of Defence should appreciate the restrictions on use and the planning factors likely to apply - and likely to have a formidable effect on commercial value, were that to be an issue."

The threat receded, for the moment.

General Fraser's period as Colonel of the Regiment was coming to an end and on 19 January he visited the 1st Battalion to say goodbye for the last time. "It is no exaggeration to say," commented the Journal, "that the standing of the Regiment has grown in the last five years." As tokens of appreciation, Brigadier C.G.T.Viner had already presented General Sir David with a fine edition of the complete works of Jane Austen on behalf of the Regiment and the Comrades' Association, and Colonel Freemantle now presented him with a silver tiger from all ranks of the 1st Battalion. On 26 January 1987 Brigadier R.G.Long, OBE, MC, succeeded General Sir David Fraser as Colonel of the Regiment. Brigadier Bob Long, it will be recalled, had commanded the 1st Battalion some ten years previously and was currently commanding 42 Infantry Brigade and Chester Garrison. Some details of his career have already been given, but it worth mentioning once again that he possessed a unique Regimental background, having originally served as a National Service Officer, as a Territorial Officer with the 4th Battalion, and then as a Regular Officer with the 1st Battalion.

On 21 January 1987 the 1st Battalion assumed responsibility for the most troubled area of Ulster. It had been four years since it had last served in the Province and, in the nature of things, for many of its members it was their first experience of Northern Ireland. Only a handful remained of those who had served in South Armagh fourteen years earlier, and they found that in the intervening period the military situation had changed almost beyond recognition. There were, for example, many more troops on the ground within a smaller operational area, including those manning the new interlinked, ground-dominating, observation posts. Life in South Armagh, however, was never simple and differed from everywhere else in Ulster due to the introversion of the predominantly nationalist community and the consequent inability of the RUC to carry out what could be called normal policing, even in Northern Ireland. Quite apart from the internal security situation, in which the IRA sought to exploit any weakness, smuggling provided a lucrative hobby for many people and in such circumstances the presence of troops and police was bad for business.

The Battalion was deployed with Battalion HQ and Y Company (Major Trevor Finklaire and WOII Young) at Bessbrook Mill, A Company (Major Adrian Pryce and WOII Nye) at Forkhill joint military/RUC base with responsibility for three observation posts, B Company (Major Paul Newton and WOII Clay) manning four OPs along the border south of Crossmaglen, and Z Company (Major Mike Cornwell and WOII Lane) at Crossmaglen. Because of the ever-present threat posed by culvert bombs and cross-border ambushes, road movement of military vehicles was deliberately restricted, insertions and extractions being carried out by helicopter. The permanent observation posts were large affairs consisting of an observation tower and mortar-proof underground accommodation. The large quantities of sandbags and corrugated iron employed in their construction gave them a World War I look, but they were surprisingly comfortable within, being equipped with telephones and video equipment, and each post had its own ACC personnel to supply hot food round the clock. Less attractive was the cesspit sanitary system, which was emptied periodically by the Royal Engineers. Within each OP a routine of three six-hour shifts was maintained, six hours in the tower being followed by six standing by as a quick reaction force and six resting. In other respects the Battalion was engaged in the usual round of patrolling, arrests, finds, bombs and being sniped at, both on the ground and aboard helicopters.

The largest undertaking of the tour was Operation Bullet, the purpose of which was to refurbish several observation posts. Since the IRA had issued death threats to contractors who worked for the Army special measures had to be taken for their protection. This involved picquetting either side of the routes taken by the contractors' plant, material and men, plus top cover flown by helicopters and extra patrols. Naturally, the demands on manpower were heavy and additional companies, drawn from the 1st Battalion The Duke of Wellington's Regiment and the 1st Battalion The King's Own Royal Border Regiment, were placed under

Colonel Freemantle's command for the operation, which was successfully completed during an intense three-week period. "It was quite heartbreaking," wrote Second Lieutenant Mark Hanscomb, the author of B Company's Journal notes, with ringing insincerity, "for us to look out from our warm OP to see our guests soaking wet and tramping around the fields. It even became quite common to hear enquiries about the weather booming over the loud hailer as a patrol went past, generally followed by much laughter!"

Visitors during the tour included the Colonel of the Regiment; the then Secretary of State for Northern Ireland, Mr Tom King; the Mayor of Winchester, Councillor Sue Gentry; Keith Hamilton of the *Southern Evening Echo;* and Miss Karyn Miller, the reigning Miss Royal Hampshire, together with her escort, Miss Angie Gyandeo.

A week in South Armagh without a significant terrorist incident was regarded as a success. In fact, fully half the Battalion's tour passed without such an incident and the Hampshires were obviously inhibiting the IRA's activity to such an extent that it decided to mount one of its major efforts against them. At 11:25 on 16 April it fired sixteen home-made remotely-controlled mortars into Bessbrook Mill from the back of a flatbed lorry. Most landed in the yard, destroying some vehicles and badly damaging others. There was also a great deal of glass broken in the building itself. Fortunately, only half the bombs exploded, leaving others lodged in the roof. Colour Sergeant Robinson and Lance Corporal Moorhouse had been on the point of leaving the Mill in a car when the attack took place but escaped with comparatively minor injuries. There were no other casualties and the work of the Operations Room team was barely disrupted.

The attack, therefore, was hardly an unqualified success and indeed a Y Company patrol managed to cordon off the "base plate" position shortly after the final explosion. More often than not, these weapons were wildly inaccurate and, as the bombs sometimes straddled housing estates, their use by terrorists was disliked by civilians of every persuasion. Thus, when security around Bessbrook was tightened and three permanent VCPs were set up, the local population made it clear they were quite prepared to tolerate the inconvenience. In addition, a company from 45 Royal Marine Commando was placed under command at Bessbrook. The Marines, having gone to some trouble to earn their green berets, wore them on every possible occasion until Colonel Freemantle insisted that they don steel helmets like everyone else, pointing out not only the safety factor but also that badged berets were an immediate disclosure of a unit's identity to the enemy. In passing, it is worth mentioning that during this tour the Battalion wore the new pattern of steel helmet for the first time on active service. The new helmet, having been based on the medieval bascinet, was found to be more comfortable and stable than its predecessor, which had more in common with the long-tailed sallet.

The mortaring of Bessbrook Mill was the most serious attack made on the the Battalion during this tour. On 25 April, however, a heavy explosion was heard from Battalion HQ and Colonel Freemantle, accompanied by RSM Rodda, immediately set out by helicopter to discover its cause. On the main road from the Republic to Belfast he found a large crater around which were strewn human remains and vehicle debris. Some distance from the centre of the explosion he came across the engine block and from the number on this the RUC were able to establish that the car belonged to a Dublin car rental company and had been hired by Lord Chief Justice Gibson and his wife, who had travelled to Ireland by sea and were on their way home. The IRA, aware of this, had obviously monitored the couple's progress and prepared a 300-lb bomb which had been detonated as the car drove over it. Y Company was involved in the subsequent follow-up operation.

There were no further major incidents during the tour and on 3 June the Hampshires handed over the area to the 1st Battalion The Queen's Regiment and returned to Tidworth. On 7 July Colonel Andrew Freemantle relinquished command to Lieutenant Colonel T.A.L.Glass on being appointed Commander of 19 Infantry Brigade. He had enjoyed an interesting period of command spanning Berlin, Tidworth and South Armagh, during which the 1st Battalion had distinguished itself in a number of areas and received its new Colours. He had maintained a high standard of physical fitness within the Battalion and in recognition of this was towed out of Lucknow Barracks on a jogging machine!

Colonel Tim Glass had long-established family connections with the Regiment, in which both his father and grandfather had served, the latter having commanded the 37th over a century earlier. He had himself been commissioned into the Regiment in December 1965 and served as a platoon commander with the 1st Battalion in Sabah, and subsequently with the Battalion in

Germany, Ulster and Hong Kong. As a company commander in the 2nd Battalion Royal Brunei Malay Regiment he was decorated by the Sultan for his services and was later a student at the Indian Army Staff College at Wellington, Southern India. His more recent appointments included that of Second-in-Command of the 1st Battalion in the Falklands and Berlin, and Infantry Tactics Instructor at the Royal School of Artillery, Larkhill.

Flexibility and adaptability are two of the basic requirements of the modern soldier. The Battalion, therefore, expressed little surprise when it was required to provide detachments for ceremonial occasions in London as soon as it returned from post-Ulster leave. The first was route lining for the state visit of King Hassan of Morocco on 14 July, and the second, at the Colonel-in-Chief's request, was to mount a Guard of Honour at the Guildhall when she was granted the Freedom of the City of London on 22 July. For the latter, a Guard of eighty-four men, commanded by Major T.S.Finklaire, was provided. Led by the Band, now under WOI (BM) C.C.Gray, who had taken over from Mr Wood in January 1987, it was to march through the City from Armoury House, the Headquarters of the Honourable Artillery Company, before mounting at the Guildhall, and no complications were expected. However, the Adjutant, Captain R.W.Dennis, aware that the Square Mile was a hotbed of mysterious customs, had done considerable research and the day before the parade he informed the Guard Commander that he would be challenged by the Marshal of the City of London as soon as he crossed its boundary. "He will appear from a side street riding a white horse," he said. "He will be wearing a full length scarlet and gold coat and a tricorn hat with a big feather." Major Finklaire, in no mood for what he took to be adjutantal frivolity, made an appropriate response. Nevertheless, all came to pass as predicted and the Guard gave a creditable performance.

In sporting arena, the Battalion sailing team, consisting of Lieutenant C.N.Macdowell, Lance Corporal Ellis and Private Haswell, won the Infantry Sailing Association's Inter-Unit Cup, which was presented by Major General A.S.Jeapes, OBE, MC. In so doing they qualified for the Army Regatta, finishing a respectable 13th out of 20 in a field that included a number of Olympic yachtsmen. On 31 July the Battalion held its annual inter-company ahtletics day, which was won narrowly by Y Company with 102 points, Z Company coming second with 99 points. Lance

Corporal Hurst of Y Company was awarded the Victor Ludorum for the best individual performance of the day, having established a new Battalion shot-put record with a throw of 12.81 metres and won the long jump. At the end of the meeting the prizes were presented by Mrs Sarah Glass.

In August the Battalion began preparing for several important events which were to take place in the autumn. It had been selected to represent the Army in the Northern European Command Infantry Competition against teams from the Royal Marines, Denmark, Norway, West Germany, Canada and Holland. The competition was known to be challenging in every way with very high standards, reflected by the fact that it had been won only once by the Royal Marines in eighteen years and by a British regular infantry battalion never. Competition for places in the squad was fierce, the original fifty-two volunteers eventually being reduced to the twelve who would actually compete. Training was equally fierce, lasting thirteen weeks, and included visits to the Depot at Lichfield, the Brecon Beacons and the Depot of The Parachute Regiment. The team consisted of: Trainer - Captain C.F.Warren; Captain (non-participating) - Lieutenant J.J.Eldridge; Admin NCO - Sergeant M.R.Day; Squad Commander - Sergeant C.Cockram; Squad Second-in-Command - Corporal A.Marshall; Reserve Squad Commander - Corporal G.Matthews; Privates D.Allen, S.Ashmore, A.Cooper, J.Cooper, M.Domingo, P.Stratton, R.Wake and L.Walton.

The competition was held at Camp Borris, near Esjberg, Denmark, during the first week of October. The first phase, a skills circuit involving assault course work, shooting, map reading and grenade throwing, resulted in disappointing results for the team, which finished in fifth place. During the second phase, night firing, the team produced the remarkable score of 445 points out of a possible 500, only 40 Royal Marine Commando coming close with 400 points; significantly, the nearest score to this was 255 points. The third phase, an 18-km cross-country run interspersed with demanding physical tasks designed to test leadership, teamwork and determination, was the most gruelling, but from it the team again emerged in the lead with 903 points, their closest rivals being the Canadians with 862. During the final phase, day firing, the team hit 99 targets out of 100, scoring 495 points and tying with the Royal Marines for first place. When the results of all phases were consolidated, the Hampshires were pronounced overall winners of the competition, and carried off every trophy but one, having scored a total 2370 points; second were the Royal Marines with 2132, and third were the West German Jäger Battalion 512 with 2129. Astounded disbelief among the team quickly gave way to joy and celebration, echoed in Tidworth when the result was telephoned through.

Meanwhile, a dispute between firemen and their employers in Wales had escalated into a strike and the civil power had requested assistance from the armed services. As a result of this, on 5 October A, B and Y Companies found themselves manning elderly Green Goddess fire engines and driving to West Glamorgan where, respectively, they were stationed at Neath, Swansea and West Cross. B Company were kept very busy and at times had all six vehicles deployed; in sharp contrast, Y Company were left with little or nothing to do. However, just as everyone was getting into the swing of things the strike ended and the Green Goddesses had to be driven back to Tidworth.

Some months earlier, the Regiment had commissioned the artist Emily Patrick to paint a portrait of its Colonel-in-Chief. This was unveiled by the Colonel of the Regiment at Serle's House on 15 October. Four days later, in what was proving to be a very eventful month, the Regiment was granted the Freedom of the Borough of Christchurch during a parade held on the town's Recreation Ground. The parade, commanded by Colonel Glass, consisted of two guards of ninety-six men, the Colours, the Band and Drums, and the Standards of the Comrades' Association.

In his speech the Mayor, Councillor David J.Fox, commented that although, as a result of boundary changes imposed some thirteen years earlier, Christchurch now belonged to the County of Dorset, it had previously, from time immemorial, formed part of Hampshire. The Royal Hampshire Regiment, he said, had a long and illustrious history going back nearly 300 years, during which it had gained no fewer than 153 Battle Honours and won ten Victoria Crosses. Presenting the Freedom Scroll to the Colonel of the Regiment, the Mayor continued, "This Honour is not freely given. It is given by grateful people to deserving people. I hope, Sir, that by this ceremony and by the presentation of this Scroll the gratitude of the people of Christchurch will be conveyed to the Men of The Royal Hampshire Regiment. I also hope that in some small way this famous Regiment, and all those associated with it, may be encouraged by today's ceremony to go on to maintain at all times your proud traditions, pray God in peace, but if necessary in war. In this way our traditions and our heritage will not only be preserved from aggression without but also strengthened and purged from meaningless friction within."

After his reply thanking the Mayor and the Borough, Brigadier Long presented the Mayor with a Regimental plate. The parade then exercised the Regiment's privilege as Honorary Freemen and marched through the town with usual Honours, being entertained afterwards to lunch at the Leisure Centre.

On the morning of 23 October 1987 the 1st Battalion carried out another Freedom March in Winchester. The parade consisted of two guards of ninety-six men, the Battalion's Old and New Colours and the Band and Drums. Its purpose was twofold, firstly to lay up the Old Colours in the Cathedral, and secondly the Dedication of the Regiment's *Third Book of Remembrance,* which already contained the names of seventy-two men who had given their lives since 1946.

After marching down the High Street the parade was drawn up in front of the Guildhall to receive the Colonel-in-Chief with a Royal Salute. Having invited the Mayor of Winchester, Councillor Major D.F.Covill, MBE, DCM, to inspect her Regiment, the Princess, accompanied by the Colonel of the Regiment, followed the Mayor and Colonel Glass during the inspection.

At the Cathedral the Old Colours were marched up the nave to the slow march *Scipio* and, on their reaching the altar, Colonel Glass requested the Dean, the Very Reverend Trevor Beeson, to accept them into the safe-keeping of the Cathedral. Together, the setting, the ritual and the music, in which the Band accompanied the Cathedral's full choir, provided a moving service for the congregation of almost 1400 people. The 1st Lesson was read by the Colonel of the Regiment and the 2nd Lesson by the Reverend John Berry, who had been Chaplain to the Battalion during the Malayan Emergency.

After the Dean had dedicated the *Third Book of Remembrance* in the presence of the Colonel-in-Chief and relatives of those whose names were inscribed therein, he gave a sermon which reinforced the themes addressed by the Mayor of Christchurch a few days earlier, namely remembrance, gratitude and dedication. In a reference to those in society who seemed incapable of understanding the power inherent in tradition, he said:

"Those of us who have served in any great institution, whether it be a regiment, or a school, or a parliament, or a church, know that its ability to move forward depends not only on its insights and technical excellence in the present but also on the powerful thrust it receives from the past. The accumulation of loyalty and commitment, devotion and service, from the past generates, mysteriously, tremendous power in the present, and those of you who have served in fighting units will know this better than anyone."

After the service the Battalion and their families were entertained to a ploughman's lunch by the City in the Guildhall, at which the Colonel-in-Chief was present. There were also buffets for the officers and the Comrades, and their guests, at, respectively, Serle's House and Newburgh House.

The remainder of the autumn was spent by the Battalion in conversion training with the new SA 80 rifle and the Saxon wheeled APC. The SA 80, which had already been used in the Northern European Command Infantry Competition, was a short, automatic rifle the design of which had not sacrificed barrel length. It was handy to carry and possessed a high rate of fire. It had from the outset been designed for use with an optical sight, but in the event of this being damaged folding conventional sights could be used. It weighed 11lbs and, unlike the SLR, could be sloped for drill and ceremonial parades.

The Saxon had been designed as a replacement for the now-ancient Pig and, although it clearly had an application in the internal security role, its defined use lay in providing "protected mobility out of direct contact with the enemy." The Battalion's establishment was forty-three Saxons, each of of which could carry a complete infantry section for whom firing ports were provided, and was fitted with a commander's fixed cupola on which a GPMG could be mounted. The MT Platoon, notably Sergeant Meopham, Corporals Tyrrell and Gloyn, and Lance Corporals Ingram, James and Brackstone, ran a series of cadres to equip drivers and commanders with the necessary skills, which were tested during Exercise Saxon Tiger. The Battalion also introduced the rest of the Brigade to the Saxon and ran a series of study days for the 1st Battalions The Queen's Regiment and The Devonshire and Dorset Regiment.

Everyone returned from Christmas leave keenly anticipating Exercise Grand Prix, which would take the Battalion to Kenya for six weeks' training - so much so that Essential Swahili was much used and "Jambo, Bwana!" became the accepted form of greeting in Lucknow Barracks. Training, including the Battalion Skill-at-Arms Meeting on 18/19 January 1988, was geared to the exercise and from 10 to 21 February the Battalion flew out.

In Kenya, Battalion HQ was located at Nanyuki with a main resupply depot at Kahawa, near Nairobi. The companies rotated for the various phases, which included a course at a Jungle Training Camp, run by Captain Chris Warren and two SAS instructors, at Kathendini on the southern slopes of Mount Kenya; field firing at an isolated training area known as Mpala Farm; rest and recuperation at Watumu on the coast; adventure training in various areas; and a final exercise.

The objects of Exercise Grand Prix were to develop individual self-confidence and allow junior commanders to develop their independence. At any one time the Battalion was dispersed in ten widely separated places, many of which provided extremes of terrain and climate, but everyone coped with these. Professionally, the training was invaluable, but perhaps the least expected by-products of the exercise were the dozens of unsolicited letters received by Colonel Glass from local residents, tourists and others, complimenting the Battalion on the good nature, cheerfulness and professionalism of its soldiers.

There were, too, for those taking part, unforgettable experiences including, among others, climbing on Mount Kenya, expeditions to Lake Naivasha, Lake Turkana (formerly Lake Rudolf), Thompson's Falls and the Masai Mara Game Reserve. Some were fortunate enough to visit Elsamere, the house where Joy Adamson, the author of *Born Free*, lived, watch the video of her life there and enjoy tea on the lawn while colobus monkeys played nearby.

The Battalion returned to Tidworth during the first week of April, having genuinely enjoyed its East African experience. There was, however, much to occupy its collective mind, including administering the Ten Tors race on Dartmoor, two Freedom Marches and an exercise the following month. The first Freedom March took place at Romsey on 12 May. This was the first occasion on which the Battalion was inspected by two Mayors, as the town now formed part of the Borough of Test Valley; it may also have been the first occasion on which the SA 80 was used ceremonially in the United Kingdom. The march through the streets was joined by a mounted contingent including Saxon APCs, Fox armoured cars and Land Rovers carrying Milans, the Salute being taken at the Corn Exchange in the Market Place by the Mayor of Test Valley, Councillor Mrs Doris Bunting, and the Town Mayor of Romsey, Councillor Air Commodore Peter Ruston. Afterwards, the Battalion was given a civic reception at the Crosfield Hall. The second Freedom March took place two days later at Portsmouth, with two ninety-six-strong Guards marching in sixes to the Guildhall Square, where they were inspected by the Lord Mayor, Councillor K. Hale. The parade ended with the firing of a *feu de joie*, after which the soldiers were generously entertained in the Guildhall. During the evening the Band and Drums joined the Bands of the 1st Wessex (Rifle Volunteers) and 2nd Wessex (Volunteers) to Beat Retreat on the Square before a large and appreciative crowd which included 500 international submariners. The Comrades and their Branch Standards were on parade for both Freedom Marches, during which the Regiment received a fine welcome from the public. On 25 May the Colonel-in-Chief honoured Regimental Headquarters with a short visit during which she was shown round the Museum and the Memorial Garden as well as attending a meeting of the Regimental Committee.

At the end of May the rifle companies deployed for Exercise Saxon Rose in Norfolk, where the Saxons were put through their paces as part of the build-up for the year's major exercise in Denmark. June provided a varied month with B Company hosting a day's visit by the Winchester College CCF and a composite company acting as prison guards for a week at Rollestone Camp, near Larkhill, which had been opened by the Home Office to alleviate overcrowding elsewhere. On 17 June the Battalion hosted a party for civic dignitaries from Hampshire who spent a busy morning watching the companies at work and were then entertained at an informal reception in the Officers' Mess. The month ended with Exercise Wiltshire Pheasant, in which the UKMF (United Kingdom Mobile Force), commanded by Brigadier D.P.Thompson, MC, put the final touches to its deployment plans for Denmark. This was followed on 12 July by a Brigade-sponsored training week intended to hone a variety of individual skills ranging from cross-country driving to vehicle recovery and morse. Lest future readers regard the last as being a little archaic, it should be remembered that the Warsaw Pact was expected to indulge in wholesale radio jamming and in such circumstances, as one brewer claims for his product, morse can often reach parts that other means cannot.

Meanwhile, the Band and Drums, Sergeant S.J.Tubb now being Drum Major, were taking part in the Royal Tournament at Earl's Court, providing two performances a day for three weeks. The theme marked the 400th Anniversary of the Spanish Armada with a finale including massed bands, motorised galleons and fireworks. Taking part in the Tournament were over 600 musicians, fifty horses, three Royal Naval field gun teams, the Hong Kong Motor Cycle Display Team, and a tribe of Red Indians; luckily, as one member of the Drums Platoon recalled, someone had found room for an audience as well!

The UKMF Exercise Bold Grouse, involving a Battalion move by road and ferry to Denmark, occupied most of September. Altogether, some 1600 troops took part, making it the largest NATO exercise ever held in that country. The first phase involved co-operating with the Danish Home Guard and thereafter the exercise took the usual form of holding a defensive position followed by a counter-attack. It was adjudged to have been a very successful conclusion to a two-year period of training. Among those observing was the Commander UK Field Army, Lieutenant General Sir David Ramsbotham, who was entertained with coffee and Danish pastries prepared in the depths of 5 Platoon's command trench by Privates Greig and Illingworth.

On its return home the Battalion devoted much of October to adventure training, including climbing, caving, fell walking and canoeing. In response to an idea put forward by Lance Corporal Williams, a keen cyclist, an eleven-strong team led by Second Lieutenant Gareth Babbs, Intelligence Corps, undertook a sponsored cycle ride covering the 880 miles from Land's End to John o' Groat's in aid of Cancer Research.

The Ulster order of battle had now been adopted in preparation for a two-year accompanied tour in Londonderry, with Z Company again becoming a rifle company and, after due process of selection, the Reconnaissance Platoon transformed itself into the Close Observation Platoon. Concentrated training for Northern Ireland began in November with a commanders' cadre and courses for those required to perform specialist tasks. December passed with the usual festivities and on return from block leave in January 1989 the NITAT training cycle began, with visits from

General Sir Charles Huxtable, Commander-in-Chief UK Land Forces, and Major General Jeapes. Once again, this opportunity was used for platoons to compete for the Winchester Trophy, which was won by the Milan Platoon for the second year running.

On 25 March a Battalion Service of Dedication, attended by the Colonel-in-Chief, was held in Winchester Cathedral. The 250 soldiers in combat dress, accompanied by some of their families, were joined by the civic dignitaries of the County and serving and retired members of the Regiment and Comrades. During the service, the Colours having been placed on the altar by the Dean, the 1st Lesson was read by Colonel Glass and the 2nd Lesson by the Colonel of the Regiment. The sermon was given by the Reverend Alexander Boyd who, in July, was to follow the Battalion to Londonderry to become the Senior Chaplain of 8 Infantry Brigade. After the service, the Princess conversed with members of the Battalion's families at Prior's Hall and then attended a buffet luncheon at Abbey House, where she met representatives of the city and the Regiment.

Few of those present in Winchester Cathedral that day could have imagined that this was the last time in the Regiment's long independent history that the 1st Battalion would go forth against The Queen's enemies.

* * * * * * * * *

TIDWORTH AND SOUTH ARMAGH 1986 — 1989

STATISTICS RELATING TO THE 1st BATTALION'S
1987 TOUR IN SOUTH ARMAGH

Major Incidents
17 January   Find of sawn-off shotgun and imitation pistol in Newry.
30 January   Arson at Council offices in Newry.
21 February Find of 300lbs of explosive in Crossmaglen.
14 March   Irish National Liberation Army member's body discovered
               at Border Crossing Point No 3.
29 March   Find of hand grenade in Newry.
7 April   Bomb explosion in shop in Newry.
12 April   Body found on Border Crossing Point No 5.
16 April   Mortar attack on Bessbrook base.
25 April   Murder of Lord Justice and Lady Gibson.

Terrorist Equipment Recovered
2 imitation pistols
1 sawn-off shotgun
26 rounds of 5.56mm ammunition
601lbs of homemade explosive
1 set of bomb-making equipment

Vehicles checked
16,342 private cars
238 motor cycles
5019 commercial vehicles, including two attempting to smuggle large quantities of petrol to the Republic, the discovery of these resulting in GOC's Commendations for Captain A.M.Prior and Lance Corporal Domingo.

Movements by Air
333,250 people (enough to fill 1190 VC10s)
300 tons of rations
513,000 litres of water (enough to fill a junior Olympic swimming pool)
100 tons of sandbags
300,000 litres of generator fuel

Aviation: 1520 flying hours involving the consumption of 2,100,000 litres of aviation fuel, enough to drive the average car 400 times around the world.

CHAPTER 20

LONDONDERRY 1989 — 1991

IRA activity - the Battalion's operational cycle - car bomb attack on married quarters - changed attitude to security forces - friendly policy produces results - Colonel Tim Glass hands over the Battalion to Lieutenant Colonel P.A.Davis - further anti-terrorist successes - collapse of the Warsaw Pact - manpower problems - visits of the Colonel-in-Chief and Freedom Town Mayors - Regimental visit to Tunisian war cemeteries and battlefields - *Options for Change* - implications and questions arising - outbreak of the Gulf War - Minden Day 1990 - welfare donations from Freedom Towns - murder of five soldiers of The King's Regiment and a civilian worker by proxy bomb - contrasts with 1979 tour - Christmas 1990 - course of the Gulf War - the Battalion returns to England

In Londonderry the IRA was concentrating on the murder of what it called "soft" targets. Just a few days before the 1st Battalion took over from the 1st Battalion The Green Howards, the RCT driver of the services' school bus was shot and killed as he went to collect the children during the afternoon. Again, on the night of 8/9 March 1989, only hours before the Royal Hampshires were due to assume operational control, a Land Rover carrying eight gunners from 18 Battery, 32 Field Regiment, RA, was blown up by a 400-lb landmine on the Buncrana Road, within the city boundary. Two of the gunners were killed instantly and a third lost an eye, but the remainder miraculously survived with minor injuries.

The Battalion was based east of the Foyle in Ebrington Barracks, which it shared with HQ 8 Brigade, commanded by Brigadier J.W.Parker, OBE, and its married quarters were situated at various locations including Campsie and Ballykelly. During the first half of the tour, A, B and Y Companies, commanded respectively by Majors Nick Sim, Rory Steevenson and Bob Russell, would work on a fifteen-week cycle, with five weeks west of the Foyle in Fort George and independent bases in Rosemount and Masonic Camps. They would then have two weeks' leave after which they carried out guards and duties and acted as the Battalion reserve for five weeks before final work-up training prior to their return to the city. Z Company had permanent control of the Waterside district but rotated its platoons through a similar cycle.

Shortly after the Battalion's arrival one area of the married quarters was attacked with a car bomb. A telephone warning was given and there were no casualties, but several quarters were severely damaged. As a result of this incident the quarters were fenced off and patrolled. If the bomb had been intended to intimidate the families it failed dismally. They remained perfectly steady, supporting Wives' Club events and attending to their children's education which, in the Ulster tradition, placed great emphasis on the three Rs. The Battalion was proud of them.

Despite the increased level of terrorist activity, Colonel Glass sensed that there had been a change of mood among the local people. "It is clear that the inhabitants of Derry are totally fed up with the Troubles. Walking around the hard Catholic estates one cannot escape the underlying feeling of goodwill and sympathy that exists towards us as soldiers. More people are prepared to speak to us than I can ever remember from previous tours. More people recognise that in searching their cars or houses we are just doing our jobs - providing we do these things professionally and with humour and sensitivity. In short, they realise it is the IRA alone who perpetuate this ghastly state of affairs. Thus, although things appear worse in Londonderry and Ulster than they have for some few years, there is in my mind an unjustified but nevertheless persistent feeling of optimism."

Having been a company commander during the Battalion's 1979 tour in the city, Colonel Glass recognised that once again the essential character and good nature of the Hampshire soldier could be used to improve the situation. It came quite naturally to the Hampshires to be fair, firm and friendly in their dealings with people, and also to greet those they had met before in their daily round of patrols. Furthermore, many of the senior ranks were familiar with the city and its problems from the previous tour so that it was possible to reactivate the feeling of goodwill between the Battalion and the local people which had existed then. This was true also of the relationship which developed between it and all the churches in the city and the practical assistance given to youth groups. By now, too, weariness with the Troubles had produced a Peace and Reconciliation Group with which the Battalion worked closely, winning more friends. It was, of course, understood that there were those in the loyalist and republican communities who would never accept each other, and indeed that some on both sides had a vested interest in maintaining the Troubles, but overall the atmosphere was lightening. The results of the Battalion's friendly policy were so rapid as to be tangible, for the level of violence dropped by comparison with that which had preceded its arrival and with the remainder of Northern Ireland. This was achieved by a huge and relentless work rate involving immense pressure on NCOs and soldiers, and eternal guard duties, all performed under the constant threat of bomb, mortar and sniper attack.

Nothing, however, could be taken for granted. July marked the 20th anniversary of the beginning of the Troubles. Tension increased to the extent that the Battalion was fully deployed for a whole week and the media began making block bookings in the city's hotels. The IRA, planning a mass murder that would have led to bitter communal violence, planted a 180lb bomb on the route of the Apprentice Boys' March, but this was discovered by one of the Battalion's patrols and rendered harmless. Elsewhere, good policing by the RUC, with the Battalion's support, saw to it that trouble was stopped before it could get properly started. The crisis passed without a major incident and the media departed.

Among the numerous visitors received by the Battalion during its first nine months in Londonderry were General Sir John Chapple, GCB, CBE, ADC, Chief of the General Staff; Lieutenant General Sir John Waters, KCB, CBE, GOC Northern Ireland; Major General R.J.Hodges, OBE, Commander Land Forces Northern Ireland, and Major General David Thompson, CBE, MC, his successor; the Colonel of the Regiment; Mr Tom King,

Secretary of State for Northern Ireland; Sir Patrick Mayhew, the Attorney General; and Mr Neil Kinnock, Leader of the Opposition, who entered into the spirit of his visit by conducting the Band while wearing a beret with a Regimental badge.

On 11 September, after an eventful and memorable period of command, Colonel Tim Glass handed over the 1st Battalion to Lieutenant Colonel P.A.Davis on being appointed Commander of 48 Infantry Brigade in Hong Kong, the second successive commanding officer to be appointed directly from the Battalion to a Brigadier's Command. Colonel Paul Davis was commissioned into the Regiment in 1969 and had served as a platoon commander in Minden Company. During subsequent service with the 1st Battalion he was Anti-Tank Platoon Commander, Regimental Recruiting Officer, Adjutant and a rifle company commander, serving in Germany, Ulster, Hong Kong and the Falklands. His external appointments after Staff College, Camberley, included Chief of Staff to 7th Armoured Brigade, British Exchange Officer at the US Army Infantry School, Fort Benning, Georgia, and, immediately prior to assuming command of the 1st Battalion, he was a member of the Directing Staff at the Staff College. He could not believe his luck at teaming up again with RSM Baker, whom he had first known as his platoon radio operator in 1971 in Malaya. Such associations lie at the very heart of the Regimental system.

During the next five months there were a number of serious incidents, including the destruction of vehicles in Major Bob Russell's rover group, the members of which were fortunately some way from their vehicles when two devices exploded. Large quantities of terrorist hardware were captured as a result of routine operations and, as Colonel Davis recorded at the time, the Battalion's community relations policy was beginning to pay substantial dividends:

"The hijacking of vans on the Creggan Estate [19 December 1989] that eventually led us to the find of six mortars the following day, was initiated by a number of telephone calls to the RUC from local inhabitants in the Creggan. Again, on 1 March 1990 similar warnings were given and, in a joint Army/RUC operation, we netted an RPG-7 with warhead, a machine gun, a pistol and four arrests. These warnings, given while the hijackings and house take-overs were actually taking place, were unprecedented. Also, civil disorder in estates like the Creggan, Bogside, Brandywell and Gobnascale is now almost non-existent. Youths throwing stones at Army Land Rovers or foot patrols are equally rare. The vast majority of the population are totally fed up with the terrorists and realise that they have nothing at all to offer the community. More are now prepared to publicly denounce them."

Before proceeding further it is necessary to examine events which would lead to a major turning point in the world's, and the Regiment's, history. The experience of the Soviet Army following its invasion of Afghanistan in 1979 had been catastrophic. Faced with a large-scale rebellion by the Islamic fundamentalist Mujahideen, it opted instinctively for a counter-productive policy of brute force rather than winning hearts and minds. In 1986 Mikhail Gorbachev's public reference to Afghanistan as a "bleeding wound" revealed the effect that the war was having. By 1989 the Soviet Union was virtually bankrupt and, unable to sustain either the war or its global commitments, it abandoned the puppet regime in Kabul to its fate.

Suddenly, the incredible happened. One of history's mightiest and most evil empires simply collapsed within the space of a few months. Throughout the Warsaw Pact countries there had emerged a new generation of politicians who were quick to take advantage of Soviet impotence. Poland had already gone some way down this road, but the real rot began when Hungary and Czechoslovakia opened their borders to East Germans seeking passage to the West. Unable to staunch the flow, the East German regime fell apart, the hated Berlin Wall was demolished and the reunification of Germany began. One after another, the remaining members of the Pact threw out the tyrannical old demagogues who had ruled them for so long, and finally the USSR itself disintegrated into a number of independent republics. Remarkably little blood was shed, the only serious resistance to change being offered by isolated pockets of secret police who clearly had much to lose.

The Cold War was over and since the possibility of armed conflict between East and West in Europe was now extremely remote, both sides agreed to proportional reductions in their forces and the destruction of surplus armaments. Just how this would affect the British Army, and particularly the Regiment, was to be revealed shortly. In the meantime, life for the 1st Battalion in Londonderry continued as before.

A shortage of manpower remained a problem throughout the tour although the Regiment was making every effort to retain trained men and attract new recruits. To ease the situation and release men for active duty, the first elements of a WRAC platoon joined the Battalion at the end of December. Ultimately, this would include drivers, clerks, cooks, mess stewardesses and medical assistants. Further men were obtained under the Divisional reinforcement scheme, involving platoon-sized drafts from other regiments within the Prince of Wales's Division joining the Battalion for six months in succession, as well as attachments from regiments outside the Division.

On 25 January 1990 the Colonel-in-Chief, wearing combat dress, paid an informal visit to the Battalion and spent much time talking with the soldiers at various locations. Her presence was a huge boost to morale. Miniature uniforms and helmets, obtained by the outstanding Quartermaster, Major Bob Le Galloudec, were presented by Corporal Havers to the Princess for Prince William and Prince Harry. The much-photographed visit attracted world-wide attention and was fully reported even in such organs as the *Kansas City Star* and the *Alabama News*. On 20 February the Colonel-in-Chief also attended the Colonel of the Regiment's Dinner at Serle's House.

Between 16 January and 6 March nine Mayors from the Regiment's Freedom Towns and the Mayor of Medina each paid a two-day visit to the Battalion, including Councillor Mrs M.Weston, Mayor of Basingstoke and Deane; Councillor N.A.Best, Mayor of Southampton; Councillor F.G.Allgood, JP, Mayor of Winchester; Councillor H.Bostock, Mayor of Bournemouth; Councillor J.C.Ritchie, Mayor of Medina, Isle of Wight; Councillor J.Moss, Mayor of Christchurch; Councillor E.A.Sier, Mayor of Test Valley, Councillor B.A.Oliver, Mayor of Rushmoor; Councillor G.Mead, Mayor of Romsey; and Councillor Miss G.Howard, Lord Mayor of Portsmouth. They were given a tour of the Battalion's operational area and naturally spent some time with soldiers from their own towns, discussing local matters. All left having made the same three points. Firstly, they were astonished by the superb council housing in the Bogside, now said to be the best in Europe, which showed how much had been achieved socially and economically in the past twenty years. Secondly, they were surprised by the soldiers' spartan living conditions in the outstations. And thirdly, despite this, they were deeply impressed by the cheerful and competent manner in which the soldiers carried out their difficult and dangerous tasks. Once again, the fact that Hampshire's civic dignitaries had taken the trouble to visit "their" soldiers in the Battalion went down extremely well with all ranks.

In March Z Company (Major Graham Martin) were relieved of responsibility for the Waterside area and entered the Battalion's operational cycle, which was extended to sixteen weeks. Training presented obvious difficulties, although Colonel Davis was able to arrange for each company to undergo a three-day exercise at Ballykinler. Whenever possible, too, small groups of soldiers were sent off on adventure training expeditions, some of which took them as far afield as the United States, Corsica, Sardinia, Gibraltar, Morocco and France. Both the training at Ballykinler and the expeditions were essential to allow soldiers to escape the pressures and tensions of Northern Ireland operations for a little while.

In March 1990 the Colonel of the Regiment, accompanied by the Bishop of Sherborne, the Right Reverend John Kirkham, a former National Service Officer in the Regiment, Colonel B.Gater, TD, Lieutenant Colonel H.E.Wingfield, MC, and Lieutenant Colonel H.D.H.Keatinge, led a fifty-nine-strong party to Tunisia. The party included representatives of the 2nd, 1st/4th (TA), 2nd/4th (TA) and 5th (TA) Battalions. Altogether, 270 soldiers of the Regiment are buried in the Commonwealth War Graves Cemeteries in Tunisia, a further 122 soldiers who have no known grave being commemorated on memorial panels. The cemeteries at Medjez-el-Bab, Beja, Massicault, Oued Zarga and Enfidaville were all visited and wreaths laid at their Cross of Sacrifice. They were carefully tended, beautiful and peaceful places. Next, the party visited the battlefields of Tebourba, Sidi Nsir and Hunt's Gap. It was then invited to tea at the Residence of the British Ambassador to Tunisia, where Brigadier Long presented the Ambassador, Mr Stephen Day, with a print of the painting showing Major Le Patourel winning the Victoria Cross at Tebourba. On 29 March a service was held at St George's Church, Tunis, during which the Colonel of the Regiment and Mr S.J.Ferbrache, DCM, unveiled a Regimental Memorial Tablet.

The spring and summer months in Londonderry were one of the quietest periods on record since the Troubles began, reflecting the considerable amount of work undertaken by the 1st Battalion in support of the RUC. However, on 25 July Mr Tom King, now Secretary of State for Defence, provided the House of

Commons with details of the anticipated reduction in the strength of the armed services. The proposals were contained within a document entitled *Options for Change,* which was in itself something of a subconscious apology as no options were on offer. The effect of the proposals would be to produce a Royal Navy similar in size to that which the first Elizabeth had sent out against the Armada, an Army smaller than that available to Marlborough, when the country's population was a fifth of today's, and the smallest Royal Air Force in history. Within the infantry, the number of battalions was to be reduced from fifty-five to thirty-six, a reduction of over one third.

The shock within the armed services was shared by the general public. In the light of recent events the public accepted that some cuts were inevitable, but those proposed went dangerously deep. Indeed, one had only to look around to see the damage already wrought by previous cuts. For example, in the entire south-eastern corner of England, not one of the original County regiments remained; by degrees, the Queen's Royal Regiment (West Surrey), the East Surrey Regiment, the Middlesex Regiment, the Buffs (Royal East Kent Regiment), the Queen's Own Royal West Kent Regiment and the Royal Sussex Regiment, had been amalgamated to form The Queen's Regiment, consisting of three Regular and two Territorial battalions. With the example of the Falklands before them, the public was aware that wars came suddenly and from nowhere, yet apparently the government had learned nothing from the experience since, under the new proposals, the services would be severely stretched to meet their commitments with no margin left for contingencies.

The government seemed genuinely surprised at the intensity of public and media reaction. In vain would it reiterate such phrases as "maintained nuclear deterrence," "collective defence with our allies," "smaller but better," and, of course, "increased flexibility." The public had heard them all so often before that they had become mere catchphrases. There was, too, a promise to "preserve the regimental system." It has now become clear that *a* regimental system is a more accurate description than *the* regimental system.

To save yet more money, the Ministry of Defence imposed a ceiling on the number of recruits who could be accepted by regiments in any one year; it then appeared to target battalions known to be under strength. To those such as The Royal Hampshire

Regiment, whose retention rate was among the best in the Army and who had a waiting list of recruits, the integrity of Whitehall seemed akin to that of the double-headed penny. History would remember *Options for Change* as it had the Cardwell Reforms over a century earlier, but whereas the verdict of posterity was that Cardwell had been constructive, it seems unlikely that *"Options"* will be regarded in so generous a light.

With supreme irony and appropriate timing, another war blew in from nowhere. On 2 August 1990, Saddam Hussein, the ruthless dictator of Iraq, invaded the tiny oil-rich state of Kuwait in an attempt to restore his finances after a costly eight-year war with Iran. He chose to ignore United Nations Resolution 660, condemning the action and calling for him to withdraw. Likewise, diplomatic and financial pressure failed to change his mind. It was clear that he would have to be removed by force and, since he possessed the fourth largest army in the world, this would require considerable effort. A military Coalition, including the United Kingdom, the United States, France and members of the Arab League, began assembling troops in Saudi Arabia for the task. The British contingent included an armoured division of two brigade groups, drawn mainly from Germany. For the moment, *Options for Change* became a prisoner of circumstances and was temporarily shelved.

Meanwhile, faced with the more immediate problems of Londonderry, the Regiment's 1st Battalion celebrated the 231st Anniversary of the Battle of Minden with a march around Ebrington Barracks, led by the Band. Among those present were the Colonel of the Regiment, Mrs Long and very popular Miss Samantha Jane Williamson, the reigning Miss Royal Hampshire. After the parade Brigadier and Mrs Long, Colonel Davis, RSM Mulligan and Miss Williamson toured the Battalion's outstations to distribute roses, which were worn with pride by those setting out on patrol. During the evening a Minden Day Celebration Dinner was held in the Officers' Mess, at which the guests included Lieutenant General Sir John Waters, Lady Waters, Major General David Thompson, Assistant Chief Constable Maurice Johnston and Chief Superintendent Clive McComb of the RUC.

Another visitor, early in September, was Councillor Derek Burdle, Chairman of the New Forest District Council. As mentioned earlier, all the Freedom mayors had expressed concern at the poor living and recreational facilities for those soldiers operating in the city outstations. They had evidently continued to discuss the subject afterwards and to help improve the situation they had each contributed £300, making a total of £3000; in addition, Rushmoor contributed a brand new pool table. The Battalion felt itself very fortunate indeed to have such loyal and supportive Freedom Town Councils. All these welcome visits needed much organisation by the Adjutant, Captain Christopher Warren, and his successor, Captain Johnathan Eldridge.

During the autumn the Brigade Commander carried out his official Staff Inspection, subsequently writing to Colonel Davis as follows: "My official report will be with you within a week. It will reaffirm the extent to which I now find 1 R.Hamps fully fit for their exacting and tricky role....Thank you for a thoroughly pleasant day which made me feel close to a Battalion that I admire and whose friendship and support I cherish."

IRA activity continued at a low level with periodic sniping and hijacks, but on 24 October there occurred the worst incident of the tour. Having achieved very little since the Battalion's arrival, the Provisionals decided to employ a new and particularly cowardly form of attack for the first time. This was the so-called "proxy bomb" which involved holding a civilian's family hostage while he drove a vehicle packed with explosives into the designated objective where, if he was lucky, the bomb would be detonated by remote control when he had got clear. At this period the Battalion had under command a company of the 1st Battalion The King's Regiment which was responsible for manning the permanent vehicle checkpoint on the Buncrana Road. This was the terrorists' target and the ensuing explosion killed five Kingsmen and a civilian kitchen worker at Fort George, Patsy Gillespie.

"None of us who saw the results of this 1000-lb bomb will forget either the devastation it caused or the resulting feelings of anger and shame within the local community," wrote Colonel Davis. "The condemnation of this outrage was unequalled. The address by the [Roman Catholic] Bishop of Derry at Patsy Gillespie's Requiem Mass was moving, and I have yet to hear such a blistering and unequivocal attack against the IRA."

This tragic incident apart, it was clear that in Londonderry great change was under way. Major G.J.Martin, commanding Z Company, recalls some of changes which had become apparent since the 1979 tour. "A large expressway sweeps traffic around the city centre. Now there is just a huge gap where the Rossville Flats used to be. The flats used to be a difficult obstacle to cross on patrol, providing a high platform for dropping missiles on unwary troops below. There was an OP on top of the flats which often experienced crack and thump. The gas works has disappeared and the nearby housing of the Bogside has undergone a massive rebuilding and renovation programme. This has undoubtedly improved the living standards of the Bogsiders. The routine of guards and patrols is much the same. More gratifyingly, whilst we complain about the number of static guards we do now, the dreaded gates that controlled access to the city centre, which was then full of bombed out derelicts, has gone. We had to shut the gates each evening with a ceremony nearly as complex as that of the Keys at the Tower of London. It was, however, far more deadly and very nearly claimed some Royal Hampshire lives. Once shut, some of these gates then had to be guarded all night. The city centre was then deserted. Now it is a vibrant shopping centre by day and the pubs and clubs are full at night. Then, the RUC were unable to operate anywhere outside the city centre. Now, the public expects to deal with the Police and not the Army in most areas."

Events such as the annual Lundy parade, when up to 5000 Orangemen and 200 bands converged on Londonderry to burn in effigy the wretched Colonel Lundy, who had wished to surrender the city to James II three centuries earlier, or the republican commemoration of Bloody Sunday, when a number of people had been killed during the major disturbances of 30 January 1972, required large-scale clearance and patrolling prior to and during the day, but the Battalion's friendly, even-handed approach ensured that these passed without serious incident.

The Colonel of the Regiment paid another visit shortly before Christmas and on 22 December the new Brigade Commander, Brigadier John Sutherell, OBE, attended a party in the Officers' Mess. On Christmas Day itself Colonel Davis visited all the outstations with the traditional "gunfire," which was especially enjoyed by the sangar sentries.

Half a world away, the Gulf War had begun in earnest on 17 January 1992 with a sustained air offensive designed to destroy the Iraqi command, communications, control and logistic structure. Within days the enemy's air force had fled abroad. Saddam's divisions, of which no fewer than forty-one had been crammed into Kuwait, were then subjected to several weeks of continuous air attack. No army could endure such a battering for long and when the Coalition opened its ground offensive on 24 February it found that all the fight had been knocked out of its semi-starving opponents. In 100 hours of fighting the Iraqi army in Kuwait was completely destroyed. The Allies sustained very few casualties, of which the majority were caused by battlefield accidents. Brief as it was, two aspects of the campaign were of interest to the Regiment. The first was that the planning and execution of the final ground offensive bore marked similarities to Megiddo 1918, in which the 1st/8th Battalion took part, and the second was that the five Royal Hampshires serving with the 1st Battalion The Staffordshire Regiment in 7th Armoured Brigade were the last members of the Regiment to take part in a major campaign.

It had been hoped that the Gulf War would provide the government with time and reason enough to reconsider its *Options for Change* policy, but apart from the cancellation of a couple of regimental amalgamations, this had not been the case, and its proposals would be implemented as quickly as possible.

The final months of the 1st Battalion's tour in Londonderry were very quiet. It had made many friends and, as it handed over to the 3rd Battalion The Royal Anglian Regiment in May 1991, it was sorry to leave them behind. Shortly after its departure for Roman Barracks, Colchester, Colonel Davis received the following message from Lieutenant General Sir John Wilsey, GOC Northern Ireland:

"Your Battalion has made a most positive contribution to the overall security situation and community relations in Londonderry. Throughout the tour all members of the Battalion have shown a friendly, dedicated and flexible approach to their various tasks."

In fact, as recorded elsewhere, the Battalion had acquired an international reputation for its expertise in the fields of peace keeping and community relations, not least in Russia.

* * * * * * * * *

LONDONDERRY 1989 — 1991

ADVISING THE RUSSIANS

During the 1st Battalion's second year in Londonderry, John Lampen of the Peace and Reconciliation Group contacted Colonel Davis with a request that he would speak to a delegation from Russia. Their visit was made on behalf of the Russian Centre for Political Studies and the Institute of Conflict Studies in Moscow and co-ordinated in London by Quaker Peace and Service. The delegation included mediators and leaders from the Northern Caucasus, which was afflicted by troubles similar to those in Ulster, and members of other Russian groups interested in the subject of conflict resolution. After clearance had been obtained the delegation arrived on 15 January 1991. It was clearly most interested in the Royal Hampshires' approach to peace keeping and the role of the Peace and Reconciliation Group in mediating between the security forces and different sections of the community. Having contrasted this very favourably with the Soviet forces' violent behaviour in the Baltic republics, which appeared on television during its visit to Northern Ireland, the delegation expressed a wish that Colonel Davis and Mr Lampen should visit Moscow to describe the Ulster conflict in the interests of reducing violence.

In due course invitations to attend a seminar in Moscow that September were received from the Soviet Peace Committee and the Ministry of the Interior (MVD) Academy. Colonel Davis and Mr Lampen were asked to contribute to the seminar and join in discussions, met a number of senior officers and two Deputies of the Russian Parliament's Security Committee, and gave a television interview. They received the impression that their views were taken very seriously and even actively endorsed by some of those present.

The MVD possesses its own army, the function of which is to deal with civil disorder, and its members wear military or police uniforms, depending upon the role they are required to perform. A day spent with the MVD's Dzherzhinsky Division was therefore one of the more interesting highlights of the visit. The divisional commander explained that he was unable to demonstrate active training as most of his men were helping with the harvest, a yearly task for the armed services. However, weapons, vehicles and training aids were freely exhibited. As crowd control weapons evidently consisted of live ammunition and stun grenades, some discussion took place on the merits of baton rounds. Having presented the divisional museum with a Regimental plaque, Colonel Davis was asked to sign the visitors' book; the last British visitor to do so was Winston Churchill!

It was, as Colonel Davis commented, difficult to assess the practical value of the visit, but Russian senior officers were certainly keen that further exchanges should take place. The possibility exists, therefore, that when inter-communal strife has broken out within the new Russian Federation, it is with Royal Hampshire methods that the MVD has contained it. We shall probably never know.

CHAPTER 21

AMALGAMATION

Discussions regarding amalgamation - press reaction to announcement - celebration of Minden Day 1991 at Portsmouth - Freedom March at Basingstoke - the Regiment honoured with the Freedom of Eastleigh - training in Kenya - A Company disbanded 19 December 1991 - Colonel Paul Davis relinquishes command of the 1st Battalion to Lieutenant Colonel T.M.Reeve-Tucker - emergency tour of Y Company in Northern Ireland - acceleration of amalgamation process - the Regiment honoured with the Privilege of Jersey - Farewell Freedom Marches at Southampton, Romsey, Bournemouth, Lyndhurst, Christchurch and Aldershot - final Farewell Parade, Freedom March and Service of Remembrance at Winchester - the last days

It is necessary now to return briefly to the events of the previous months. Once the Berlin Wall had come down even the lowest-powered crystal ball gave clear indications that cuts in the armed services were inevitable, albeit perhaps, not on the savage scale actually inflicted. It was also apparent that The Royal Hampshire Regiment was terribly vulnerable, partly because it was one of the very few of the original County Regiments to have retained its independence, and partly because the recruiting strictures unfairly imposed by the Ministry of Defence rendered the 1st Battalion a natural target.

Immediately after the government's announcement on 4 June 1991 that the strength of the Army was to be reduced by 40,000 to 116,000, Brigadier Long attended two meetings with his fellow Colonels of the Prince of Wales's Division to examine the implications and discuss the options for amalgamations. On the basis of geography alone, if two amalgamations were required between the four former Regiments of the Wessex Brigade, The Gloucestershire Regiment would amalgamate with The Duke of Edinburgh's Royal Regiment (Royal Berkshire and Wiltshire) and The Devonshire and Dorset Regiment would amalgamate with The Royal Hampshire Regiment. The option of amalgamation with The Gloucestershire Regiment, which had nearly materialised in 1970, was never seriously considered, not least for logical geographical reasons.

For Brigadier Long and the Regimental Committee the essential priority was to safeguard the career prospects of serving officers and soldiers of the Regiment, in addition to preserving the link with the County. The Regiment's submission to the Army Board accepted with reluctance the possibility of amalgamation with either of its neighbouring Regiments, The Devon and Dorsets or The Duke of Edinburgh's Royal Regiment, but also included as an option what Brigadier Long proposed as an imaginative idea to resurrect a famous County Regimental name; that was, to form a single-regular-battalion Regiment from the counties of Hampshire and Sussex, to be called The Royal Sussex and Hampshire Regiment. The same submission included a caveat, since the danger was apparent, that the Regiment was not inclined to amalgamate with The Queen's Regiment, whose traditions as a large multi-county Regiment were so in contrast with those of a closely-knit single-battalion County Regiment with the closest of County ties. It came almost as a physical shock, therefore, when Tom King, Secretary of State for Defence, announced to the House of Commons on 23 July 1991 that The Queen's Regiment and The Royal Hampshire Regiment were to amalgamate to form a Regiment of two regular battalions, thus saving two battalions out of the four which existed.

Shortly afterwards, having insisted on their right to meet the Chief of the General Staff, the Colonels of the two Regiments began a series of meetings to discuss the terms of the amalgamation. It was soon clear that the particular association between Sussex and Hampshire was a non-starter. It was also evident that the Colonels would have to agree to delegate detailed negotiations to an Amalgamation Committee consisting of serving officers, and, in the case of the Regiment, a Warrant Officer.

AMALGAMATION

Each side discussed matters with goodwill, and in the spirit of compromise eventually came up with a formula that was acceptable to both. Perhaps it can be said that the Royal Hampshire team negotiated at a slight advantage in that they spoke only for their own Regiment, whereas the Queen's team were simultaneously conscious of their six forbear Regiments. Yet, valued differences apart, The Royal Hampshire Regiment and the forbears of The Queen's Regiment had much in common. Over the centuries, they had served together on many battlefields around the world and at Salerno in 1943 the three Hampshire battalions of 128 Brigade and the 2nd/4th Battalion had fought alongside no fewer than six battalions of the original Queen's Regiment (2nd Foot). The question of title caused much difficulty and in the end the decision was left to the Army Board, which from the alternatives submitted chose the title The Princess of Wales's Royal Regiment (Queen's and Royal Hampshires). It was decided at the time that the new Regiment would come into being towards the end of February 1993.

The reaction to the news within Hampshire itself was encapsulated in an Editorial of the *Southern Evening Echo*

DEFENCE AXE CUTS HEART OF HAMPSHIRE

A very special part of Hampshire history came to an end yesterday as a result of a heavy blow inflicted by the axe of Government defence cuts. Although Tom King's announcement of amalgamation probably comes as no surprise to the Tigers, now based at Colchester, it does not lessen the degree of sadness and measure of pain which greeted the news. Sad for the Regiment, as it changes its traditional identity forever, and sad for the County of Hampshire. The Regiment is deeply proud of its centuries-old links with Hampshire, and keeping the connections was one of the main priorities it insisted on during the high-level, behind the scenes negotiations leading up to yesterday's House of Commons announcement. It is time for everyone to say a heartfelt and sincere thank you to our very own soldiers for all they have done on our behalf. Wherever the "Happy Hamps" have served, they have brought credit and pride to the name of Hampshire. In their quiet way they set a standard in all they do that few regiments have ever come near to beating. Whatever lies ahead, the Tigers can be assured Hampshire will always be a special place for them.

Meanwhile, following post-Northern Ireland leave, the 1st Battalion had returned to Roman Barracks, Colchester, where it became part of 19 Infantry Brigade, commanded by Brigadier C.D.Farrar-Hockley, MC. Its first task was to prepare for a number of ceremonial occasions, beginning with Minden Day, which was celebrated in Portsmouth at the invitation of the Lord Mayor, Councillor Brian Reed, in the presence of the Regiment's Colonel-in-Chief. The day began at Portsmouth Cathedral with a Service of Thanksgiving to mark the 1st Battalion's safe return from Northern Ireland. On her arrival at the Cathedral the Princess of Wales was greeted by a Guard of Honour from the Hampshire and Isle of Wight ACF and presented with her Minden Rose by In-Pensioner WOII Terry Hyatt. The Colours were borne up the nave to the slow march *Minden Rose,* composed by Bandmaster C.C.Gray, and placed upon the drums by the Cathedral's Provost, the Very Reverend David Stancliffe. During the service, attended by a 1200-strong congregation, the Lessons were read by Colonel Davis and the Colonel of the Regiment, and the Address was delivered by the Bishop of Portsmouth, the Right Reverend Timothy Bavin. At the end of the service the Colonel-in-Chief made a symbolic presentation of roses to the Colonel of the Regiment, the Vice Lord Lieutenant of Hampshire, General Sir David Fraser, the Lord Mayor of Portsmouth, Colonel Davis, the Parade Guard Commanders, Major S.A.C.Frere-Cook and Major G.J.Martin, and the Chairman of the Comrades' Association, Lieutenant Colonel Hugh Keatinge.

The 1st Battalion then exercised the Regiment's Freedom by marching through the city from the Cathedral to the Guildhall Square, where 180 members of the Comrades' Association and the ACF contingent were already drawn up. Just one week had passed since the amalgamation had been publicly announced and an enormous crowd had gathered, wishing to demonstrate its affection for the Regiment. The Regiment had always received a hearty welcome in Portsmouth, but this occasion surpassed all others, for, as the 1st Battalion marched through the arch leading into the Guildhall Square, it was greeted with a roar of spontaneous cheering and sustained applause that echoed around the buildings. Having been accorded a Royal Salute on her arrival, the Colonel-in-Chief invited the Lord Mayor to inspect the parade. After he had done so, he gave a speech emphasising the strong ties which existed between the city and the Regiment, and to this Brigadier Long replied. The parade continued with a Troop by the massed bands of the Regiment and The Duke of Edinburgh's Royal Regiment and the 1st Battalion's Corps of Drums, ending with a spectacular display of drumming, after which the 1st Battalion fired a *feu de joie*. The parade concluded with a march past by the Battalion, the ACF and the Comrades, the Salute being taken by the Lord Mayor. Afterwards, the city entertained the participants to a magnificent buffet luncheon during which the Colonel-in-Chief mingled freely with soldiers and civilians alike.

The following day the 1st Battalion exercised the Regimental Freedom of Basingstoke, where it received an equally warm and enthusiastic welcome. Here, because of security considerations — the IRA having already carried out attacks on parades and bands in mainland UK — the police recommendations regarding the route to be taken were accepted. This complicated the format of the parade somewhat but all went well and the 1st Battalion, represented by two half Guards of forty-eight men and the Colour Party, followed by a contingent of the Comrades' Association, marched past the Town Hall where the Salute was taken by the Mayor of Basingstoke and Deane, Councillor R.A.O'Bee, accompanied by the Colonel of the Regiment. After the parade the Regiment enjoyed truly generous hospitality at a civic reception held at a marquee in the park.

The third ceremonial occasion took place on 14 September when the Borough of Eastleigh conferred its Freedom on the Regiment. The parade took place at Leigh Memorial Park, the 1st Battalion being represented by two half Guards of three officers and forty-eight men each, the Colour Party and the Band and Corps of Drums. Councillor Michael Buckingham, the Mayor of Eastleigh, presented the Colonel of the Regiment with a silver casket containing the Freedom Scroll, and received a Regimental plate in return. During the subsequent march past the Salute was taken by the Mayor, accompanied by Brigadier Long, and, once again, the Regiment was warmly applauded by a large and appreciative crowd.

In the meantime, the Battalion had been honing its basic infantry and sporting skills which, of necessity, had taken second place to operational requirements in Londonderry. There had, for example, been no competition for the Minden Trophy during the past two years, and in July it was fiercely contested in nine sports with Y and Z Companies tying for first place. The contest for the Winchester Trophy took place over three days in September and involved speed marches, assault and obstacle courses, a 12-mile march-and-shoot and tests in all manner of military skills. The contest was won by 9 Platoon of Y Company, commanded by Second Lieutenant Leigh Young, the most recently joined subaltern, and Sergeant Shaun Cummings, who was himself newly promoted.

Elsewhere, the Band had been extremely busy. Among its other engagements it had travelled to Vienna to play at The Queen's Birthday Reception at the British Embassy, where a former Band President, Lieutenant Colonel Peter Hughes, was serving as Military Attaché, and also participated in a parade with the Band of the Austrian Guards Battalion, its hosts. On its return home it gave concerts in Romsey Abbey, St Mary's Church, Portsmouth, as a result of which the Regiment was able to donate £1100 to the completion Appeal for Portsmouth Cathedral, and at the Portsmouth Guildhall.

In October the Battalion began flying out to Kenya for Exercise Grand Prix, which was to last until 11 December. This had been the subject of much pleasurable anticipation and followed the form of the previous visit to East Africa, with companies undergoing in turn jungle training at Kathendini, section and platoon training at Dol Dol, live firing at Mpala Farm, adventure training, a rest and recuperation period with trips to the coast and a final exercise at Archer's Post. Visitors included the UKLF Field Army Commander, General Wilkes, Brigadier Farrar-Hockley and the Colonel of the Regiment. Unfortunately, the early stages of what proved to be valuable and enjoyable training were marred by the tragic death of Lance Corporal Trevor Ring, who sustained fatal injuries when struck by a civilian vehicle.

Colonel Davis's stated aim for the exercise was that all ranks should experience the most challenging, satisfying and enjoyable training of their careers so far. The vast training areas provided total freedom both for original and imaginative field training and tactical training. The variety in climate and terrain - jungle, bush and semi-desert — and the altitude fully tested the fitness and self-discipline of all ranks and the initiative and leadership of junior commanders. There was also immense scope for adventurous training and unique opportunities to climb Mount Kenya or fish for sailfish and blue marlin in the Indian Ocean.

The capping of manning levels was already making serious

inroads into the Battalion's strength. A Company was therefore disbanded on 19 December 1991 and its personnel were transferred to the other companies or posted. This marked the first major step in reduction towards the designated amalgamation level. After Christmas leave all soldiers were asked to complete pro formas indicating where they would prefer to continue their service. During the ensuing months many hours would be spent negotiating the best possible deal for them and frequent briefings were held in the gymnasium to keep everyone informed. Some members of the Battalion would continue their service with the 1st Battalion of the amalgamated regiment, some with its 2nd Battalion, and some would be posted to other infantry regiments. Some would be leaving the Army anyway as their engagements expired and others would be content to end their service with a redundancy payment. However, involuntary redundancy could not be avoided altogether and this was applied as fairly as possible at every level. Occurring as it did in the middle of a severe economic depression it would hit some men hard, despite the temporary cushion provided by their severance payments.

On 5 February 1992 Colonel Paul Davis relinquished command of the 1st Battalion to Lieutenant Colonel T.M.Reeve-Tucker on being appointed Military Assistant to the Quartermaster General. Colonel Mike Reeve-Tucker had originally been commissioned into Minden Company and had subsequently served with the 1st Battalion in Malaya, Hong Kong, Northern Ireland, Germany and England as a platoon commander, anti-tank officer, operations officer, and company second-in-command. In 1984 he had commanded a company in Berlin and then served as a Military Assistant to the Chief of the General Staff. In 1988 he became the 1st Battalion's Second-in-Command while it was based at Tidworth. Prior to passing through Staff College his extra-Regimental tours included periods as an instructor at the Brigade Depot in Exeter and on the Platoon Commanders Division at the School of Infantry, and as a staff officer with 20th Armoured Brigade. More recently he had been posted to the German Army's School of Infantry at Hammelburg as British Liaison Officer, with accreditation to the German Parachute and Mountain and Winter Warfare Schools in southern Germany. His father, it will be recalled, had commanded the 1st Battalion in Münster 1964-1966, and while it was, therefore, sad that he would preside over the Battalion's last months, he had already been designated as the first Commanding Officer of the 1st Battalion The Princess of Wales's Royal Regiment.

Within twenty-four hours of taking over Colonel Reeve-Tucker received orders to deploy one company to serve with the 2nd Battalion The Queen's Regiment on an emergency tour in Northern Ireland. The task fell to Major Paul Newton's reinforced Y Company, which thus became the last formed body of The Royal Hampshire Regiment to see active service.

The tour lasted from 10 February until 28 March. Initially the Company was based in Magherafelt but later moved to Dungannon in County Tyrone. During its first week in the Province four IRA terrorists were shot dead in Coalisland and it was given the task of protecting the RUC from the crowds of republican supporters attending the funerals, which took place over a period of two days. Although the potential for trouble clearly existed, the event passed with little more than turgid graveside orations delivered by Gerry Adams. There were the usual patrols, shootings and several finds. The tour also provided a welcome opportunity for the Hampshires and the Queensmen to get to know each other. Each pretended never to have heard of the football teams supported by the other, but both laughed and groused at the same things and the final verdict was that there was no real difference between them.

In February B Company took part in Exercise Phantom Bugle, the concluding exercise of the School of Infantry's current Combat Team Commanders' Course, on Salisbury Plain. For five days the Company manned Warrior IFVs, making the pleasant discovery that for once the infantry vehicles outpaced the Chieftain tanks with which they were working.

During the spring it was learned that two Queen's Battalions would be returning from Germany and Cyprus and be based at Colchester and Canterbury. The Director of Infantry accepted Colonel Reeve-Tucker's submission that it was in no one's best interest to have the 1st Battalion and a Queen's Battalion, both under strength, sitting about in Colchester awaiting amalgamation the following February. It was therefore agreed that the amalgamation should be brought forward and take place on Salerno Day, 9 September 1992. Brigadier Long then contacted the Freedom cities, towns and districts proposing that the Regiment should exercise its rights for the last time with a farewell parade during the summer. The response was favourable and meant that within the last year of its existence the Regiment would have exercised all its Freedoms.

First, however, because of its long association with the island, The Royal Hampshire Regiment was to receive the Privilege (Freedom) of Jersey, a unique honour which had never been accorded to any other military unit before. The 1st Battalion sailed from Marchwood to the island aboard the LSL *Sir Galahad* and were joined there by a contingent of Comrades for the parade which took place in Royal Square, St Helier, on 9 May, the anniversary of Jersey's liberation from German occupation. After the Lieutenant Governor, Air Marshal Sir John Sutton, KCB, had inspected the parade, the Privilege was conferred on the Regiment by the Bailiff of Jersey, Sir Peter Crill. In his reply the Colonel of the Regiment referred to the many Jersey men who had served or were still serving with the Regiment and presented the Bailiff with a Regimental Plate. The Corps of Drums then gave a short display and the Battalion fired a *feu de joie*. Accompanied by ninety-three Comrades, their Standards and the Standard of the Royal Militia Island of Jersey, the Battalion marched through the narrow streets of St Helier, receiving much appreciative applause, and on to the Town Hall, where the salute was taken. After the march the Battalion, the Comrades and their ladies were generously entertained at a civic reception. The following day the Battalion returned to the mainland aboard *Sir Galahad*.

The Winchester Trophy was competed for during 1 and 2 June on the Thetford training area and won by Second Lieutenant Young's 9 Platoon. On 18th June the 1st Battalion entertained most of the Freedom Mayors and representatives of the Hampshire press. Brigadier Long expressed the Regiment's thanks for their past support and the hope that they would continue to support the new Regiment. They were then conducted round a series of stands illustrating the modern soldier at work, fired the pistol and the SA 80 and, under WOII Wright, underwent a period of drill on the square. During lunch Colonel Reeve-Tucker thanked Alan Cairns of the *Basingstoke Gazette* and Larry Signy of the *Aldershot News* who had always given the Battalion sympathetic coverage after their many visits in England and Northern Ireland. He also paid special tribute to Keith Hamilton of the *Southern Evening Echo* and, on behalf of all members of the Officers' Mess, presented him with a silver tiger to mark a special relationship extending back many years.

A week of farewell Freedom Marches began on Saturday 27 June. The form of each parade was similar, the Regiment being represented by the Colours, two Guards and the Band and Corps of Drums. Marching with them were a contingent of the Comrades with Standards and, where appropriate, a contingent of the Hampshire and Isle of Wight Army Cadet Force. The parade, having formed up, marched through each town with "Drums Beating, Bayonets Fixed and Colours Flying," being cheered and applauded by the crowds lining the pavements.

At a suitable point on the route the local Mayor took the salute accompanied by the Colonel of the Regiment. After each parade, all those taking part were generously entertained by the Councils to a civic buffet reception. Because of the very short routes at Romsey and Lyndhurst, at these two towns there was an additional bonus of an inspection of the parade by the Mayor and the firing of a *feu de joie*.

To recount the course of these parades would be needlessly repetitious, but the following notes from the Journal convey the special atmosphere of each occasion.

"At Southampton on 27 June the sight of the Regiment marching through the historic Bar Gate and the pedestrian precinct, which was thronged with Saturday morning shoppers, will long be remembered by those present. Afterwards, the kind words of the Mayor, Councillor Nora Goss, were particularly appreciated by the Regiment, especially as she had discharged herself from hospital that very morning in order to take the salute and entertain those on parade.

"The parade at Romsey (29 June) was highlighted by the cosy and intimate atmosphere created in Palmerston Square, dominated by its statue and flanked on one side by the Town Hall. There, the Regiment sensed the warmth and heartfelt support of the townspeople, who had turned out in force.

"The enduring memory of Bournemouth (30 June) was the splendid arena created by the Pier Approach as the Colours were marched on parade. This was followed by a very long and undulating route around the perimeter of the Lower Gardens. At the reception in the ballroom of the Pavilion we were all privileged to meet Mr William Farr, MM, aged 97, who had won his Military Medal at

Passchendaele and who, sadly, was to die shortly after this parade.

"The terrible weather at Lyndhurst (1 July) totally failed to detract from the wonderful setting of Bolton's Bench in the middle of Hampshire's ancient and beautiful New Forest. Although our spirits might have been slightly dampened, they were soon raised by a reception held in marquees on the lawn of Apple Tree Court, which was second to none.

"The welcome given by the citizens of Christchurch (2 July) to their County Regiment confirmed it all. The boundary changes of 1974 were irrelevant. Once a Hampshireman, always a Hampshireman!

"There was a fitting climax at Aldershot (3 July), when once again the weather left much to be desired. On this occasion, the Comrades stole the show with the participation of 101-year-old Bill Pearce, the oldest Tiger on parade during the whole week. Almost exactly 76 years after he had gone over the top on the first day of the Somme, he insisted on staying in the front line and was pushed in his wheelchair along a rain-soaked route by former Corporal Tony Robinson."

The competition for the Minden Trophy took place between 7 and 16 July and was based on performance in a number of representative sports including athletics, cricket, soccer, cross-country running, sailing, basketball, volleyball and swimming, B Company emerging as the final winners. On 17 July a twelve-strong team under Second Lieutenant Young and Corporal Jones left for the Nijmegen Marches, the last day of which attracted over a million spectators. The team succeeded in raising £800 for the Great Ormond Street Children's Hospital.

The final Farewell Parade and Freedom March took place in Winchester on 23 July in the presence of the Regiment's Colonel-in-Chief. Winchester contained the heart of the Regiment and Tigers of all ages had converged on the city from far and wide. They included very large contingents of officers, from all the Comrades' Association Branches, and from the Sergeants Past and Present. The sky had looked ominous when some 800 serving and retired members of the Regiment began to assemble on the square of Peninsula Barracks but as ranks were formed the

sun broke through. On the stroke of 11:00 the column, commanded by Brigadier Tim Glass and headed by the Band and
Corps of Drums, left the Barracks, paying its first compliments
of the day to the Chairman of the Hampshire County Council,
Mr Dudley Keep. It then took the traditional route down the High
Street to the Broadway, lined with appreciative crowds waiting to
welcome it and, as always, windows were thrown open to watch
the Regiment go by. Though it marched in sixes, the column
stretched for almost the full length of both thoroughfares. Behind the Band came the 1st Battalion's No 1 Guard, followed by
the Colour Party and No 2 Guard; then the officers led by Brigadier Gordon Viner; the Comrades, marching in two Guards with
their massed Standards between; and finally the Sergeants Past
and Present under their Chairman, Major Roger Coleman. If the
public's welcome for the Regiment as a whole was warm and heartfelt, it was especially so for the bemedalled Comrades, for here
were men who had survived the hideous trench battles of World
War I; men who had kept the peace in India and elsewhere in the
Empire; veterans of Dunkirk, Malta, Tebourba, Sidi Nsir, Salerno,
Cassino, the Gothic Line, D Day, the Normandy Beachhead and
the Rhineland; and those who, in more recent years, had fought
terrorists in Palestine, Malaya and Northern Ireland, as well as
saving countless lives in the hurricane-torn Caribbean; all marching like younger men with heads up and shoulders back, demonstrating their pride in the Regiment and their part in its long
history. Warmest of all was the welcome for those who, disabled
or too infirm to march, joined the parade in their wheelchairs,
accompanied by the Regiment's In-Pensioners from the Royal
Hospital, Chelsea.

As the parade approached King Alfred's statue prior to
wheeling for the march past it was joined by Brigadier Bob Long,
who thus almost certainly became the first Colonel to march at
the head of the Regiment since the eighteenth century. The
Salute at the Guildhall was taken by the Mayor of Winchester,
Councillor Wing Commander John Nunn, accompanied by the
Colonel-in-Chief. Among those marching past were seven brigadiers and the oldest Comrade on parade, centenarian William
Pearce. The column then marched to Winchester Cathedral for a
Service of Remembrance while the Princess of Wales, who had
earlier been presented with a posy by four-year-olds Kirsty Brown
and Emma Hack, the daughters of serving soldiers, delighted the

crowd with a walkabout before rejoining her Regiment.

Within the Cathedral, which was filled to capacity, the Colours were borne up the aisle to the slow march *Minden Rose* and placed upon the altar. During the service there were readings by the Colonel of the Regiment and Brigader Gordon Viner, and while the hymn *I Vow To Thee My Country* was being sung the pages of the three volumes of the Regimental *Book of Remembrance* were turned by Mr Ernie Billett (World War I), Brigadier David Warren (World War II) and Private Watkins (post 1946). The Last Post followed by Reveille was then sounded by Band Sergeant Major Maddocks. As the passage quoted below shows, the Sermon delivered by the Bishop of Winchester, The Right Reverend Colin James, was notable for the understanding and comfort with which it addressed the profound sadness and sense of loss giving rise to this proud occasion:

"No one knows better than a soldier the horrors of war, and its evil. It is a strange paradox that out of the misery and wretchedness of war some of the finest human qualities can emerge. Courage, yes; comradeship in adversity, the determination to overcome in dreadful conditions, unselfishness, trust and reliance on one another, the refusal to let others down; the strong bond between officers, NCOs and private soldiers; without false sentiment, a band of brothers. And their friendships are sustained by the Comrades' Association, and these values are acknowledged and affirmed by Hampshire people in our quiet and understated way. We recognise that a good Regiment, well led, trained and resourced, clearly identified with the County from which it is recruited, is a force for good. It contributes to the stability of our Country and its strength. The Freedoms conferred by our cities and boroughs are public testimony to this.

"The conviction that out of evil good can be wrested and secured lies at the heart of the Christian faith. God, who identifies Himself with our human lot in Jesus Christ, enters into the richness of His creation and all that is good in human life. He also experiences the pain and the evil and the rejection that man can inflict, and in that suffering He forgives and reconciles, and brings and offers resurrection. We therefore have hope — hope and confidence that life conquers death, that good prevails over evil, justice over wickedness; that God is at work in the world to heal, to transform and renew, and that ultimately He reconciles all things to Himself; 'nothing of good or value is forever lost', and we have eternal life in Him and fellowship with one another."

After the service the Freedom Mayors were presented to the Princess of Wales in the Regiment's Memorial Garden. Before the party moved on, she was photographed with them, and with all the serving officers who could be present. The congregation, meanwhile, had been making its way to the two receptions. One was held in the Great Hall of Winchester Castle, one wall of which was dominated by the huge Round Table, and here the County and the city had combined to entertain magnificently over 400 members of the Regiment. Nearby, on the square at Peninsula Barracks, another 1000 members of the Regiment and their families were entertained in four marquees. The Colonel-in-Chief was present at both receptions, meeting as many people as possible, including officers of the 49th (Sault Ste Marie) Field Regiment, Royal Canadian Artillery, who had travelled to Winchester for the occasion. If the day could hardly be described as a happy one, the Regimental family still contrived to enjoy itself.

Back at Colchester the 1st Battalion celebrated Minden Day with a parade during which, at the command 'Fall In The Officers', the Band struck up the theme from *The Muppet Show*, causing considerable laughter. Roses were distributed and, for the last time, the Battalion marched past the Colonel of the Regiment. During the evening the Band and Drums Beat Retreat and, while the buglers sounded Sunset, the Battalion flag was lowered by Corporal M.R.Slater, accompanied by the Adjutant, Captain M.R.Hanscomb. For many, this was the worst moment of the entire amalgamation process and will not be dwelled upon; those who know what is involved do not need reminding, and those who do not can imagine. The bad moment over, the evening continued with an excellent All Ranks Ball during which celebration of happy times past was combined with optimism for the future. The party continued well into the early hours of the following day. "It was," reflected the B Company scribe, "the very best way to bid fond farewell to the Regiment. It was an Irish wake of the highest order and the mother of all parties!"

It also effectively marked the end of the 1st Battalion, which went on leave next day, although there would be an Officers' Farewell Dinner, to which the Warrant Officers were invited, and much administrative work remained to be done. The Band, which had numbered among its summer engagements performances at the Seville Expo, at Cardiff Castle with representatives of all the Regiments of the Prince of Wales's Division, and at a Buckingham Palace garden party, gave its last concert at the Milner Hall, Winchester. This was followed by a dinner at Newburgh House, attended by 130 Band members past and present.

The days passed and at midnight on 8 September 1992 the 290-year independent history of The Royal Hampshire Regiment came to an end. Simultaneously, that of The Princess of Wales's Royal Regiment (Queen's and Royal Hampshires) began.

* * * * * * * * *

EPILOGUE

"NOTHING OF GOOD OR VALUE
IS FOREVER LOST"

The Right Reverend Colin James, Bishop of Winchester   *23 July 1992*

I t is one of history's eccentricities that armed bodies of worth should continue to exercise a fascination centuries after they have ceased to exist. Learned archaeologists still discuss the possible fate of Legio IX Hispana, which once formed part of the garrison of Britannia and, despite the bad press accorded them by Sir Walter Scott, the forcibly-disbanded Knights Templar are the subject of a stream of books; indeed, some of their customs remain in use to this day in certain legal and masonic circles. Nothing seems more certain than that, at the end of the next millennium, military historians will be examining the British regimental crests carved into the cliffs of the Khyber Pass and in many other places around the world. They will find further traces of those regiments on the best preserved memorials in our cathedrals, churches, towns and villages, and they will reach the inevitable conclusion that they were the work of a people who, in their own special way, were just as remarkable as the Greeks and Romans. Yet, the military historian of the year 3000, possessing all the advantages of highly developed information technology, will have no more difficulty than his counterpart today if he wishes to trace the steps of the 37th at Minden, or the 67th at the Taku

Forts, or the 2nd Battalion The Hampshire Regiment in the Tebourba Gap.

More immediately, there is much of The Royal Hampshire Regiment that has survived. Serle's House, now the Western Head-quarters of The Princess of Wales's Royal Regiment, also contains the Regiment's archives and its excellent Museum, which receives several thousand visitors from all over the world every year, and of course, the Memorial Garden is still carefully tended. The Royal Hampshire Regiment Officers' Association continues, as does the Warrant Officers' and Sergeants' Dinner Fund, the Comrades' Association, The Malaya and Borneo Veterans' Association, and the 6 oh 70s Club, founded by and presided over by Barnie Thompson, the founder of *Tiger Rag*, for those who served in the Regiment during those decades, including several brigadiers. The Hampshire and Isle of Wight Military Aid Fund also continues to make benevolent grants to former Royal Hampshire soldiers who find themselves in need or distress.

The perception with which Brigadier Bob Long and the Regimental Committee led the Regiment along the difficult road to amalgamation has also resulted in many more important survivals, not least that Hampshire still possesses a Regiment to call its own and that this will carry the County's name forward into the future. In recognition of the fact, the County's cities, boroughs and districts which conferred their Freedoms on The Royal Hampshire Regiment have transferred them to The Princess of Wales's Royal Regiment, as was the Privilege of Jersey in 1995.

The Princess of Wales's Royal Regiment (Queen's and Royal Hampshires) numbers among its forbears the 2nd, 3rd, 31st, 35th, 37th, 50th, 57th, 67th, 70th, 77th, 97th and 107th Regiments of Foot, so it is not surprising that it has inherited some 380 Battle Honours, spanning almost the entire experience of the British Army from 1662 onwards. Some arranged marriages do not fare well, but that between the Queen's Regiment and The Royal Hampshire Regiment has been a good one because, from the outset, both parties were determined to work for the common good and, in justice to their forbears, produce a happy and efficient Regiment. The professional soldier does not live in the past, although he respects it and at times will draw great strength from it; the professional soldier lives in the present and prepares for the future.

EPILOGUE

The Hampshire influence within The Princess of Wales's Royal Regiment is very strong. The Regiment celebrates three Regimental Days: Albuhera (Queen's) 16 May, Minden (Hampshires) 1 August, and Salerno (common to both) 9 September. The Hampshire Rose forms a prominent part of the combined cap badge, the Royal Tiger badge is worn on the left upper sleeve of all uniforms save combat dress, and bronze buttons are worn with service dress. The Minden Trophy and the Winchester Trophy are still the subjects of keen competition. The entire Princess of Wales's Royal Regiment, Regulars and Territorials alike, have adopted with enthusiasm the nickname of The Tigers.

Thus, if change, however regrettable, there had to be, it has been approached in the most positive spirit imaginable, and the results have been equally positive. As I said in the opening sentences of my Introduction, if there is a point to be made the Hampshires will make it, quietly, without fuss, and in the manner of a Regiment that never sought to be grand but was always great.

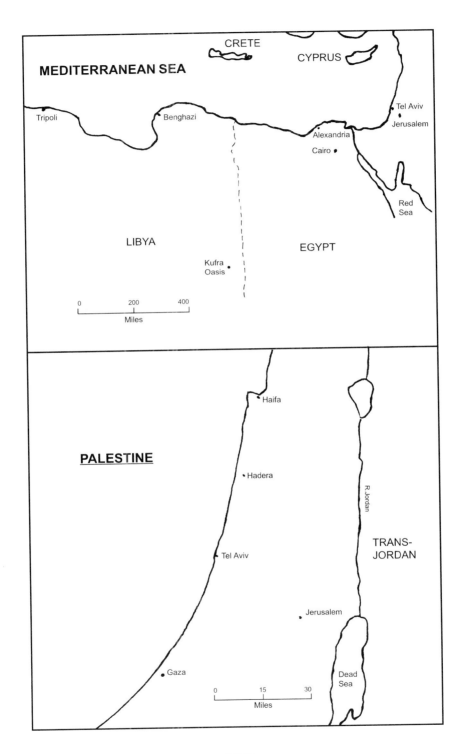

425

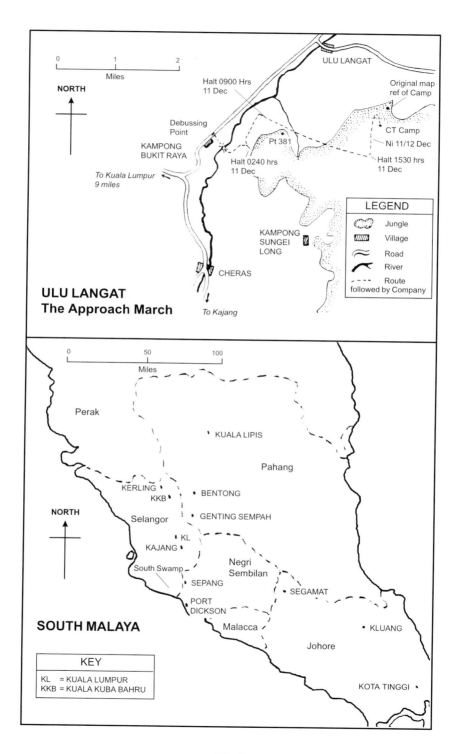

ULU LANGAT
The Approach March

SOUTH MALAYA

426

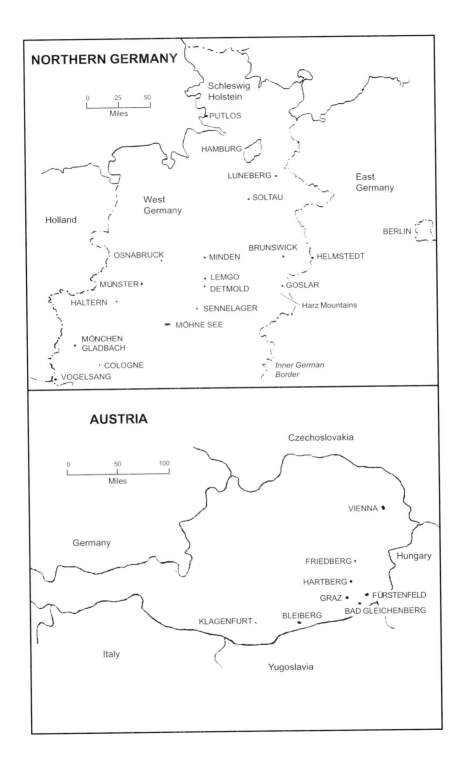

NORTHERN GERMANY

0   25   50
Miles

Schleswig
Holstein

PUTLOS

HAMBURG

LUNEBERG

East
Germany

SOLTAU

West
Germany

Holland

BERLIN

OSNABRUCK

BRUNSWICK

MINDEN

HELMSTEDT

LEMGO
MÜNSTER
DETMOLD

GOSLAR

HALTERN

Harz Mountains

SENNELAGER

MÖHNE SEE

MÖNCHEN
GLADBACH

COLOGNE

Inner German
Border

VOGELSANG

AUSTRIA

Czechoslovakia

0   50   100
Miles

VIENNA

Germany

FRIEDBERG

Hungary

HARTBERG

GRAZ   FÜRSTENFELD
BAD GLEICHENBERG

KLAGENFURT   BLEIBERG

Italy

Yugoslavia

427

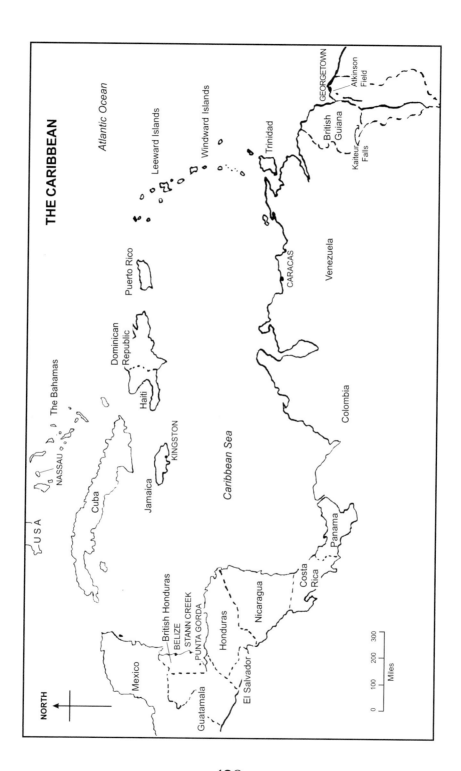

THE CARIBBEAN

NORTH

Atlantic Ocean

Leeward Islands

Windward Islands

Trinidad

GEORGETOWN
Atkinson Field

British Guiana

Kaiteur Falls

CARACAS

Venezuela

Puerto Rico

Colombia

Dominican Republic

Haiti

KINGSTON

The Bahamas

NASSAU

Cuba

Jamaica

Caribbean Sea

U S A

Panama

Costa Rica

Nicaragua

Honduras

British Honduras
BELIZE
STANN CREEK
PUNTA GORDA

Mexico

El Salvador

Guatamala

0   100   200   300
Miles

428

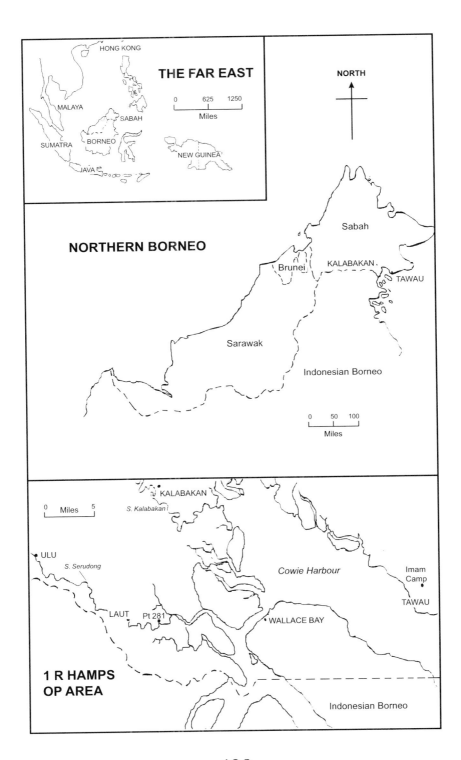

NORTHERN IRELAND

LIMAVADY
BALLYKELLY
LONDONDERRY · KILREA
MAGHERA
STRABANE · MAGHERAFELT · TOOME
HOLYWOOD
Lough Neagh
BELFAST
DUNGANNON · LURGAN
Lough Erne
BELLEEK
ENNISKILLEN ARMAGH BALLYKINLER
LISNASKEA KEADY
NEWTOWNBUTLER NEWRY
NEWTOWN HAMILTON
CROSSMAGLEN

0   10   20   30
Miles

430

APPENDIX 1

THE ROYAL HAMPSHIRE REGIMENT
ROLL OF HONOUR
1946 - 1992

L/Cpl	R	Abel
L/Cpl	K F	Adams
Pte	J R	Ainsley
Pte	T A	Allo
Maj	A E	Amor
Pte	G	Andrews
Pte	P J	Archer
Pte	I	Ashton
Pte	W R	Bartlet
Pte	D H	Bath
Pte	A	Bennett
Cfn	A	Bowen REME
Cpl	R	Birch
Pte	C A	Bishop
2/Lt	D W	Bolam
Pte	D J	Bray
Pte	E G	Bull
Pte	K J	Callaway
Pte	A	Clark
Capt	P B	Chambers MC
Pte	C P	Clifford
Pte	A J	Cockwill
Pte	J	Colley
Lt the Hon	R	Collier
Pte	T	Cotton
Pte	J	Downer
WO2	C F	Dummer
L/Cpl	K A	Falder
Pte	F A	Fallows CHESHIRE
Pte	R W	Ford
Sgt	A	Fox
Pte	R J	Gold
Pte	M	Hogan
Pte	W	Hill
Pte	D J	Hussey
Pte	I R	Jeeves
Cpl	T	Keating RAPC
Pte	T E	Keith

Pte	G	King
Pte	J W	King
Cpl	J W	Leahy DERR
Pte	D	Le Page
Pte	M A	Mason
Pte	P W	Masterman
Pte	M S	Matthews
Pte	T M	McDonald
Sgt	P H	Messham
Pte	B T	Metherill
Pte	T	Mildenhall
Sgt	J W	Morris
Maj	C J G	Mumford MC
Pte	A G	Oram
Pte	D J	Philpott
Pte	K	Randall
Pte	C C	Rawles
Pte	M V	Reeder
Lt-Col	T S W	Reeve-Tucker
Pte	A	Reid
Pte	G H	Richards
L/Cpl	A T	Ring
Pte	A	Roberts
Pte	W R C	Robins
Pte	M A	Sanger
Sig	N J	Saville R SIGNALS
Pte	R E J	Sawyer
Pte	A C S	Sheperd
Pte	B D	Smith
Pre	A C	Sutton
L/Cpl	B D	Swain
Pte	R D	Thorne
Pte	G S	Trickey
L/Cpl	R D	Turkington
Sgt	M P	Unsworth
Pte	A T	Watkins
L/Cpl	R C	Watton
Col	J D	Wellings OBE

Lt   C B   Winchester

APPENDIX 2

THEATRES OF SERVICE
1946 - 1992

AUSTRIA

BORNEO

BRITISH GUIANA

BRITISH HONDURAS

CYPRUS

CYRENAICA

ENGLAND

FALKLAND ISLANDS & SOUTH GEORGIA

FEDERAL REPUBLIC OF GERMANY

GIBRALTAR

GREECE

HONG KONG

JAMAICA

MALAYA

NASSAU, BAHAMAS

NORTHERN IRELAND

PALESTINE

WEST BERLIN

APPENDIX 3

HONOURS AND AWARDS

This list contains the honours and awards made to officers and soldiers of The Royal Hampshire Regiment. The officers given are those who, with certain exceptions, were commissioned into the Regiment. The rank given is usually that held at the time the award was made.

Companion of the Order of the Bath (CB)

Maj Gen	R H	Batten CBE DSO	Maj Gen	R G F	Frisby CBE DSO MC
Col	L W S	Blackmore	Maj Gen	P H	Man CBE DSO MC

Commander of the Order of the British Empire (CBE)

Brig	R H	Batten DSO OBE	Brig	R G	Long OBE MC
Brig	G D	Browne OBE	Col	L J P	Morrish
Col	G J A	Dewar	Col	C C	Smythe MC
Brig	R G F	Frisby DSO MC	Brig	C G T	Viner MC TD
Brig	A C F	Jackson OBE	Col	B J	Willing OBE

Lt Col   J B   Young

Distinguished Service Order (DSO)

Lt Col   P H   Man OBE MC

Officer of the Order of the British Empire (OBE)

Lt Col	V A	Blake	Lt Col	B R	Hobbs DERR
Lt Col	P	Branwell	Lt Col	H D H	Keatinge
Lt Col	J B	Buckmaster	Col	R G	Long MC
Lt Col	K C	Came	Lt Col	P D T	Powell TD
Lt Col	P A	Davis	Lt Col	E S	Purcell
Maj	J G	Dukes TD	Lt Col	T M	Reeve-Tucker
Lt Col	J S S	Gratton	Col	P R	Sawyer MC
Lt Col	D A C	Hannah	Col	D J	Warren DSO MC
Lt Col	R D	Hanscomb	Lt Col	B J	Willing

Lt Col   M F A   Wilson

Member of The Royal Victorian Order (MVO)

Maj   M G P   Chignell

Member of the Order of the British Empire (MBE)

Capt	G W	Alderman
Capt	J	Allen
Maj	H	Baker MC TD
WO1(RSM) H L		Barnard
Maj	J A	Barrow DERR
Maj	H	Brammell
Maj	R G	Bate-Jones
		D AND D
Lt	R W	Coleman
Maj	J E B	Conder
WO2(RQMS) P G		Croucher
Capt	G J A	Dewar
WO2	D E	Duffy
Maj	T S	Finklaire
Lt Col	A W	Freemantle
WO2(RQMS) F		Hale
Maj	F J H	Hayes
Maj	P W L	Hughes
WO2	J M	Jenkins
Maj	R J	Jordan
Maj	W G	Juckes TD
Maj	E C	Kimberley
Maj	B J	Lambert
		STAFFORDS
Maj	S G B	Matthews
WO2	W J	Mills
Maj	W	Parrott
Maj	A	Pearson MC TD
WO1(BM) J		Plant
Maj	W F	Pollard
Capt	W F	Stockdale
Capt	G S	Thomas
Capt	R N	Tillard
WO1(RSM) W R		Watton
WO2(ORQMS) F		Welch
Maj	A R	Withers
Maj	A P	Wright WFR
Maj	E G	Wright MC

The Queen's Gallantry Medal (QGM)

Cpl	A W	Johnson

British Empire Medal (BEM)

WO2	P J	Bailey
C/Sgt	M P	Bardwell
Cpl	L C	Bentley
Cpl		Clarke RE (att 1 R HAMPS)
L/Cpl		Clayforth R SIGNALS (att 1 R HAMPS)
Sgt	E J R	Cook
Cpl	J A	Hartigan
Sgt	W	Hale
Sgt		McLaren
C/Sgt	R	Mitchell
Sgt	W H	Moss
Sgt	G R	Price
Sgt	D G	Scrivens
Cpl	G	Turner
Cpl	K	Walters

Bar to Military Cross

Maj	J M	Symes MC

Military Cross (MC)

Capt	C W E	Coppen-Gardner
Maj	R G	Long

Military Medal (MM)

Cpl	J J	Clarke	Cpl	H T	Smith
Pte	P P	O'Callaghan	Sgt	G	Westall
Sgt	M F E	Pike	Cpl	J H	Wheeler

Bisley - The Queen's Medal

Sgt	J H	Wheeler MM

Mention in Despatches

Lt	N S	Alderman	Lt Col	R G	Long
Cpl	D R	Allen	Cpl	C J	McLaughlin
Sgt	S J	Barter	Lt Col	P H	Man OBE MC
Rev	J R	Berry RAChD	Lt Col	M J	Martin (twice)
Capt	L D	Brown	Maj	W A F	Maynard
Maj	C A	Bulleid	Sgt	J G	Morris
Cpl	J A	Burrell	Lt Col	L J P	Morrish
Sgt	P N	Chadwick	Sgt	M F E	Pike
Maj	E G	Churcher	A/Sgt	R W	Remsbury
Capt	C D	Darroch	Maj	R P	Russell
Maj	G J A	Dewar MBE	A/Cpl	G F	Savage
C/Sgt	A J	Dicker	Lt	N A	Sim
WO2	L B	Edmonds	Capt	A H T	Smith
Maj	A J B	Edwards	L/Cpl	R M	Smith
A/Cpl	K P	Faithful	Maj	J G T	Southwood
Lt Col	T A L	Glass	L/Cpl	R W	St John
Maj	P A T	Halliday	Maj (T/Lt Col) W B Thomas		
Lt	D A C	Hannah	A/Sgt	G F	Townsend
Capt	M R	Hanscomb	Maj	J E	Tull
Cpl	E G	Harris	Cpl	R D	Turkington
Sgt	D E	Henderson	C/Sgt	R J	Wells
Maj	E P G	Hillman	A/Sgt	G A R	Westall
Lt Col	A H T	Hogge	Sgt	J A	Wiles
Lt	J E	Horton	Maj	B J	Willing
Lt Col	P W L	Hughes	Lt Col	M F A	Wilson
WO2	A W	Johnson QGM	Sgt	W T	Winter MM
Lt Col	J R E	Laird	Capt	C G	Wissett-Warner
Sgt	N	Lihou	Pte	W L	Wolland
Maj	V T G	Liles	Sgt	K	Wood

Maj   E G   Wright MC

Meritorious Service Medal

Mr	A	Baird	Mr	W	Gumbley
C/Sgt	M P	Bardwell	WO2(RQMS) F		Hale
WO2	P J	Ferris	Maj	H	Herrington MBE MM
Capt	A	Finnemore	Mr	J E	Palmer MC DCM
Mr	S	Finnemore	WO1(BM) J		Plant
Maj	G	Greenway	Lt(QM) H A J		Plummer

Mr   H Stone

Foreign Orders and Decorations

Malaya

Lt Col	P H	Man DSO OBE MC	The Sultan of Selangor's Meritorious Service Medal

Brunei

Maj	J R E	Laird	Bintang Perwira Agong Negara Brunei 1st Class
Maj	T A L	Glass	Paduka Seri Laila Jasan 3rd Class
Maj	J D K	Kellie	Paduka Seri Laila Jasan 3rd Class

Singapore

Maj	C R	Chandler	Singapore Public Administration Medal

C in C - GOC - Area Commander's Commendations

Sgt	T	Allen	Cpl	K	Dodd
Lt	R H	Arden	Pte	R F	Greaves
Cpl	D A	Ashton	Pte	T	Jackson
Sgt	H K	Baker (twice)	C/Sgt	B R	Jenkins
Pte		Barnes	WO2	D M J	Lawless
Capt	R G	Bate-Jones	Cpl	D	Mort
Cpl	J	Black	Pte	S	Parkes
Pte		Braithwaite	Cpl	K J	Paterson
Lt	C H	Cann	Cpl	T	Purser
L/Cpl		Carter	Sgt	V	Rodda
L/Cpl	C	Cockram	Cpl	D F	Smith
WO2	J	Cockwill	Cpl	A	Thurley
Sgt	A J	Crawley	Sgt	J A	Wiles
Sgt	S	Cummings	Pte		Williams

WO2   D J   Wright

APPENDIX 4

COLONEL-IN CHIEF
H R H The Princess of Wales
1985 - 1992

COLONELS OF THE REGIMENT

1945 - 47	Gen	Sir George D Jeffreys
		1st Lord Jeffreys KCB KCVO CMG DL JP
1948 - 54	Brig	P H Cadoux-Hudson MC DL
1954 - 64	Brig	G D Browne CBE DL
1964 - 71	Maj-Gen	R H Batten CB CBE DSO DL
1971 - 81	Brig	D J Warren DSO OBE MC DL
1981 - 87	Gen	Sir David Fraser GCB OBE DL
1987 - 92	Brig	R G Long CBE MC DL

COMMANDING OFFICERS
1st BATTALION (37th)

1946	Lt-Col	R G F Frisby DSO MC
1947	Lt-Col	R Chandler DSO
1947	Lt-Col	J S S Gratton
1948	Lt-Col	J H H Robinson DSO OBE

COMMANDING OFFICERS
2nd BATTALION (67th)

1946	Lt-Col	J P Fowler-Essen DSO MC
1947	Lt-Col	J H H Robinson DSO OBE
1948	Lt-Col	R Chandler DSO

COMMANDING OFFICERS
1st BATTALION (37th/67th)

1949	Lt-Col	R Chandler DSO
1950	Lt-Col	R H Batten DSO OBE
1951	Lt-Col	R G F Frisby DSO MC
1953	Lt-Col	P H Man DSO OBE MC
1956	Lt-Col	A H T Hogge
1959	Lt-Col	M C Hastings DSO
1961	Lt-Col	D J Warren DSO OBE MC
1964	Lt-Col	T S W Reeve-Tucker
1966	Lt-Col	M F A Wilson OBE
1969	Lt-Col	W R B May MC

MINDEN COMPANY (37th/67th)

| 1970 | Maj | B R Hobbs DERR |
| 1970 | Maj | D A Protheroe |

COMMANDING OFFICERS
1st BATTALION (37th/67th)

1972	Lt-Col	L J P Morrish
1974	Lt-Col	F D J Dickenson
1977	Lt-Col	R G Long MC
1979	Lt-Col	M J Martin
1982	Lt-Col	D H Neville
1985	Lt-Col	A W Freemantle MBE
1987	Lt-Col	T A L Glass
1989	Lt-Col	P A Davis OBE
1992	Lt-Col	T M Reeve-Tucker OBE

ADJUTANTS
1st BATTALION (37th/67th)

1945	Capt	H E Wingfield MC
1947	Capt	W R B May MC
1948	Capt	G S C Balleine
1950	Capt	D J Warren DSO MC
1951	Maj	H E Wingfield MC
1953	Maj	J B Buckmaster
1955	Capt	C D Darroch
1957	Maj	S G B Matthews
1958	Capt	J D Wellings
1960	Capt	R J Russell
1961	Capt	D L Stephens
1962	Maj	R J Freeman-Wallace
1963	Maj	J E Horton
1965	Capt	J G T Southwood
1967	Capt	M J Martin
1969	Capt	B J Willing

MINDEN COMPANY (37th/67th)
[1971]

ADJUTANTS
1st BATTALION (37th/67th)

1972	Capt	B J Willing
1972	Capt	J P B Hooley
1975	Capt	P J W Shepherd
1975	Capt	D A C Hannah
1976	Capt	P A Davis
1978	Capt	N S Alderman
1980	Capt	R P Russell
1982	Capt	S A C Frere-Cook
1984	Capt	I Passingham
1986	Capt	R W Dennis
1988	Capt	C F Warren
1990	Capt	J J Eldridge
1991	Capt	M R Hanscomb

QUARTERMASTERS
1st BATTALION (37th/67th)

1941 - 48	Capt	A B Stone MBE
1949	Maj	W H Hall
1949	Capt	A J Truran MBE (Assistant QM)
1949	Capt	H J Hardwidge
1950	Maj	F R A Read
1958	Maj	H A J Plummer
1963	Maj	L B Edmonds
1967	Capt	W C Harris
1968	Capt	J E Venn MM DERR
1969	Capt	H L Barnard MBE
1972	Capt	F J Thomas RWF
1972	Maj	R G Bate-Jones MBE
1976	Maj	J A Barrow MBE DERR
1979	Capt	R W Coleman MBE
1981	Capt	L D Brown MBE
1983	Capt	E C Kimberley
1986	Maj	E C Kimberley
1987	Capt	A L Gay WFR
1989	Capt	L B Le Galloudec
1990	Maj	L B Le Galloudec
1991	Capt	M R Power

TECHNICAL QUARTERMASTERS (37th/67th)

1960	Capt	A J Tregidgo
1964	Lt	J E Venn MM DERR
1966	Capt	H L Barnard MBE
1972	Capt	G S Thomas MBE GLOSTERS
1975	Capt	M W Neville STAFFORDS
1977	Capt	R W Coleman MBE
1979	Capt	W C Walter D AND D
1981	Capt	P D Stacey
1983	Capt	P Goss GLOSTERS
1986	Capt	L B Le Galloudec
1989	Capt	C D Burnett
1990	Capt	M R Power
1991	Capt	G M Shave

REGIMENTAL SERGEANT MAJORS
1st BATTALION (37th/67th)

1944 - 46	RSM	R W Shave
1947	RSM	K Ryder
1950	RSM	L Garlick
1951	RSM	W R Watton
1955	RSM	E V Cole
1957	RSM	W R Watton
1957	RSM	H L Barnard
1961	RSM	R C Daws
1963	RSM	G House
1967	RSM	G S Thomas GLOSTERS

MINDEN COMPANY (37th/67th)

| 1970 - 72 | CSM | A J Rumbold |

1st BATTALION (37th/67th)

1972	RSM	R W Coleman
1975	RSM	M D Terry
1975	RSM	E C Kimberley
1978	RSM	A J Rumbold
1981	RSM	L B Le Galloudec
1983	RSM	M W Gibson
1985	RSM	D Sutton
1987	RSM	E V Rodda
1989	RSM	H K Baker
1990	RSM	M J Mulligan

REGIMENTAL BANDS AND CORPS OF DRUMS
BAND MASTERS(WO1): BAND WARRANT OFFICERS (WO2)
BAND COLOUR SERGEANTS: DRUM MAJORS

1946 - 1950 REGIMENTAL BAND

BANDMASTER (WO1)	J A	Gilbert ARCM
BANDMASTER (WO1)	L	Fereday ARCM

1st BATTALION (37th/67th)

1951	Bandmaster (WO1)	J A	Gilbert ARCM
	Band C/Sgt	F	Keens
	Band Sgt	W	Butt MM
	Drum Major	R	Gray
1953	Bandmaster (WO1)	G S J	Fidoe
1955	Drum Major	R E	Bryant
1958	Bandmaster (WO1)	J	Plant
1959	Band BSM (WO2)	W	Butt MM
1960	Band C/Sgt	V	Pawson
1962	Bandmaster (WO1)	G E	Gregory
1962	Band C/Sgt	P J	Bailey
1964	Drum Major	P J	Ferris
1968	Band BSM (WO2)	P J	Bailey BEM

MINDEN COMPANY 1970 - 1972

1972	Bandmaster (WO1)	C J	French ARCM LTCL LGSM
	Band BSM (WO2)	P J	Ferris
	Band C/Sgt	A	Nunn
	Drum Major	D	Lord WFR
1974	Drum Major	D W	Barnes
1976	Band C/Sgt	T	Marston
	Drum Major	R W	Highmore
1977	Band BSM (WO2)	T	Marston
1978	Band C/SGT	R G	Glasspool
	Drum Major	A F	Widebank
1979	Bandmaster (WO1)	D W	Wood
1982	Band BSM (WO2)	R G	Glasspool
1984	Drum Major	D R	Beer RWF
1987	Drum Major	S J	Tubb
1987	Bandmaster (WO1)	C C	Gray ARCM BRCM
1990-92	Drum Major	B D	Pierce

4th (TA) BATTALION

1949	Bandmaster (WO1)		A	Burgess
	Band Sgt	A A	Earl	
1950	Band Sgt	R	Streeter	
1952	Bandmaster (WO1)		H T	Pallister MM
	Band Sgt	T W	Marsh	

5th (TA) BATTALION

| 1956 | Bandmaster (WO1) | C L | Jones |

4th / 5th (TA) BATTALION

1961-67	Bandmaster (WO1)	J	Parrot
	Band C/Sgt	J	Henn
	Drum Major	G	Urry

THE DEPOT
THE ROYAL HAMPSHIRE REGIMENT

COMMANDING OFFICERS

1946	Maj	H J	Jeffrey
1947	Maj	E R S	Westropp
1948	Maj	C AT	Halliday OBE
1950	Maj	H D	Nelson Smith MC
1951	Maj	D J	Warren DSO MC
1954	Maj	F M	Shaw
1956	Maj	T H N	Keene
1957-58	Maj	H E	Wingfield MC

TRAINING MAJORS / ADJUTANTS / QUARTERMASTERS / REGIMENTAL SERGEANT MAJORS

1948	WO1(RSM)	J	Baxter	
1948	Capt	L M M	Stewart	
1948	Capt(QM)	A W	Garlic	
1948	Capt	H W	Parry	
1949	Maj(QM)	G A	Greenway MBE	
1949	Capt	J H G	Low	Administrative Officer
1949	Capt	C H G	Dees	
1949	WO1(RSM)	V	Hamilton	
1950	Capt	J E	Tull	

1950	WO1(RSM)	V Lawson	
1951	Maj(QM)	V A Blake MBE	
1952	Lt	M J Ponting	Adjutant
1952	Capt	J E Tull	Training Capt
1952	WO1(RSM)	W R Southcott	
1952	Lt	J D Wellings	Adjutant
1953	Capt	WRB May MC	Training Captain /Adjutant
1954	Maj	J S S Green	
1954	Maj	H W Watts	
1954	Capt	WRB May MC	Adjutant
1955	WO1(RSM)	W R Watton	
1956	Capt	P B Chambers MC	Adjutant
1956	Maj	A R Denne Bolton MC	Training Major
1957-58	Lt Col	H E Wingfield MC	
1957-58	WO1(RSM)	E V Cole	
1957-58	Capt	G W Alderman	Adjutant
1957-58	Maj(QM)	F R A Read	
1957-58	WO1(RSM)	W R Watton MBE	

REGIMENTAL HEADQUARTERS

REGIMENTAL SECRETARIES

1959	Brig (RO2)	R	Chandler DSO
1961	Maj (RO2)	G A	Greenway MBE
1963	Col (RO2)	J M	Clift
1974	Lt Col (RO2)	C D	Darroch DL
1989-92	Lt Col (RO2)	D C	MacDonald-Milner

ASSISTANT REGIMENTAL SECRETARIES *

1961	Lt Col (RO3)	J H	Fitzsimon
1971	Lt Col (RO3)	F M	Shaw
1981	Lt Col (RO3)	A W	Freemantle
1983	Maj (RO3)	G C	Phipps
1986-92	Maj (RO3)	J D K	Kellie

*Editor — Regimental Journal
Secretary — The Royal Hampshire Regiment Comrades Association

4th (TA) BATTALION
THE ROYAL HAMPSHIRE REGIMENT
COMMANDING OFFICERS

1947	Lt-Col	F Mitchell DSO MC
1950	Lt-Col	C A T Halliday OBE
1953	Lt-Col	T G Tucker MC
1955	Lt-Col	P R Sawyer OBE MC TD JP
1959	Lt-Col	B Gater TD

14th BATTALION THE PARACHUTE REGIMENT (TA)
(5th BATTALION THE ROYAL HAMPSHIRE REGIMENT)
COMMANDING OFFICERS

1948	Lt-Col	A F G Monro TD (The Parachute Regiment)
1949	Lt-Col	R G F Frisby DSO MC
1951	Lt-Col	H D Nelson Smith MC
1954	Lt-Col	H W Le Patourel VC
1956	Reverts in title and role to	

5th BATTALION THE ROYAL HAMPSHIRE REGIMENT (TA)

1956	Lt-Col	H W Le Patourel VC
1957	Lt-Col	G J A Dewar MBE
1960	Lt-Col	J B Young TD
1961	Amalgamation with the 4th (TA) Battalion to become	

4th/5th (TA) BATTALION
THE ROYAL HAMPSHIRE REGIMENT

1961	Lt-Col	B Gater TD
1962	Lt-Col	J B Young OBE TD
1965	Lt-Col	P D T Powell OBE TD

TRAINING MAJORS / ADJUTANTS / QUARTERMASTERS
/ REGIMENTAL SERGEANT MAJORS
4th (TA) BATTALION

1947	Capt	T F	Knott	Adjutant
	Capt (QM)	V A	Blake MBE	
	WO1 (RSM)	G T	Bugden	
1948	WO1 (RSM)	F G	Drake	
1950	Capt	A R	Denne Bolton MC	Adjutant
	Maj (QM)	V A	Blake MBE	
1952	Capt (QM)	W H	Watts	
	WO1 (RSM)	H	Dimmack	
1953	Maj	C E S	Perkins	Adjutant
1953	WO1 (RSM)	E	Stares	
1954	Lt (QM)	H A J	Plummer	

TRAINING MAJORS / ADJUTANTS / QUARTERMASTERS / REGIMENTAL SERGEANT MAJORS - continued

4th (TA) BATTALION

1955	Capt	H W	Parry	Adjutant
1955	Maj	C G T	Viner MC	Training Major
1957	WO1 (RSM)	L B	Edmonds	
1957	Maj	J B	Buckmaster	Training Major
1957	Capt	D L	Hudson	Adjutant
1957	WO1 (RSM)	G	Street	
1957	Maj (QM)	W H	Watts	
1958	Maj	J B	Buckmaster	Trg Major/Adjutant
1959	Maj	C D	Darroch	Trg Major/Adjutant

14th BATTALION THE PARACHUTE REGIMENT (TA)
(5th BATTALION THE ROYAL HAMPSHIRE REGIMENT)

1952	Capt	K C	Cane	Adjutant
1953	Capt (QM)	A J	Truran MBE	
1954	Capt	A	Imrie	Adjutant
1955	Capt	G C	Phipps	Adjutant
1956	13th July: 14th Battalion reverts in title and role to			

5th BATTALION THE ROYAL HAMPSHIRE REGIMENT (TA)

1956	Capt (QM)	A J	Truran MBE	
1956	Capt	G C	Phipps	Adjutant
1956	WO1 (RSM)	A	Pyke	
1958	Capt	A H T	Smith	Adjutant
1959	Capt	R F	Dorey	Adjutant
1959	Lt (QM)	L B	Edmonds	
1960	WO1 (RSM)	F S	Godden	
1961	1st April: Amalgamation with 4th (TA) Battalion to become			

4th/5th (TA) BATTALION

1961	Maj	C D	Darroch	Training Major
1961	Maj	G C	Phipps	Training Major
1961	Capt	J C	Munday	Adjutant
1961	Capt (QM)	L B	Edmonds	
1961	WO1 (RSM)	F S	Godden	
1962	WO1 (RSM)	R	Thomas BEM	
1963	Maj (QM)	H A J	Plummer	
1964	WO1 (RSM)	H L	Barnard MBE	
1964	Maj	W R	Dugmore	Training Major
1966	Maj	W G	Alderman MBE	Training Major
1966	Maj (QM)	A	Cainey DERR	
1966	WO1 (RSM)	J	Hutchison	

APPENDIX 5

THE ROYAL HAMPSHIRE REGIMENT
COMRADES ASSOCIATION

PATRON
H R H The Princess of Wales 1987 - 1992

PRESIDENTS
Colonels of the Regiment (Ex.Officio Appointments)

CHAIRMEN
Executive Committee

1946	Lt Col	B B	von B im Thurn DSO MC
1947	Lt Col	J M	Lee DSO
1948	Col	J L	Spencer DSO OBE MC
1949	Maj	C A T	Halliday OBE (CO, Depot)
1950	Maj	H D	Nelson Smith MC (CO, Depot)
1951	Maj	D J	Warren DSO MC (CO, Depot)
1954	Maj	F M	Shaw (CO, Depot)
1956	Maj	T H N	Keene (CO, Depot)
1957	Maj	H E	Wingfield MC (CO, Depot)
1959	Brig	R	Chandler DSO
1961	Col	C C	Smythe CBE MC DL
1967	Col	J M	Clift
1971	Col	P R	Sawyer OBE MC TD JP DL
1974	Lt Col	C D	Darroch DL
1989-92	Lt Col	HDH	Keatinge OBE

FREEDOMS / AFFLIATIONS / PRIVILEGE

Borough of Aldershot	11th September 1945
Borough of Bournemouth	13th September 1945
City of Winchester	15th September 1945
City of Southampton	25th April 1946
City of Portsmouth	20th May 1950
Borough of Romsey	26th September 1959
Borough of Basingstoke	16th July 1966
Borough of Rushmoor	20th May 1981
New Forest District (Affiliation)	8th July 1986
Borough of Test Valley	25th June 1986
Borough of Christchurch	19th October 1987
Borough of Eastleigh	14th September 1991
The Privilege of Jersey	9th May 1992 (Liberation Day)

INDEX